ACTS OF GALLANTRY

VOLUME TWO

BEING

A DETAILED ACCOUNT OF DEEDS OF BRAVERY IN SAVING LIFE, 1871 - 1950

FOR WHICH THE ROYAL HUMANE SOCIETY AWARDED THE SILVER MEDAL AND THE STANHOPE GOLD MEDAL

Compiled by

WILLIAM H. FEVYER

The Naval & Military Press

ACTS OF GALLANTRY
VOLUME TWO
1871 TO 1950

Also by W. H. Fevyer
The George Medal 1940 - 1945
The Distinguished Service Medal 1939 - 1946
The Distinguished Service Medal 1914 - 1920
The Distinguished Service Cross 1901 - 1938

First Published 1996 By

The Naval & Military Press

© W.H.Fevyer 1996
© Royal Humane Society 1996

All rights reserved. No part of this publication may be reproduced, stored in a retrieval system or transmitted in any form by any means, electrical, mechanical or otherwise without first seeking the written permission of the copyright holders.

Set By Wilson & Fevyer

FOREWORD

Lambton J.H. Young was the longest serving Secretary of the Royal Humane Society (1859 -1879). In 1872, he had published a book "Acts of Gallantry" which gave a detailed account of deeds of bravery, for which the Society's Silver Medals were awarded, for saving life in all parts of the world between 1830 - 1871.

At that time the Silver Medal was the Society's highest award, the Stanhope Gold Medal only being inaugurated in 1873. To appreciate the importance of the Silver Medal's degree of bravery, Mate (later Lieutenant) Charles David Lucas, Royal Navy, was awarded the Silver Medal in 1854 for his gallantry in action in the Baltic. H.M. Queen Victoria subsequently invested him with the Victoria Cross for the same action and this was gazetted on 24th February 1857. Lucas thereby became the first recipient of the highest award for valour.

This latest book "Acts of Gallantry, Volume Two" is a natural sequel to Lambton Young's book and covers the period, 1871 - 1950. Furthermore, it records details of the Stanhope Gold Medal, only one of which is awarded annually.

I have known Bill Fevyer for the past decade. He is a collector of gallantry awards, a meticulous researcher and editor of a most valuable periodical "Life Saving Awards Research Journal", now in its eighth year.

I am delighted to have been asked to write an introduction to this book and would commend it to all.

A.J. Dickinson
Brettenham House, 1995

INTRODUCTION

The details in this volume have been taken from the records of the Royal Humane Society. Wherever possible the date of the incident and the occupation of the recipient have been included. I am indebted to the Secretary of the Society (1978 - 1995), Major A.J. Dickinson and his staff, for all their assistance and help. Although Bronze Medals and Testimonial citations are not covered in this work, where other awards have been mentioned they have been indexed.

Reading through these citations, it can be readily seen, that the geographical locations are truly world wide. Not only do the awards cover many continents but also many nationalities.

The time span of this book, 1871 to 1950, covers the South African War, 1899 to 1902, and the two World Wars; these are reflected in the citations for those periods. The advance from sail to steam, land to air, horse to motor transport, gas to electricity and indeed the emancipation of women can also be seen from the various incidents rewarded by the Society

This Book is dedicated
to

Major A.J. Dickinson
Secretary of the Royal Humane Society
1978-1995

&

Mrs. Marjory Robson

For all their help and assistance
which has made this book
possible

CONTENTS

STANHOPE GOLD MEDALS 1873 - 1950	page	1
R.H.S. SILVER MEDALS 1870 - 1950	page	30
INDEX TO STANHOPE & SILVER AWARDS	page	171
INDEX TO BRONZE AWARDS	page	179
INDEX TO TESTIMONIALS	page	182

R.H.S. STANHOPE GOLD MEDALS

1873 to 1950

Webb, Matthew   Case 19158

First Stanhope Gold Medal 1873.

On the 22nd of April, as the Steamship *Russia* was proceeding on her voyage from New York to Liverpool, a stiff breeze blowing, and the ship cutting through the water at the rate of 14 ½ knots, a seaman, named, Michael Hynes, while on the rigging performing his duty, fell overboard. Immediately on perceiving this a fellow sailor, Matthew Webb, jumped overboard and swam to the place where his comrade had disappeared; he was too late, however, and could recover nothing or see anything of the unfortunate man except his cap, which he brought on board. The Steamer was stopped and turned about, a boat lowered and sent to the rescue; after cruising about for nearly half-an-hour they returned to the ship with Webb, who was found swimming about, nearly a mile from the ship; he was not at all exhausted but had suffered somewhat from the cold.

Some kind hearted gentlemen immediately started a subscription for the benefit of the man who had so nobly risked his life to save his comrade. In about an hour £100 was raised. Two more subscriptions were also taken for the benefit of the parents of the man who had lost his life, and for the boat's crew who went to the rescue.

Hoghton, J.de, Lieutenant, 10th Foot.   Case 19498

Stanhope Gold Medal 1874.

On Thursday, the 10th of September, 1874, at half past 9 p.m., in the gateway between the outer and inner harbour at Lowestoft, Suffolk, James Dorling fell overboard from the Yacht *Dart* whilst she was making for the inner harbour in a strong half-flood tideway, the night was very dark, blowing and raining hard, and going about five and a half knots. Lieutenant J. de Hoghton, 10th Foot, jumped overboard, swam to Dorling, and supported him in the water for about a quarter of an hour in the tideway between narrow high pilework, without cross beams or side chains to lay hold of, and the head of the pilework twelve or fifteen feet above the water. The yacht was carried away into the inner harbour and there was no other vessel or boat in the gateway to lend assistance; the darkness prevented any immediate help being obtained from the shore. The length of the gateway about 350 yards, width 15 to 20 yards, depth 10 to 15 feet. Lieutenant de Hoghton and Dorling were ultimately drawn up the pilework by ropes from the shore.

Rogers F.H., Sub-Lieutenant, R.N.   Case 19580

Stanhope Gold Medal 1875.

On the 26th of November, 1874, at 9.15 a.m., a cry of man overboard was heard, the ship was hove-to with mainyard aback, & etc., a lifeboat was sent away in a very rough sea. The lifeboat was pulled in the direction where it was thought the man would be. When the boat got near to pick him up, he cried out that there was a man's cap to leeward and that we must endeavour to pick him up first. We pulled past Mr. Rogers, Sub-Lieut of H.M.S. *Raleigh*, with great reluctance, as it was thought that in such a rough sea he would be in great danger. The man who had fallen overboard was not seen, although his cap was, as Mr. Rogers stated, to leeward; but after some hard pulling, and a quarter of an hour had elapsed, we pulled back to Mr. Rogers, who had been swimming bravely and waiting his time. After a tedious pull of nearly three quarters of an hour Mr. Rogers was put on board the *Raleigh*, considerably fatigued after his gallant attempt to save life. It appeared afterwards that a blue-jacket had fallen off the cross-jack or mizzen-topsail-yard arm of the *Raleigh*, who was just on the lee bow, and that Sub-Lieut Rogers had gallantly jumped after him. The man was supposed to have struck an upper half-port in his fall, and had not this occurred the chances are that Mr. Rogers gallant efforts would have been successful.

Storey, Geo. W. Bennett, Land Owner, Tasmania.   Case 19824

Stanhope Gold Medal 1876.

During the afternoon of Monday, 16th August, 1875, three persons attempted to cross over the bridge at Henbury in a gig whilst the South Esk River was flooded, running some feet over the bridge and still rising; the depth of water at the spot was about fifteen feet. Mr. Geo W. Bennett Storey, land owner, at Henbury, near Avoca, Tasmania, plunged into the river and swam seventy yards to the spot and brought each one safely to land separately, and from the extreme coldness of the water, being winter-time, was completely exhausted and benumbed, so that with great difficulty he reached the house of a friend some two miles off, on the opposite side of the river, which he dared not recross to his own home.

Montgomerie, R.A.J., Sub-Lieut., R.N.   Case 20109

Stanhope Gold Medal 1877.

On a dark night, 6th April, 1877, H.M.S. *Immortalite* was under sail, going about 4 knots before the wind, the sea rough for swimming, and abounding with sharks, when T.E.Hocken, O.S., fell overboard. Sub-Lieut. Montgomerie, jumped overboard from the bridge, a height of twenty-five feet, to his assistance, swam to him, got hold of the man, and hauled him on to his back, then swam with him to where he supposed the life-buoy would be; but seeing no relief, he states that, after keeping him afloat some time, he told the man to keep himself afloat whilst he took his clothes off. He had got his coat and shirt off, and was in the act of taking off his trousers when Hocken, in sinking, caught him by the legs and dragged him down a considerable depth. His trousers luckily came off clear, and he swam to the surface, bringing the drowning man with him. Hocken was now insensible, and too great a weight to support any longer, and finding that his only chance of saving himself was to swim for it, he reluctantly gave up the hope of saving his companion, and struck out for the ship. He was eventually picked up by a second boat that was lowered, after having been over twenty-one minutes in the water, the first boat having missed him. The life-buoy was not seen. Awarded the Albert Medal for the same act.

Wintz, Lewis E., Lieut., R.N.   Case 20297

Stanhope Gold Medal 1878.

This officer, being already in possession of the Silver Medal for a former act of gallantry in 1867, was awarded a Silver Clasp.

On the 19th December, 1877, H.M.S. *Raleigh* was running before a fresh breeze at the rate of seven knots off the Island of Tenedos, when James Maker fell from aloft into the sea. Lieut. Wintz immediately jumped overboard and supported the man for twenty minutes at considerable risk (not being able to reach the life-buoy). The man would undoubtedly have been drowned (being insensible and seriously injured) had it not been for the bravery of this officer.

Baboo Kristo Chunder Chuckerbutty, Medical Man.   Case 20523

Stanhope Gold Medal 1879.

On the 15th February, 1878, the body of a native woman was being taken to Ghat on the Ganges for cremation, but, showing symptoms of returning animation, the natives threw her into the river, being under the impression that she was possessed with an evil spirit. Mr. Chuckerbutty, hearing the cry of "Bhutt-Bhutt" (goblin), ran to the spot, and not being able to obtain assistance from a concourse of affrighted natives, promptly plunged into the water and swam out to the assistance of the woman. The place was a dangerous whirlpool twenty-five feet deep. In effecting the rescue, Mr. Chuckerbutty ran very great personal risk, not only from the well known eddies of the

Hooghly, but from becoming entangled in his cloth and having his hand violently clutched by the drowning woman. In addition to showing great physical courage, the salvor had the moral strength to risk the native opinion, which might have reduced him to the position of outcast from his friends, or compelled him to renew his caste by a severe penance. It is considered that the loss of caste must follow the act of touching what might have been a corpse.

Fremantle, Edmund R., Captain the Hon., C.B., C.M.G., R.N.   Case 20932

Stanhope Gold Medal 1880.

On the 7th February, 1880, H.M.S. *Invincible* was on a voyage from Alexandria to Aboukir Bay, when one of the leadsmen slipped out of his brace and fell into the sea. The man retained hold of the lead line for some time, and was consequently dragged under water. Becoming insensible he let go his grasp.

Captain Fremantle, encumbered with heavy sea boots and uniform, jumped from the bridge of the ship, dived after the man, and brought him to the surface; with much difficulty he retained hold of him until the cutter arrived.

The ship was going seven knots when the accident took place, and the man must have been drowned had it not been for the prompt action displayed by Captain Fremantle.

Senior, H., Major, 34th Bengal Native Infantry.   Case 21249

Stanhope Gold Medal 1881.

On the 9th February, 1881, several gentlemen were proceeding by country boat from Moonshegunge to Shichar, when the boat struck on a rock in the centre of the river. The gentlemen succeeded in landing safely, but the boat had to be abandoned. Immediately afterwards a large native boat with coolies on board struck the hidden rocks at the same place, and all the crew were immersed.

Major Senior immediately swam out and succeeded in rescuing six persons, but not until he had repeatedly swam to and from the bank. He encountered great personal risk in venturing into the midst of twenty-five terror stricken men and women, most of them totally unable to help themselves.

The River Barrack is a large and fast running river, and like most Indian rivers, abounding in under currents.

Jenkins, John, Constable, E Division, Metropolitan Police.   Case 21845

Stanhope Gold Medal 1882.

Constable Jenkins was on duty on Waterloo Bridge at 2.45 a.m. on the 14th July, 1882, when he saw a man mount the parapet and throw himself into the river. Without hesitation the constable unfastened his belt and jumped from the bridge after him. Not withstanding a determined resistance on the part of the would-be suicide, Constable Jenkins succeeded in seizing the man and supporting him above water until both were picked up some distance down river by a boat which was promptly sent from the Thames Police Station.

The danger incurred in this rescue may be fairly estimated when it appears that the height jumped was forty-three feet, the tide was running out under the arches at the rate of six miles an hour, and a thick mist covered the river, so much so, as to render it impossible to see any object in the centre of the river from either side. The place where the men entered the water was 170 yards from shore.

Simpson, William, Captain of the Foretop, R.N. Case 21997

Stanhope Gold Medal 1883.

At 7.45 p.m., on the 28th January, 1883, H.M. Schooner, *Harrier*, was anchored in Pomony Harbour, Johanna Island, when William Pond fell overboard. The night was pitch dark with a chopping sea, and the force of the wind was so strong as to render the noise of the splash almost inaudible to those on board.

Simpson, on looking over the side, heard a gurgling sound, and surmising that a man had fallen overboard called away the lifeboat's crew, and then jumped into the sea; he found the man and supported him above water for some time until hauled on board. The danger incurred appears to have been very great, as the coast here abounds with sharks, a large one having risen to the surface alongside the ship the previous day. There was also great danger in being carried towards the adjacent reefs and being dashed against them.

Cleverley, Walter, Passenger on the Steamship *Rewa*. Case 22191

Stanhope Gold Medal 1884.

On the 13th September, 1883, the Steamship *Rewa* was proceeding through the Gulf of Aden, when a lascar fell overboard. Being unable to swim he drifted astern rapidly.

Walter Cleverley, a passenger, promptly jumped overboard, swam to the man - then fifty yards from the ship - and assisted him to a lifebuoy which was previously thrown.

The vessel was going about thirteen knots. Captain Hay, commanding the ship, states, "The danger incurred was incalculable, as the sea thereabouts is infested with sharks. The salvor was forty minutes in the water, supporting the man. Cleverley jumped off the top of the poop, a height of thirty feet to the water."

Collins, Alfred, Fisherman. Case 22611

Stanhope Gold Medal 1885.

The fishing lugger *Water Nymph* of Looe was seven or eight miles east-south-east of the Eddystone, on the night of 16th December, 1884, when a boy named Hoskings fell overboard, and was soon about eighty feet astern.

The captain of the boat, Alfred Collins, immediately jumped in to the rescue, carrying the end of a rope with him; he was clothed in oil skins and sea boots. After a great deal of difficulty Hoskings was reached and pulled on board. At the time this gallant act was performed there was a gale of wind blowing with heavy rain, and the night was dark.

McRae, H.N., Captain, 45th (Rattray's) Sikhs. Case 23343

Stanhope Gold Medal 1886.

At 5 a.m. on the 5th October, 1886, a trumpeter of the Royal Artillery was crossing the compound of Captain Holmes's bungalow at Rawal Pindi, when he fell down a well. On hearing the alarm, Captain Holmes, Captain McRae, and Lieutenant Taylor proceeded to the spot. On arriving they found that Mr. Grose had preceded them, and had let down a well-rope which was of sufficient length to reach the soldier, and capable of sustaining him for a time.

Both Captain McRae and Captain Holmes volunteered to go down, but as the former was a light weight it was decided that he should make the trial, Captain Holmes demurring, as he wished to undertake the risk himself. The rope being very weak, it could not possibly have borne Captain Holmes great weight.

Captain McRae was accordingly let down by means of a four-strand tent rope, and on reaching the water found the soldier practically insensible; he therefore decided to go up with him.

Captain Holmes was at the head of the rope, and his strength enabled him to lift both completely. At every haul the amount gained was held in check by the other persons above. After hauling up about ten or fifteen feet the rope broke, precipitating Captain McRae and his charge to the bottom of the well. A second attempt was then made, and both were brought to the surface.

The depth of the well was eighty-five feet of which twelve feet was water. It was quite dark at the time.

Hill, Hedley, Medical Student.　　　　　　　　　　　　　　　　　　　　　　　　　　　Case 23798

Stanhope Gold Medal 1887.

On the 18th October, 1887, about 7.30 p.m., owing to the darkness of the night, a girl walked by mistake into the Avon at Bristol. She was rapidly carried away by the current when Mr. Hedley Hill's attention was called to the accident. He at once plunged in without divesting himself of clothing, and succeeded after much difficulty in bringing her to the bank.

Battison, Albert, Boy, H.M.S. *Impregnable*.　　　　　　　　　　　　　　　　　　　　Case 23861

Stanhope Gold Medal 1888.

On the 29th December, 1887, the Soar at Leicester being frozen, a girl named Annie Freer attempted to cross it on the ice when she broke through and became immersed in fourteen feet of water. A man went out part of the way to the girl's assistance but returned, failing in his attempt to reach her.

Battison then went on the ice, actually dived under it, got hold of the girl, and in coming up broke the ice with his head; he succeeded in bringing the girl to the surface and afterwards to the shore.

The officer commanding the boy's ship states that he cannot imagine a greater risk than that attendant on the act. "If the lad had not been able to break the ice he would in all probability have been drowned." He considers "diving under the ice for a drowning person perhaps the greatest act of bravery that anyone can perform, the risk being so great."

Meyer, William, Works Foreman.　　　　　　　　　　　　　　　　　　　　　　　　　Case 24388

Stanhope Gold Medal 1889.

In the month of March, 1889, at the Municipal Works, Kim Seng Bridge, Singapore, an accident occurred which resulted in the death of two natives. The coolies work in cylinders under water, ascending and descending in buckets three feet in diameter. A rush of foul gas appears to have entered a cylinder, and a man fell backwards and lay insensible at the bottom. Another man went down and succumbed also, and a third appears to have been pulled up in a bucket insensible.

Mr. Meyer then gallantly volunteered to descend. He went down and made fast one of the men to a rope round his waist, and both were hauled to the surface. Meyer again descended and brought up the other man, who was still breathing, but who died, two minutes after coming to the surface. The letters received from Singapore show the great danger incurred by Mr. Meyer, and his knowledge of what the danger would be in descending to the place of the accident.

Cooper, Alfred John, Fourth Officer.   Case 24825

Stanhope Gold Medal 1890.

On the 8th April, 1890, whilst the Steamship *Massilia* was proceeding from Bombay to London, a lascar fell overboard in the Gulf of Aden. The ship was going at thirteen knots. Mr. Cooper who was in the saloon at the time, on hearing the cry of man overboard rushed on deck, jumped overboard, swam after the man, seized hold of him, and kept him afloat until a boat was lowered and went to his assistance.

The officer encountered serious risk, as he was encumbered with clothes and the native clung to him in the water. The gulf is known to be infested with sharks. Awarded the Albert Medal for the same act.

Huddleston, W.B., Second Grade Officer, Royal Indian Marine.   Case 25291

Stanhope Gold Medal 1891.

On the 15th December, 1890, the Indian Marine survey ship *Investigator* was trawling in 1800 fathoms of water in the middle of the Bay of Bengal. Whilst engaged in the operation the men observed two sharks swimming round the ship, and on lowering a baited hook they succeeded shortly afterwards in hooking one of them. The shark, however, dashed forward and fouled the trawl-rope by swimming round it. Mr. Peterson, the gunner, thereupon fetched a rifle with the intention of shooting it, but while getting over the head rails he fell overboard. Mr. Huddleston, the officer of the forecastle, being aware the gunner could not swim, immediately jumped overboard to his assistance, and the two were afterwards got on board without hurt.

The personal risk incurred in this act is apparent from the following circumstances.

One shark, seven feet long, was a captive dashing round and round under the ship' bows, while a second was in attendance free, and at no great distance off. The shark line might have been at a moment's notice entwined around the seamen's bodies, in addition to the usual risk incurred in entering the water in the presence of sharks.

McDermott, Thomas, Boatswain, R.N.   Case 26221

Stanhope Gold Medal 1892.

On the 9th September, 1892, the sailing cutter of H.M.S. *Swallow* was cruising off the south end of Zanzibar Island. About 6 p.m. the boat was anchored off Uzi Island, and half the men were landed to cook supper. Two of the men left with the boat were bathing, when a large shark was seen within six feet of them, and making towards one of them.

McDermott without any hesitation, with all his clothes on, jumped overboard, right over the shark, and by the splash created frightened the fish from its prey, and the men were enabled to regain the boat.

Scrase-Dickens, Spencer Wm., Capt., 2nd Bn Highland Light Infy.   Case 26389

Stanhope Gold Medal 1893.

On the 27th April, 1893, at 2.11 p.m., the steamship *Peshawur* was on her voyage from Aden to Suez, steaming at eleven and a half knots, in a strong head wind and a moderately high sea, when a lascar fell overboard. Captain Dickens, who was in a chair on deck, suffering from sea-sickness at the time, at once jumped overboard to rescue the man. After securing a life-buoy, subsequently thrown, swam with it to the lascar, and with this help supported the man above water for seventeen minutes, until picked up by a boat which was promptly lowered. The risk incurred in this case was undoubtedly very great, as the sea was so high it was impossible at times to see the boat, and this part of the Red Sea is notoriously dangerous, being infested with sharks. The rescue is described by the captain of the ship as "a deed of daring."

The salvor and the lascar were one and a half miles from the ship when picked up. Awarded the Albert Medal for the same act.

Mugford Wm., Foreman of Works.   Case 27411

Stanhope Gold Medal 1894.

A violent thunderstorm, accompanied by rain, broke over Torquay at 2.30 a.m. on the 20th October, 1894. The flood rushed from all points with terrific force into the town sewer, the water of which rose about three feet in as many minutes. A party of eight or nine men were dispatched to carry out some repairs to the interior of the main sewer. They had been at work about a couple of hours, when the man who was set to watch signalled to them that the water was rising, and William Mugford, the foreman, ordered the men up. Three men, Callicot, Beasley, and Potter started off in the direction of the manhole, Mugford remaining behind to make fast the staging upon which they were working. The water rushed down in a perfect torrent, and before the foremost man had reached the manhole it had overflown the dam, and was whirling about down the sewer in a resistless flood. Beasley managed to clutch a barrow which was made fast to the dam, and by means of a life-line was pulled up on the staging. Callicot was overcome and carried away, nor was anything seen of him until his dead body was found lodged against the staging upon which the men had been working. Milton, one of the workmen, again and again was carried off his feet by the rushing water, and would have undoubtedly have been drowned but for the coolness and presence of mind of William Mugford, who is a powerful man, and held on to him, half carrying him out of danger. Potter who was further up the drain, also owes his life to the foreman. The two men, under the direction and supported by Mugford, finally hauled themselves up to the foot-irons and chains, and remained seven hours there before they were finally rescued. It is stated that had it not been for Mugford's brave devotion to his fellow workmen all would have been drowned, as the outlet discharges directly into the sea on a rocky and dangerous coast.

Hatton, E.A., Seaman.   Case 27714

Stanhope Gold Medal 1895.

On the 3rd March, 1895, at 6.30 p.m., J. Smith, carpenter of the steamship *Dunbar Castle*, was washed overboard at sea off the coast of South Africa. The ship was under steam running at ten knots. There was a fresh head-wind with a high sea, and to add to the danger, darkness was setting in, and the water swarming with sharks.

Hatton a seaman, at once ran aft, jumped over the stern, and swam after the drowning man. He had almost reached him, when the latter threw up his hands and disappeared, having been probably seized by a shark.

Collin, John H., Second Officer.   Case 28627

Stanhope Gold Medal 1896.

On the 28th July, 1896, Esmolla, a lascar fireman, belonging to the steamship *Sultan*, fell overboard at sea in lat 11 14 N., lon 6 22 E. A life-buoy was at once thrown to him, which he secured, and the steamer was manoeuvred in order to pick him up, but owing to the immense sea which was running at the time, the man aloft was unable to keep him in sight. After wearing the steamer several times he was sighted on the port beam, but by reason of the high sea it was impossible to launch a boat, as it would have endangered the lives of those who might have volunteered to man her. At once J.H. Collin, second officer, without any previous warning sprang overboard with a line and swam after the man, who had now been three hours in the water. He succeeded in reaching him, and in making fast the line, by which he was hauled on board in an exhausted state.

Extreme risk was incurred, not only from the high sea running but from sharks, several being seen around the steamer, and their presence was known to Mr. Collin before the rescue.

Chainey, Geo. B., Gunner, R.N.   Case 29005

Stanhope Gold Medal 1897.

At 6.50 p.m. on the 9th July, 1897, the 28-feet cutter of H.M.S. *Dryad*, with a bathing party on board, was capsized in the Mediterranean off Retimo, Crete, throwing the occupants into the water. Gunner Geo. B. Chainey, who was one of the party, immediately on the cutter capsizing saw Frank A. White, a stoker, floundering in the water, and at once swam to shore with him, a distance of 150 yards.

He then returned and rescued private Arthur H. Staines, R.M.L.I., who although able to swim was in distress and nearly drowned, owing to his trousers having slipped down round his knees, thus preventing him using his legs.

Again entering the surf he saved Daniel Bull, leading stoker, who had fallen exhausted after saving two other men.

Chainey now undressed, and went out through the breakers to where leading seaman W. G. Fuller was struggling, and finding himself unable to bring him to shore through the surf, supported him in the water with the help of a broken oar for nearly half an hour, till both were picked up by a boat. Three of the men were unconscious when rescued, and the fourth much exhausted. The accident occurred about 200 yards from the beach, the depth of water being three fathoms, with rollers breaking from fifty to one hundred yards from land.

O'Neill, Francis, Miner.   Case 29817

Stanhope Gold Medal 1898.

At noon on the 29th September, 1898, an explosion occurred in the Annagher Pit, Coalisland, Co. Tyrone. Four men were working at the time; two of these reached the surface alive, one of whom died the same evening. The other two men named Hughes and Murphy were rendered unconscious by the deadly after-damp.

Francis O'Neill, miner, who was acting as underground manager and had been down the pit the same morning, at once determined to try and effect the rescue, and made three attempts to descend the shaft, which is sixty-five yards deep, but was on each occasion driven back. Hearing Hughes' voice, the gallant fellow made a fourth attempt, and although his light was extinguished at a depth of ten yards, he succeeded in reaching the bottom, and finding Hughes, put him in the cradle, when he himself became unconscious, and they were drawn to the top.

On recovering consciousness, O'Neill, accompanied by Thomas McKenna, went down and recovered the body of Murphy, but all efforts to restore animation were fruitless. Great risk was incurred, the pit being full of after-damp, the deadly effect of which is well known.

The Silver Medal was voted to O'Neill and the Bronze Medal to McKenna.

Hall, William, Gunner, R.G.A.   Case 29865

Stanhope Gold Medal 1899.

At 3.40 p.m. on the 28th December, 1898, a man named Carrington Franklin was at work in an electro-plating establishment in an upstairs room at 42, Clerkenwell Close, Clerkenwell, London, when he was visited by his wife and three children aged respectively ten, four, and two years. On the floor were various vessels containing chemicals used in the business, and it is supposed that the children in their play upset two basins containing cyanide of potassium and vitriol. Fumes of prussic acid were at once generated and filled the room, rendering Franklin and the children unconscious.

Mrs Franklin managed to escape, and called for help. Gunner Hall, who was on furlough, happened to be passing, and on being told what had occurred he, without hesitation, stuffed his handkerchief into his mouth, and rushing in found the eldest boy near the bottom of the stairs and carried him out. He then made three journeys up the stairs and into the room where the others lay, bringing out first the children and last of all the father. From inhaling the fumes he was now so exhausted that he fell with Franklin at the foot of the stairs, and was assisted out by his brother, who had come on the scene. When outside he became unconscious, but soon recovered.

Extreme risk was incurred, and without doubt all four persons would have lost their lives but for his prompt action and presence of mind.

Allen, William, Factory Worker, Wear Fuel Company, Sunderland.   Case 30582

Stanhope Gold Medal 1900

At 7 a.m. On the 15th March, 1900, Francis McLeod, a fitter in the employ of the Wear Fuel Company, Sunderland, entered a tar still for the purpose of making some repairs. The still is 9 feet 6 inches in diameter and 8 feet 6 inches deep. McLeod acted against instructions in entering the still at the time, it being hot from previous use and in a most dangerous condition from the gaseous fumes being given off, and he at once fell down in an unconscious state. Richard Lawson at once went in to his assistance, but was also overcome. John Weddle then went in, but shared the fate of the others - being at once rendered insensible. William Allen now went in with a rope, and was successful in bringing McLeod out. Going in a second time, he succeeded in like manner in bringing up Weddle. Going in for a third time, he managed to place the rope round Lawson but was so overcome with the fumes that he had much difficulty in reaching the outside. It was then found that Lawson's feet were fast in some machinery at the bottom of the still, and Allen for the fourth time went in and freed him so that he could be pulled out. All the men were much affected, and Allen ran great risk in entering the still four times, knowing as he did the danger of doing so.

The Silver Medal was voted to William Allen, and Bronze Medals to John Weddle and Richard Lawson.

Lowry, A.C., Lieutenant, R.N., H.M.S. *Empress of India*.   Case 31111

Stanhope Gold Medal 1901

At 9.15 p.m. on the 18th September, 1900, while Her Majesty's ship *Empress of India* was entering the Doro Channel, Cape Fassa, Isle of Andros, a steamer was observed firing signals of distress, and on nearer approach, about 10.45 p.m., was found to be anchored off a lee shore, and riding by a hawser only. She proved to be the steamship *Charkich* of London, bound from Piraeus to Constantinople, commanded by an Austrian, with a crew of forty to fifty hands, and carrying upwards of thirty passengers. Lieutenant Lowry communicated with the ship in the cutter, and learning that the shaft was broken, asked the captain what he could do for him, and whether he wished his crew to be taken off. The captain asked for a hawser to take him in tow, but by the time the cutter had returned with it the ship had drifted too close to the shore for this plan to be feasible. Immediately afterwards she disappeared from view. It was evident by the sudden extinction of the lights that she had taken ground.

All efforts to find the vessel by search-light proved useless, and as the wind and sea made it impossible to search the coast with boats, the *Empress of India* stood off at 12.50 a.m. until daybreak, when the masts of the *Charkich* were seen standing out of the water. Three men were on the foremast, and three others on detached rocks close to the wreck. A heavy sea was running with a cross current, and much wreckage was about. Lieutenant Lowry at once went in the cutter, and endeavoured under oars to float a line and lifebuoy to the foremast to windward of the wreck. He failed owing to the cross current, but one man swam from the mast to the buoy, and was hauled into the boat. Having tried again for some time to get the buoy to the mast, with no success, and the men seeming unable to move, Lieutenant Lowry jumped overboard at about 7 a.m. and swam to the wreck with a lifebuoy and line. As he reached the rigging, he lost the line, which fouled some wreckage, and he was cut off.

Throughout the forenoon efforts were made to establish communication with the wreck. The cutter first made another attempt, but was struck by a heavy sea and half filled with water. Both sea boats were then sent in with oil to throw on the water, rockets, and grass lines, but all in vain.

The *Empress of India* then proceeded to Pargo Bay and landed a party to try and reach the wreck from shore. On her return it was found that the back of the wreck was broken. One of the men had got ashore on a large piece of wreckage. Lieutenant Lowry, with the other man, was still in the fore-rigging, which might now give way at any moment. His own life-belt would possibly have enabled him to reach the shore, but he would not leave his companion, who had none.

Another attempt was made about 3 p.m., both by the shore party and by Lieutenant Vereker in the cutter, to reach the wreck. Lieutenant Lowry directed the cutter from the mast of the wreck, and succeeded at last in throwing a line into her. With the aid of this the rescue was accomplished, Lieutenant Lowry assisting the last man into the boat before leaving the wreck. Meanwhile one of the three men on the detached rocks managed to reach the shore. The others were washed off and drowned.

Henderson, Alexander C., Third Officer, S.S. *City of Corinth*.   Case 31967

Stanhope Gold Medal 1902

On the 1st February, 1902, the s.s. *City of Corinth*, while crossing the Bay of Biscay on her voyage to London, encountered a tremendous hurricane with a mountainous sea running. About 8.30 a.m., the storm being then at its height, the French brig *Eugene Raoul* was sighted, she being then in distress, labouring heavily, and shortly after was seen to founder at a distance of about half a mile. The *City of Corinth* was then circled round the place where the brig disappeared in the hope of picking up any survivors one man was seen hanging on to some wreckage which was floating about. Lifebelts and ropes were thrown, but he was too exhausted to avail himself of them. Alexander Henderson, third officer of the steamer, then went over the side with a line, but had great difficulty in reaching the man. Several times he got quite close to him, when a huge wave would cause the ship to lurch, and drag him away. At one time he would be high on top of a wave, and next down in the trough of a sea, and once he was right under his own ship. Eventually he managed to reach him, and fastened the line round him, when both were hauled on board, the rescued man, who was the sole survivor, did not regain consciousness for five hours.

Great risk was incurred owing to the fearful storm then raging.

Shearme, J., Fourth Officer, S.S. *Malacca*.   Case 32467

Stanhope Gold Medal 1903

At 2 p.m. on the 15th December, 1902, whilst the P. & O. s.s. *Malacca* was lying at anchor below the bar about two miles from land, at Woosung, China, A. Aveston, quartermaster of the ship, in attempting to go down a bamboo ladder, fell into the sea between the ship and a lighter, to which he intended going. The night was dark, with an ebb tide running five to six knots, there being a considerable sea on and the temperature below freezing point. Mr. Shearme, fourth officer of the ship, was standing near, and he at once jumped in, fully clothed, and having caught Aveston, succeeded in maintaining his position until ropes could be lowered and both pulled up. Owing to the fact that the boats were bumping heavily there was great danger of being crushed.

On the previous voyage Mr. Shearme jumped overboard and saved a European in the Shanghai river.

Mackenzie, Thomas C., Captain, Royal Army Medical Corps.   Case 33669

Stanhope Gold Medal 1904

At 9.30 a.m. on the 22nd September, 1904, while the Messageries Maritimes Company's Steamer *Saghalien*, from Mauritius to Marseilles, was in the Ionian Sea, steaming at the rate of twelve and a half knots, an apprentice accidentally fell from the ship. Hearing the cry "man overboard!" Captain Thomas C. Mackenzie, R.A.M.C., who was being sent home invalided after a severe attack of pneumonia and typhoid, and was a passenger on the vessel, at once jumped after him. A lifebuoy was thrown, which fell 75 yards from him, but this he secured, and with it reached the youth, who, although able to swim, was in difficulty owing to his waist-belt having got twisted round his legs. Capt Mackenzie released him, and with the waist-belt lashed him to another buoy which had drifted near, and tying this buoy to his own they awaited rescue. Owing to the choppy sea they had been lost sight of from the steamer, and it was not till forty minutes had elapsed that they were again sighted, when a boat was lowered and they were picked up.

Great risk was incurred, not only by jumping from a steamer going over twelve knots, but also on account of Capt. Mackenzie's weak state of health, as when embarking three weeks previously he had to be carried on board.

Stockton, John, Baker's Carter, Warrington.   Case 3786

Stanhope Gold Medal 1905

At 9 p.m. on the 6th March, 1905, a number of men were engaged in cleaning a sewer at Warrington. The first man to go down the manhole was Frank Donoghue, the sewer being about seven feet below the street level. On reaching the bottom he was overcome by foul gas and fell down unconscious. A fellow-workman, R.W. Bretherton, at once went down to try and save him, but failed, and had to be assisted out. John Mitchell then went down, followed by James Baxter, but both men succumbed to the noxious fumes without being able to render any assistance to Donoghue. John Stockton, a baker's carter, who was without any experience of sewer work, then volunteered to try and rescue the three men. At the first attempt he was badly affected by the gas, and had to come up for air. At the second attempt he succeeded in getting a rope round Baxter who was then pulled up. A third and fourth time Stockton descended, and succeeded in recovering the bodies of the other two men. Artificial respiration was at once resorted to, with the result that Mitchell and Donoghue recovered but Baxter succumbed. Extreme risk was incurred from the deadly gas present in the sewer.

The Silver Medal was voted to John Stockton, Testimonials on Vellum to Mitchell and Bretherton, and an "In Memoriam" to relatives of Baxter.

Noble, D.J.D., Sub-Lieut., R.N., H.M.S. *Leviathon*.   Case 34505

Stanhope Gold Medal 1906

At 6.30 p.m. on the 12th March, 1906, W. Mulligan, A.B., whilst employed in getting in the accommodation ladder on the cruiser *Leviathon*, then in the Gulf of Lyons, was washed overboard from the port sea gangway. It was nearly dark at the time, there being a heavy sea with considerable overfall, and the ship steaming at about eight knots.

Sub-Lieut. Noble at once jumped from the quarter-deck, but unfortunately failed to reach Mulligan before he sank, and was himself only just able to reach the lifebuoy by which he was got on board.

Parr, William Henry, Able Seaman, S.S. *Illovo*.   Case 35726

Stanhope Gold Medal 1907

At 5 p.m. on the 13th December, 1907, the s.s. *Illovo*, belonging to the Aberdeen Line of Direct Steamers, was lying at anchor in the Inhambane river on the East Coast of Africa, when a boat, containing James Moore, A.B., and some thirty natives, was swamped in trying to reach the ship.

Moore was unable to swim, and many of the natives, in their frantic efforts to save themselves, clutched him and he was dragged under water. William H. Parr, seeing this from the ship, at once jumped overboard and swam to the place, where he succeeded in liberating Moore from the grasp of the natives, and then swam away with him, he being in a half drowned state.

Eventually they were picked up by a boat from the ship after being twenty minutes in the water and drifting about half a mile. It was blowing hard at the time, with a strong wind and choppy sea. Extreme risk was incurred, not only from the danger of being dragged down by the natives, but from the sharks which infested the locality.

Smith, George Henry, Brick Worker, Woburn Sands Brick Works. Case 36435

Stanhope Gold Medal 1908

At 9.20 a.m. on the 24th October, 1908, Charles Griffin was engaged cleaning ballast from the top of a brick-kiln at the Woburn Sands Brick Works, when part of the roof gave way and he fell into the kiln, being buried up to his waist in the red hot ballast. The kiln is about eighteen feet by twenty with a domed roof, on which many tons of brick earth are placed in order to retain the heat when the kiln is working. This ballast, when bricks are being burnt, gets red hot, and holds its heat for a long time. The entrance to the kiln is by a wicket at the bottom through which a man can readily pass, but when the fall took place the barrow which Griffin was using blocked this opening, leaving a space of only about a foot across. Through this opening Smith made his way and dug away the hot earth from around Griffin, and in about fifteen minutes succeeded in getting him out in a fearfully injured state, when he was removed to hospital, where he died some days later.

Great risk was incurred from the danger of a further fall of the tottering roof, the intense heat, choking dust and poisonous gases with which the kiln was filled.

Bouttell, Thomas, Able Seaman, R.N., H.M.S. *Glory*. Case 36480

Stanhope Gold Medal 1909

At 11.30 a.m. on the 25th November, 1908, the s.s. *Sardinia* was ashore off Ricasoli, Malta, and burning fiercely, a heavy sea running at the time.

A sailing pinnace from H.M.S. *Glory*, with a crew of sixteen men, was endeavouring to rescue passengers and approached her weather quarter, and for a short time established communication by means of a rope, down which four Arabs climbed into the boat. At that moment, however, owing to the heavy sea and the boat's anchor dragging, the officer in charge was forced to haul away from the ship. Meanwhile three Arabs lowered themselves down the ship's side until they were awash and were being thrown heavily against the ship's side with each succeeding sea. Two were picked up, but the third man became in some way entangled with the rope and was in great distress, collapsing from the effects of the submersion and knocking about.

A volunteer being called for, Able Seaman Thomas Bouttell sprang overboard, successfully detached the man from the rope, and supported him for a sufficient time to enable a customs whaler to pick them both up.

Great danger incurred, as there had been frequent explosions on board the ship up to that time; and, owing to the fierceness of the flames in many places, the ship's side was nearly red hot.

Fraser, Frank, Chief Engineer, Aberdeen Trawler *Donside*. Case 37760

Stanhope Gold Medal 1910

At 12.30 a.m. on the 27th August, 1910, the Aberdeen trawler *Donside* was fishing on what is known as the Viking Bank, about 225 miles north-east by east of Aberdeen. Although it was blowing hard with a heavy sea running the captain decided to shoot the trawl, and when he thought everything was clear shouted to let go, but unfortunately the deck hand John Fraser, was standing on part of the net, and was carried over the side of the vessel. Hearing the shouting on deck the chief engineer, Frank Fraser, rushed up from below and instantly leapt overboard and managed to reach the man, both then drifting to windward. There being a light in the after rigging the men could be seen, and a rope was thrown which the chief engineer succeeded in grasping, but his hands being greasy with oil from the engine room he had the utmost difficulty in retaining his hold and continually slipped back, and it was only after fifteen minutes patient work that both were got safely on board, the salvor being much bruised from knocking against the side of the vessel. Extreme risk was incurred, the night being pitch dark, and the sea very rough.

Halliday, Charles C., Second Officer, S.S. *River Clyde*.   Case 38006

Stanhope Gold Medal 1911

At 9.40 a.m. on the 29th November, 1911, while the Glasgow steamer *River Clyde*, on her way home, was in the Red Sea and going full speed, a Chinese fireman, with the intention of committing suicide, threw himself overboard from the fore deck. Charles C. Halliday, R.N.R., Second Officer, without hesitation at once sprang after him, but as the man never came to the surface he was unable to effect the rescue. The steamer was stopped and a boat got away which picked Mr. Halliday up after he had been twenty minutes in the water.

Great risk was incurred not only from drowning, but of being cut to pieces by the propeller and from the numerous sharks which infest these waters

Palmer, D., Second Engineer, S.S. *Meifoo*.   Case 38997

Stanhope Gold Medal 1912

On the evening of the 23rd April, 1911, the s.s. *Meifoo*, belonging to the China Merchants Steam Navigation Company, was at anchor some four miles south by west of Elgar Island, off the Chinese coast, when she was run into by the same Company's steamer *Kwanglee*, there being a dense fog at the time. The *Meifoo*, which had a large number of native passengers on board, rolled over and sank four minutes after in a depth of fifteen fathoms. The chief officer, James Smith, who could not swim, was going down with the ship, when D. Palmer, the second engineer, jumped after him and succeeded in getting him clear of the wreck, supporting him in an unconscious state for an hour, when they were picked up by a boat. About forty of the *Meifoo*'s passengers were drowned.

Great risk of being clutched and pulled under by the drowning passengers and of being lost in the dense fog then prevailing.

Tomkinson, Wilfred, Commander, R.N., H.M.S. *Wolf*.   Case 40545

Stanhope Gold Medal 1913

At about 11 a.m. on the 20th November, 1913, William H. Ball, A.B., was washed overboard from submarine B4 off Bigbury Bay, Devon, the water being very cold with a heavy sea running. In response to a signal from the submarine the destroyer *Wolf* raced at full speed to the place, and on the man being seen in an apparently helpless state Commander Tomkinson at once plunged in from the *Wolf*, and having caught the man, succeeded in bringing him close to that vessel. A lifebuoy was then thrown, to which he held on to with a view to both being pulled on board, but unfortunately the buoy broke, throwing them again into the water. On coming to the surface Commander Tomkinson, who was now much exhausted, grasped a line which was thrown, but would not come on board until all hope of saving the seaman had gone.

Owing to the rough sea and the heavy motion of the ship Commander Tomkinson ran extreme risk of being taken under the *Wolf* as she drove down to leeward.

Hales, Edward John, Chief Officer, S.S. *Mineric*.   Case 41120

Stanhope Gold Medal 1914

At 11 a.m. on the 3rd June, 1914, the British s.s. *Mineric*, belonging to the Andrew Weir Line, on a voyage from Kobe to Shanghai, was in the Sea of Japan when she encountered a violent typhoon with a heavy sea. During the storm a Japanese fishing schooner, which had been upset, was sighted, four men being seen clinging to the bottom and shouting for help. The master turned the vessel's head and approached near enough to be able to get them on board, when it was found that a woman was inside the schooner and unable to get out.

Edward John Hales, chief officer of the *Mineric*, taking an axe was lowered by a rope into the raging sea and reached the overturned vessel, cut through her bottom, and got the woman out, when the steamer was brought near enough to get them on board, a boat which had been got out to pick them up being blown away. Mr. Hales was about an hour on the bottom of the upturned craft, with the sea breaking over him and in constant danger of being swept away.

Hetherington, Cecil, Apprentice, S.S. *Jacona*.   Case 41910

Stanhope Gold Medal 1915

At 11.35 p.m. on the 12th August, 1915, the s.s. *Jacona* on a voyage from Middlesbrough to Montreal was crossing the Moray Firth when she was either torpedoed or struck a mine and sank in two minutes. There was no time for launching boats, all hands going down with the ship. The captain and nine others came to the surface clinging to some wreckage. Some ten to fifteen minutes later what appeared to be a boat was seen floating about 75 yards away. Most of the men being exhausted, Cecil Hetherington, who was an apprentice on the ship, volunteered to try and reach the boat and was successful, although he had great difficulty in getting on board after his long swim fully dressed. He then brought the boat back, picking up one man on the way, and those clinging to the wreckage were then got on board. In all thirteen persons were thus saved, the remainder of the crew, twenty-five in number, being drowned.

The boat was eventually picked up five hours after the ship sank.

Paxton, John, Fireman, S.S. *Swedish Prince*.   Case 42938

Stanhope Gold Medal 1916

At about 10.30 a.m. on the 17th August, 1916, the s.s. *Swedish Prince* had to be quickly abandoned in the Mediterranean, owing to being shelled by a German submarine. When the last boats put off Paxton, who was a fireman on board, and three other men, none of whom could swim, were left behind.

At once jumping overboard, Paxton called on the first man to follow, which he did, and Paxton swam with him to the nearest boat. Returning, he called to the second man to jump, and he also was conveyed to the boat; again Paxton returned to the ship, and the third man, jumping in, was taken to the nearest boat. One of the men had a lifebelt on, nothing being used in saving the other two.

Great risk was incurred, there being a high wind with heavy sea.

Lewin, Francis H.L., Commander, R.N.   Case 43242

Stanhope Gold Medal 1917

At 8.15 p.m. on the 8th February, 1917, one of H.M. ships struck a mine at sea about 4 miles off Dungeness, and sank in a few minutes, there being a heavy sea running at the time. With the intention of picking up survivors a trawler steamed over the position, but in putting out her boat it was damaged, and broke adrift, thereby losing the only means of rescuing those in the water.

Shortly afterwards Commander Lewin drifted alongside with two men clinging to him, and though well knowing that he might drift away again at any moment, as others had already done, he called out to those on board the trawler to take the men, first supporting the second man while the first was being dragged on board. Eventually, all three were rescued in a state of great exhaustion after being thirty minutes in the water. The weather was very cold the deck of the trawler being covered with ice.

Ritchie, Hugh Lownie, Skipper, Motor Fishing Boat *Grace*.   Case 44519

Stanhope Gold Medal 1918

At 5.10 a.m. on the 9th October, 1918, the motor fishing-boat *Grace* was at sea about 4 miles E.S.E. from Gourdon on the Fifeshire coast going at about five and a half knots, the sea being rough and the weather dull and threatening, when a heavy wave broke over the boat, washing Robert Davidson, one of the crew, overboard. When the water cleared the man was seen about 10 yards to windward.

Fully clothed and wearing heavy sea-boots Hugh L. Ritchie, skipper of the boat, at once went after him and bringing him to the surface supported him for nearly half an hour, when the boat was brought round, and both were hauled on board in an exhausted state.

Grey, Aubrey A.D., Lieut., R.N.   Case 44748

Stanhope Gold Medal 1919

During action on the 12th December, 1917, Lieut. Grey jumped into the water to the help of Lieut. Walters who was exhausted, and although badly wounded in the leg, swam with him for more than a quarter of a mile and placed him on the only vacant place on a raft. Seeing that his own added weight would endanger the raft, he then swam away and was eventually picked up by a German destroyer in a very exhausted state. There was a heavy sea running at the time and the weather intensely cold.

Twentyman, Ernest, Captain, Harbour Master, Levuca, Fiji.   Case 45272

Stanhope Gold Medal 1920

About noon on the 1st September, 1919, George Rosendale, Captain of the American schooner *King Cyrus*, then in harbour at Levuka, Fiji, in order to get a piece of wire went into the fore-peak of the vessel and became unconscious owing to an accumulation of carbonic acid gas. Captain Ernest Twentyman, Harbour Master, who was following him, caught him by the shoulders, and was pulling him towards the hatchway when he felt himself collapsing, and letting go, mounted the ladder and reached the deck. Two members of the crew then went down, but collapsed before they could do anything. Two Fijians then went down and managed to get a rope round Captain Rosendale, when they also succumbed to the effects of the gas. Meanwhile Captain Twentyman had somewhat recovered, and again going down secured the rope, with which he went on deck, and eventually, after considerable trouble and difficulty, Captain Rosendale was drawn clear of the hatchway and recovered soon after reaching the deck. The two members of the crew and one of the Fijians who attempted the rescue unfortunately lost their lives.

Brannon, Thomas, Coal Miner, Newcastle-on-Tyne.   Case 46228

Stanhope Gold Medal 1921

At 4.30 a.m. on November 14th, 1921, Nicholas Passmore, deputy overman at the Hall Pit Netherton Colliery, Nedderton, near Newcastle-on-Tyne, in the course of his examination found that "stythe" had accumulated in some of the working places. In order that the miners might begin work in other parts of the pit he rashly entered these places to bring out their gear, and was overcome by the gas at a point about 40 yards from the entrance. The men who were waiting tried to enter the place but were driven back by the gas, so sent for assistance.

Brannon was called, and he at once went in and tried to reach Passmore, but this part of the pit being strange to him, with two places branching off and the whole in absolute darkness, it was not until the third attempt that he succeeded in locating Passmore and dragging him out by the heels. The deputy had been unconscious for some time but eventually recovered.

Brannon showed exceptional coolness, courage, and powers of endurance, and was in extreme danger owing to the peculiar virulence of the "stythe" or gas.

Hutton, Peter C., Midshipman, R.N., H.M.S. *Raleigh*. Case 46560B

Stanhope Gold Medal 1922

When H.M.S. *Raleigh* stranded near Armour Point on the 8th August, 1922, a cutter was lowered to try to get a line ashore. Midshipman Hutton and Herbert R. Reynolds, A.B., were both in this boat, which was driven on the rocks and capsized, eleven men being swept away and drowned. Able Seaman Reynolds was carried back into deep water, Mr. Hutton and others succeeded in reaching the rocks. Still fully dressed Mr. Hutton jumped into the surf, which was breaking heavily over the rocks, swam out to Reynolds, who was rapidly drowning in deep water, and succeeded in saving him. There was a strong wind and heavy sea.

See Case 46560A.

Clayton, Harvey, Gentleman, Cape Province, South Africa. Case 46782

Stanhope Gold Medal 1923

At 7.30 a.m. on the 1st April, 1923, Mrs Marion Fox was bathing in Palmiet Bay, Cape Province, South Africa, when she got into deep water and was quickly carried seaward by the strong current. An alarm was at once raised, and three gentlemen Cecil Penny, Athol Timm and Harvey Clayton after running 300 yards entered the water, but Penny and Timm were swept away and drowned, Clayton was caught by the current and carried out beyond Mrs. Fox, who was then about two miles from land. He, however, managed to reach Mrs. Fox, and succeeded in bringing her back for about half the distance, when they found footing on a sand-bank for a few moments. On leaving this the lady lost consciousness, but Clayton stuck to his task and eventually brought her to land, he himself being in a most exhausted state, having been about one and a half hours in the water.

In Memoriam Testimonials being awarded to the relatives of Penny and Timm.

No Silver Medal having been awarded during 1924, the following cases in which Bronze Medals were awarded were selected by the Committee for further consideration :-

Harold F. Milner	Case 47165
George Ingham	Case 47262
Benjamin Miller	Case 47356
Henrietta Kirk	Case 47503

Ingham, George, Dye Worker, Smedley Bridge Dyeworks, Lower Crumpsall, Manchester. Case 47262

Stanhope Gold Medal 1924

At 2.45 p.m. on the 30th January, 1924, two men, named Marriott and Bamford, in the course of their work entered a keir on the premises of the Smedley Bridge Dye Works, Lower Crumpsall, Manchester, and were overcome by the fumes from some tetralene which was being used. A keir is a perpendicular boiler used for boiling two tons of cotton cloth at a time, and is 9 feet 5 inches deep and 7 feet wide, with two manholes at the top, 12 inches by 7 inches, a ladder being used for entering, it being dark inside.

On an alarm being given, Ingham, with a fellow workman named Porter (to whom a testimonial on vellum has been awarded), entered the keir, and with considerable difficulty got Marriott out, and he recovered. Ingham then went down to try and save Bamford, but could do nothing, and came out. On recovering he got a rope, and again going down, he fastened the rope round Bamford, and he was pulled up but did not recover. Ingham ran extreme risk by entering the keir three times, knowing the nature of the fumes to which he was exposed.

Souter Duncan L., Seaman, Steam Trawler *Honoria*. Case 47801

Stanhope Gold Medal 1925

At 1.30 p.m. on the 16th May, 1925, the steam trawler *Honoria*, belonging to the Grimsby Fishing Vessel Owners Exchange Co., was engaged taking up her lines and gear about 90 miles off the coast of Iceland, the weather being exceedingly rough, with half a gale blowing and heavy cross-seas running. The trawler was steaming slowly, head to sea, when it was discovered that the mate, John M. Lee, had been washed overboard and was seen well astern of the vessel. Two lifebuoys were thrown towards him, but he failed to reach either of them, and in about twenty minutes he was seen to give up and lay face downwards in the water. A member of the crew, Duncan L. Souter, then threw off his heavy boots, and plunging overboard, secured one of the lifebuoys, which he took to Lee, and with this supported him until the vessel was got into a position from which it was possible to throw a line, by which means both men were got on board. The Captain states that if the first attempt to throw a line had been unsuccessful, it would have been impossible, owing to the wind and heavy seas, for a second attempt to have been in time to effect a rescue. When got on board Lee was unconscious, and Souter collapsed on reaching the deck. Extreme risk was incurred, it being impossible to launch a boat.

Smith, Harry, Mate, Steam Drifter *Sarepta*. Case 48693

Stanhope Gold Medal 1926

At about 4 p.m. on Sunday, the 31st October, 1926, the Steam Drifter *Sarepta* was returning to Lowestoft from the fishing grounds in heavy squalls and very cold weather. When some 4 miles east of the Corton Lightship, Alfred Marjoram, while cleaning the nets with others of the crew, was thrown overboard by a heavy lurch of the vessel. He was wearing heavy sea-boots and oilskins, and was soon some 300 yards astern. The engines were reversed and the boat brought round, a lifebuoy being then thrown to him, but he was too exhausted to make use of it.

Seeing this, Harry Smith, the mate, having thrown off his oilskins and sea-boots, jumped overboard and reached Marjoram as he was sinking. A line with lifebuoy attached was then thrown from the vessel, and Smith, getting his arm over the line, they were hauled alongside and with difficulty got on board, both men being washed under the vessel's quarter, Marjoram being now unconscious and Smith exhausted and bruised.

During this time the boat was drifting to leeward, and had the line attached to the lifebuoy broken by a sudden strain caused by the rolling of the boat, both men must have been drowned.

Johnson, Ernest T, Plumber, Higher Crumpsall, Manchester. Case 48761

Stanhope Gold Medal 1927

Between 4 and 5 p.m. on the 10th December, 1926, two men, David Inglis and Ernest T. Johnson, were working in a trench which was being excavated in the garden of Mayvern House, Bury Old Road, Higher Crumpsall, Manchester. The trench was 16 feet deep, the subsoil at this depth being quicksand. Without warning the trench suddenly collapsed, partially burying Johnson and completely burying Inglis. Johnson could easily have released himself, but realized that if he did so Inglis would have been suffocated, as he was entirely covered, only his hair showing, and he decided at the risk of his own life to remain where he was, and thus try to save his mate. He had constantly to scrape the earth away from Inglis's head so that he could breathe, and at the same time carry the weight of the crumbling earth above, and so prevent a further collapse.

Assistance was summoned, but owing to the shifting nature of the sands it took eight hours before the men were finally got out, and during this time the weight of earth Johnson was supporting forced him down to where Inglis was buried, making his position one of great danger.

Heyns, Andries H, Farmer, Mossel Bay, South Africa.   Case 49214

Stanhope Gold Medal 1928

On the morning of the 28th December, 1927, several persons were bathing at Little Brak River Beach, near Mossel Bay, the sea being calm with very little wind. Suddenly a large shark appeared in the water, and seizing a lad named Ockardus J. Heyns, aged 17, dragged him by his foot some 20 yards back into deeper water, where it bit off his leg above the knee, his right foot being also completely crushed.

At this stage Mr. A.M. Heyns went to his rescue, and found him in deep water with the shark still circling round him; seizing the exhausted lad he managed to get him into shallow water and carry him out of the sea; and he was taken to hospital, 9 miles distant, where he died six hours later.

Thomson, Leonard R., Deck Hand, Steam Drifter *Forethought*.   Case 49862

Stanhope Gold Medal 1929

At 3.30 a.m. on the morning of the 25th June, 1929, E.E. Bulley, Mate of the Steam Drifter *Forethought*, was accidentally knocked overboard owing to a heavy sea. He was dressed in full length oilskins and thigh boots. The vessel was lying at her nets, 37 miles south of Bressay Light, 20 miles east of Fair Isle off the Shetlands.

L.R. Thomson, a deck hand, aged 18, who was working in the hold, came on deck and went overboard to the man's aid, also wearing oil skins and thigh boots, and got hold of Bulley who now became unconscious. It took some 20 to 30 minutes before the drifter could be cut away from her gear and brought alongside and the men hauled on board. Throughout this time, in a heavy sea and a bitterly cold morning, Thomson held on to the mate and kept him afloat.

All efforts to restore Bulley failed.

Singleton, Colin H.C., Lieut., R.N., H.M.S. *Peterel*.   Case 50623

Stanhope Gold Medal 1930

On the 13th August, 1930, at 11 p.m., Lieut. Singleton, who had been ashore on duty to ensure that the libertymen from his ship all returned from the Naval Canteen at Hankow, was returning to H.M.S. *Peterel* together with six libertymen in the ship's motor sampan - a boat with very little draft and very little freeboard.

On arrival alongside H.M.S. *Peterel* Lieut. Singleton got out of the boat and stood by the gangway to watch the libertymen come inboard-libertymen being inspected by an officer on all occasions of arriving on board.

Two of the six ratings had stepped on board, when Stoker O'Brien came out from under the canopy of the sampan, paused a moment before stepping inboard, and, for no apparent reason, fell backwards into the river. He was the only non-swimmer in the ship, a fact which was known to Lieut. Singleton, who, without waiting to remove any clothing, leapt from the ship on to the sampan and dived after Stoker O'Brien. Lieut. Singleton caught O'Brien about 20 yards astern of H.M.S. *Peterel* but he was struggling so violently that both sank, and the rescuer was forced to relinquish his hold, and in spite of every effort could not locate O'Brien. About half a minute later Lieut. Singleton picked up a lifebuoy. The motor sampan by this time had again got under way and came alongside the officer, who instructed it not to stop but to go on down stream and continue the search for the deceased. The boat then proceeded down as far as the Installation of the Asiatic Petroleum Co. (about three and a half miles from the scene of the accident) and then returned, and then with considerable difficulty found Lieut. Singleton (who hailed them) and returned to the ship. Had the officer not hailed it is extremely probable he would not have been picked up.

The Yangtse River is notoriously dangerous, owing to the very fast current (at the time at least 4 knots) a powerful undertow and the very real danger of acquiring disease from contact with its waters. Innumerable cases of drowning have occurred where the victim has fallen in and never appeared again, owing to the aforementioned undertow. Lieut. Singleton was in the water approximately twenty minutes, and suffered from nausea for two to three days after as a result.

Jenkin, G, Ship's Cook, Auxiliary Schooner *John William V.*   Case 50673

Stanhope Gold Medal 1931

At about 7.30 a.m. on the 5th October, 1930, at sea, lat 47 50 N., lon 47 50 W., Alexander Samuel, Seaman on Auxiliary Schooner *John William V* was washed overboard from the jib-boom, while furling the inner jib. Engines stopped and helm put hard-about and lifebuoys thrown in and lifeboat launched. Before the lifeboat reached the water, Jenkins the cook, had gone overboard, and was seen to reach a lifebuoy and endeavour to reach Samuel, but the man sank, and though the lifeboat cruised round for about an hour was not seen again. Jenkins was picked up by the boat after being some twenty minutes in the water, and was nearly exhausted when reached.

Weather very rough and ship unmanageable when the engines were stopped. S.W. gale with confused swell. Lifeboat smashed in attempting to take on board, and had to be abandoned.

Spencer, Benjamin R, Manager, Klipspruit Sewage Farm, Johannesburg, South Africa.   Case 51523

Stanhope Gold Medal 1932

About noon on the 13th October, 1932, a native worker went down a manhole at the Klipspruit Sewage Farm, Johannesburg, to remove a blockage, and collapsed, being overcome by sewer gas. Another native went down with the same result, followed by a third, who also was overcome.

Then Mr. Spencer, having been sent for, went down with a rope tied round himself and a cloth soaked in hypotheosulphate round his face, and on reaching the bottom of the manhole, fastened a second rope round the three men, who were hauled to the surface in succession, he himself being drawn out last in an unconscious state which lasted 20 minutes, when he recovered.

Manhole 24 feet deep and a diameter of 2 feet 6 inches at top.

Jones, H.E.B, Rubber Planter.   Case 51726

Stanhope Gold Medal 1933

At 10 a.m. on the 6th March, 1933, owing to an abnormal current, with mist obscuring the land, the s.s. *Antung* on a voyage from Swatow to Hong Kong stranded at Mofu Point on Hainan Island, and the Captain decided to abandon ship as the seas were very rough and the vessel pounding heavily. The Captain placed his wife and child in the gig along with some native passengers in charge of the Third Officer. When the boat got level with the main deck it was rushed by panic-stricken passengers, which caused the gig to list heavily towards the ship's side and the falls jammed. To get the boat into the water the falls had to be cut, and when the boat hit the water it capsized and threw everybody out.

The sea was rough and thickly coated with fuel oil from the burst double bottom fuel oil tanks. It was extremely hazardous for anyone to go into the water from the ship on account of the panic-stricken people in the water who were clutching one another and fighting to get to the ropes that were thrown to their aid.

P. Sherevera went in and rescued the Captain's child, but was played out with the effort and was unable to help Mrs. Ashby. The Third Officer was in the water, but was unable to do anything on account of the injuries he had received.

Mr. Jones slid down a rope and swam off to Mrs. Ashby and brought her to the ship's side. He had great difficulty in bending a rope on to her on account of the passengers in the water clutching him in their efforts to save themselves. When Mrs Ashby had been pulled aboard, Mr. Jones remained in the water and assisted in the rescue of quite a number of Chinese passengers. When he was himself hoisted aboard he was in a very exhausted state. When the ship was abandoned, the boats were rushed, and approximately 50 passengers and 20 of the crew lost their lives. Survivors eventually transferred in a lifeboat to the s.s. *Anhui* and later to Hong Kong.

Silver Medal awarded to H.E.B. Jones, and Bronze Medal to P. Sherevera, Sergeant, of the Anti-Piracy Guard.

Richardson, Hugh N.A., Lieut., R.N., H.M.S. *Wolfhound*.   Case 52037

Stanhope Gold Medal 1934

On the 7th January, 1934, H.M.S. *Wolfhound* was at anchor in 16 fathoms in Lamlash Harbour, Isle of Arran. It was a cold, dark morning, with strong south-westerly squalls (force 6-8, Beaufort scale), which caused a nasty choppy sea and considerable spume. About 7.30 a.m. an ordinary seaman fell overboard and was quickly swept astern into the darkness. Two lifebuoys were thrown at once in his direction, but failed to reach him.

Lieut. Richardson called away the lifeboat's crew, threw off his overcoat and seaboots, dived in fully clothed and swam straight to the man, whom he endeavoured to tow to the nearest buoy. Being unable to do so, he left the man with words of encouragement, swam back and returned with the buoy, which he placed under the man's shoulders, whilst he himself grasped one of the beckets. A boat had now been manned and lowered, and with the aid of a searchlight, the man was picked up after about 10 minutes in the water. Lieut. Richardson assisted to get the man into the boat, and in so doing lost hold of the lifebuoy and was again swept to leeward into the darkness. The boat eventually found him some 10 minutes later in a very exhausted condition. As the boat was now on a dead lee shore and unable to make any headway against the wind and sea, it had to be beached, Lieut. Richardson and the crew wading ashore. Lieut. Richardson had been swept nearly half a mile from the ship before he was finally rescued by the boat.

Irons, Evelyn Graham, Miss., M.A., Cardigan Bay.   Case 52938

Stanhope Gold Medal 1935

About 4 p.m. on 29th July, 1935, Mrs MacSweeney, a good swimmer, was bathing in a rough sea at Tresaith Beach, Cardigan Bay, was caught in a cross-current, swept seaward, and got into difficulties.

Miss Irons was swimming about 50 yards away, heard her cries, swam over and supported her, whilst calling for assistance. A strong swimmer tried to get through the breakers, failed and had to desist. A small boat was launched and capsized. Attempts to launch a larger boat failed. The beach was crowded, but no one could do anything effectual. Mrs MacSweeney became semi-conscious and Miss Irons continued to support her, the waves breaking over them continuously.

At this stage there was small prospect of any rescue. Miss Irons who could then probably have saved herself, decided to stay by her friend and save her, or perish in the attempt. After about one hour the current changed and swept the two ladies nearer inshore. A strong swimmer put on a line and succeeded in swimming out to them, others on the beach holding the line and forming a human chain close to the breakers, and all were hauled ashore. Mrs MacSweeney was unconscious and was with difficulty brought round; Miss Irons was very exhausted.

Fresh gale blowing. Sea rough and choppy. Rescue at least 200 yards out from shore and in deep water.

Kinch, Noel Augustus Fisherman, Steam Trawler *Northern Pride*.　　　　　　　　　　　　　　　　Case 53640

Stanhope Gold Medal 1936

At 3 p.m. on 13th August, 1936, whilst the Steam Trawler *Northern Pride* was steaming at 10 knots and shooting her gear off Dyrafiord, Iceland, the messenger wire jumped out of its sheave, caught the bos'n in the small of the back and knocked him overboard. Kinch, seeing the accident, ran aft, discarded his heavy seaboots, dived overboard in full fishing kit, swam 500 yards to the bos'n and supported him and encouraged him to float until the vessel could be manoeuvred back to them.

Meanwhile the warps were eased off, the vessel turned and headed for the two men, who were seen to be in difficulties, due to the coldness of the water. When approaching them, Wright seized a handline, dived overboard, swam out to them with the line and thus enabled all three men to be hauled back to the ship. The rescue took about 40 minutes in all to effect.

Silver Medal to Noel Augustus Kinch and Vellum Testimonial to John Robert Wright.

Hill, Ernest, Deck Hand, Steam Trawler *Northern Spray*.　　　　　　　　　　　　　　　　　　　Case 53819

Stanhope Gold Medal 1937

At 11 p.m. on Sunday, 8th November, 1936, whilst the Steam Trawler *Northern Spray* was preparing to shoot her trawl off the West Coast of Iceland, Daniels, a deck hand, caught his foot in a bight of the fore-quarter rope and was dragged overboard before he could be released. Buoys were thrown, but were not seen by him as he drifted across the head rope of the trawl, to which he held on to.

Hill, a deck hand also, was working the Gilson on the opposite side of the vessel, heard the alarm, ran across, jumped overboard in full fishing kit, including heavy sea boots, swam astern and found Daniels in a state of partial collapse and suffering from cramp in both legs due to the coldness of the water. Hill supported Daniels, and by means of the trawl head rope, both men were hauled alongside the vessel, where great difficulty was experienced in getting them inboard, due to the size of the vessel, the height of her bulwarks and the heavy confused sea and swell running at the time. Hill was also suffering from cramp by now, and it is doubtful if either man would have been saved but for the Skipper climbing down a rope and relieving Hill of the by now semi-conscious Daniels.

The rescue, which took 15-20 minutes to effect, was carried out under very cold conditions, and in pitch darkness.

Mountain, Ralph, 1st Officer, Flying Boat *Cygnus*.　　　　　　　　　　　　　　　　　　　　　Case 54911

Stanhope Gold Medal 1938

At 8.30 a.m. on 5th December, 1937, the Imperial Airways Flying Boat *Cygnus* was taking off in Brindisi Harbour, Italy, and when about 600 yards from shore it crashed at 50/55 knots, smashed the forepart and commenced to sink fairly rapidly in deep water. Mountain, the 1st Officer, who was sitting abaft the two pilots, was hurled through the windscreen, sank deep, and on coming up to the surface again, somewhat dazed by the impact, was unable to find any means of re-entry to the partly submerged hull, until the after-loading hatch was opened from the inside by three passengers, who then dived overboard and swam to a nearby boat.

Mountain then swam back on to the hull, divested himself of his outer garments, climbed in through the open hatchway, found the after-compartment much congested with wreckage and with three passengers in it. Seeing that one of the passengers was unconscious, he propped his head up on a luggage-rack to prevent him from being drowned, then swam through the entrance to the after-hold and forward through the promenade saloon, which was filled with water to within two feet of the roof. Realizing that opening the emergency hatch in the roof of the fuselage would completely flood the compartment, he swam back and got the two conscious passengers in position beneath the hatch, which he then opened and helped them out, being assisted outside, from on top of the hull, by the Station Superintendent, who had arrived in a boat. Mountain then swam back again through the fuselage to the unconscious man and got him out of the after-loading hatch into a boat which had just arrived. The *Cygnus* sank shortly afterwards.

Lee, Martin, Able Seaman, S.S. *Harmanteh*. Case 55180

Stanhope Gold Medal 1939

At 9.33 p.m. on 21st May, 1938, at Penguin Rocks, Messier Channel, Chile, South America, the s.s. *Harmanteh*, in ballast and proceeding northwards up Smythe's Channel, and after passing through the English Narrows, ran into a strong N.E. gale with heavy rain squalls. The Master then decided to anchor in a sheltered anchorage for the night, but was informed by the Chilean Pilot that there was no place, due to the great depth of water. The vessel was then headed for the open sea to get sea room to ride out the gale until daylight. The gale having increased, the vessel was driven to leeward on to San Pedro Light.

The vessel was then turned round to leeward to try and get under the shelter of Sombrero Island, and after doing so an island was sighted close to starboard. Seeing that it would be impossible to clear the rocks, the engines were put astern and the vessel struck the rocks with her forefoot and was flung broadside on to the reef, where she pounded heavily. Due to the outward list of the vessel, it was impossible to lower any boat on the weather side. As the vessel was forming a breakwater to the heavy seas, it was thought that a line might be got ashore by a man scrambling over the rocks between the successive waves.

Lee volunteered to do so, descended over the bows by means of a rope ladder, waited his chance, and then scrambled the 30 feet or so over the low rocks, and attempted to scale the higher rocks, was caught up by the next wave, and was swept up against them. Luckily he was able to hold on to the rock, and when the water receded, scrambled up and hauled the heavy line ashore. A bosun's chair was rigged up, and an able seaman (Bugeja) was sent ashore to help Lee to rig up breeches buoy apparatus. The vessel was unfortunately driven still further ashore, resulting in the rope sagging and Bugeja being washed out of the chair and swept away in the swirl of the waters. Lee, seeing this, scrambled down off the high rocks, seized Bugeja, and held on to him, in spite of a huge wave which rolled inshore and covered the high rocks also. The two men got ashore again, and the whole crew were landed safely by 10.30 p.m. The vessel became a total wreck, necessitating the crew being repatriated in two home-coming vessels.

Lee, though wearing a lifebelt, incurred considerable risk in getting ashore with the line, as the rocks were wet and slippery and swept by heavy seas. It was pitch dark at the time, with heavy rain squalls. The vessel was steaming full speed at the time she was grounded.

Lucas, Harry, Leading Seaman, R.N., Sheerness. Case 55833

Stanhope Gold Medal 1940

At 12.30 a.m. on the 30th January, 1940, Leading Seaman Harry Lucas and Stoker Thomas L. Phillips, Royal Navy, were crew of a motor-boat which capsized in a choppy sea about 300 yards from the Martello Tower, Isle of Grain, Sheerness, and 700 yards from shore. They were both thrown into the water, Phillips being a poor swimmer.

Lucas gave Phillips his own inflatable lifebelt and secured it on to him, also obtaining a petrol drum, which he gave to Phillips in order that he might use it to support himself. Lucas remained with Phillips about ten minutes during which time he undressed. Telling Phillips to hold on to the drum, and kick out with his legs towards shore, Lucas swam ahead, encouraging Phillips with shouts, Phillips having become somewhat hysterical.

Lucas reached shore, and as there was no one about, ran across two fields covered with thick snow, the temperature at this time being 28 degrees F. He badly lacerated his feet on barbed wire in scrambling through hedges. Reaching the Isle of Grain Tower, Lucas reported to the Military Authorities and then collapsed. A search party was sent out, and finding Phillips unconscious on the beach, had him taken to hospital by ambulance, where he was in a serious condition for some time, having been in the water for one and a half hours.

On recovering consciousness, Lucas insisted on reporting by telephone to his Commander. The River is 1,500 yards wide and 13 fathoms deep. Tidal stream flooding S.W. at one and a half knots. Dark at the time of rescue with a temperature of 28 degrees F. Depth of water 11 feet.

Fairley, Douglas S., Radio Operator.   Case 56486

Stanhope Gold Medal 1941

When in convoy at sea, on the 13th June, 1941, the s.s. ---- received a direct hit from a bomb on or near the bridge. She was immediately enveloped in flames, burning fiercely. H.M.S. ---- 50 minutes after the attack arrived to assist two trawlers carrying out rescue work. Hearing cries, ship closed two severely injured men in the water, one holding on to a lifebuoy with one hand, using the other to support the second man. The first man was seen to pull the second back to the lifebuoy four times in ten minutes, encouraging him not to give up. They were picked up by H.M. ship and found to be Radio Operator Fairley and Seaman John Miller.

Fairley, when the ship was hit, made his way from his cabin to the deck to reach his boat and just below the bridge came across Miller seriously injured. Making efforts to save Miller he missed his boat and somehow, though both had broken legs, managed to get him into the water. Finding a lifebuoy, he held it with one hand, supporting Miller with the other for a period of fifty minutes until picked up.

Injuries sustained:-

> Miller: Almost complete severance of right leg; fracture of left leg; severe burns to hands and face.
> Fairley: Compound fracture dislocation of right ankle joint; severe burns to hands and face.

Case reported by H.M.S. *Whaddon*.

Bengough, Arthur, Miner, Pontypridd.   Case 57007

Stanhope Gold Medal 1942

At 3.45 p.m. the 6th June 1942, Wendy Williams, an evacuee, with her aunt and other children was walking across the farm land at Llan Farm, Craigwen, Pontypridd. The child, playing, jumped into a small trench, where the ground gave way due to a colliery subsidence and she disappeared.

The Police and Fire Services were called to the scene with ropes and ladders. The hole in the trench was examined and found to be just wide enough to allow a very thin man or a small boy to get in. The earth was soft and loose, and there was definite danger of another subsidence if the hole was tampered with.

Leslie Richards, aged 14, volunteered to try and locate the child, whose cries could be heard. A rope was tied round his feet and he was lowered head first into the hole, but was unable to see anything and was hauled out. After a few minutes he was provided with a torch and was again lowered some 7 ft., and when brought out said that he could not get any further.

Brown then volunteered and was lowered in the same way, but could not get very far and reported that the child was some way down. He suggested that an excavation should be made a few yards from the hole and after sufficient depth had been reached a tunnel to the position of the child should be made. This was started, Brown taking charge. Brown made another descent, later assisting in the final rescue.

Hazell, a youth, was then lowered head first, but failed to locate the child. He also descended later, assisting in the final rescue.

Digging was being continued through the night, with the aid of miner's lamps, and reaching rock it was smashed partly with sledge hammers. The ground under the workmen caved in, but they carried on. About 6.30 a.m. next day they were 18 ft. down and had to exercise great care to prevent a further fall of earth.

Jones now volunteered and was tied by the feet and lowered head first. When brought out he said the child was some 12 ft. below and near another crevice. The child's cries could still be heard.

Archer was then lowered head first, going down 9 ft. He shouted that he had got hold of the child and asked to be raised. He lifted the child about 2 ft. but, owing to an overlapping piece of rock, could not get her through and had to leave go. He was brought up, and at once made another attempt. The same thing happened again and Archer was brought up completely exhausted. The child was now silent.

Christopher was now lowered, and getting no reply to his shouts it was feared that the child had fallen further down.

Bengough and others, who had just finished night-shift in the colliery, arrived, and, though the workings were now definitely unsafe, Bengough volunteered to go down. He was tied by his feet and lowered 7 ft., then asking for a walking stick. With this he chipped away some earth and shouted to be lowered further. He was lowered another 5 ft. He then shouted that he had found the child dead or unconscious. When he grasped her she began to cry, and taking off his vest he wrapped it round her feet and called for a length of rope, which was lowered. Tying it round her feet he shouted for a pull to be given. Not being able to get the child past his body he asked for a thin boy to be lowered. Hazell was again lowered, and, after doing as Bengough directed, he was hauled out absolutely exhausted.

Bengough then gave instructions for the child to be raised slowly, but when she reached the position of his feet near rock it was impossible to get her head past. He then directed the men on top to lower him further. This was done, but the child was still jammed. Brown now again went down head first and with difficulty pulled her clear and she was hauled to the surface.

Bengough, still head first down the hole, was in a dangerous position. He was raised a few feet and his body became jammed, and it was only after a difficult struggle by the men on top and much wriggling by Bengough that he was finally raised to the surface. He was a mass of cuts, scratches and bruises, and though the pressure of the rope on his ankles caused agonizing pain he stuck to his task.

The child, taken to hospital, recovered.

Crevice: Mountain district. Subsidence 25 ft. deep; 2 ft. wide at the top narrowing downwards.
Rescue : 12 ft. down. Bengough head down in hole for half an hour. Child in hole 16 hours - throughout the night.

Silver Medals awarded to Arthur Bengough and Bryn Brown.
Bronze Medals awarded to Malcolm Hazell and George Archer.
Testimonials on Vellum awarded to Leslie Richards, Emlyn Jones and Thomas Christopher.

Drake, Francis C., Schoolboy, aged 14, Parys, Orange Free State. Case 57996

Stanhope Gold Medal 1943

On the morning of the 6th January, 1943, Neville Roberts, aged two, was playing near a well which supplies water to a boarding house named Bonnie Banks at Parys, Orange Free State, South Africa. The well is 70 yards from the house, is 40 ft. in depth, containing deep water. It is 8 ft. in diameter, surrounded by a low concrete border and covered with an iron platform with a loose sheet of iron in a dilapidated state, and just large enough to cover the hole.

Drake had just passed the well, and hearing a sound looked back and noticed that the child Roberts had disappeared. He ran back and peering into the well shouted "Neville" and saw the child's head sink below water. He at once, without waiting to summon assistance, lowered himself into the mouth of the well and dropped into the water. Recovering the child he then discerned for the first time a pipe running up the side of the well to the pump above. Using this he climbed up to a point underneath the iron platform with the child in his arms. By this time two young natives who had heard Drake shout arrived and assisted to pull the child out through the hole from the arms of the boy Drake.

The natives in their excitement, took the child to the house, forgetting all about the now exhausted Drake, clinging to the pipe underneath the platform. He managed to get out through the 2 ft. aperture in the centre of the platform, but was in such a dazed state that he has never been able to explain how he did get out, and it is still a mystery.

The child recovered consciousness after a considerable time, but was speechless and motionless for two days. The promptitude with which Drake accepted the appalling risk of dropping into the well without assistance at hand indicates great courage and devotion. Without such promptitude the child's life would hardly have been saved.

The Bronze Medal was awarded to Francis C. Drake.

Alexander, James, Group Captain, Royal Australian Air Force.   Case 58467

Stanhope Gold Medal 1944

At 4.15 a.m. on the morning of the 2nd September, 1944, Flight-Sergeant Glynne B. Standring, R.A.F., and Sergeant Maurice K. Davis, R.A.F., and another were, owing to an impending gale, detailed to do emergency duty on an aircraft moored in Plymouth Sound.

A gale of 65 miles per hour developed, and a fishing vessel dragging her anchor and driven before the wind smashed into the nose and port mainplane of the aircraft. In disengaging the aircraft was damaged, and a call for assistance was sent out. A pinnace sent out but owing to the abnormal conditions was unable to get near the aircraft. At 5.30 a.m. the crew were ordered to slip moorings, which was accomplished with great difficulty, owing to the buffeting by waves which were breaking over the cockpit. On leaving the buoy a second ship crashed into the starboard mainplane, collapsing the starboard float. To balance the plane the crew of three crawled out on to the port wing. The third man on the aircraft was washed away by a large wave and managed to reach the shore. It was now 6 a.m. and still very dark.

There were jagged rocks in the vicinity and Standring and Davis decided to jump in an attempt to reach the pinnace. They jumped both wearing heavy clothing, Davis wearing an inflated Mae West and Standring being unable to inflate his. Visibility was practically nil, and after previous strain both were in serious difficulties.

Group-Captain Alexander, seeing this, jumped from the pinnace fully clad, and wearing a deflated Mae West, swam 50 yards, reaching Davis. Supporting him, he then swam to Standring and kept them both afloat until the pinnace manoeuvred into position and picked them up in an extremely exhausted state.

The sea was confused, with waves 8 ft. high. It was also pitch dark with heavy rain squalls. Rescue took place 120 yards off a rocky lee shore, the water being 17 ft. deep.

Brown, Cyril G.L., National Fire Service, Chesil Beach, Portland.   Case 58610

Stanhope Gold Medal 1945

At Chesil Beach, Wyke Regis, Portland. On the 13th October, 1944, at 4.23 p.m. information was received at the Coastguard Station that H.M. Landing Craft 2454 was close inshore in a rough sea. Naval Authorities informed said they would send a tug, which they did. The tug, unable to reach the Landing Craft, was recalled. The Coastguards arrived off-shore and signalling the vessel which was riding comfortably on a long stay of wire replied that they were all right. At 6.40 p.m. the stay parted and the vessel drove ashore rapidly. Striking the beach, a tremendous sea struck her, taking ten of the crew and washing everything moveable overboard. Stoker James Botton and Leading Motor Mechanic Ernest W. Shirley were then seen huddled together helpless to the lee side of the wheelhouse with seas continually breaking over them. Several lines were fired by rocket until one passed over the vessel held seaward by the spent rocket shell and became foul of the vessel.

Captain John A. Pennington Legh, D.S.C., R.N., with Coastguard Robert H. Treadwell and another seized the shore-end of the line and made their way down to the wreck now lying diagonally to the shore. During a lull the line was cleared and moved aft towards the two men.

Cyril G.L. Brown then appeared wearing a lifebelt and line and managed to board the vessel just forward and below the two helpless men. A tremendous sea then struck the vessel and Legh and Treadwell were washed away and drowned. The back of the vessel was broken. Brown, knocked down and pounded by the terrific seas, succeeded with superhuman efforts in hauling off enough line to pass to each of the survivors, working in all about 40 minutes. Brown then jumped, being hauled to safety and removed to hospital, followed by Botton, who was also hauled to shore. The line of the second survivor then parted leaving him still on the vessel. Albert Oldfield then seizing a chance dashed out from the beach with a line round him and with great determination succeeded in placing a line in the hands of Shirley, who was then hauled ashore in an exhausted state.

Weather -	Wind S.W. 6-8 o.m.r.q. Visibility half a mile.
Sea -	Heavy swell. Seas 30 ft. high.
Rescue	Off sloping beach.

The Silver Medal was awarded to Cyril G.L. Brown, the Bronze Medal to Albert Oldfield, and In Memoriam Testimonials to the relatives of Captain John A. Pennington Legh and Coastguardsman Robert H. Treadwell, H.M. Coastguard

Ravani, Alan Edward, Commercial Traveller, Peacehaven.   Case 59579

Stanhope Gold Medal 1946

Two Flight Sergeants, R.A.F., left Brighton for Newhaven about 2.30 p.m. on the 9th September, 1946, in an 11 ft. dinghy with outboard motor. About 3.30 p.m., when off Portobello Outfall Works, Peacehaven, the dinghy shipped a heavy sea which cut out the motor and before the water could be baled, another sea came onboard causing the boat to fill up and float level with the surface. The two men paddled about for about one hour, before being swept towards the beach by the onshore wind, and their cries for help being eventually heard when about one mile out. Both men by this time were suffering from cramp and were more or less helpless, and would have sunk but for the support of the waterlogged boat.

Ravani (aged 17 1/2), who was working in his parent's shop at Telscombe Cliffs, was informed by a man who ran in to telephone the Police that two men were in difficulties out at sea. Ravani ran 350 yards to the cliff edge, saw the men supporting themselves on the waterlogged boat, slid down a wire on to the beach (which is often used for that purpose as`no other ready means of access to the beach) ran to the Sewer Outfall where some men were working, and was advised by them not to enter the sea there due to the swirl and dangerous current off the "Barrell" of the Sewer Outfall Pipe.

Ravani then proceeded further along the beach until almost in line with the boat, removed his outer clothing and swam out to the men, one of whom was sitting in the waterlogged boat and the other hanging on to the stern. He then pushed the boat towards the shore until it grounded and all were helped ashore by the onlookers, police, etc., who had assembled by then. Ravani was very exhausted by his efforts, all three being taken to hospital by ambulance, but allowed to leave later.

The rescue was effected about 4.30 p.m. in the face of numerous difficulties, i.e. in a rough sea, ebb tide and onshore wind. Dangerous current around the Sewer Outfall Pipe, rocky cliffs without ready access to the beach, and no boats in the vicinity.

Ferguson, Petronella, Mrs., Housewife, Windward Islands.   Case 59718

Stanhope Gold Medal 1947

At Victoria, Grenada, Windward Islands, West Indies.

About midnight on the 4th October, 1945, there was a cloudburst in the St. Mark's District, and many people were trapped in their homes by the flood water from the nearby river, which rose so rapidly that 12 houses in all were swept away and 14 lives lost in consequence.

Mrs. Ferguson, who was in an advanced state of pregnancy, was in her house with her husband and son when it broke loose and was swept seaward by the flood waters, both the husband and son being drowned. While in the drifting house, she heard cries for help from a young girl, aged 13 years, unable to swim and clinging on to a floating log.

Mrs. Ferguson went to her aid and, still swimming, started to push the log with the girl on it shoreward, as she thought. Later a flash of lightning revealed that they were heading seaward and were being carried out to the open sea by the flood waters. After about two hours swimming in the right direction she brought the exhausted girl to the shore, Mrs. Ferguson herself then being in a state of collapse. In view of her condition at the time, her bravery was considered locally as deserving of the highest commendation.

The rescue was effected about 250 yards out in 30 fathoms of flood water.

Roberts, Thomas Matson, Ironmonger and part time Coy. Officer, N.F.S.   Case 60194

Stanhope Gold Medal 1948

At Graig Cae, Pen Cae, Cader Idris, near Dolgelly, Merionethshire.

On the afternoon of 26th September, 1947, a man attempted to climb the mountain face, 1,200 ft. high, and when about 700 ft. up became stranded on an almost inaccessible ledge. The ledge was screened by "overhangs" and "buttresses," and these rock formations so upset the acoustic conditions that it was impossible to locate the man's position by his voice signals alone. Directions for the rescue were given by shouting across the valley.

At 7.30 p.m. the Police were informed that the man was stranded on the cliff and rescue parties were formed. Thomas Matson Roberts led two other part time N.F.S. men. Other parties were formed from N.F.S., Police and Royal Marine Commandos and local guides accompanied the parties.

Roberts with his two companions, climbed the cliff by a circular route, leaving another party to work up from the bottom. after reaching the top Roberts with companions had to give up the idea of a straight climb down, and returned by the circular route to wait until the lost man had been properly located.

On their arrival at the foot of the cliff at about 11.30 p.m. they found that the lower party had, as they thought, located the man by shouting. They decided, however, to wait till dawn before making a further attempt to make the climb.

Roberts, however, thought it worth while making a further attempt, and his two N.F.S. companions agreed to come with him. At 1 a.m. Roberts and one N.F.S. companion, after climbing the sheer face of the cliff to within 50 feet of the top, found they could not go further and decided to come down again. Actually they has passed within 200 yards of the man, but owing to the acoustic "clutter" due to rocks and buttresses, had missed him.

Roberts and his companion rested from 4 to 6 a.m. Then seeing the mist descending, they shouted to the lost man to light a fire. He did this and it was possible to locate him. Roberts now sent one N.F.S. man across the valley where he could see the cliff and fire to give directions while he and the other N.F.S. man made the climb again. They got within 100 feet of the lost man but were forced to give up and return to the cliff foot.

They then decided to try again by another route, Roberts assistant got stuck, but Roberts himself found a chimney and went on alone backing up the chimney with elbows and knees, leaving his companion with the rope. He found himself on a ledge, still below the lost man, but, guided by directing shouts of the man across the valley, made his way, with great difficulty, to the lost man, who was suffering from shock, exposure, and loss of nerve. Roberts persuaded the man to make a try to get down, but actually had to carry him in places. Finally they reached the chimney where the N.F.S. companion was waiting with the rope. From then on the descent was relatively simple.

Robert's two companions were awarded the Society's Bronze Medal and Testimonial on Parchment respectively.

Pearson, Robert Colin, Lieut. (E) (A.E.), R.N., H.M.S. *Vengeance*.   Case 60717

Stanhope Gold Medal 1949

In the sea at Freetown, Sierra Leone, West Africa.

At 10.55 p.m. on the 27th November, 1948, H.M.S. *Vengeance* was anchored off Sierra Leone. The night was very dark, it being described as "complete blackness," a strong ebb tide was running and sharks were present in the waters surrounding the ship. At this time, and in these conditions, Canteen Assistant William Parr fell from a gun sponson and was swept away from the ship.

Lieutenant Pearson dived from the quarterdeck into the water 23 feet below, and within seconds of entering the water was lost to sight in the total blackness of the night. Although this officer is a strong swimmer, there was no chance whatsoever that he would be able to swim against the tide and return to his ship; there was also very real danger from sharks, and Lieutenant Pearson was fully aware of the risks he was facing.

When the accident happened two lifebuoys were released, Lieutenant Pearson sighted one of these, swam to it, and discovered that Canteen Assistant Parr was not clinging to it. He then searched and found the second lifebuoy, but Parr was not on this either. Lieutenant Pearson left the comparative safety of the lifebuoy and searched the surrounding waters.

When picked up by a boat Lieutenant Pearson had fought his way back to the first lifebuoy, which was by now between half and three-quarters of a mile from the ship. In all, Lieutenant Pearson spent nearly twenty minutes in the sea, making every effort to save Canteen Assistant Parr, whose life was unfortunately lost.

Bulteaux, Roland, Citizen of the French Republic, Le Havre. Case 61403

Stanhope Gold Medal 1950

In the Seine Estuary, Le Havre, France, M. Bulteaux saved four British subjects in the following circumstances:-

Four British nationals two men and two women, sailed from the Isle of Wight to Le Havre in a yacht for the Easter holiday in 1950. They encountered foul weather and after a night spent on board the yacht with the weather at gale force, reached Le Havre just before dawn on 9th April, 1950.

On arrival their auxiliary engine had ceased to function, and one of the men on board the yacht had lost the top of his finger while attempting to repair a defective rudder. He was bleeding freely. In the storm the yacht could not be worked and anchored in the harbour, but in water too shallow for regular tugs to operate in.

M. Bulteaux came to the sea wall and answered the signals of the four Britons on board the yacht. He realized that they needed both seamanlike and medical help, and as no regular salvage vessels could operate in the shoal water in which the yacht was anchored, secured the assistance of two volunteers and came out in a small fishing smack. With great difficulty they came alongside the British yacht, and M. Bulteaux leapt on board with a tow rope which he made fast to the yacht. This unfortunately parted on the strain being taken, so at considerable hazard, a second rope was passed and secured. This, in turn parted and the British yacht drifted on to the rocks 50 yards away and broke up. The rocks protruded 8 feet from the harbour wall and were covered with pounding waves. The harbour wall has an iron ladder up it but the top ten rungs had been removed during the German occupation and not replaced.

As soon as the vessel hit the rocks M. Bulteaux sprang ashore with a line but was washed away and found himself 30 feet from the wreck. With great difficulty he struggled back to the rocky ledge and secured a line to the ladder. Then he returned through the heavy seas and brought one lady and then the other to the ledge below the ladder. In the meantime the two men, one of whom was in considerable pain from his lost finger, had been swept away, and M. Bulteaux brought them to the ledge.

A crowd had gathered on the harbour walls and sent down ropes. All four Britons were then hauled to safety. M. Bulteaux, despite the fact that he had himself sustained abrasions, drove the most injured Briton to hospital. All four Britons were taken to hospital and detained with abrasions, M. Bulteaux was treated in hospital and allowed to go home.

R.H.S. SILVER MEDALS
1870 to 1950

Poulden, E., Commander, R.N. T/S *Formidable*. Case 18635

At 9 a.m., October 24th, 1870, at Portishead, near Bristol, depth of water about six and a half fathoms alongside the ship at the time; a gale of wind had been blowing all the night before, and a heavy sea was on at the time with a very strong ebb-tide. Captain Poulden, without a moment's hesitation, jumped in to rescue the boy Thomas Evans; the tide carried them both down the channel over 200 yards before the boat could reach them, which was only just in time as Captain Poulden had quite given up.

Harrison, John, Sydney, Australia. Case 18653
Bayley, Samuel B.

Sydney; 17th May, 1870. The gallant efforts that were made by John Harrison and Samuel Bayley, of this city, are particularly worthy of recognition, the former of whom twice swam through the heavy surf, accompanied by the latter one. On the second attempt he reached the wreck, and succeeded in making a line fast for the purpose of establishing communication with the shore, but which unfortunately broke before any assistance could be rendered to the unfortunates on the wreck. Especial notice has been taken of them by the Government of the Colony, and it is hoped that such meritorious conduct will be noticed by the Humane Society: perhaps by the donation of a medal to each.

McGran, H., Sub-Constable, Royal Irish Constabulary. Case 18660

On the 26th July, 1870, about 11.40 a.m., Sub-Inspector J.G. French, R.I.C., went to bathe at a place called the Point on Thompson's Bank, accompanied by Sub-Constables McGran, P. Marron and J. Campbell; on arriving there the three Sub-Constables undressed and entered the water, and in about seven minutes their attention was attracted by the cries of Sub-Constable Marron for help; perceiving his danger they called loudly to McGran, who immediately hastened to render assistance, and during the interval Marron was several times completely submerged from view, his position was exceedingly perilous from the following reasons, he knew not how to swim, he was in a current of water no less than ten feet deep. His incessant exertions to regain footing or safety were useless, and he was gradually borne away into deeper water by the force of the receding tide. When McGran reached Marron, the latter seized the former whereupon both became invisible, and, on reappearing, Marron seized McGran round the waist with extended arms which led to a violent struggle which threatened at the time to terminate alike disastrous to them both; but when McGran released himself from the grasp of Marron, which he accomplished by sheer force, he instantly turned on his back and pushed Marron with his feet a distance of about five feet towards the shore, thereby drifting him clear of the current into shallow water, where he obtained a footing, and thus was a sad event averted.

Gibbons, William, Stoker, R.N. Case 18665

On the 1st January, 1871, at 7.30 p.m., as H.M.S. *Minotaur* was lying at Spithead, in seven fathoms of water, it being a very dark night and freezing hard, John Hutchings, who was on the hammock netting, missed his footing and fell overboard, upon seeing which, and that he was unable to swim, William Gibbons, who was also on the netting, sprang overboard to his assistance and with a great deal of difficulty and at the risk of his own life, succeeded by swimming in bringing him to the gangway, where they were both taken on board. The height of the netting from the water was 22 feet.

Lowrey, Amos Case 18667

On the 11th October, 1870, at 9 p.m., lat 45 N., Lon. 40 W., night clear but dark, whole sail breeze, as the ship *Dauntless*, of Newcastle, was on the starboard tack and going three and a half knots, chief officers' watch on deck, the order was given to loose the mizzen topgallant staysail (the sail is stowed in the maintop) and Albert Rirt at once throws off his sea-jacket and proceeds aft by the weather side of the main top for the purpose of carrying out the order, but, when in the act of climbing the futtock rigging, he missed his hold and fell, striking the lower rigging in his descent, and went overboard, the alarm was given and all hands called on deck. One of those whose watch it was below, and who was in bed at the time of the accident, with a very vague recollection, at present, whether he was asleep or awake, but hearing a commotion rushed up on deck in his shirt, and seizing a life-buoy threw it over the taffrail and jumped after it.

It is only necessary to refer to the foregoing account of time, position and circumstances, to show the noble deed of Amos, the son of Captain Amos Lowrey, the second officer, but a stripling, who pushed the life-buoy ahead of him towards the lad, or where he supposed him to be, and found him. It's true the lad himself had in the meantime found and caught hold of the life-buoy which had been thrown overboard, but, with sea-boots and other clothes on, he seems to have had but little consciousness left in him to know how to avail himself of it, but Lowrey held by him and supported him until a boat, manned by the carpenter and two seamen, came to their rescue and brought them alongside.

Hookum Ally, Native of Calcutta. Case 18695

On the 20th July, 1870, the stream which runs past the town of Deoree, Nagpore, Central India, was much flooded and running with great force, a poor lame boy, who was on part of the Deoree Bridge, fell into the river and was at once carried down the stream. A large number of persons were present but no one dared to go to the rescue of the child, till Hookum Ally, who is a strong swimmer and a brave man, dashed into the water and managed to get to the boy just as he was sinking for the third time, and after a severe struggle brought the child safely to the bank.

Also on the 29th August last, a man fell into the river and was being carried down by the rapid stream, Hookum Ally, who had come down the river with the Chief Constable, went to the man's assistance, but before he could get him up the man had sunk once or twice. On Hookum Ally at length getting near enough to seize the drowning man, he took him by the arm and endeavoured to drag him out of the current, but the man put his arms round the policeman's neck and they both went down together and seemed to turn over and over in the stream. When Hookum Ally came to the surface he appeared to be gasping for breath but still retained his hold of the man, and after some time succeeded in bringing him to the bank; both men were in a most exhausted state when they reached land.

McCalmont, James M., Lieut., 8th Hussars. Case 18741

On Wednesday, the 24th May, 1871, McCalmont saved the life of Denis Harrington a clerk in the Chief Secretary's office, Dublin, under the following circumstances;

About 9.30 p.m., he was standing on the balcony of the Royal St. George Yacht Club, when he heard cries of distress in the water near Carlisle Pier, Kingstown Harbour, he rushed at once to the pier and jumped into the sea, a distance at that time of twenty-six feet and succeeded in catching Harrington, who was at that time insensible. As soon as possible Colonel Atkinson and Geo. Putland got into a boat and brought them ashore, when Dr. Simms attended Harrington and with difficulty succeeded in restoring suspended animation; had it not been for Lieutenant McCalmont's activity Harrington would in all probability have lost his life.

Browne, W.L.H., Sub-Lieut R.N. Case 18759

On the night of the 31st March, 1871, at about 10 p.m., I was standing at the Entry Port of H.M.S. *Ocean* and saw Lieut. Edye, Royal Marine Light Infantry, who was leaning against the rail of the accommodation ladder, suddenly fall overboard, Sub-Lieut. Browne who was standing by and hearing he could not swim, instantly jumped overboard after him; Browne laid hold of him and kept him on the surface of the water, and owing to all the boats being hoisted up at the time it must have been a quarter of an hour before they were picked up. There was a strong tide running at the time.

Bean, Harry Ralph, Seaman Instructor. Case 18794

On the 7th of August, 1871, a boy named Thomas Harris, aged 11, fell from the starboard rigging of the Training Ship *Goliath*, at Grays, Essex, about 40 feet from the water, struck the fore chains and bounded overboard. An alarm was given, when Harry Ralph Bean, Seaman Instructor, jumped overboard from the starboard gangway, all his clothes on except jacket and cap, a strong ebb tide running at the time. The boy was carried away eighty or ninety yards by the current before Bean reached him, and supported him until a boat arrived; the boy was brought on board very much exhausted. Bean was slightly injured in the right thigh.

McCarthy, Patrick K., Throstle Doffer.　　　　　　　　　　　　　　　　　　　　　　　　　　Case 18797

Patrick McCarthy is 15 years of age and employed as a throstle doffer at Messrs Pearson's mill, Stockport. About a quarter to two o'clock on Wednesday afternoon, the 9th of August, 1871, a girl called out, "There's a boy drowning, and no one will go after him." McCarthy ran to the window and saw a lad struggling in the water. He sank, and McCarthy ran down the yard, taking off his clothes as he did so. When he arrived at the river the boy was under the water; he jumped in and swam towards the spot where he was told he had gone down; when he got to the middle of the river he saw two hands out of the water and swam towards them, but they had disappeared before he reached them. He dived and took hold of him by the hair, and brought him up and pushed him towards the opposite bank swimming after him; he was sinking again, when McCarthy caught him by the hand and swam towards the shore. McCarthy was exhausted and let the boy go, and he sank; he swam down, and in doing so one of his legs touched some part of the boy's body; he turned round and caught him, swam with him to the shore and got him on a rock and called for assistance, when the boy's life was saved.

Butterfield, John, Surgeon Dentist's assistant.　　　　　　　　　　　　　　　　　　　　　Case 18811

On Wednesday evening, the 21st August, 1871, one of the most daring rescues from drowning was effected at Cork. It appears that a Mr. Boyde and a Mr. Ogilvie, both commercial gentlemen, went for a sail on the river, and when they had got down as far as Lough Mahon, and opposite the Castle, they were caught by a squall which upset the boat and turned her bottom upwards, at about 100 yards from the railway embankment. Both gentlemen were immersed, and as neither could swim, they were in a very perilous position. There were but very few persons on the lower Glanmire Road at this hour (8.30), but the incident was seen by a young gentleman named Butterfield, assistant to Mr. Joseph Corbett, jun., Surgeon Dentist, South Mall, who immediately jumped into the water, and reaching the ill-fated craft, succeeded in getting on to her bottom, from which position he saved Mr. Boyde. Mr. Ogilvie had sunk at this stage twice, and on his appearing a third time on the surface Mr. Butterfield saw him at about 10 yards distant, and immediately sprang from the boat's bottom and seized him. With a great deal of difficulty he got him near enough to haul upon the craft. A rapid tide soon drifted all three of them a long way down the river, but they soon got ashore by paddling with their hands. Mr Ogilvie was very much exhausted, and received medical treatment in the course of the evening, but is now convalescent. Too much cannot be said in praise of Mr. Butterfield, who acted in the most courageous manner, he having but *one leg*.

Parkes, Gustavus, Ordinary Seaman, R.N.　　　　　　　　　　　　　　　　　　　　　　　Case 18821

At 11.40 a.m., 4th July, 1871, lat. 18 26 S., lon. 107 19 W., John Anderson fell overboard from the lee quarter of H.M.S. *Scylla*, when the ship was going at the rate of four and a half knots. The life-buoy was immediately let go and he swam for it; Gustavus Parkes, O.S., who did not know the other could swim, on hearing the cry of "Man overboard", jumped from the taffrail and swam to his assistance; they both succeeded in getting to the life-buoy; the risk incurred was being taken by sharks, which abound in these latitudes. They were about twenty minutes in the water before they were picked up by the boat. See case 20955.

Smith, Sydney G., Lieut. R.N.　　　　　　　　　　　　　　　　　　　　　　　　　　　　　Case 18838

On the 14th of July, 1871, at 11.45 a.m., lat. 35 26 S. lon. 155 50 E., in making sail to a fresh breeze, with a rough tumbling sea on, Mark Didymus fell into the water, from the fore-yards of H.M.S. *Basilisk*. Lieut Sydney G. Smith R.N., who was at his station on the forecastle, instantly plunged after him; the man passed under the paddle wheel (providentially without being struck) before Lieut. Smith could seize him (Lieut. Smith barely escaping a stroke from the wheel himself). On the man coming to the surface abaft the wheel, Thomas Dalton, captain of the fore-top, jumped from the after sponson and seized him, Lieut. Smith coming to the rescue at the same time; a boat was then lowered and thus the man was saved.

Rawson, H.H., Lieut., R.N.
Aitken, John, Engineer.

Case 18839

On the afternoon of the 30th August, 1871, while Her Majesty's Yacht *Victoria and Albert* was lying in the Scheldt, off Antwerp, a boat containing four women, one man and two boys, was capsized abreast of the after ladder. Three of the passengers were saved at the gangway, but the others were swept astern by the tide which was running past the ship at the rate of four knots.

The accident was observed by Lieut. H. H. Rawson and Mr. John Aitken, engineer, who immediately lowered themselves over the stern and swam to the assistance of the drowning people, and succeeded in rescuing two of the women, while boats went to the assistance of the others, so that all were happily saved.

Both the officers were for some time under medical treatment for severe laceration of the hands resulting from the precipitation in lowering themselves by a lead line over the stern. The circumstances having come to the notice of the Belgium Government, the principal naval officer was directed by the King to tender his Majesty's thanks for the gallantry shown by these two naval officers in hastening, at the risk of their own lives, to the rescue of the women.

Whitlock, H.C., Major (British Army).

Case 18845

On Sunday evening on the 8th of October, 1871, a workman, named Louis Coquelin, was rolling about the pier at Havre in a state of drunkenness. Suddenly an idea seemed to strike him that it was a very good thing to take a sea bath. No sooner thought of than done. He quickly undressed and threw himself in to the sea. It was evident, however, that he was too drunk to be able to swim and was rapidly drowning. As he was disappearing, Captain H.C. Whitlock (British Army) jumped in dressed as he was, and on coming to the surface it was seen that he held Coquelin by the hair. At this moment a sailor (Felix Delahaye) followed Captain Whitlock's example, and taking Coquelin by one arm whilst Captain Whitlock supported him by the other, they were enabled to land the drunkard on *terra firma*, then more dead than alive. At this point, however, matters changed; Coquelin was rapidly brought to his senses (about twenty-five minutes after the occurrence), but Captain Whitlock, after making a few steps on the beach fell on his face, and the usual symptoms of death by drowning set in. Happily, however, by the care and attention he received from a medical man present, Dr. Faliz, as also from the unremitting exertions of the chief of the Humane Society (who possess a building on the pier), and his wife (M. and Madame Dusecu), Captain Whitlock was sufficiently restored some two or three hours later to be taken to his home. It is satisfactory to add that he has completely recovered.

The Bronze Medal of the Society was awarded to Felix Delahaye.

Savill, Henry, Scholar.

Case 18846

On the afternoon of Wednesday, 18th October, 1871, on going down to a large pond on the College Farm, at Ardingly, Sussex, one of the masters (Mr. Mosley) and two boys were seen to be in a most perilous predicament in the very centre from the upsetting of a small punt, all means of rendering them any assistance having failed until the arrival of one of the scholars, Henry Savill, who in spite of the coldness of the weather, the amount of obstruction from the weeds, and the additional risk of being grasped by the sufferers (only one of whom was less than himself), at once plunged into the water and succeeded in taking out a rope, by means of which all were relieved from the immense danger which had been threatening them for fully twenty minutes. Had it not been for the courage of the boy H. Savill there is little doubt that three persons would have lost their lives.

Yonge, Gustavus H., Sub-Lieut., R.N.

Case 18871

Extract from a letter from Captain J.D. McCrea, R.N., H.M.S. *Bellerophon*, Lisbon, 10th February, 1872.

I have the honour to report that at 3.35 p.m., on 7th inst., The second launch of H.M.S. *Northumberland*, while under sail was carried by the tide foul of our starboard swinging boom and instantly capsized.

The ship's Steward's assistant who had been in the boat shouted loudly for help as the five knot tide swept him past. Mr. Gustavus H. Yonge, Sub-Lieutenant of this ship, very gallantly plunged overboard to assist him, rendering material aid by picking up a life-buoy and swimming to the man with it and remaining by him until both were picked up. I have great pleasure in reporting this case of gallantry and request you will move the Rear-Admiral Commanding to bring it under the notice of their Lordships and recommend him for the Albert Medal, or that of the Royal Humane Society.

Smith, Charles Alfred, aged nine years.   Case 18874

Extract from a statement by Caroline Matthews of Saint Hillier, St. Abbotsford, Victoria, New South Wales.

On Wednesday, the 13th day of December, 1871, I was engaged at the house of Mr. Smith, about twenty-five yards distant from the River Yarra, when suddenly I heard screams near the river, I immediately ran towards the water, and I then heard Sarah Froggitt screaming "Leslie's drowned!" I ran back towards the house screaming "the baby's drowned," and met Charles Alfred Smith running towards the river, pulling his waistcoat off as he ran. When I reached the house, Mrs. Smith rushed out and ran towards the water, I ran after her; when I reached the water I saw Charles A. Smith with the baby struggling in the water and swimming towards the shore; Mrs. Smith ran down to the water and lifted the two children out of the stream. At the time the river was very high and the current near the bank was very strong, and the baby must have been drowned but for the promptness and energy of his brother, C.A. Smith, who is only nine years of age.

Alexander, H. McC., Mate, R.N.   Case 18880

Extract of a letter from Captain W.S. Wiseman, R.N., H.M.S. *Penelope*, Simon's Bay, 19th April, 1856 (Awarded 1872).

I beg to bring to your notice the gallant conduct of Mr. H. McC. Alexander, mate of her Majesty's ship under my command, on the evening of the 18th April, 1856, when the dinghy upset alongside; although a dark night, and twenty men were in the water, most of them unable to swim, Mr. Alexander jumped overboard and saved the life of three of them, and in so doing was in great danger of being pulled under by the men in the water who were unable to swim and struggling for life.

Mr. Alexander's conduct during the fifteen months he has served under my command has been so correct and satisfactory, and his gallantry in jumping overboard on this occasion so conspicuous, that I venture to hope you may be able to bring his name before my Lords Commissioners of the Admiralty.

Brenton, R.O.B.C., Sub Lieutenant, R.N.   Case 18901

Silver Clasp

Henry Hull, Ordinary seaman, H.M.S. *Minotaur*, fell into the harbour at Portsmouth on 1st May 1872. Sub Lieutenant R.O.B.C. Brenton jumped overboard from the poop and supported the man until a boat arrived.

Necton, Robert, A.B., R.N.   Case 18906

James Connell, bandsman, H.M.S. *Royal Alfred*, fell into the harbour, at Nassau, West Indies, at midnight on the 17th March, 1872, into three fathoms of water, the tide was running about two and a half knots, and sweeping him out of the harbour, when Robert Necton, A.B. of H.M.S. *Fly*, jumped overboard and supported him until a boat was sent and picked them up; there are sharks in the harbour.

Dowdney, James, A.B., R.N.   Case 18916

Extract of a letter from W.E. White, 3rd Officer of the *Highflyer*. Arthur Steele, midshipman of the ship *Roxburgh Castle*, aged 19, fell overboard at noon, 19th March, 1869, in lat. 1 30 N., lon 21 15 W., whilst getting into a boat, the ship was going from six to seven knots and there was a heavy sea on. It was known that Steele could not swim, and one of the men, James Dowdney, A.B., jumped overboard, swam to a life-buoy which had been thrown from the ship, conveyed it to Steele, who was in an exhausted state; the ship's way was stopped in about 10 or 15 minutes, and a boat lowered which picked them up.

Margary, A.R., British Consular Service.   Case 18920
Dodd, John, British Merchant and Consul for the United States.

On the night of the 9th and 10th August, 1871, a typhoon burst upon the coast of Formosa, causing frightful havoc among the shipping. Three vessels were totally destroyed in the harbour of Kelung, on the north coast of the island of Formosa, they were the British barque *Westward Ho*, manned by eighteen Malays. the French barque, *Adele*, with a crew of fifteen Europeans, and the British schooner, *Anne*, with a crew of seven Englishmen, these ships were torn away from their anchors and shattered upon the rocky shores of the harbour although they had been moored in apparently sheltered safe berths.

The whole of the crews of these vessels were saved by the efforts of a handful of Europeans, who were stationed at this most isolated spot. The violence of the typhoon itself called forth the energies of those on shore, although the blinding rain and pitchy darkness added to their utter bewilderment and apparent helplessness.

By the aid of the brilliant light of burning camphor, the perilous position of the ships was soon defined. The next moment a rope was secured and Mr. John Dodd, a British merchant and Consul for the United States together with Mr. A.R. Margary, of the British Consular Service, attempted to carry it through the surf to the aid of the schooner *Anne*. The rope, however, proved too short, and these gentlemen had to throw it away and swim on board, after which they attempted to bring a rope on shore in a boat, having obtained two volunteers from the crew; this, however, proved abortive, as the boat was swamped and the two men nearly perished.

Messrs. Dodd and Margary next proceeded to the aid of the French vessel which lay a mile further out, heaped up in ruin together with the *Westward Ho*, on the worst rocks in the harbour. Here Mr. Hough, of the Imperial Customs, had been searching with his men, under the utmost difficulties, and with their aid, after several hours of sustained effort, Messrs Dodd and Margary again effected a junction with the remains of the French ship and brought the crew safe to shore, including a man with a broken leg. Both also awarded the Albert Medal.

Niven, John, Second Officer.   Case 18937

Statement from the Captain and Officers of the ship *Asia*, May 2nd, 1872. We beg to draw your attention to the brave conduct of John Niven (of Greenock), Second Officer of the ship *Asia*, 2054 tons, on her voyage from Melbourne to London. The particulars are as follows - On the 1st May, 1872, at 2.45 p.m., in lat 35.33 S., Lon 20.26 E., the ship under all studding sails with a moderate breeze; George Peck fell overboard from the fore rigging, a life-buoy was thrown to him, which he could not catch. Mr. Niven who was in bed (it being his watch below) hearing the cry of a boy overboard rushed to the stern of the ship, and plunged overboard to his assistance; he succeeded in getting him, much exhausted, to the life-buoy, and had great difficulty in holding his head above water the boy being heavily dressed and with his sea boots on.

Mr. Niven was obliged to strip himself in the water. Before the ship could be rounded to and a boat sent to their assistance about half an hour elapsed, and they were about a mile distant when they were rescued from their perilous situation, rendered doubly so by sharks having been seen round the ship in the morning.

Speed, George E., Signalman. R.N.   Case 18981

Statement from Lieut. R.F.W. Henderson, H.M.S. *Glasgow*, at sea lat 6 26 S., lon 81 27 E., 25th June, 1872. This is to certify that on the 24th of June, 1872, George E. Speed, signalman, jumped overboard from the poop after John Langley, Private, R.M.L.I., who had fallen overboard from the lower rigging, where he was hanging his clothes up to dry, and was passing under the quarter in a helpless state, either from an injury received in his fall or being unable to swim, and who was seen to go down before Speed, in spite of his efforts, could reach him.

Buttle, Richard, Waterman. Case 18986

Extract from letter of W.M. Rackham, St. Peter's, Norwich.

I appeal to your most benevolent Society in a case (a most deserving one) on behalf of Richard Buttle, in which a life was saved with great unselfish promptitude.

The case happened thus:- On the 4th July, 1872, ten persons, including two children, were sailing in a pleasure cutter on the river between Norwich and Yarmouth, one of the boys, when the boat was lurching and on a tack, was shot into twenty feet of water, mid-stream, boat going five or six miles an hour; Buttle made a grab for the boy, missed him, instantaneously he plunged in and at forty or fifty yards in the wake of boat he secured him; unfortunately the youngster grasped Buttle tightly round the neck and partially throttled him, so that he had to swim with his head under water partially drowning; he reached the rushes and was there sinking in sixteen feet of water when the boy was pulled from him and their lives saved. Buttle was prostrate and unfit for work during the trip. Buttle bears an irreproachable character and is respected for his honesty and general manly bearing. I must add that this is no isolated case, he (Buttle) having been the means, directly and indirectly, of saving between forty or fifty lives from drowning.

Le Fleming, Stanley Hughes, aged seventeen. Case 18993

On the 22nd August, 1872, Amelia Brown, aged 14 of 2 Bloomfield Terrace, South Sea, Hants., was carried out by the tide whilst bathing from the beach at South Sea; an alarm was given by the bathing attendant, when Mr. Stanley Hughes Le Fleming, of Rydall Hall, Ambleside, Westmoreland, aged 17, who was walking on the beach with his sister at the time, rushed into the sea, swam out, and brought her to the shore insensible; the bathing attendant did not aid in the rescue, but called to Mr. Le Fleming to go to the young girl's aid, which he at once did, with the happy result above detailed.

Steel, Michael, Hop Picker. Case 19007

Letter from H. Hilder, East Malling, Maidstone, 16th September, 1872.

I beg to call your attention to an act of great bravery performed by Michael Steel in attempting to save the life of Sarah Ann Allchin, aged 5, who fell into a draw-well at Sprigett's Hill, East Malling, on the 11th September; the circumstances are briefly these. The child whilst at play incautiously stepped upon the lid of the well, which was a sliding one and badly fitting, tilted up precipitating the child down the well; on alarm being raised the above named man rushed from a beer-house close by, threw off his jacket, seized the chain, and descended the well with fearful rapidity (the distance down to the water being seventy-five feet). He grasped the child and kept it above water until assistance came, but unfortunately, while being drawn up, his own weight with that of the child caused the chain to break when raised up about thirty feet; he consequently dropped a second time into the water, and although the man was severely bruised as well as the child, he again brought it to the surface, and held it until ropes could be obtained, when they were drawn up, but from the elapse of time after the second immersion and injuries received, life could not be restored to the child.

The man with careful attention, was able to be removed to the Malling Union Infirmary on Friday last. He is a married man without family, and came from London for the purpose of hop picking.

Apper, Abaran. Case 19018

Letter from W.H. Gregory, Governor of Ceylon, The Pavilion, Kandy, 16th of August, 1872.

I am desirous of bringing under the notice of your Society the conduct of a man named Abaran Apper who on the night of the 8th of June rescued fifty-three persons at the town of Gampola from the most imminent risk of drowning.

This man, in the dark, at great personal risk, brought down two canoes which he had lashed together, and braving the flood, laid his craft alongside the roofs of two houses and carried of the inhabitants to a place of safety.

I visited the spot on the Monday following, the 10th of June, and saw the scene of the disaster of the 8th. I found the inhabitants loud in their expressions of gratitude to the man for having by his own unaided energy come to their rescue when all hope seemed to them at an end.

These acts of self-devotion are so rare, I regret to say, among the inhabitants of this island, that I am anxious such an act as this should receive every possible distinction. I have already conferred local rank on Abaran Apper, and I am convinced that a medal of the Royal Humane Society would be looked upon as a very great honour, and be received with gratitude by him.

Fudge, James, aged fifteen.   Case 19024

Extract from a letter from Captain A.O. Molesworth, R.A., to the officer commanding Royal Artillery, Guernsey.

I have the honour to bring to your notice, in forwarding accompanying report of the wreck of the barque *Thames*, at Alderney, on the 28th of May last, the exertions made and help rendered by the men of the Coast Brigade, R.A., here and especially the brave conduct of a boy named James Fudge, aged 15, the son of James Fudge, Coast Brigade, R.A.

On the night of the 28th of May last there was a dense fog overhanging both land and sea, continuing until midday, 29th of May. At about 11 p.m., Lieut. Robinson, was roused by some of his men, and on proceeding to the shore, about a mile distant, found the men mentioned in his report endeavouring by shouting and showing lights to guide the boat of the *Thames*, which had gone down into the small bay, the circumstances of the wreck being detailed in the report annexed. There was a heavy ground swell on, and the boats attempting to get in, instead of following the light, got on to a rock; the boy Fudge then took a rope in his mouth and swam off in the fog, some fifteen yards to reach them and did so, thus establishing communication with them to the shore.

Christian, George Henry Perkins, Seaman.   Case 19040

Letter from Stephen P. Brown, Newton, 12th August 1872.

This is to certify that on the 16th of April, 1872, during a passage from Auckland to the Bay of Islands in the schooner *Ariel*, when off Omahes, and about four miles from shore, George Henry Perkins Christian saved from drowning my daughter, a girl of twelve years of age, under the following circumstances.

It was almost dark, and the vessel running before the wind, when the girl came on deck and became dizzy, the vessel lurching, she fell overboard; there was no person on deck save Christian steering, he saw the incident, and had only sufficient time to cry out "the girl's overboard!" Leaving the helm he plunged into the sea, and succeeded in reaching her ere she had sunk the second time. In the meantime the vessel had gone a considerable distance from the scene of the accident, during which time Christian was swimming and keeping the girl up until a boat was lowered and reached them in about fifteen minutes. Christian although an expert swimmer, speaks of the act as one attended with great risk, as he could not have borne up the girl much longer from the weight of the clothes upon each.

Heaton, Henry W., Signalman, R.N.   Case 19049

Extract of a letter to Admiral Sir Rodney Mundy, K.C.B., from Captain E. Madden, H.M.S. *Endymion*, Portsmouth, 7th of November, 1872. I have the honour to bring before your notice the gallant conduct of the man Henry W. Heaton, signalman, who jumped overboard on the night of 28th of October, at Spithead, and rescued Joseph Goff, ordinary seaman, who had fallen overboard; the ship was steaming five knots at the time, and the night was very dark and rough. I beg to enclose the usual form of recommendation for the Royal Humane Society's medal, which I consider him highly entitled to.

Wood, Robert T., Sub-Lieut., R.N.   Case 19100

Letter from Captain E. Madden, R.N., to Admiral Sir Rodney Mundy, K.C.B. H.M.S. *Endymion*, Spithead 19th of January, 1873.

I have the honour to report to you that while reefing top-sails yesterday, John Butler, A.B., fell from the maintopsail-yard into the sea. Sub-Lieut. Robert T. Wood immediately (with all his clothes on) jumped overboard after him, there was a high sea running and a strong wind blowing at the time, and Mr. Wood subjected himself to a great risk of drowning, and showed distinguished courage in endeavouring to save John Butler, who was unfortunately drowned.

I have the honour to request that you will be pleased to mention Mr. Wood to my Lord Commissioners of the Admiralty for their favourable consideration. This attempt at rescue occurred when returning to Portsmouth from the Channel in a gale of wind.

Kennett, Barrington, Barrister.   Case 19114

Letter from J. Milsted Spencer, 7 Old Palace Yard, 19th April, 1873.

I have very great pleasure in testifying to the praiseworthy and courageous conduct of Mr. Barrington Kennett, on the occasion of the upsetting of a boat between Putney and Hammersmith, on the 26th of March. After watching the practise of the University Crews, I was walking towards Hammersmith when I saw a boat containing four young men overturned, and its occupants struggling in deep water; three of the men were rescued by passing boats, but the fourth sank almost immediately. Mr. Kennett pulled to the spot, and without divesting himself of his clothing, dived after him, he swam about the place and dived seven or eight times without success, until becoming exhausted, he was obliged to cling to a boat and was thus assisted ashore. The day being very cold greatly increased the risk.

As an old boating man, I can say that were there many such men on the river the number of lives lost by boat accidents would be very few. Such noble conduct certainly deserves the encouragement of your Society.

Dowson, Phillip, a resident of Yokohama.   Case 19116

Letter from Russell Robertson, British Consul, Kanagawa, 10th of March, 1873.

I venture to bring to your notice a very gallant act performed by a British subject, Mr. Phillip Dowson, a resident at this port, and under exceptionally hazardous circumstances.

The harbour of Yokohama is really an open roadstead, where a slight breeze will soon raise an angry sea, and put a stop to communication between the shipping and the shore; on the 12th ult., a coal barge was proceeding from the wharf to one of the American Mail Steamers, when, owing to the freshening breeze and being loaded down to the gunwhale, she foundered. Fifty Japanese and one European were on board and were soon struggling for their lives, no boat was near, but Mr. Dawson (sic), whose Iron Works border on the Creek, which empties into the Bay, proceeded in his Steam Launch to the scene of the accident and threw himself in among the drowning; the gallantry of the act being enhanced from the fact that there was a fresh wind, the thermometer stood at about freezing point, and the unfortunate Japanese were sinking one by one around him. Rapidly he seized four of the drowning men, one after the other, in one instance diving to a considerable depth after a drowning man, and brought them ashore; animation was restored to two, but the others, owing to their long immersion, were beyond human aid, the loss of life amounted to eighteen.

Westaway, J.G, Lieut., 13th Light Infantry.   Case 19167

Letter from John H. Keough, Queen's Bench Office, Four Courts, Dublin, 8th March, 1873.

One day in June last, hearing cries on Inno Quay, I looked from the office window and saw an excited crowd pointing to some object which was but occasionally visible, as it was carried along with the receding tide; a gentleman (who I afterwards heard was Mr. Westaway, 13th Lt. Infantry) walking on the opposite side of the roadway, ran across, and, without an instant's hesitation jumped up on the parapet and down into the river, the tide being more than half ebb and the height, from where he sprang, about 30 feet. Mr. Westaway struck the bottom, cutting his head and face severely, he rose again and swam with him to the wall, when standing up to his neck in mud and water, he held up the boy until a rope was let down, to which he made him fast, and by which he was brought safely up; Mr. Westaway was in like manner got up the wall streaming with blood from head and face.

Osborne, William, aged twelve. Case 19172

On the 3rd July, 1873, Samuel Westhorpe (aged 15) and another boy (whose name is not known) were bathing together; the other boy, who could not swim, got out of his depth and Westhorpe went to his assistance, but as he could only swim a little he was in danger of being drowned in consequence of the other lad clinging to him. William Osborne (aged 12), who was on the bank dressed, seeing what was going on and hearing the boys calling out for help, began to undress to go in after them, but when he was partly undressed noticing that both boys had sunk (as he states) for the fourth time, and knowing that the water was beyond their depth, he dived in after them with the remainder of his clothes on. Both the drowning boys clung to Osborne, who pulled them both near to the bank and then pushed off Westhorpe and brought the elder lad to shore; Westhorpe was brought out by a man named Hensly.

McCoy, Henry, Sub Constable, R.I.C. Case 19183

Letter from F.J. Canty, Clonakety, County Cork.

On 10th of July, 1873, an Annual Regatta was held at Courtmasherry, and sub-constable, Henry McCoy, R.I.C., stationed in this town, was at the Regatta on duty, and at the time of the accident was sitting at the window; he immediately jumped through the open window, at a height of 9 or 10 feet, rushed, as well as he could, through the dense crowd and gallantly jumped into the water with uniform and side arms on, and swam to the capsized boat. As soon as he reached her, he found the legs of one of the women sticking out from under the gunwale, he dragged her out and swam with her to a lighter, rested her on an oar, from which she was taken on board, and immediately turned round and swam to the boat again. He saw some air bubbles at the stern, and although greatly exhausted, he dived under the boat and caught the other woman, who immediately on his touching her, grasped him by the hand and buried her nails in it, he dragged her from under the boat and pushed her towards the shore, swimming with one hand; when he reached the land he was completely exhausted.

Brownbill, James Henry, aged eleven. Case 19325

James Henry Brownbill, of Newbridge, Victoria, Australia, aged eleven years, was passing along the river Loddon at about 5 p.m. on the 2nd of January, 1874, on horseback, and hearing screams galloped forward. Casting his horse adrift and without waiting to undress he plunged in to the rescue. The only visible object on the surface was Harriet Cherry's hand, which was grasped and brought to shore by Brownbill, when without delay, he dived down in search of the others and succeeded in getting Letitia Grant (aged 14), who, when brought to shore, was found to have the apparently lifeless boy Bayley (aged 6) clinging to her dress, the depth of water about eight feet.

These three people were saved through the unaided energy and pluck of this child 11 years of age.

Ellis, John, Bristol General Steamship Company, Case 19328

Letter from C.G. Star, Master, s.s. *Juno*, Cork, 15th April, 1874.

On the 14th April, 1874, I was just in the act of sailing from Bristol and had let go the ropes and moved the engine ahead, when a soldier jumped on the paddle-box and turning round to shake hands with a woman fell between the paddle-wheel and the quay wall. John Ellis, who was standing by, immediately slid down the fender rope, putting the ship's papers in his mouth, and calling out to stop the engine, caught the man before he got into the wheel; life-buoys were in readiness, but could not be used, as the whole affair occurred under the paddle sponson. John Ellis has been many years in the employ of the Bristol General Steamship Company, and is a most deserving man of high character.

Macmeikan, C.H, aged nine.   Case 19361

At noon on the 18th of March, 1874, some schoolboys were bathing in the Salt Water River at Footscray, near Melbourne, Victoria, South Australia, when one of them, aged 14, being unable to swim, got beyond his depth, and was in imminent danger. His elder brother, who could swim a little, went to his assistance, but the former seized and clung on to him so that both disappeared under water. Two sons of Mr. James Macmeikan, seeing their danger, began to strip; the elder could not get his boots off, but the younger, aged 9 years, getting his shoes and jacket off, plunged in, dived under water and happily succeeded, unassisted, in bringing first one and then the other to the shore, both boys being too far gone to struggle. The water was twelve feet deep where the boys lay, and this child had to dive for them.

Nadal, Laurent, Fisherman.   Case 19374

On the afternoon of the 28th March the ship *Chrysolite*, bound from Volemar, in Madagascar, to Port Louis with a cargo of 270 bullocks, struck upon a coral reef to the eastward of the Island, about five miles from shore.

The vessel began to break up rapidly and several sailors were washed overboard; the land could not then be seen from the ship nor could she be perceived from the shore, owing to the thick rain. On the following morning, however, the land was perceived by those on board and signals of distress were hoisted. These signals having been observed by a fisherman named Laurent Nadal, he immediately collected some other fishermen, chiefly relatives of his own, who proceeded to the wreck in two piroques or country canoes, one, the larger, commanded by himself, and the other by his brother, Donald Nadal. Each of the brothers was accompanied by four men.

The undertaking was one of extreme danger, as the hurricane, though diminishing, still continued in heavy squalls accompanied by much rain and the sea was high, whilst the distance from land to be traversed was considerable, amounting to several miles, nor is a piroque, even in the most practised hands, a craft well adapted for rough water. However, they succeeded with great difficulty in boarding the *Chrysolite* and rescuing her crew.

The larger piroque returned safely to shore with the captain, chief officer, and fifteen of the crew; the smaller piroque of Donald Nadal, manned by himself and four other men, which had the remainder of the crew, five in number, had entered, was capsized and all on board drowned, with the exception of two of the crew of the *Chrysolite* who were drifted among a number of dead bullocks floating on the water, by means of which they supported themselves and were, after being many hours in the water, ultimately floated to a little islet on the reef. Those in the larger piroque were wholly unable to render any aid to their unfortunate comrades.

Harvey C.L., Captain, 71st Regiment.   Case 19447

Letter from Major C.Eccles, 24th Regiment, Cork Barracks, 7th of August, 1874.

I have the honour to state for your information that on the night of Tuesday last, the 4th inst., at about 10 o'clock, when the steamer which conveyed the detachment of the 24th Regiment arrived at the quay at Cork, the wife of Drummer Thompson in attempting to get ashore fell into the water and got under the paddle-wheel; she had a child under her arms at the time. Captain Harvey, 71st Regiment and D.A.A. General, Cork district, with great presence of mind, and with great risk to his own life, jumped into the water and succeeded in rescuing both the woman and the child.

I beg to add that had it not been for the presence of mind displayed by Captain Harvey both the woman and the child must have been drowned, as it was quite dark at the time.

Robson, Henry, Gunner, R.A., Fort Trincomalee, East India.   Case 19465

At 5 p.m. on the 4th of July, 1874. two men belonging to H.M.S. *Glasgow* having jumped over board from a canoe on their way to the ship when returning from leave, were in imminent danger of being drowned at about 300 yards from the Town Pier, when Henry Robson, Gunner R.A., swam to their assistance and after considerable difficulty succeeded in bringing them to the shore, one of them, Bombardier Armstrong, R.M.A., being insensible was restored to consciousness with considerable difficulty on his being sent to the Naval Hospital.

Smith, W.E., Midshipman, R.N.   Case 19583

About five minutes past midnight of the 7th of March, 1875, at the Peraeus of Athens, Edwin Payne, engine-room artificer, being delirious with fever, jumped overboard through the Sick Bay port on the forepart of the main deck, the night being very dark and cold, blowing hard from the north-east, with showers of snow. Mr. W.E. Smith, Midshipman, H.M.S. *Pallas*, jumped overboard from the after-sponson and succeeded in keeping the man's head above water till picked up by a shore boat, which after a little time reached them, Mr. Smith being unaware at the time this man could not swim. Depth of water 30 feet. Temperature of water 57.

Brenton, Reginald O.B.C., Lieut., R.N.   Case 19716

Second Silver Clasp

Letter from Capt T. Branditt, H.M.S. *Excellent*, Portsmouth, 21st August, 1875.

I beg to report that on Wednesday 18th of August, whilst the launch of the *Vernon* was laying down torpedoes the electric cable of one caught round the leg of John Patterson, A.B., and dragged him overboard. He was seized and his mouth was with great difficulty just held above water. There was a strong tide running, and the whole weight of the boat broadside was hanging on the man. I consider from the evidence that the man would certainly have drowned had not Lieut. Brenton, R.N., gone overboard and after diving three times succeeded in clearing the cable from the man's leg.

J. Patterson was much exhausted, and his leg was found to be broken. Lieut. Brenton has already a Royal Humane Society's Medal with one clasp, and I have to request you may be pleased to apply for a second clasp for him.

Isaac, F.V., Lieut., R.N.   Case 19846

On the 6th September, 1875, when entering Simon's Bay at the rate of nine knots, an ordinary seaman, named Rees Williams, of H.M.S. *Narcissus*, fell overboard from the mizzen rigging, striking against the mizzen-channels, which bruised and rendered useless his left leg. Lieut. F.V. Isaac, R.N., immediately jumped overboard from the poop (a height of about twenty-five feet) to his rescue. He came up to him just as he became exhausted and insensible, and supported him until the cutter arrived, having been in the water for about ten minutes. The weather was cold, temperature of the air 55, water 57. Lieut. Isaac was on the sick list for twenty days owing to the chill incurred by being in the water.

Moores, Alfred, Resident of Pouch Cove, St. John's, Newfoundland.   Case 19858

At a late hour on Monday night last, the 29th November, 1875, a man named Langmead, living at the extreme north of the village of Pouch Cove, was aroused by shouts from some persons near his house. Lighting a lamp, and partially dressing himself, he opened the door and discovered three men wet and well-nigh exhausted, who proved to be the captain and two of the crew of the fore-and-after *Waterwitch*, of Cupids. He soon learned from them the sad news that their vessel had gone ashore in an adjacent cove, that a number of the crew had perished, but that some were still clinging to the rocks. Getting the half dead men into the house, and seeing them comfortably disposed of, Langmead immediately started up the settlement, rousing the inmates of the various houses as he went along, telling them what had happened. It was not long before most of the persons on the north side of Pouch Cove were up, and many prepared to start, some by boat and others by land, for the scene of the disaster.

This is a deep and narrow inlet or gulch about a mile and a half to the north-east of Pouch Cove, well called HORRID GULCH. In it the water is deep right to the foot of the shore, which is very steep. On the north side, and at the bight of the gulch the rocks run up. almost perpendicularly to the height of 600 feet, as against them the sea dashes with tremendous force. On the north side they are somewhat less precipitous, and a narrow ledge runs close to the water's edge. On this ledge it was that the captain, his son, and two other men jumped, the others who were saved being on the other side in a position I shall presently describe. Immediately opposite the ledge I have mentioned a peaked shelving rock rises, evidently broken off from and close to the perpendicular cliff.

The first party of rescuers started from the village, about one in the morning, and reached the spot where the captain and his party had landed, and where he had left his son to keep in good heart the poor creatures on the other side of the gulf. Arriving there they could hear through the darkness and drift the screams of those so near them, whom they were so powerless to help; and endeavoured by their shouts of encouragement to give them assurance that help would soon be afforded them. The names of the men composing this family are Robert Moulton, Thomas Noseworthy and Adam Noseworthy.

Meanwhile, other parties had reached the top of the cliffs on the other side, and were endeavouring to devise plans for the rescue of those below. The only way possible was by lowering a man over the cliff by a rope, for by that means alone could the position of the shipwrecked men be known. A worthy man, named Alfred Moores, volunteered for this dangerous service, and accordingly a strong rope was fastened around him and he was lowered over the precipice. Three times was the brave fellow swung into the dark, but he could not find a suitable place to descend. A fourth time he was lowered, and half swinging, half sliding along a crevasse in the rock, he succeeded in reaching a ledge immediately over the spot whence the cries proceeded. Guided and supported by his rope other brave fellows followed him, and took up positions between him and the top of the cliff, so as to be in readiness to help. The names of these were David Baldwin, Eli Langmead, William Noseworthy, and Christopher Munday. At the top, with the end of the rope hitched round a tree, was William Langmead. To get any idea of the pluck of these men you have to picture to yourself their position on that bleak hill side in the darkness and cold, clinging for dear life to a rope, the length of which, from the top to where Alfred Moores stood with the end around his body, was eighty-five fathoms.

How to reach the poor men was the question. Away down below him, twenty fathoms further, on the small jutting rock which I have described, Moores could now make them out through the grey dawn - eight poor creatures huddled as closely together as they could lie, and clinging with all the power they possessed. Twice he threw down a hand-rope he had with him, and twice he had to haul it back. "In the name of God", he makes a third cast, and this time is successful, it had caught. A stronger rope is handed down, made fast around the body of one of the men, and he is hauled up to where Moore stands. There this rope is untied, and helped along by those on the crevasse and supporting himself by the rope which supports them, he reaches the top, while the rope which hauled him up goes down for another. In this way they all reach the top in safety, and the skill and courage of their rescuers is rewarded by success. But these are not all the survivors, for on a ledge by himself is crouching a poor young fellow, who has been left till the last, because he was supposed to be in the least danger. There, alone, some hundreds of feet from his companions, he has clung through the terrible night, half dressed, hatless, and with but one boot. A rope is flung to him, he has just strength left to fasten it around him, and he, too, is safe. Soon all are in Pouch Cove, and cared for with the utmost kindness.

Silver Medal awarded to Alfred Moores and Bronze Medals to Eli Langmead, William Noseworthy, David Baldwin, and Christopher Munday.

Drake, Charles Edwin, Lieut., R.N.   Case 19894

Silver Clasp

At 7 p.m. on the 9th May, 1876, Hugh McBain, Assistant Sick-Berth Attendant, fell overboard from the port gangway of H.M.S. *Philomel* at sea, in lat. 4 S., lon 86 E. Navigating Lieut. Charles Edwin Drake, R.N., jumped overboard from the ship's quarter and swam to McBain, who was in an exhausted state, took him on his back, and swam twenty yards off to a life-buoy, and were both picked up by the lifeboat; the ship was under steam at the time, going five knots.

Mr. Drake received the Society's Silver Medal in 1868.

Strickland, J., Sub-Constable, Royal Irish Constabulary   Case 19963

On Tuesday a man named Connolly, for some time residing in Cahir, was seized with a sudden fit of insanity, to which it appears, he had been occasionally subject. Divesting himself of his clothing, he made his escape in a state of nudity through the upper window of his dwelling, which is some twenty feet from the ground. He, however, sustained little or no injury in his fall and he immediately fled towards the River Suir, being hotly pursued by some of his friends. Intelligence of the occurrence having reached the Police-barracks, Sub-constables Strickland, Mullany, and Brosnahan, of the Cahir station, were quickly in pursuit. Connolly in the meantime had gained the summit of a rock overhanging the river, and, on the near approach of the three constables named, he flung himself into the river, the water being at this spot at least fifteen feet deep. Sub-constable Strickland immediately divested himself of his tunic and boots, and gallantly plunged after him. The Sub-constable having caught hold of Connolly, who is a man of superior build and an expert swimmer, succeeded in putting Strickland under water, and fears were entertained that the Sub-constable was drowning, when Mullany and Brosnahan swam to the assistance of Strickland, and eventually they succeeded, after much exertion, in saving their comrade and Connolly, whom they brought to the bank in safety.

Silver Medal Awarded to Strickland and Bronze Medals awarded to Mullany and Brosnahan.

Cox, W. Private, 2nd Battalion, Royal Welsh Fusiliers.   Case 20084
Dornin, A.   "
Kirby, H.   "

On the night of the 30th November, 1876, the boat of a Spanish gun-boat was upset in a squall in Catalan Bay, at the back of the Rock of Gibraltar. The night was so dark that the direction of the wreck could only be traced by the cries of the men. A guard of the 2nd battalion of the 23rd or Royal Welsh Fusiliers, who were on duty at the Eastern Beach, assisted by three Spanish boatmen, with difficulty launched a boat, and, being joined by one of the wrecked crew, rescued four men who were clinging to the wreck. On reaching the shore it was ascertained that one of the crew was missing. The boat was again launched, and on reaching the wreck Privates Cox, Dornin, and Kirby swam about the wreck in search of the missing man, whose body was subsequently recovered. Houghton remained in the boat.

Shortland, T.W., Midshipman, R.N.   Case 20121
Ford, W.H., Ordinary Seaman, R.N.

A boat was under sail from the *Pallas*, at Salonica Bay, on the 17th May, 1877, when she capsized, all her crew being thrown into the water. They got on the bottom of the boat, except for W. Nicholls, O.S., who was about two boat lengths' to windward, in a drowning state, when Mr. T.W. Shortland, midshipman, seeing his danger, swam to his rescue, and endeavoured to bring him to the boat. The drowning man struggled with him, and in sinking grasped him by the legs. Becoming exhausted, Mr. Shortland called for assistance, when W.H. Ford, O.S., came to his aid. On reaching the spot he found that Nicholls had sunk, upon which he dived, and, bringing him up by the hair, swam with him to the boat. Mr. Shortland, though much exhausted, assisting to the best of his power.

Scotcher, George, A.B., R.N.   Case 20157

Her Majesty's Ship *Danae* was at sea off Sierra Leone, on the 8th May, 1877, when Henry Mindry, boy, 1st class, fell off the fore yard whilst he was assisting to make sail. The sea was smooth, but frequented by sharks. George Scotcher, A.B., jumped after him from the upper deck port, and supported him until assistance arrived. The ship was going five knots. The boy, when saved, had been ten minutes in the water.

Marx, J.L., Lieut., R.N.   Case 20179
Heyland, W.O.L., Lieut., R.N.

On the 15th July, 1877, when H.M.S. *Achilles* was at sea in lat. 36.45 N. lon. 0.46 E., a first-class boy, J.J. Burke, fell from aloft when setting studding sails. On seeing this accident Marx and Heyland, jumped overboard to his assistance, and as the rod of the life-buoy jammed and could not be let go, great exertions were necessary to save the boy's life. The sea was running very heavily, and the ship was going ten knots. Both these officers had already received the bronze medals of the society for saving life on former occasions.

Eyre, G.S., Lieut., Bengal Staff Corps.   case 20195

On the 15th April, 1877, Lieuts. Deane and Mansell attempted to swim across a branch of the Ganges at Baghalpur, Bengal, in all their clothes, when Deane became faint. Mansell did all he could to sustain him in the water, but, through being clasped round the neck by Deane, would have been drowned with him had not Eyre with great promptitude, come to their assistance. The moment he saw them in difficulties he had on all his clothes (heavy shooting boots etc.) but he swam some eighty or ninety yards, and succeeded in separating them, and then brought the insensible body of Deane to the shore. A strong stream was running, and the bottom was very muddy; also the bank was steep. The risk was very great.

Brant, James, Lieut., R.N.   Case 20199
Lawrence, R., A.B., R.N.

When off Port Said, on 3rd July, 1877, a cry of "Man overboard!" was raised on board H.M.S. *Research*. Engines were at once stopped and reversed, when Henry Godwin, A.B., drifted past, just under water, with one hand raised. At this moment Brant jumped overboard from the hammock netting, followed by Lawrence. They both swam towards Godwin, who was still under water. At this moment a middle sized hammer-headed shark was observed fifteen or twenty yards from the men, swimming rapidly, the three men in the water drifted about four hundred yards astern, where they were picked up by the life-boat. Godwin's life was most undoubtedly saved by the two men, as all three were thoroughly exhausted when brought on board.

Thomas, Daniel, Colliery Proprietor.   Case 20235
Beith, William, Mining Engineer.
Pride, Isaac, Collier.
Howell, John William, Collier.

On the 11th April, 1877, the Tymwydd Colliery, situated near Porth in the Rhonda Valley, South Wales, was inundated with water from the old workings of the adjoining Cymmer Colliery. At the time of the inundation there were fourteen men in the pit, of whom four were unfortunately drowned, and one killed by compressed air, leaving nine men imprisoned by the water. Of this number four were released after eighteen hours imprisonment. It was in effecting the release of these latter five that those distinguished services were rendered by Thomas, Beith, Pride and Howell, which the conferring of the Society's Silver Medals is intended to recognise, and for which the Albert Medals of the first-class were awarded by Her Majesty the Queen.

The rescuing operations consisted of driving through the barrier of coal, thirty-eight yards in length, which intervened between the imprisoned miners and the rescuers, and kept back a quantity of water and compressed air. This task was commenced on Monday, April the 16th, and was carried on until Thursday, April the 19th, without any great amount of danger being incurred by the rescuers; but about one o'clock p.m., on that day, when only a few yards of the barrier remained, the danger from an irruption of water, gas and compressed air was so great as to cause the colliers to falter. It was at this juncture that the above four men volunteered to resume the rescue operations, the danger of which had been greatly increased by an outburst of inflammable gas under great pressure, and in such quantities as to extinguish the Davy lamps which were being used. The danger from the gas continued at intervals until half past three on the following morning; and from that time the above four men, at great peril to their own lives, continued the rescuing operations until three o'clock p.m., when the five imprisoned men were safely released.

Bartlett, Alex. Edward, Surgeon.   Case 20257

During some repairs being made to a well at Goudhurst, Kent, on the 21st September, 1877, W. Buss a plumber, who was down the well, made a signal to be hauled up, which was immediately acted on, and when within eight feet of the top he became quite insensible from the foul air, and slipping through the rope by which he was fastened, fell to the bottom, a distance of thirty-four feet from the surface. An alarm was raised, and Mr. Alex. Edward Bartlett, surgeon, was sent for. On his arrival a light was lowered into the well, but went out. No one present would venture down to the assistance of Buss; when, as the stertorous breathing of the man was clearly audible at the surface, Mr. Bartlett, on a short piece of ladder attached to a rope, was let down to the man's aid. On reaching the bottom he found the man quite insensible, with his head just out of the water. He tied him to the pipe of the pump to prevent him drowning, and then had to come up to the surface for fresh air, not being able to carry up such a heavy man. No one would go down to the man's aid. Mr. Bartlett went down again three times, and succeeded in fastening a rope round the man, but he was dead when brought to the surface. Mr. Bartlett was very ill and weak for some time after, from the foul air.

Barnes, Frederick, Capt-Coxswain.   Case 20274

During the terrible gale on the 15th October, 1877, which swept over the country, the look-out on board H.M.S. *Turquoise* in Plymouth Sound, at 2.30 a.m., saw some wreckage floating by, and faint cries were heard from it, but no boat could be lowered in the fearful sea, with spars and wreckage floating about. At this moment Barnes, with great gallantry offered to swim to the wreckage from which the cries came, so as to render any assistance needed. A line was obtained, and with it Barnes went overboard, swam to the timbers, secured the man to the wreckage, and returned with him to the bows of the *Turquoise*, when both were safely drawn on board. It was found that the rescued man was one of the crew of the barque *Harriet Jones*, which had been carried by the sea right over the breakwater, her anchors being outside, and the chain cables right over into the sound. The ship was totally destroyed by the force of the sea and storm.

Bussell, Grace Vernon, Miss.   Case 20278

On the 1st December, 1876, a native stockman brought the alarm that there was a wreck some miles down the coast, and on ascending a hill near their house at Wallscliffe, Western Australia, they could make out a vessel among the rocks and breakers about seven miles down the coast. Miss Grace Vernon Bussell then took her father's horse (an exceptionally good one) and galloped off with the stockman to the place. Upon arriving there she found the sea breaking heavily over the stranded ship, which lay about seventy yards from the beach; and in endeavouring to land a number of the passengers in the only remaining boat it was overturned in the sweep, just as Miss Bussell and her attendant reached the top of the cliff opposite. Without a moment's hesitation she dashed her noble steed down the cliff and into the raging waters, closely followed by the stockman, reached the boat, and dragged many of the passengers ashore. This was repeated many times until all were safely landed. Miss Bussell then galloped home for more assistance. She ran great risk, as, when her horse was swimming ashore it caught its legs in a rope, and nearly turned over at the time some women and children were clinging to her saddle. The stockman, Samuel Isaacs, swam his horse in and saved the last man. Samuel Isaacs was voted the Bronze Medal.

Labat, Felix.   Case 20286

On the 4th August, 1876, two young men (one Batty, an Englishman, and a Frenchman) were bathing in the sea at Biarritz. They being ignorant of the locality got into a current which carried them out into the breakers, where they must have perished had not M. Felix Labat, who knew the neighbourhood, gallantly swam out to their assistance, and seizing the two supported them (one in each hand) for some minutes. Unfortunately the two young men, in their fright, began to struggle, and seizing Labat, all three sank. Freeing himself, Labat alone rose to the surface, and recovering his breath he dived, and a second time took hold of both the drowning men, and, seeing the life-boat approaching he supported them for about sixty yards, swimming out to sea from the breakers, the current rendering it impossible to reach the shore. Unfortunately the life-boat came up at such a rapid rate that it passed over Labat's shoulder, hurting him much, and striking Batty on the head, took him from Labat's grasp, and he sank never to rise again. M. Labat, however, notwithstanding the injury he had himself received, held on to the other young man, and ultimately the boat took both on board and saved their lives.

White, George, Gentleman.   Case 20303

About 9 a.m., on the 27th October, 1876, two brothers (George and Harry White) became immersed in the Mississippi Lake, three quarters of a mile from shore, by their canoe upsetting.

George could have saved himself, but finding his brother Harry unable to keep afloat, went to his assistance, and, with his arm passed around him, continued to support him for a considerable time, until he himself became insensible. Unfortunately his brave exertions were of no avail in saving his brother Harry, and he was only rescued himself, several hours after the accident, in an exhausted state.

Boyer, Francis Henry, Lieut. R.N.   Case 20310

On the 11th November, 1877, in the Inland Sea in Japan, W.C. Gibbon, seaman of H.M.S. *Modeste*, was washed off the accommodation ladder. The night was intensely dark, a cross sea and strong current running.

Lieut. Boyer, immediately jumped overboard to rescue the seaman, but his brave efforts were unsuccessful, the man was drowned and, Boyer was picked up by the cutter in an insensible state.

Saul, Arthur E., Navigating Sub-Lieut., R.N.   Case 20349
Eade, Henry H., Ordinary Seaman, R.N.

On the 3rd of February, 1878, the pinnace of H.M.S. *Vestal*, in charge of Navigating Sub-Lieut Saul, with a crew of thirteen hands, foundered in deep water six miles from the coast of Madagascar. Most of the boats gear went down with her, and there was not sufficient supports for all the struggling seamen.

Lieut. Saul was supporting himself on an empty barricoe, when he saw Frederick Suter, a seaman, in a distressed state. He gave up the barricoe to him and swam for the shore, successfully attaining it in seven hours.

Henry Eade, ordinary seaman, was also supporting himself on the awning, and seeing another seaman named Rowsell sinking, gave the support up to him, and struck out for the shore.

The Commander of the ship remarks - That the conduct of all reflects the highest credit upon the discipline and spirit of the service. The gallant conduct of Mr. Saul and Henry Eade is enhanced by the fact that at the time of the accident there seemed little chance of their brave performances ever being brought to light.

Hawkes, Thomas, Sail Maker, R.N.   case 20364

On the 23rd of March, 1878, Thomas Hawkes, a sail maker of H.M.S. *Sapphire*, jumped overboard from the poop to the rescue of M. Begley, who had fallen into the sea from the flying boom. The ship was going six and a half knots in a heavy cross sea. He succeeded in saving the man.

Hawkes has jumped overboard six times to save life during his service.

Pearce, Thomas Richard, Midshipman.   Case 20444

On the 1st June, 1878, the ship *Loch Ard* was lost off the coast of Australia, when all the crew and passengers perished excepting Thomas Richard Pearce and Eveline Carmichael. Pearce was washed ashore in a heavy sea. Some time afterwards he saw a female clinging to a spar about seventy yards from shore. He immediately swam out, brought her to the shore, and then climbed an almost perpendicular cliff for further assistance. His gallant exertions were successfully rewarded.

Holt, Hugh W. Lea, Station Master.   Case 20446

On the 28th April, 1878, C.M.Tuke was bathing in a gulf near Newcastle, N.S.W., and becoming exhausted when swimming in rough water called out for help. Mr. Holt at once plunged from a rock twelve feet in height and swam a distance of thirty yards to his rescue. Seizing Tuke by the arm he succeeded in landing him on a rock, from which he was again washed off. Holt again went to his assistance, and with some trouble brought him to land much injured and helpless. This gentleman has been the means of saving several other persons from drowning.

Rourke, John, Sergeant, R.A.   Case 20481

Silver Clasp

Morris Ford, a gunner in the Royal Artillery fell into the Bristol Basin, on the 29th July, 1878.

John Rourke (fully accoutred in marching order) jumped in, a height of fifteen feet, succeeded in keeping the man afloat until a rope was thrown, which he fastened round Ford's body, and by which he was hauled on board the ship.

The fact of Rourke having a sword and great coat on at the time very much enhanced the personal risk.

Agassiz, Roland L., Captain, R.M.L.I.   Case 20510

On the 23rd of September, 1878, H.M.S. *Agincourt* was going seven knots under steam in the Sea of Marmora, when F.Peel a seaman, fell overboard.

Captain Agassiz immediately jumped overboard and supported the seaman until a life-buoy was thrown. The night was very dark.

Donner, C.S. Lieut., R.N.   Case 20542

Silver Clasp

On the 17th of September, 1878, H.M.S. *Euryalus* was at sea when a ship's boy fell overboard. Lieut. Donner, who was in his berth at the time, on hearing the alarm, jumped through an upper deck port, placed a Kisbie life buoy over the lad, and guided him to the ship's buoy, remaining in the water until the arrival of the boat. The ship was going six knots, with a fresh breeze astern. This officer was already in possession of the Society's Silver Medal, for saving life at sea in 1867.

Hodge, Charles H., of the West Indies.   Case 20567

C.H. Hodge of Roseau, Island of Dominica, West Indies, was the means of saving five lives from drowning off St. Joseph.

On the 14th December, 1878, a boat containing six persons (the salvor being one of them) started a plank when under sail about four miles from shore. The crew turned her over and got rid of the ballast; they then attempted to pull towards shore, but the boat became waterlogged and they could make no headway, on the contrary they found themselves drifting out to sea. Hodge volunteered to swim ashore for assistance, which almost incredible feat he accomplished against the wind and tide, arriving on the beach at 4 a.m. on the morning of the 15th. Obtaining assistance, he pushed off again in a boat, and succeeded in rescuing his companions, who were found still clinging to the boat seven miles from shore.

The waters off St. Joseph are infested with sharks.

Warburton, James, Forgeman.   Case 20644

On the 18th July, 1879, a small steamer, with upwards of 100 passengers, was returning from Pyewipe to Lincoln, when the supports of the upper deck gave way and stove in the sides of the boat; the whole of the passengers were precipitated into the water. Warburton was walking on the bank at the time of the accident; he plunged in several times without divesting himself of clothing, and succeeded in rescuing many of the people.

Voisard, Edward, Captain, French Merchant Service. Case 20653

On the 7th July, 1879, during the International Yacht Race at Havre, Douglas Yates a seaman of the yacht *Hildegarde*, belonging to His Royal Highness the Prince of Wales, was washed overboard from the bowsprit while bending the jib topsail. Capt. Voisard most gallantly jumped overboard from the *Hermine*, a small screw steam vessel, and succeeded in rescuing the man from being drowned, although he died soon after from congestion of the brain. The wind was blowing fresh with a chopping sea on, and both vessels were going fast through the water. The seaman was unable to swim. Her Majesty the Queen was most graciously pleased to grant a gold medal to the salvor.

Lang W.M., Commander, R.N. Case 20715

On the 26th July, 1879, the Chinese fleet of gunboats constructed in this country were anchored in Plymouth Sound, and about to proceed to China under the command of Captain Lang, when a boy fell overboard from a steamer. Captain Lang promptly jumped overboard without divesting himself of his clothes, dived after the boy, and rescued him.

Fry J.W., Colonel, late 88th Foot (Connaught Rangers). Case 20761

Several young ladies were bathing at Boulogne on the 24th of September 1879, when they were swept off their feet and overwhelmed in the surf by the violence of the sea.

Colonel Fry, seeing their danger, ran a considerable distance to the spot, dashed to their assistance; first he grasped the body of Miss Wiseman, but was knocked down and lost his hold of her. He then returned and found Miss Clarke, and succeeded in bringing her safely to shore. He again attempted to find the others, but without success.

A gale of wind was blowing and the sea unusually rough.

Falconer J., Quartermaster, Royal Engineers. Case 20772

On the 6th September, 1879, John Ruber became immersed by falling from Gillingham Pier. The salvor, fully clothed, jumped a height of fourteen or fifteen feet into the water, and after diving brought the lad to the surface, and succeeded in rescuing him. Falconer was already in possession of the Society's Bronze Medal for saving life from drowning on a former occasion, and this is the ninth life he has rescued from imminent danger.

Duggan, Richard J., Barrister at Law, Ontario. Case 20779

On the 25th August, 1878, in Burlington Bay, Hamilton Ontario, two men were knocked off the deck of a yacht whilst endeavouring to get into Hamilton in a strong gale of wind.

The salvor was on the deck of his own yacht at her moorings, and hearing the alarm he at once jumped overboard, and swam to the aid of the drowning man. The night was quite dark, and he was only guided to the spot by the cry. He succeeded in finding one man, and swam 100 yards with him to the nearest wharf, running great personal risk from drowning by getting entangled in thick seaweed. Mr. Duggan again entered the water and attempted to save the other man, who was unfortunately drowned.

Knight, Frederick, Boy, 1st Class., R.N. Case 20782

At 11 p.m. 17th August, 1879, H.M.S. *Ready* was at anchor at Jask when a stoker fell overboard. The salvor was asleep on deck, and waking up he promptly jumped overboard and supported the man above water until a boat arrived. The roadstead was infested with sharks.

Cunningham, Henry Ward, Missionary Student.   Case 20830

On the 2nd February, 1880, at Lake Sherewater in Wilts., Adam C. Laughlin, a student of St. Boniface College, broke through the ice whilst skating, becoming immersed in ten feet of water, fifteen yards from the bank. Cunningham skated up to the place, and, without any hesitation jumped in (encumbered as he was with clothes and skates on), and succeeded in rescuing the other gentleman from under the ice.

Tardival, Francois, Quartermaster on board a French Gunboat.   Case 20888

The gunboat *Monette* was lying at the South Quay, Lowestoft. On the evening of the 28th March, 1880, about 9 o'clock p.m., two ladies fell into the water between the quay and the boat. Tardival hearing the screams rushed on deck and jumped from the bow of the vessel, caught hold of both ladies, and at great personal risk, succeeded in supporting them above water until a boat came to his assistance.

McGarritty, Francis, Miner.   Case 20912

On the 3rd of May, 1880, at great personal risk, repeatedly ventured down the shaft of a mine near Binchester, and brought to the surface the bodies of three men, who unfortunately succumbed to the effects of carbonic acid gas.

Prosser, Ephraim, Shoe Maker.   Case 20930
Dykes, Wm., Constable.
Maddox, Jas., Shepherd.

On the 28th May, 1880, Wm. Maddox went down a well, about forty-five feet deep, which he was engaged in sinking, and became insensible from the effects of gas. E. Prosser, without taking any precautions, at once went down to his assistance, and succumbed also.

The bystanders then called Wm. Dykes, who, comprehending the danger, at once went down with a rope attached to his body, placed it around Prosser.

Jas Maddox, seeing that none of the bystanders were willing to descend, was lowered down the shaft, and succeeded in bringing his uncle, Wm. Maddox, to the surface, who, however, died immediately afterwards.

Parkes, Gustavus, Leading Seaman, R.N.   Case 20955
                                    Silver Clasp

On the 6th July, 1880, H.M.S. *Vestal* was steaming up channel with square sail set, going six knots, when Charles Summers, an ordinary seaman, fell overboard.

Gustavus Parkes at once jumped over to the rescue of the seaman, and succeeded in supporting him above water until a boat arrived. There was a considerable sea on at the time, and both men were much exhausted when reached by the boat. See case 18821

Arscott, James, Labourer.   Case 20972

On the 17th August last, descended the unfinished shaft of a well, and worked for six hours at great personal risk, in extricating William Greenslade from suffocation.

Westley, Yetta P., Miss.   Case 21007

On the 22nd July, 1880, at St. Andrew's, Fife, a young lady whilst bathing was carried out of her depth by the tide, and being unable to swim, was in imminent danger of drowning.

Miss Westley plunged in to her assistance, and succeeded in bringing the lady to shore, a distance of fifty yards.

Nizam Din, Native Police.   Case 21013

Nizam Din, a chokidar in the Punjab, was awarded the Silver Medal for having gone down a well, at considerable personal risk, and saved the life of a water carrier who had fallen therein.

Lewis, J.W., aged fifteen.   Case 21023

For having saved a man from drowning at Aberrayon, under difficult circumstances, where a previous attempt was unsuccessfully made to rescue the person, on the 26th March, 1880.

Colville, Blanche, The Hon. Miss.   Case 21035

On the 24th August, 1880 year a young girl got out of her depth whilst bathing in the sea at West Cowes. The Hon. Miss Colville at once plunged in, without divesting herself of clothing, swam out, and rescued the girl.

Chambers, Wm., Well Sinker.   Case 21059

For having, on the 25th August, 1880, at great personal risk from noxious gases, descended the shaft of a well, at Ashford, and rescued Thomas Rogers, who was lying insensible at a distance of thirty-one feet from the surface. The salvor again descended, and recovered the body of another man who had succumbed from the effects of the poisonous air.

Newland, George, Labourer.   Case 21090

On the 11th September last, George Newland, a labourer, descended the shaft of a well, at Plymouth, and rescued a man from drowning.

Graham, E.F.C., Lieut., R.N.   Case 21107

For having, at Portsmouth, on a dark night, the 14th September, 1880, jumped from the taffrail of the Royal Yacht, *Osborne* to the rescue of a waterman who became immersed by his boat capsizing. Lieut. Graham, although encumbered with his uniform, succeeded in saving the life of the man.

His Royal Highness the Prince of Wales honoured Lieut. Graham by presenting the Medal in the presence of Her Royal Highness the Princess of Wales, the Committee having had the honour of being present by invitation.

Bayley, C.H., Lieut., R.N.　　　　　　　　　　　　　　　　　　　　　　　　　　　　　　　　　Case 21119

Jumped overboard from H.M.S. *Encounter* at sea and saved the life of a seaman. The ship was under steam, going eight knots, and at the time was in proximity to a coast where sharks abound.

Aitken, F.M., Lieut., 93rd Highlanders.　　　　　　　　　　　　　　　　　　　　　　　　　　Case 21172
Middleton, A.H., Lieut., 93rd Highlanders.
Orde, C.R., Lieut., Rifle Brigade.

On the 28th November, 1880, they were out sailing in Gibraltar Bay in a yawl belonging to the officers of the 93rd Highlanders.

At 6 o'clock p.m. the wind, which had been blowing hard all day, suddenly dropped, and an attempt was made to tow the yawl by the means of the dinghy, in which Mr. Campbell and Private Buchanan commenced rowing. The other officers manned the sweeps of the larger boat, keeping the mainsail and jib set. The wind suddenly sprung up and the yawl forged ahead, dragging the other boat swiftly through the water; at this juncture an attempt was made to transfer the tow line from the stern to the bow of the dinghy, and in doing so, the boat became swamped, immersing Mr. Campbell and the soldier. The latter succeeded in reaching the yawl at once, but Mr. Campbell was unable to see the boats in the darkness, and after swimming a considerable time, became exhausted and found himself sinking.

Mr. Aitken, who was steering the yawl at the time of the accident, seized a life-buoy and jumped overboard without divesting himself of clothing, and swam to the assistance of his brother officer. Mr. Middleton followed only removing some of his clothes, and taking with him another life-buoy. After swimming about fifty yards they heard Mr. Campbell calling for help; they went in the direction of the sound, and at first could see nothing until the phosphorescent light in the disturbed water showed where Mr. Campbell had gone down.

Mr. Aitken dived and succeeded in reaching the body, but owing to Mr. Campbell's struggles and the loss of his life-buoy, he had difficulty in keeping on the surface and holding the other. Mr. Middleton then arrived and assisted in placing the other life-buoy under Mr. Campbell; in doing so, the three officers sank several times.

Mr. Orde in the meantime went overboard, swam to the dinghy, then forty yards off, and brought it to the officers; they succeeded in making Mr. Campbell hold on to it, and shouted to Private Buchanan to pull on the attached tow rope. Mr. Campbell then became unconscious, and the dinghy, which hitherto had floated right way up now, turned over.

Mr. Middleton then succeeded in getting Campbell on the keel, and with Mr. Orde's assistance they reached the yawl. It was now found that Mr. Aitken was missing; they went in the dinghy and found him 250 yards off. Thunder and lightning with heavy rain continued all the time.

The case was sent by desire of His Royal Highness the Field Marshall Commanding-in-Chief, strongly recommending the above named officers for honorary reward, especially Lieutenant Aitken.

Stuart, Stonehouse, Boatman.　　　　　　　　　　　　　　　　　　　　　　　　　　　　　　Case 21180

On the 18th January, 1881, during a snowstorm and hurricane F. Carter, a boy of twelve years of age, was standing on Harwich Pier watching the heavy sea, when he was blown into the water.

Stonehouse Stuart, a boatman, without waiting to divest himself of heavy clothing, jumped in after the lad. A life-buoy was thrown, which Stuart attempted to place over the boy's shoulders, but was unable to do so on account of the lad clinging to him; he, however, succeeded in saving him with the aid of a plank and line which was thrown from the pier, but not before he incurred great personal risk from being dashed against the piles.

Dr. A. Kinsey Morgan attended the boy after immersion and successfully treated the case.

Coleman, Michael, Commissioned Boatman, Coast Guard. Case 21186

At 9 o'clock p.m., on the 14th January, 1881, Samuel Whitcombe was attempting to cross the River Yealm on broken ice when he became immersed in deep water about eighty yards from the shore. Coleman hearing his cry for help, rushed out of his house, jumped over the quay wall into the river of broken ice; when he reached the scene of the accident he found the man about a foot under the surface, face downwards, arms outstretched, and to all appearance dead. He succeeded with great difficulty in bringing the man to the bank, and spent three quarters of an hour in successful endeavours in restoring animation.

Coates, Jennie, Miss. Case 21207

On the 31st January, 1881, Miss Coates went out skating on Lough Derg, Co. Galway, whilst her sister and a gentleman named Lewis were walking on the ice close by. When the party were upwards of 100 yards from shore the ice gave way under Miss Coates and she became immersed in twelve feet of water. Mr. Lewis started for the land with a view of obtaining a rope from a boat on the other side of the lake, but before going made an ineffectual attempt to rescue the lady, becoming immersed himself.

Miss Jennie Coates took off her boots and ran across the rotten ice of the bay, nearly half a mile distant, and procured a rope, returning by the same route, followed by Mr. Lewis, who endeavoured to hand the rope to the lady, who was holding herself above water with the aid of a branch thrown by her sister.

In doing this Mr. Lewis lost his life, as the ice gave way and he sank beneath the surface. Miss Jennie Coates, nothing daunted, with great presence of mind succeeded in getting the rope to her sister, but could do nothing more by herself excepting to encourage her sister to hold on. In this awful position the ladies remained for nearly two hours. Miss Jennie, retaining her hold on the rope, supporting her sister, and crying aloud for help. At this juncture the lady's younger brother appeared, who at once procured another rope. Here, again, the young lady added to her former presence of mind by handing the rope to which her sister was clinging to her brother to hold, whilst with the other rope she crept along the ice to the place where Mr. Lewis had gone down and tied it round her sister's waist, stooping over the edge of the ice and reaching into the water, then getting back to her brother on the firm ice, they pulled the almost lifeless girl out of the water and carried her to land.

The Committee of the Royal Humane Society were unanimously of the opinion that the courageous conduct of the late Mr. Lewis should be recorded, and if he had survived his gallant exertions, he would have been awarded the Silver Medal also.

Eccles, Robert, Lieut., 43rd Regiment. Case 21248

On the 26th May, 1879, several gentlemen were sleeping on board a steamer at anchor in the River Irrawaddy. About midnight a native servant accidentally fell from the paddle box, and would in all probability have been drowned, owing to the rapid current and the darkness of the night, had not Mr. Eccles (who was sleeping on deck) promptly jumped overboard, seized hold of the man, and grasped something which protruded from the ship's side; in this position they were found and assisted out by other gentlemen on board. It is stated that the current was running six or seven knots and the night was intensely dark.

Beazor, Elias, Labourer. Case 21274
Teague, Thos., Seaman.

On the 10th February, 1881, a vessel was wrecked on the north reefs of the Island of Barbuda. Three boats in attempting to rescue the crew were upset, and two boatmen were in imminent danger of drowning. Elias Beazor, one of the immersed crew, swam to the assistance of Thomas Hudson (who was caught under a boat head downwards); after extricating the man he swam with him to the shore. Thos. Teague, who had safely landed, went out in a small boat to render assistance, and in doing so the boat capsized; he had to support himself on a barrel for some time, this he willingly gave up to a drowning man who was eventually saved by means of it.

Two other men, named Bryant and Wilson, behaved courageously, and rendered good assistance in saving life.

Cusack, J.W.H., Lieut., 87th Regiment.   Case 21275

At 1.20 o'clock a.m. on the 22nd May, 1881, whilst H.M.S. *Dasher* was laying alongside the transport ship *Holland* in Guernsey Roads, Private W.S. Clarke, 87th Regiment, fell off the after sponson; being unable to swim he would inevitably have been drowned had not Lieut. Cusack promptly jumped overboard, seized the man, and brought him to the ship's ladder. The night was dark, and the tide was running at three knots. Lieut. Cusack incurred considerable personal risk, as he jumped between two ships riding alongside one another in a tideway.

For Clasp see case 23016.

Lee, Richard J.   Case 21323

At 7.30 p.m. on the 21st June, 1881, Thos. Molloy, aged nine years, whilst playing on the quay at Limerick, fell into the River Shannon. Mr. Lee, who was near the place at the time, without hesitation flung off his coat, jumped off the pier (a height of twenty feet), seized hold of the lad, and supported him until a boat came to his assistance.

The personal risk incurred by Mr. Lee on this occasion was very considerable, as the bed of the river was rocky, the height jumped very great, and the water was shallow.

Sawdie, George, Pier Master, Eastbourne.   Case 21427

At 1 p.m. on 21st August, 1881, Miss E. Mitchin fell off Eastbourne Pier-head. Mr. Sawdie, the pier-master, was engaged in the toll house at the time of the accident, but on hearing the alarm he ran the full length of the pier, took off his coat, and plunged into the sea. He succeeded in reaching the lady (who had then drifted some distance to the westward of the pier), and held her above water for twenty-five minutes before a boat came to their assistance. A fresh gale was blowing at the time, and a heavy sea running. There was great danger of being dashed against the piles of the pier.

Place, Wm. T., Private, R.M.L.I.   Case 21448

On the 25th August, 1881, whilst H.M.S. *Invincible* was at sea O.S. Phillip Branton fell overboard from the fore rigging, striking the swinging boom in his fall. Private Place jumped overboard and kept the man afloat until the cutter reached them. The ship was going four and a half knots under steam only, the night was dark, and the sea calm.

Montgomery, W.H., The Reverend.   Case 21450

On the 29th July, 1881, E. Parkhouse whilst bathing at Bude in Cornwall was carried out of his depth by a strong current, and having become exhausted, was drifted rapidly out to sea. Mr. Montgomery swam out about four hundred yards, and succeeded in bringing the gentleman to shore in an apparently lifeless state. The place is extremely dangerous, as there is a conflux of several currents. Mr. Montgomery ran the risk of being carried out to sea.

Jones, Joseph G., Captain of the Forecastle, R.N.   Case 21451

H.M.S. *Garnet* was at anchor in Monte Video roads, Rio-de-la-Plata, on the 28th July, 1881, when Mr. B. Gwynne, Navigating Lieutenant, in the execution of his duty on the top-gallant forecastle veering cable, fell overboard. The night was dark, and a gale of wind blowing with a heavy breaking sea.

Joseph G. Jones hearing the alarm rushed on deck, seized the nearest rope and jumped overboard out of the upper deck port, he swam to

Gwynne, brought him to the ship's side, then with great courage supported him until rescued by a boat from the ship. The ship was one mile distant from the shore at the time.

Cunningham, Jas., Engineer. (Combined cases.)

Case 21467
Case 21468

At Limassol, Cyprus, on 24th December, 1880, a torrent from the mountains flooded the town.

Mr. Cunningham at great personal risk entered the falling houses and extricated several women and two men. He had to procure a ladder and make his way through a rush of water six feet deep, running at the rate of six or seven miles an hour; in doing this he fell into a native well, fifteen feet deep, and encountered numerous perils from falling debris. The temperature of the water was at freezing point.

On the 24th June, 1881, Mr. Cunningham again rescued a person from drowning near the pier at Limassol. Brought to the notice of the Society by General Sir R. Biddulph, K.C.M.G., C.B., High Commissioner of Cyprus.

Cronch, H.J., United States Consul at St. Helena.

Case 21469

On the evening of the 31st August, 1881, near Jame's Town, St. Helena, a woman threw herself off the rocks into the sea with the intention of committing suicide.

Mr. Cronch (who was in ignorance of the locality) ran to the nearest point where he could approach the woman, divested himself of coat and boots, jumped into the water and swam a distance of thirty or forty yards. He succeeded in seizing the woman and bringing her in an unconscious state to the rocks, where he had much difficulty in effecting a landing. The night was dark.

The case was sent to the Society by desire of the Right Honourable the Secretary of State for the Colonies.

Trench, F.P., Lieut., R.N.

Case 21531

At 4.30 o'clock p.m., on the 6th June, 1881, H.M.S. *Miranda* was running under steam off the Island of Upolnu, when a man fell overboard. The life-buoy was thrown but the man was unable to swim and could not reach it. Lieut. Trench at once jumped from the poop (a height of fifteen feet), swam to the man, and supported him until a boat came to his assistance. The ship was going four and a half knots when the accident took place.

The risk incurred was considerable, as sharks were seen alongside the ship on the day of the accident and on the following one.

McLean, John, Chief Officer.

Case 21553

On the 16th October, 1881, a man named McDonald was bathing in the Harbour of Pensacola, Coast of Florida. Soon after entering the water he was seen struggling, and apparently sinking.

John McLean, chief officer of the ship *Labrador* of Greenock, jumped off the wharf and succeeded in seizing hold of the lad, who, however, pulled him under water, and he was obliged to let go his hold to save his own life.

It is supposed that a shark had bitten McDonald, as his mutilated body was found next day.

Leonard, Ernest, Fisherman.   Case 21584

On the 20th December, 1881, a vessel was driven ashore in a gale of wind at St. Owen's Bay, Jersey, two men were left on board in a helpless state.

E. Leonard, a fisherman, swam off to render the men assistance, hoping to find a rope on board for the purpose of communication with the shore.

The vessel was driven still higher upon the beach, and then a gentleman named Nicolle made his way through the surf with a line which was eventually made fast to the mast, and by this means all the men were conveyed to the shore.

Mr. St. John Nicolle received a Testimonial on Vellum.

Johansson, Julius, Norwegian Sailor.   Case 21596

At 10 o'clock p.m., on the 28th July, 1881, the barqe *Compadre*, of Liverpool, was running at five knots through a heavy sea, in the Pacific Ocean, when an apprentice named Griffiths fell from the foretop into the water.

Julius Johansson, a Norwegian sailor, at once jumped overboard, caught hold of the lad, and supported him until the vessel dropped down to them, and they were assisted on board without launching a boat.

The personal risk incurred in this rescue was considerable, as it was some time before the ship lost her way and the rope could be thrown to the sailors.

The seaman was dragged under water whilst holding the lad.

Swaine, Arthur, Private, R.M.L.I.   Case 21617

At Shanghai, on the 26th February, 1882, private Arthur Swaine, of H.M. Gunboat, *Sheldrake*, made a gallant attempt to save Wm. Venney, stoker of the same ship, from drowning.

The man, in attempting to step on board from a native boat, missed his footing and fell into the tidal stream. The night was dark, and the tide running rapidly.

Swaine, heavily clothed, jumped from the taffrail, swam to the drowning man, and succeeded in seizing hold of him; he was, however, unable to retain his grasp (being twice dragged under water), and in the attempt was in imminent danger of losing his own life.

Verney was unfortunately drowned, and Swaine was picked up by the ship's boats.

Ramaswami, Constable, Madras Police.   Case 21618

In the North Arcot District of the Madras Presidency of India a native prisoner, in the custody of the police, was being conveyed to the station, when he made his escape, and jumped down a well, with the intention of committing suicide.

Ramaswami, a first-class constable of the Madras Police, without waiting to divest himself of his uniform, jumped into the well and succeeded in keeping the prisoner on the surface of the water until ropes were procured, though the prisoner struggled, bit the salvor, and made a desperate attempt to carry out his object. This rescue was effected in June, 1880.

On the 29th December, 1881, Constable Ramaswami again jumped into a well and rescued from drowning an old woman who had fallen therein. In this act of bravery the salvor effected his object with promptness, and did not wait to divest himself of his uniform.

Kirk, Joseph, River Inspector, Salford.   Case 21652

At 11 o'clock p.m., on the 28th March, 1882, Joseph Kirk, River Inspector of the Corporation of Salford, was passing over a bridge which spans the River Irwell, at Salford, when he heard screams, and immediately afterwards he found that a woman had thrown herself into the water.

Mr. Kirk ran to the scene of the accident, and finding that the woman had sunk he dived in, and succeeded in bringing her to the surface. The woman struggled to such an extent that the salvor had great difficulty in saving her. It appears that the water was impregnated with dye refuse and in so foul a condition as to render it a matter of much personal risk to enter it.

Carus-Wilson, Ernest J., Sub-Lieut., R.N.   Case 21855
Harding, William, Quarter Master, R.N.

At 7.40 p.m., on the 7th September, 1882, Thomas Payne, able seaman of H.M.S. *Euryalus*, jumped overboard in Suez Roads with the intention of committing suicide. Quartermaster Harding jumped in after him and held him up with great difficulty, as the man seemed determined to drown himself. At this juncture Sub-Lieut. Carus-Wilson also jumped overboard, swam to the struggling men, and assisted Harding in bringing the man on board.

The night was very dark, and sharks had been seen near the ship.

Sheedy, Daniel, Town Councillor.   Case 21863

At Clonmel, at 9 p.m., on the 18th October, 1882, the River Suir was unusually flooded, and a violent gale was blowing. A man named Coffey accidentally walked into the river in the darkness, and in a few moments was carried down by the rapid current to the mill; here he managed to get hold of the iron bars protecting the large mill wheel, and in this position remained calling loudly for help. Several people came to the banks of the river, but it seemed utterly futile to attempt a rescue without gaining admittance to the mill (which was locked up for the night.)

Mr Sheedy (living in an adjacent house) was roused from his bed by demands for ropes and lights. He at once dressed, ran to the nearest bank, and, contrary to the advice of bystanders, plunged in and swam to where the drowning man was last seen holding on to the sluice-bars.

With great difficulty he grasped the man's body, but was unable to do more than assist in keeping his head above water. At this juncture two other persons gallantly came to his assistance, and by their united efforts held Coffey up until the keys of the mill were obtained, and the whole party rescued, with the help of the police.

Bronze Medals were awarded to Thomas Ahern and John Quirke.

Tudor, Frederick C., Tea Broker.   Case 21898

At 12.0 p.m., on the 17th December, 1882, a boy fell from the lower stage of the Chain Pier at Brighton. Frederick C. Tudor, who witnessed the occurrence, gallantly jumped with his clothes on into the sea to the rescue. The drowning boy was carried off a considerable distance by the tide, and when Tudor reached him and swam back with him to the pier there were no means at hand to complete the rescue. Mr. Tudor, held fast to the piles until his brother Mr. J. Tudor, fastened a rope to the pier-head and descended to his assistance.

There was a heavy sea at the time, therefore the personal risk incurred in the rescue was considerable.

Connolly, Patrick, Captain.   Case 21903

On the 19th May, 1882, a passenger accidentally fell overboard from a steamer plying between Sydney and Balmain, New South Wales. The night was dark, and the place infested with sharks. Notwithstanding the personal risk incurred, the master of the boat, P. Connolly, at once jumped overboard, dived and brought the drowning man to the surface.

Captain Connolly is already in possession of a Bronze Medal for another act of gallantry.

Scott, James, Waterman.   Case 21911

At 7.30 a.m., on 24th November, 1882, Thomas Tate fell into the River Tyne, near Newcastle; the accident occurred between the quay wall and a large steamer.

James Scott, a waterman, jumped into the river (a height of thirty feet), caught hold of the man, and succeeded in keeping him above water until assistance came. In effecting this rescue Scott struck some floating object and dislocated his ankle.

Cochrane, C. Home, Lieut., R.N.   Case 21921
Bennett, George, A.B., R.N.

About 7.30 p.m., on the 28th January, 1883, off Tarbet, Andrew Hooper was getting from the steam launch to the Jacob's ladder, preparatory to coming on board H.M.S. *Valiant*, when he fell into the water; the man could scarcely be seen owing to the darkness.

George Bennett jumped over the stern and supported him. Lieut. Cochrane observing by the light of a signal that the men were floating astern in the darkness, also jumped overboard and assisted them to the buoy which was hanging over the stern with a grass hawser attached. It was blowing a gale of wind at the time with a considerable sea on, and the night was very dark.

Joste, Captain.   Case 21942

On the 8th January, 1883 the s.s. *Medoza* was proceeding south along the western coast of South America and going at ten knots, when a third class female passenger jumped overboard.

Captain Joste at once stopped and reversed engines, then ran aft and jumped overboard; he was drawn down into the vortex of the water caused by the sudden reversal of the engines, but on coming to the surface he succeeded in seizing hold of the woman, and in supporting her until a boat came to their assistance.

Donald, Captain.   Case 22003

On the 31st March, 1883, a seaman belonging to the Ship *Alumbagh* fell overboard whilst at sea.

Captain Donald rushed on deck, threw off his clothes and jumped overboard; he was however unsuccessful in saving the man, and had to remain in the water more than half an hour before he could be picked up.

The water was infested with sharks, one having been caught soon after the accident.

Paterson, John, Esq., Provost of St. Andrews, N.B. Case 22056

On the 16th July, 1883, a lad of sixteen whilst bathing at St. Andrews, got beyond his depth and was being carried out by a strong ebb tide, when Mr. Patterson (who was passing at the time) promptly divesting himself of clothing, jumped from the rocks, swam out, and succeeded in bringing him to the shore.

Kough, Philip, Assistant Light-House Keeper. Case 22188

On the 4th August, 1882, the ship *Octavia* during the prevalence of thick fog got in proximity to a dangerous reef at Burnthead, Newfoundland. Kough (the Assistant Light-House Keeper) hailed the ship from the cliff and told them to heave a line ashore, which was accordingly done and caught by him; he then tied the hawser to the cliff, divested himself of the heavier portion of his clothing, fastened the line round his body and went through the surf. He was instrumental in rescuing nine persons.

Brimelow, William, Son of the proprietor. Case 22206

On the 21st September, 1883 a furnaceman in the employ of Mr. Brimelow, of Deansgate, Bolton, entered the cupola of a blast furnace for the purpose of replacing some lining fire bricks which had fallen during the charging process. The fires had been lighted with coke some hours previously. The man succumbed from the effects of the noxious gases and fell insensible. William Brimelow, son of the proprietor, rushed to the stage, went through the opening for charging the furnace and by means of a ladder (inconveniently longer than the purpose required) descended and succeeded at extreme personal risk in bringing the insensible man out.

McCulloch, David. Case 22207

On the 11th November, 1883, at 2 a.m., the Barque *Ennomia* was wrecked at Cairngawn, Wigtonshire, the crew were cast on the rocks beneath the high cliffs. Owing to the tempest it was impossible to pass a rope to the men.

Mr. McCulloch allowed himself to be lowered from the cliffs (a height of 200 feet) by a single rope fastened round his waist; he carried another rope in his hand, which he attached to the men below, and had them pulled up one by one.

The salvor had no footing, and hanging merely by a rope at the mercy of the wind, he ran extreme danger of being dashed against the rocks. The men who lowered him were expert cragsmen, and considered the feat too dangerous to attempt.

Bell, Thomas William, Quarter-master, R.N. Case 22309

On the 12th April, 1884, at 7.30 p.m., H.M. Corvette *Curacoa* was anchored in the River Woosung, China. Private Ogden, R.M.L.I., in attempting to come on board from a boat alongside, fell in the water and was quickly carried astern by the current.

Thomas Bell, Quarter-master, at once jumped overboard, dived, and caught hold of the man as he disappeared beneath the surface; he succeeded in holding him above water until another man came to his assistance with a life-buoy. The night was dark.

Shooter, Frank, Bathing Ground Superintendent. Case 22473

At 5 p.m., 16th July, 1884, Mr. F.K. Hartnol was in a canoe on the mill-stream, Exeter, when the boat upset, and the swift current carried him under the mill-fender, and through the opening of the mill-leat, which runs for 180 yards through a dark tunnel. The leat varies in depth from four to six feet, with pits at intervals, and is cut in the solid rock, with jagged projections on each side. The stream was running nine miles an hour. The fender at the opening was let down seven or eight inches below the water surface, under which the salvor had to enter the tunnel. This feat he succeeded in effecting, and, being guided by the sound, he found Hartnol clinging to a projecting rock. Finding it impossible to stem the current he took Hartnol on his shoulders, proceeded down the tunnel with the stream, and landed him safely at the outlet.

He had all his clothes on, and ran great risk of being dashed against the rocky rough sides.

Grimston, William, Lieut., the Hon., R.N.   Case 22524

On the 29th August, 1884, off Beyrout, H.M.S. *Alexandra* was steaming at the rate of four knots, when a man fell overboard.

Lieut. the Hon. William Grimston dropped from his port into the sea, and succeeded in holding the man on the surface of the water until two seamen (who had jumped overboard) came to his assistance.

The special danger incurred in this rescue is brought to the Society's notice by Captain Rawson, R.N., commanding the ship. The port through which the officer had to drop is very small, and situated just before the double screw, which was then revolving; in fact, the salvor passed through the circle made by it.

McCluskey, John, Training Ship boy.   Case 22527

At 3.30 p.m., on the 24th September, 1884, a boy slipped off the bowsprit of the ship *Wellesley*, when at anchor in the River Tyne. One of the boats was coming off shore, but could not approach owing to the cables intervening. The officer of the boat at once jumped overboard to rescue the boy, but finding the tide and the wind too strong against him had to return to the boat. J. McCluskey, a boy on board the Training Ship *Wellesley*, jumped overboard, swam to the place where the drowning lad had sunk twice, dived, and rescued him.

Startin, James, Lieut., R.N.   Case 22537

At 11 p.m., on the 7th July, 1884, a shore boat, manned by three watermen, came alongside H.M.S. *Minotaur*, at Portland, bringing off liberty men. The men were under the influence of liquor, and on attempting to get on board capsized the boat.

Lieut. Startin at once ran to the after-gangway, jumped overboard, and with great exertions assisted each man to the ship. The last man brought on board was quite insensible. The fact of the liberty men being drunk, and the watermen unable to swim, rendered Lieut. Startin's task peculiarly difficult to accomplish.

H.R.H. the Duke of Edinburgh, Vice-Admiral commanding the Channel Squadron, states "that Lieut. Startin incurred great personal risk in performing this very meritorious service."

The night was very dark, with a fresh breeze and choppy sea.

Goodwyn, J.E., Major, 1st Battalion, East Lancashire Regiment.   Case 22545

On the 29th July, 1884, the Steamship *Nubia* was running at eleven knots, under steam and canvas, when a boy fell overboard.

Major Goodwyn gallantly jumped after him, without waiting to divest himself of any of his clothing; he swam in the direction in which the lad was seen; after remaining twenty minutes in the water searching in vain for the boy, he was picked up by the ship's boat.

The personal risk incurred in this case cannot be over estimated, as the accident occurred in the Red Sea, which is well known to be infested with sharks. The ship being under both canvas and steam made it more difficult to pick a man up.

Brassey, Thomas Alnutt. Case 22556

On the 30th September, 1884, Sir Thomas Brassey's Yacht *The Sunbeam* was lying in Loch Carron, Ross-shire. As the yacht's cutter was proceeding to shore (about three quarters of a mile distant) one of her planks started, owing to the heavy sea; she was then in a sinking condition. Thomas Brassey, being in charge of the boat, distributed the oars to those who were unable to swim, and taking off his coat advised the others to do the same. The boat soon filled and turned over in the very rough sea, several men lost their oars, but Mr. Brassey's voice was heard encouraging them all.

The special act of rescue was that Harry Timworth's oar was taken from him, and he was at once in a drowning condition. Mr. Brassey, observing his state, swam to him, gave him his own oar, and supported him against the heavy waves till *The Sunbeam*'s boats arrived. At one time Mr. Brassey lost hold of the man, and dived for him, regaining his grasp.

Whyte, William, Labourer. Case 22595
King, Patrick, Labourer.

On the 7th October, 1884, two men were engaged at Kilcoole, Co. Wicklow, in sinking a pump hole. When about thirty-two feet below the surface they had occasion to use powder in a blasting operation, and after attaching a lighted fuse to a jumper hole they ascended.

After the explosion Morgan Byrne descended and became overpowered by the foul air. James Keane then descended to see what was the matter and became insensible also. After an hour had elapsed a man named William Whyte volunteered to go down; he was accordingly lowered, and found the apparently dead bodies of the other two men lying amongst the broken rocks. He called to those above to haul him up, and in ascending the rope broke, and he fell upon Byrne, arousing him to consciousness. Although severely wounded he was able to hold the rope, and was drawn up in a maimed condition. Byrne, being then unconscious, was afterwards hauled up.

Patrick King (a labouring man) then gallantly volunteered to rescue Keane, who was still lying unconscious at the bottom of the shaft; he was accordingly lowered and was successful in his exertions.

Grainger, Edward, Fisherman. Case 22597

At Ramsgate, on the 10th November, 1884, the water was being discharged through the double sluices between the inner and outer harbours. William Crooks, a lad of seventeen, whilst watching the operation, fell into the seething mass of water, and was whirled around like a log of wood.

Edward Grainger, at great personal risk, jumped into the dock (where the water is described as rushing out with the force of a cataract) and succeeded in bringing the lad out. No boat could have lived in the spot where the accident occurred.

Betts, Peter, Sjt., 5th Battalion, Royal Irish Regiment. Case 22606

On the 15th November, 1884, a man named James Hogan was engaged in sinking a new well in the Kilkenny Prison; when at a depth of sixty-six feet below the surface he found himself sinking in the tenacious blue clay, sand and water, which was rapidly accumulating until it rose above his knees; he signalled to the workmen on the surface that he could not extricate himself.

Peter Betts, a serjeant in the 5th Battalion of the Royal Irish Regiment, descended the shaft with the manager (Mr. Purcell), and worked hard for four hours in removing the mud and the water (which at that time had risen above Hogan's chest); he then became exhausted and had to ascend for a time. He again went down and worked for upwards of two hours; and, after another interval, he resumed work for a third time, finally succeeding in rescuing Hogan, who had been nine hours immersed in the sand and water.

Betts ran the same risks as Hogan did, and at one time was in imminent danger of sinking.

Saraj Din, Foot Constable, Lahore Police.　　　　　　　　　　　　　　　　　　　　　　　　　　　　Case 22614

On the 19th September, 1884, a water carrier fell into a well at Lahore, the water surface being forty-five feet below ground; the man's brother went down to his assistance by means of a rope, when by some mismanagement it gave way and both men were in imminent danger of drowning.

Constable Saraj Din, at great personal risk, descended by a small rope (which was very much worn) and succeeded in rescuing one of the men; the other was unfortunately drowned.

Hart, Reginald Clare, Colonel, V.C.　　　　　　　　　　　　　　　　　　　　　　　　　　　　　　　　Case 22628

Silver Clasp

On the 15th December, 1884, a gunner fell of a pontoon bridge over the Roorkee Canal, and being fully accoutred, sank at once. Colonel Hart immediately jumped in to his assistance and disappeared also (being probably dragged under by the gunner). Mr. McLeod then followed with a life-buoy and it is believed sank also. The sepoy Dhan Singh then went with another life-buoy to their aid, first saved one man and was probably the means of saving all.

Bronze Medals were awarded to the others on the 17th February, 1885.

Le Mesurier, C.J.R., District Judge, Ceylon.　　　　　　　　　　　　　　　　　　　　　　　　　　　Case 22640

On the 26th October, 1884, the Judge while shooting at a tank or reservoir, saw a man struggling in the long weeds and apparently drowning; the man vainly attempted to free himself and eventually sank.

Mr. Le Mesurier swam to his assistance and succeeded in extricating him. It is stated that alligators are found in these tanks; the rescue was therefore unusually hazardous.

Brace, Henry, Sergeant, Royal Irish Constabulary.　　　　　　　　　　　　　　　　　　　　　　　Case 22674

At 3 p.m., on the 12th April, 1885, a child fell into the River Suir at Cahir; the current was very strong and carried the boy rapidly down stream.

Sergeant Brace on coming to the bank of the river, at once threw off his belt, plunged in, and succeeded in seizing hold of the drowning child; he swam with him to the boundary wall of the river, which at that place was eight feet high; here he was assisted out by another policeman.

Considerable risk was incurred by the salvor, as he was in delicate health at the time; he is a bad swimmer, and had all his clothes on, and there was much difficulty in landing.

Smith, Michael, Ordinary Seaman, H.M.S. *Duke of Wellington*.　　　　　　　　　　　　　　　Case 22677

H.M.S. *Tamar* was at anchor in the Grand Harbour of Malta on the 10th March, 1885. About 7.30 p.m. a prisoner undergoing sentence by court martial, endeavoured to escape by jumping through a scuttle into the sea and swimming to shore Smith gallantly jumped off the forecastle (a height of 22 feet), caught hold of the man, and kept him afloat until a boat arrived.

The risk incurred appears to have been considerable, as the man had a knife in his hand and threatened to strike Smith. The night was dark, and the affair occurred 200 yards from the shore.

Haveron, James Case 22691

At 11p.m. on the 5th April, 1885, near O'Connell Bridge, Dublin, screams were heard apparently proceeding from the river.

Mr. Haveron ran to the place, and on being told that a woman had fallen into the water, at once mounted the parapet of the bridge and jumped in. Two men unfastened a life-buoy that happened to be near the place and threw it towards him; he seized the woman and placed her in the buoy, directing those above to haul her up. By some mismanagement the woman again fell in when about ten feet from the water surface, and in doing so, struck Mr. Haveron on the head, rendering him almost unconscious; he, however, managed to support her until a boat came. The night was very dark.

Crook, John, Boat Builder. Case 22701

About 3.30 p.m. on the 26th April, 1885, a girl of fourteen slipped down the steep bank of the River Ribble at Preston, falling from thence over the boundary wall (a height of six or seven feet). The tide carried the girl some distance outwards. Crook ran to the place, threw of his coat, and jumped in; he succeeded in catching hold of her, but the girl clutched him around the neck, and he became entangled in her clothes, consequently both sank several times; he, however, eventually succeeded in rescuing her, although at great personal risk.

The salvor has been instrumental in saving twenty-nine lives in twenty-five years, during which time he has lived on the riverside.

Dutton, Samuel, aged thirteen. Case 22717

At 8 p.m. on the 5th June, 1885, near Bolton, a young boy fell from the top of a quarry into deep water; the height was sixty-five feet. Dutton, who was playing cricket in an adjoining field, hearing a cry for help, ran to the water, and plunged in, and succeeded (after diving) in rescuing the boy.

The personal risk incurred in this rescue was considerable, as the salvor had to descend the steep sides of the quarry-hole, and swim out to the centre of the water, where it appears, the lad had drifted.

Torrey Baz, Sepoy, Punjab Infantry. Case 22721

On the evening of the 19th of April, 1885, a native soldier went into the River Hari Rud, Afghanistan, to bathe; he was unable to swim, and was carried off his legs into deep water by the rapid current. The salvor gallantly jumped in and succeeded at great personal risk in rescuing him. The sepoy Torrey Baz, formed part of the escort of the Afghan Boundary Commission, and his conduct was recommended to the notice of the Society by General Sir Peter Lumsden, K.C.B.

Sears, H. Gunner, R.A. Case 22783

On the 24th June, 1885, about 11.30 p.m., a native was seen struggling in the Bay of Aden, and was apparently drowning; he was about 120 yards from shore. Gunner Sears ran down the rocks, and throwing off part of his clothing, plunged in to the drowning man's assistance. After swimming 40 yards or so, he took off his shirt and again proceeded, ultimately reaching the man and with difficulty bringing him to shore.
Several natives made previous attempts to swim to him, but found the sea too heavy.

The native was insensible when reached and never rallied. The attempt is said to be a plucky one as there are dangerous currents on the coast, and sharks are often seen in the same water.

See Case 23122 for Silver Clasp.

Rich, Frederick St. George, Lieut., R.N.
Walsh, William.

Case 22794

On the 21st July, 1885, about 4 p.m., H.M.S. *Hecla* and the s.s. *Cheerful* came into collision. The accident took place about eighteen miles north of the Longships. It was at once seen that the *Cheerful* was fast settling down, and within four minutes after the collision she sank.

Lieut. Rich jumped off the fore part of the *Hecla*, swam to a drowning man and was the means of saving him.

Walsh also jumped in and saved two others. Both officer and man ran considerable personal risk, not only from the broken wreckage, but in being drawn down in the vortex of the sinking ship.

Short, Edwin, Capt., 1st Leinster Regt.

Case 22859

About 6 p.m. on the 21st January, 1885, Capt. Short was steering a Nile boat down a rapid, when she struck a rock with such force as to cause one of the crew to fall overboard.

The boat was wedged so firmly on the rock that the efforts of the crew were unavailing to release her. It soon became evident that if the boat was not to go off before dark it would break up and all hands would be drowned. The only means of saving the boat was to get a rope made fast to a belt of rock in midstream, but to swim direct to this place would be impossible.

Capt. Short then conceived the idea of swimming down the rapid, coming up the backwater and thereby gaining a footing on the rock.

The danger of being drowned in the attempt was very great, but it was successfully accomplished by Capt. Short, and a rope being then thrown from the boat he was enabled to make it fast. By this means four soldiers got a footing on shore and pulled the boat off.

Skillicorn, Edward, Seaman.

Case 22918

About 11 p.m. on the 10th August, 1885, the s.s. *Tynwold* arrived at Ramsay, Isle of Man. When the passengers were leaving the ship one of them fell into the harbour.

Skillicorn, who had his heavy waterproof and sea boots on, jumped in and swam after the passenger, who was then being carried out by a strong ebb tide; he succeeded in bringing him to the ship. A strong westerly gale was blowing, and the night was very dark.

White, Joseph, Coastguard.

Case 22938

On the 11th October, 1885, at Ryhope, Seaham, six children when playing in the sands had their retreat cut off by the tide and took refuge in a cave at the bottom of the cliffs. On their situation becoming known to the salvor he obtained some small lines, twisted them together, and descended by them to the beach (a height of seventy feet). He found the children in a most exhausted state, the youngest having been washed twice out of the cave and back again.

The man took off his clothing and by means of the line managed to send five of the children in succession to the top of the cliff, the youngest being in such an exhausted state that the salvor was compelled to wade 300 yards through the surf with the child in his arms until he discovered a place where he was able to ascend.

Cusack, J.W.H.C., Lt. and Adj., 1st Bn., Royal Irish Fusiliers.   Case 23016

Silver Clasp

On the morning of the 14th January, 1886, the regiment was manoeuvring in the neighbourhood of Delhi. Whilst advancing in line through a strip of elephant grass, one of the men fell into a disused well, which had been left unprotected and concealed.

Lieut. Cusack obtained a Bhisti's well-rope, and having fastened it round his chest, under his armpits, he plunged feet foremost into the water without finding the bottom. He then tried to dive, but without any success, the narrow limits of the well preventing his descent to more than ten feet. Lieut. Cusack was then urged to come out, it being feared that the poisonous water would injure him. On the surface of the well floated the decomposed body of a pig. The diameter of the well was ten feet at the surface, but contracted towards the bottom. The depth of water was found to be sixteen feet, and the water line was five feet from the surface of the ground. The body of the unfortunate man was not recovered until after one hour's immersion.

The officer commanding states that Lieut. Cusack's attempt to save life was "both prompt and determined, especially considering the poisonous condition of the water in the well." For Medal see case 21275.

Nelson, Christian, Professional Sculler.   Case 23065

On the 27th April, 1886, about 1 p.m., a child was washed off the steps of London Bridge by the swell caused by a passing steamer, and carried out twenty yards by the fast running ebb tide.

Nelson was on the bridge at the time of the accident. He sprang down the steps, and throwing off his coat and vest, swam out and brought the child to land.

There was considerable risk encountered, as the salvor might easily have been drawn down under the large sea-going steamers and barges in the neighbourhood of the steps.

Sears, Henry, Gunner, R.A.   Case 23122

Silver Clasp

About 4 p.m. on the 15th June, 1886, a boat containing Mrs. Seymour, child and boatman, was proceeding from Spit Bank Fort, Spithead, to Portsmouth. A heavy sea capsized the boat soon after leaving. Sears on seeing the accident from the top of the fort, ran down, jumped into the water, and, after a severe struggle, succeeded in bringing the woman to the landing stage.

The salvor was assisted by Bombardier W. Thomas, who threw a life-buoy and rope towards him, and by which means he was enabled to land.

See Case 22783 for Silver Medal.

Jablouski, Paul, Ship's Barber.   Case 23173

The s.s. *Orient* was at anchor off Suez on the 5th April, 1886. About 6 p.m. an Arab dongola, with twenty-three passengers, was proceeding from the shore to the ship. Mr. Allan, one of the passengers, was knocked overboard by the sail, and for twenty minutes struggled bravely to regain the boat. Although a good swimmer his strength was not equal to the task.

The ship's barber, seeing that help was urgently needed, jumped overboard from the boat, and, regardless of the well known danger from sharks, gallantly succeeded in rescuing the drowning man.

McNulty, Michael, Constable, Royal Irish Constabulary.   Case 23335

About 7.40 p.m. on the 15th September, 1886, a large bridge spanning the Lagan River, at Belfast, suddenly collapsed, the two centre arches falling into the water. The bridge had been undergoing some repairs, and a watchman was placed on it. At the time of the accident the constable was crossing, and had just cleared the two arches in the centre of the structure, when they gave way behind him, carrying the unfortunate watchman, a woman, and two children into the river. The gas mains on the roadway of the bridge were snapped asunder and the neighbourhood plunged into darkness.

The constable at once stopped the traffic, jumped into the river, and swam to the rescue of the persons immersed. On approaching the watchman under the broken arches, the masonry fell on the drowning man and killed him. The constable then swam towards Bridget Maguire, and, with the help of others, assisted in getting her out.

The depth of the river at the scene of the accident was about ten feet, and the distance to the nearest shore forty-three feet. The constable ran considerable risk from the falling debris.

Shapter, Joseph, Captain of the Fore-top, R.N.   Case 23350

At 11 a.m. on the 26th October, 1886, H.M. Brig *Nautilus* was at sea off Plymouth. The vessel was under double-reefed topsails, going at about four knots. A boy named John Whitmore fell from the hammock netting into the sea.

The salvor, without removing his clothes, jumped after him, and assisted in supporting him until a boat arrived. There was a heavy sea on, with half a gale of wind blowing.

Joseph Shapter is already in possession of the Bronze Medal and clasp for saving life previously.

Neilson, David, 4th Officer.   Case 23360

About 9.30 p.m. on the 26th November, 1886, the S.S. *Lalpoora* was lying in the Downs; the night was dark and intensely cold. The officer of the watch heard a splash and discovered that a man had fallen overboard. The alarm was given, a life-buoy was thrown over, and a boat's crew piped away.

Mr. Neilson the 4th Officer, at once jumped overboard, swam after the drowning lascar, and succeeded in placing him in the life-buoy. The man appeared to be insensible, and numb with cold; he was unable to hold the buoy, and slipped out of it. The officer again seized hold of him, but was at last obliged to relinquish his endeavours to save him.

Mr. Neilson picked up the boat three quarters of a mile from the ship. The night was foggy and dark. The lascar was not seen again.

Bower, Hamilton, Lieut. Staff Corps, 17th Bengal Cavalry.   Case 23368

Lieut. Bower, whilst passing through Lahaul, on his way to Ladakh, had occasion to cross a jhula bridge spanning a mountain torrent called the Chandra or Bhaga river. After passing over and ascending about 200 yards he heard a scream, and on looking round, saw one of his coolies being rapidly carried away by the fast running river, the bridge having broken under him while crossing. Lieut. Bower at once ran down the hill, plunged into the water, and succeeded, with considerable difficulty, in rescuing the native.

The river was about sixty yards wide, and flowing between high rocks; the water was intensely cold, having just escaped from the snow above. The salvor had to remain in wet clothes for a day and night, his clothes being frozen.

The case is sent by the colonel commanding the regiment. The incident occurred about noon on the 1st May, 1886.

McKeen, Walter, Boatman.   Case 23380

About 12.40 a.m. on the 27th December, 1886, a barque was driven ashore at Dover whilst attempting to weather the pier. Some of the crew saved themselves by dropping into the sea and swimming ashore; others were drowned.

Mr. McKeen, at great personal risk, went out to the ship's side and rendered good assistance in getting some of the exhausted men to the shore. It was blowing a gale at the time.

Hewetson, J.B, The Reverend.   Case 23452

About 7 p.m. on the 23rd April, 1887, The Rev. J.B. Hewetson was on board a steamer proceeding down river. Just after leaving Blackfriars Bridge his attention was attracted by seeing the passengers rush to the side of the vessel, and immediately afterwards saw a man struggling in the water. Mr. Hewetson at once threw off his coat, jumped overboard, dived, and with great difficulty got hold of the drowning man. A boat was then lowered and both were picked up. The man was pronounced dead when the doctor arrived.

Fleet, Ernest Jas., Lieut., R.N.   Case 23608

On the 7th November, 1887, whilst H.M.S. *Briton* was employed on the East African Coast the boats were sent on detached service, in charge of Lieut. Fleet.

The first cutter, whilst in tow of the steam cutter, was unfortunately swamped in the breakers. Lieut. Fleet who was steering the latter boat, at once proceeded to the drowning men's assistance and succeeded in picking them all up, with the exception of a seaman named Brice, who was some distance off, and evidently in imminent danger of sinking. The officer, giving the boat in the charge of the coxswain, jumped overboard, and swam to the man's assistance. The strong surf, however, nearly overpowered him, and it was with great difficulty that he and Brice reached the upturned cutter and clung to her.

Martin, the coxswain after seeing the steam cutter anchored head to sea, then jumped overboard and swam to the assistance of both officer and man. Hennessey (another seaman) did the same, only taking with him a life-buoy, without which the exhausted man Brice could not have been saved. Martin and Hennessey were eventually the means of saving the officer.

Silver Medal to Lieut. Fleet for first going to Brice's assistance. Bronze Medals to Martin and Hennessey.

Rowe, Fanny Isabel, Miss, age Fifteen.   Case 23705

On the 19th July, 1887, a child, aged five years, fell off a jetty into the lake at Neuchatel; his brother appears to have gone to his rescue, though unable to swim. Both boys might have been drowned had not Miss Rowe promptly jumped in, swam to their aid, and succeeded in saving them.

Williams, Brian Trengrove, Captain.   Case 23717

On the 31st August, 1887, about 11.15 a.m., a lady was bathing with her five daughters and two little boys, in a secluded spot near Downderry, Cornwall. Half a gale of wind was blowing with a heavy sea.

Three of the daughters had remained in the water longer than the others; when about to return to the beach they found themselves unable to do so, and were carried out by the heavy sea. The mother at once swam to their assistance but was also carried out.

Captain Williams, on arriving at the place, found several persons attempting to reach the ladies. He at once ran along the rocks, and throwing off some of his clothes, swam to a sunken reef some distance out. Another man followed, but after facing the sea for a short time, became exhausted and commenced to return to the beach. Captain Williams, after supporting himself on the sunken reef for a few seconds, proceeded to the outer sea, where the elder lady appeared to be floating in a lifeless condition. He succeeded in reaching her, and swam about 100 yards towards the shore, when Mr. Tiltman (who at first followed) again came to his assistance, and by their united efforts the lady was eventually saved.

The rescued lady was about 300 yards from shore when Captain Williams reached her. The three young ladies were unfortunately drowned.

Silver Medal to Captain Williams. Bronze Medal to Mr. Tiltman.

Eales, George, aged fifty-eight years.   Case 23831

On the 7th November, 1887, a young woman went to draw water from one of the village wells at Dummer, near Basingstoke. Some children had followed her into the well shed, and just after the bucket had been lowered one of them (a boy four and a half years old) tripped against the lid and fell down the mouth of the well. The boy says "he caught the rope as he fell and must have kept his hold till he reached the water."

The woman at once ran to alarm the neighbours, but when the bucket was drawn up there was no trace of the child. Every effort was then made for its recovery, and as soon as a strong rope could be obtained George Eales went down, and found the boy struggling in the water. Holding on to the rope with one hand, he succeeded with much difficulty in tying with the other hand another rope round the body of the child, which was then drawn to the surface. Eales ascended afterwards.

The child was livid and had all the appearance of being drowned, but was, after several hours treatment, restored to animation. George Eales, who is fifty-eight years of age, was faint and exhausted when he reached the surface, owing to the foul air at the bottom of the shaft. The well from which he rescued the boy is 258 feet deep with 12 feet of water in it.

It took five minutes to lower the man to the water and about the same time to raise him to the top of the well, and fully twenty minutes was occupied in securing the child and tying the rope.

Eales tried, after getting the boy on his knee, to raise him to his chest and bring him to the top of the well with his arm round him, but finding himself too much overcome to attempt this he remained below until the other was drawn up, then the rope being again lowered he was brought to the surface in a similar manner.

George Eales risked his life in this rescue, and throughout showed great courage and coolness.

Whiteside, Frederick, Compositor.   Case 23842
Whiteside, Joseph, Second Officer of a ship.

On the 25th December, 1887, two young men, named James Smith and Ernest Dennison, were skating on a piece of water near Penrith when they broke through the ice and became immersed in twenty feet of water. The accident occurred about 150 to 200 yards from the bank. Joseph Whiteside ran towards the spot with all speed; Frederick skated down the middle of the pond, throwing of his top coat, then his undercoat and waistcoat. Meanwhile Joseph obtained from a gamekeeper a cord, six feet long, which was tied to a stick, and with this he crept on his hands and knees towards the hole where James Smith was evidently drowning.

When he got close the ice broke under him and he also became immersed in deep water. Smith, in desperation, got hold of his throat, dragged him under the water, fastened his legs around him, and practically prevented him from rendering any assistance.

Both, in all probability, would have been drowned had not Frederick Whiteside plunged into the hole and, after a desperate struggle, freed his brother from Smith.

Frederick then devoted all his energies to saving Smith, whom he bore up until he was able to seize the end of the stick which was held out to him, and by which Smith was finally drawn out.

Joseph Whiteside was by this time much exhausted but managed to keep himself afloat until his brother Frederick came to his help and rescued him.

Frederick then got out of the hole and skating up close to where Dennison was still struggling in the water, cleverly got his stick into the drowning man's hands and succeeded in drawing him out.

The risk incurred by both Frederick and Joseph Whiteside appears to have been very great.

Chatfield, Charles K., Lt-Col., King's Own Yorkshire Light Infantry. Case 23854

The Regiment under the command of Lieut-Col Chatfield, arrived at Mandalay from the Upper Burmah frontier in the Indian Marine Steamer en route to England. A short time after their arrival a lance corporal named Upton fell overboard. The Colonel, seeing the man in danger of drowning, at once jumped after him, but before he could reach him the man sank, and his body was not recovered. Privates A. Staton and M. Mills also jumped overboard and assisted in searching for the missing man, but their united efforts were of no avail.

In Colonel Chatfield's case the risk incurred was considerable, not only from the well known dangerous current of the Irawaddi, but from the fact that at the time of the accident one of his hands was bandaged after a recent surgical operation; the Silver Medal was awarded to him and Bronze Medals to Privates A. Staton and M. Mills, K.O.Y.L.I.

Wilmot, William Fawcett, Clerk Case 23863

At 11.20 pm on the night of 23rd January, 1888, Jane Kelso, a laundress fell from a ferry boat which was in mid-stream of the River Tyne at Shields. She was carried rapidly away. The night was very dark but Wilmot rushed on deck from the cabin, threw off his overcoat, jumped overboard and swimming he succeeded in bringing her back to the boat. It is stated that Wilmot has saved several lives.

Robinson, John, Assistant Engineer, Bengal & North-Western Railway. Case 23973

Domangarh Lake is a large expanse of water several miles broad, formed by the flooding of the Rapti and another river. On the 3rd September, 1887, a party, composed of Messrs. Henderson, Robinson, and Rogers, with Miss Beaumont and Miss Cash, were out on the lake in a sailing boat. It was blowing pretty hard from the north-east, and through some mismanagement the boat capsized when about one mile and a half from shore.

When the boat was going over Mr. Robinson seized Miss Cash for the purpose of getting her on the bottom of the boat but failed in retaining his hold. He then went to Miss Beaumont and seeing a part of the mast above water brought her to it and held her for about an hour until rescued by another boat. Henderson, Rogers and Miss Cash were unfortunately drowned.

Pochin, James W., Lieut., R.N. Case 23979

On the 28th April, 1888 a cargo of slaves had been captured by H.M.S. *Garnet*, and were temporarily detained on board and kindly treated. It was, however, a prevalent idea among the natives that they would be eventually eaten by the seamen, and one of them jumped overboard intending to swim ashore. The strong ebb-tide soon swept the man away and he called out for assistance.

Lieut. Pochin sprang overboard from the poop, swam to the slave, and supported him until picked up by one of the ship's boats. It was dark at the time, and Lieut. Pochin ran a great danger of missing the ship, owing to the drift of the current. The slave added to the danger by clinging to him.

Bradley, Wm., Pier Keeper, Southend. Case 23988

Charles Fry, on the 24th June, 1888, fell from the gangway of a steamer, head first into the sea. He was intoxicated, and incapable of helping himself. Bradley dived into the sea after him, caught hold of him and swam with him to the pier stage; he was then obliged to hold on to the pier and keep the man afloat until a rope was procured, and by which means the drowning man was hauled on board the steamer. The salvor had previously saved nineteen persons from drowning, and was in the possession of the Society's Bronze Medal and two clasps.

Waters, Michael, Master Shipwright. Case 24051

On the 10th July, 1888, at Limerick, John Tierney fell into the docks whilst passing from one ship to another. Waters dived from a ship, and found the man about five feet under the surface of the water; he succeeded in rescuing him. Mr. Waters is in possession of the Society's Bronze Medal for a previous rescue, and it is stated that he has saved seventeen lives from drowning.

See Case 25204 for Silver Clasp.

Andrews, Alfred, aged 16. Case 24085

On the 16th July, 1888, a woman had thrown herself into the River Rhondda, at Pontypridd, with the intention of committing suicide. Andrews, on hearing that some person was immersed, ran to the bank, and seeing a woman's arm above the surface of the water in the centre of the river, at once jumped in, swam out, and succeeded in bringing her to the bank. The river was much swollen, and the current running strongly. The woman had been carried 250 yards down stream before the salvor reached her.

Parker, Geoffrey, Brewery Labourer. Case 24088
Howarth, Hezekiah, Brewery Labourer.

On the 14th July, 1888, the men were engaged in running off the beer yeast from a large vat at a brewery at Burnley. When it was almost empty the valve stuck. James Hodgson then went into the vat to clear it and almost immediately became unconscious (being overpowered by the carbonic acid gas), falling with his head against the far corner. Parker was then in a cellar below, and fearing that something had gone wrong, called out, but receiving no answer from Hodgson, ran upstairs and found him as described. He called to Howarth for help, and both men got into the vat, which they knew was charged with deadly gas, and had great difficulty in raising Hodgson (who was apparently dead); they themselves then became overpowered, when two other men came to their assistance, and with great difficulty succeeded in dragging Hodgson out. It appeared as if the lives of all the men who first went in would be sacrificed, but the effect of the gas on Parker and Howarth was not so great, as they had sufficient presence of mind to drag themselves to the valve-hole for fresh air. Parker was at one time a miner, and was therefore well acquainted with the danger incurred from foul air or gas.

Porter, William, Carpenter, aged 66 years. Case 24100

Mary Pearse, whilst drawing water from a well at Kingham, Chipping Norton, on the 27th August, 1888, fell head foremost into the well. Porter descended by pushing his back against one side and obtaining a precarious hold with his feet on the other. A rake was first used to drag the girl to the surface of the water (the depth of which was about eight feet), the chain was then let down, and Porter passed it under her arms; in doing so he had nothing but his slight hold to trust to. The girl was then drawn up to the surface, a height of fifteen feet.

Troubridge, Ernest Charles Thomas, Lieut., R.N., *H.M.S. Sultan*. Case 24101

On the 26th July, 1888, Signalman William H. Davies fell overboard from a torpedo boat, at Suda Bay. The torpedo boat was going at full speed; the night was dark, and the man was lost sight of for a time. It appears that the boat passed right over him, and he rose again close to the stern. Lieut. Troubridge, seeing him sinking, jumped overboard and succeeded in holding him above water until picked up by the skiff. The accident occurred about a mile from shore, but close to several men-of-war.

Drake, Charles, Chief Boatswain's Mate, H.M.S. *Ready*.　　　　　Case 24102

On the 9th July, 1888, the ship's cutter was swamped whilst crossing the bar of the Rio Grande, Jamaica, and H. Honniball was seen in a very exhausted state floating near the breakers. Drake had been knocked overboard from the gig by the same roller that had swamped the cutter; he managed, however, to regain his boat, and afterwards jumped overboard and rescued Honniball. He also was the means of picking up several of the men by his strenuous exertions after the other boat capsized.

O'Sullivan, J., Second Officer of the *Oenone*.　　　　　Case 24107

On the 29th August, 1888, off Southend, seaman Johnson fell off the jib-boom while in the act of unbending jibs. A fresh breeze was blowing, and the ship was going about four knots. Mr. O'Sullivan, seeing the man could not reach the life-buoy that was thrown, jumped overboard and supported him until a boat was lowered. The sea was rough, and the officer was heavily clothed when he jumped over.

Maguire, John A., Porter in the General Post Office, Edinburgh.　　　　　Case 24132

On the 6th August, 1888, Alexander Pendreigh, whilst bathing at Trinity Chain Pier, became exhausted off the end of the pier, and his brother David went to his assistance, but both were evidently sinking when Maguire (partially dressed) jumped off the pier and caught hold of Alexander, who was then under water; he held him firmly and brought him to the pier steps; his companion was also helpless, and clung to them. In all probability both brothers would have been drowned had it not been for Maguire's gallantry.

Since the above occurrence Maguire has saved another life from drowning.

Stucley, Hugh Nicholas Granville, Naval Cadet, H.M.S. *Britannia*.　　　　　Case 24140

Rescued Cadet Blackwood, near Dartmouth. On the 5th May, 1888. The rescued boy had been searching for sea bird's eggs, when he slipped and fell over a cliff (a height of 100 feet), alighting on a ledge above high water mark, breaking his arm and sustaining various minor injuries. In this position he lay, bleeding and helpless, but still able to call to his companions above for help. Cadet Stucley was not at the scene of the accident at the time, but out for a walk on the Slapton Road, some little distance off; he saw a boy running towards him and calling out that Blackwood had fallen over the rocks. Stucley and his companion (Cadet Richmond) despatched some of the boys for men and ropes, and ran to the scene of the accident. Ropes being obtained and tied together, Stucley volunteered to descend, which feat he successfully carried out by tying the rope round his body and allowing the men and boys to lower him. On approaching the ledge of rock he freed himself of the rope (as it was a little short), scrambled down to the place where Blackwood lay, tied up his head with a scarf, wrapped a coat round him, and with difficulty carried him towards the rope; he then secured it round the injured boy, and called to those above to haul him up; this was successfully done. Had Blackwood not alighted on the ledge, or had fallen off it in his injured state, he would in all probability have struck some sunken rocks in the water.

Purdie, Andrew, Bookbinder.　　　　　Case 24141

On the 18th of May, 1888, a woman had attempted suicide by leaping from the quay at Leith, into the water. Mr. Purdie happened to be passing at the time accompanied by his wife; he immediately sprang off the quay without throwing off any of his clothes and succeeded in catching hold of the woman, and held her for nearly fifteen minutes above water until a boat came to his assistance. Mr. Purdie ran considerable risk, as he jumped a height of fifteen feet, into nine feet of water with a deposit of several feet of mud in the bottom; he also had heavy boots on. He has already received this Society's Bronze Medal for a previous act of bravery.

Cooling, James F., Barman. Case 24170

On the 29th September, 1888, the man who was rescued appears to have attempted suicide by jumping into the River Thames. The salvor while passing along the Victoria Embankment heard, a cry for help and saw a man struggling in the water; he took off his coat and hat, threw them on a seat, jumped into the river and rescued him from drowning. It was with much difficulty that the salvor accomplished this rescue, as the drowning man was under the influence of drink, and had to be kept above water by Cooling for a considerable time before a passing steam-tug came to their rescue and picked them up. The rescue took place at 8.30 p.m.

McKinstry, Edward Robert, Second Officer S.S. *Ionic*. Case 24188

On the 6th October, 1888, while the ship was at anchor in the Sound, Plymouth, receiving mails and passengers for New Zealand, E.A. Marshall was sent by request of the surgeon, on board the tug to be conveyed to shore. A little while after, he was seen to rush to the side and jump overboard.

Mr. McKinstry pluckily jumped in after him, and notwithstanding his struggles and violent resistance, brought him alongside the boat, when both men were picked up.

Mr. McKinstry undoubtedly risked his life in effecting the rescue.

Heathcote, William Charles Percival, Solicitor's Clerk. Case 24197

On the 21st July, 1888, a young Englishman was on Buckhorn Lake, Ontario, in a canoe with several children. He observed two women and a boy in another canoe some distance off, screaming, laughing and changing places. Presently their boat was upset. Knowing he could do nothing to rescue them with all the children in his canoe, he called to a lad in another boat, and transferred the children into it. He paddled to the place of the accident, and found the boat bottom upwards with the boy clinging to it, but the women had disappeared. He looked into the clear water and saw something white, which proved to be a part of a woman's clothing, which he got hold of, and with great difficulty and danger of upsetting the boat, got her into it. He then found the other girl, dragged her to the surface, and held her against the bows of the boat until another canoe came to his assistance.

Chappell, Herbert, Labourer. Case 24213

H. Fortescue had been for six hours working at the bottom of a well (130 feet below the surface of the ground), at Liss in Hampshire. He was being drawn up when the winding apparatus gave way, and the man fell about 100 feet into the water. The rope ran down with fearful rapidity, and the bucket dashed against the sides of the well detaching bricks and rubbish which fell on top of the man.

It was some time before another rope could be obtained, and the water in the bottom of the well was rising rapidly.

Chappell volunteered to go down, and being light he was selected for it, the rope being scarcely fit to bear a heavy man. On descending Chappell found the injured man half buried in the debris, and the water nearly covering his mouth; he succeeded in extricating him and sent him up first, remaining below at great risk to himself until the man was hauled to the surface.

Nickson, Leonard Robert, Plumber. Case 24221

At Newmarket, on the 1st November, 1888, several workmen were repairing a pump when the stone covering of the well gave way precipitating Harry King to the bottom of the shaft.

Nickson gallantly descended by means of the pump suction pipe and supported King above water until a rope was let down, and by which both were drawn up. The shaft was sunk to a depth of 95 feet with 10 feet of water in the well, and it had not been opened or cleaned for twelve years, therefore a great danger was incurred from the effects of foul air. It may be mentioned that Nickson (who is by trade a plumber) knew the risk he ran, as one of his comrades lost his life a short time before from the same cause.

The pipe by which Nickson went down was five inches in diameter for a distance of 70 feet, beyond that there were no stays for 25 feet, therefore the difficulties of the descent are apparent.

Breadalbane, The Right Hon. the Marquis of.   Case 24231

On the 6th December, 1888, a party of gentlemen were shooting in the grounds of Taymouth Castle, the Marquis of Breadalbane being one of the number. Two men named Jamieson and McLean were acting as beaters, and for that purpose went across in a small boat to an island in the River Tay below the bridge at Newhall. The river was in a flooded state, and the current running rapidly. A rope was attached to the boat, but somehow it became entangled, and was the means of swamping the boat, precipitating both men into the water. Jamieson, although an expert swimmer, had considerable difficulty, owing to the strength of the current, in gaining the shore. McLean, who was unable to swim, was carried down stream about 100 yards, and finally rescued by the Marquis of Breadalbane.

It appears that immediately after the boat capsized, the Marquis stripped off his cartridge-belt and rushed into the river to McLean's assistance, as did Mr. Robson, the Head Keeper; they were, however unsuccessful, and both had a narrow escape.

The Marquis on gaining the bank ran quickly down the river side, when he again plunged in, and after a severe struggle succeeded in catching hold of McLean, with whom he swam ashore. The river at the time was in spate (as it is called in Scotland), that is, high flood, and immediately below the scene of the rescue was a deep whirlpool, surrounded by rocks.

The rescue was rendered more difficult by the eddies and boulders. It may be said that the Marquis risked his life on each occasion on entering the river under the circumstances.

Corry, Ernest, A.B., H.M.S. *Excellent*.   Case 24232

On the 5th November, 1888, William White accidentally fell from the pier at Lerwick into four fathoms of water. Corry hearing the cry of "man overboard!" jumped from the pier head, swam out, and succeeded in seizing hold of the drowning man and held him above the surface until a boat was launched. The accident occurred at 10 p.m., the night was very dark, and there was a tide running.

Hunt, Daniel, Wharf Labourer.   Case 24253

On the 9th November, 1888, a passenger steamer was leaving her berth in Halifax Harbour, Nova Scotia. The gangway had just been hauled on shore, when an intoxicated man came running down the quay and attempted to get on board; in doing so he fell into the water. The steamer was actually moving, and a heavy sea was running with a strong wind, which caused the vessel to lurch against the dock wall as she was backing out.

Daniel Hunt, at great risk to his own life, gallantly lowered himself down a hanging rope, caught hold of the drunken man, but in doing so had his foot crushed between the ship's side and the wall; however, he held on to the man in the water, and was the means of saving him, notwithstanding the excruciating pain he endured. The salvor's foot was amputated the same evening, and he is now a cripple for life.

Piers, Hubert, Fourth Officer.   Case 24261

A most determined case of attempted suicide took place on board the ship *Garth Castle* on her voyage home from Natal on the 18th October, 1888. When near the equator a passenger of unsound mind evaded his keeper and jumped overboard. The ship at the time was steaming at fourteen to fifteen knots

A boat was lowered as soon after the accident as possible, and was pulled in the direction of the drowning man, who was seen from the masthead floating about half a mile astern. On the boat approaching he showed a determination to evade capture, and repeatedly dived.

Mr. Piers, the fourth officer, seeing this, jumped overboard from the boat, and succeeded after a most determined resistance in saving the man.

The risk incurred in this rescue appears to have been considerable, owing to the man's own resistance and the presence of sharks in those waters.

Henderson, Alexander, Machinist. Case 24262

About 3 p.m. on November 29th, 1888, a young lady slipped off some icy timber and fell into the mill race at Campbellford, Ontario; she was carried into a covered way by the force of the stream, then running six or seven miles an hour. Mr. Henderson was attracted to the spot by hearing the cries of a number of persons; he at once jumped into the race, swam down the dark aqueduct; and overtook the girl when about eighty feet from where she fell in; she was then grasping a projecting rock with one hand. The salvor held himself and the young lady above water until some spectators obtained crowbars, raised the planks covering the watercourse, and assisted the girl and her rescuer from their perilous position. The risk incurred was considerable, as the covered in watercourse had no opening for 400 yards.

Sutcliffe, Thos., Sergeant, Royal Irish Constabulary. Case 24274

About 1 a.m. on the 21st December, 1888 the ship *Etta*, in a heavy gale of wind, was driven on the rocks at Creaden Bay, Co. Waterford. Sergt. Sutcliffe observed the vessel's lights as she approached the harbour, and rightly judging her to be running into a dangerous position, he ran parallel to her course about two miles along the cliffs until he found her fast on the rocks. With the assistance of another man he climbed down the cliffs, and after several attempts succeeded, at great bodily risk, in getting a line ashore from the wreck. He seems to have crawled over the half submerged rocks at the imminent risk of drowning (being once actually washed off into the heavy sea), and succeeded in catching the line thrown from the ship and bringing it to the shore. By this means the greater part of the men on board were saved, also the captain's wife, the captain himself being drowned. Sutcliffe was ably assisted by a man named Jas. Redmond.

Whitelaw, Andrew, Engine Keeper. Case 24286
Bell, Andrew Lees, Doctor.

About 3.30 p.m. on the 2nd January, 1889, a large number of persons were skating on Townhill Lock, Dunfermline, when a portion of the ice gave way, and two men and one woman became immersed in nine feet of water. Immediately afterwards, four others, who went to assist, were also precipitated into the hole. At this juncture Whitelaw seized a ladder and ran towards the place, and at great risk to his own life plunged into the water, clutching the ladder with one hand, and using the other in assisting the drowning persons. The hole was by this time twenty feet in diameter, and it was impossible to get the ladder across it. Mr. Whitelaw appears to have been endowed with superhuman strength, as he lifted several persons out.

Dr. Bell then arrived on the scene; he threw off his overcoat, and seizing hold of one of the ladders, to which a rope was attached, pushed the apparatus along the ice, giving the end of the rope to the people on shore.

On arriving at the hole he jumped in, kept hold of the ladder with one hand, and swam with the other; he succeeded in reaching a woman, and with much difficulty got her on shore, but unfortunately, too late for restoration.

Extreme risk was encountered by Messrs. Whitelaw and Bell, especially by Whitelaw, in entering the water in the midst of six or seven struggling persons.

Lemmi, George M., Mechanical Engineer.   Case 24327

On the 28th January, 1888, a coaster carrying coals was driven, in a violent gale, on the coast of Viareggio, Italy. A boat put off to the wreck, but was capsized. Most of the crew, being expert swimmers, managed to regain the shore. Mr. Lemmi, at great personal risk, swam to the wreck with a line, followed by a seaman, and succeeded, with great difficulty, in getting the master and a boy on shore. The ship broke up almost immediately afterwards. The King of Italy presented Mr. Lemmi (who is a British subject) with a medal.

Craig, James, Wharf Foreman.   Case 24350

On the 5th of May, 1889, some boys were playing on a wherry moored in the Ousburne, which runs into the Tyne at Newcastle; one of the number slipped and fell into the water. Craig was in a house overlooking the bank of the river when his attention was called to the accident. He jumped from the window (a height of eighteen feet) into the yard below, clearing a high wall, ran about fifty yards, surmounted another wall five and a half feet high, and dived a distance of twelve feet into the water. He succeeded in rescuing the drowning boy after he had sunk twice. On reaching the nearest lighter with his charge he was in a state of complete exhaustion. It is stated that Craig risked his own life in effecting this rescue. He is in possession of the Society's Bronze Medal for a previous act of bravery, and has been the means of saving persons from drowning on many occasions.

Moore, Wm. Jas., Private, 20th Hussars.   Case 24360

On the afternoon of the 9th May, 1889, a sailing boat capsized on the River Yare, Norfolk. The accident resulted in the loss of Lieut. and Quartermaster Frederick Campbell, 20th Hussars. The boat contained Mr. and Mrs. Campbell, a waterman, and a soldier servant. The soldier, Wm. Jas. Moore, at once went to the assistance of Mrs Campbell, held her up with one hand, whilst he used the other in swimming to shore with his charge. He was also the means of saving the waterman, who clung to him whilst swimming. The accident happened about forty yards from the nearest bank in eighteen feet of water. Moore certainly risked his life in rescuing both persons.

Ishar Das, Sweet Seller, Lahore.   Case 24394

At Lahore, on the 1st May, 1889, several of the Cathedral Orphanage boys were bathing in the Ravi, and appear to have been taken out of their depths by the strong current. Four of the lads were drowned, but the fifth, who was also carried out, was rescued by Ishar Das, a seller of sweets, and a native of Lahore.

The salvor afterwards endeavoured to recover the bodies of the drowned persons.

The rescue was performed at the risk of the salvor's life, owing to the extremely dangerous current.

Sutherland, Alexander, Station Master.   Case 24459

On the afternoon of the 11th May, 1889, some lads were fishing from the piers of a bridge which crosses the river a little below Fenelon Falls, Canada; one of the number, named Archer, slipped and fell into the water. Although the river is not deep at the spot referred to, the current is very strong, and it swept the boy rapidly away towards a deeper and more dangerous place, the little fellow sinking twice in a short space of time.

Mr. Sutherland seeing what happened, rushed to the spot, threw off his coat, vest, and boots and plunged into the river. He succeeded in overtaking the boy at a place where the water boils and surges round in a strong eddy, caused by the force of the river descending a steep slide to the south of the falls. Logs of wood were being driven round and round in the eddy, making it difficult to avoid collision with them, and thereby getting maimed or stunned. It is stated that the risk was exceptionally great and the rescue unusually difficult.

Ellul, Antonio, Gunner, Royal Malta Artillery.　　　　　　　　　　　　　　　　　　　　　　　　　　　　　　Case 24593

At Pieta, Malta, on the 23rd July, 1889, two men were working at the head of a cesspool, when one of them fell into it, being overcome by the foul smell. The other labourer jumped in to help his companion, but failed, becoming helpless from the same cause. Gunner Ellul on coming to the place volunteered to go down, and did so by means of a rope, succeeding on the first attempt in rescuing one man. Notwithstanding the danger and the cautions of the bystanders he again descended, and rescued the second man.

The risk to life was very great.

Hackett, S.M., Miss.　　Case 24617

On the 30th August, 1889, a young girl, whilst out bathing at Shankill, Co. Dublin, was carried beyond her depth. Miss S.M. Hackett, being attracted by her cries for help at once rushed into the water with her clothes on, but finding that she could not reach her without swimming, returned to the shore, took off a portion of her clothing, and at the peril of her own life swam to the drowning girl, who at once clutched her round the neck and body, thus preventing her swimming back to the shore. It was only with the greatest difficulty and self-possession that Miss Hackett kept the other girl afloat until a boat came out to their assistance. They were fifty or sixty yards from shore in twelve or fifteen feet of water.

Jones, David, Miner.　　Case 24753
Williams, Aaron, Miner.

An accident resulting in the death of one man occurred at the Glanamman Colliery, Carmarthenshire, on the 6th January, 1890. Thos. Llewelyn and Thos. Roberts were being drawn up the shaft when, from some unexpected cause, the engine became unmanageable. Roberts sprang out as the tub reached the surface, and falling against a trolley at the mouth of the pit, was precipitated head foremost to the bottom of the shaft, a depth of 140 feet. Llewelyn, who failed to get out of the tub, was carried to the top, and his head coming in contact with the sheaves, he was instantly killed. His body, after hanging suspended for some time, fell down the shaft, where Roberts could be heard calling for help. A considerable time passed before a rescue could be properly organised. A rope having at last been obtained, David Jones and Aaron Williams, with commendable pluck and nerve, descended the shaft and rescued the man, Roberts, who had been up to his neck in water for upwards of an hour and a half. He had supported himself by clinging to the guides at the side of the shaft, otherwise he might have drowned, as the water at the bottom was forty feet deep. The two rescuers in this case incurred serious risk, as the rope was thin, and there was great danger in trusting to it. The broken woodwork and other debris continued falling into the shaft, and thereby constituting another source of danger.

Smith, Richard, Gas Worker.　　　　　　　　　　　　　　　　　　　　　　　　　　　　　　　　　　　　　　　Case 24756

On the 11th December, 1889, two men, named Beswick and Case, had occasion to enter a gasholder at the City Gas Works, Birmingham, for the purpose of repairing it. Half an hour afterwards the men outside became alarmed for the safety of those within, not hearing any noise or receiving any signal from the interior. Richard Smith and James Chew, well knowing the danger to be encountered, volunteered to go down, and immediately did so by a ladder; they found Beswick and Case insensible, lying at the bottom of the holder.

Smith then ran up the ladder for further assistance and got three others to go into the air-box; then, descending again, tied Beswick to the rope by which he was hauled up. Chew assisted Smith in doing this. Before they had time to do the same for Case they were almost insensible, and began to mount the ladder. Smith was pulled into the air-box and became quite insensible; he was then sent to the hospital with Beswick. Chew just as he was getting on to the top of the ladder, fell backwards into the water in the bottom of the holder and was drowned.

The risk incurred in this case is obvious, as two men lost their lives by the poisonous gases inside the holder. Smith was nearly half an hour exposed to the effects of the gas, and it is unusual for the men to stay inside the holder for more than seven or eight minutes.

An "In Memoriam" testimonial was sent to Chew's relatives.

Mackin, James, Boatman.
Rose, Isaac, Able Seaman.

Cases 24776 and 24808

On the 25th January, 1890, during a severe gale of wind, the ship *Irex* was driven ashore in Scratched Bay, Isle of Wight.

The scene of the accident was about 400 yards from the shore, and by means of the rocket apparatus communication was established between the ship and a cliff 200 feet high. On the 26th January (when the ship was first discovered) all the survivors were rescued excepting one lad, who appears to have taken refuge in the mizzen top, and being in a helpless state, was unable to gain the foremast where the shoreline was made fast. On the 27th January Mackin and Rose went on board by the cable, and at great personal risk carried the helpless lad from the mizzenmast to the foremast and sent him on shore in the cradle.

Fraser, Alex Duncan, M.D.
Fraser, Donald Lionel, Engineer.
Russell, William, Engine-driver.

Case 24786

On the 12th February, 1890, Miss Jeannie Barr, Miss Sarah Maude Robinson, and Miss Eliza Wilkie were skating on Carron Dam, near Falkirk, when the ice broke and they all became immersed.

Dr. and Mr. Lionel Fraser in attempting to reach the young ladies broke through also. The doctor managed to struggle back to shore, but Lionel Fraser succeeded in reaching one of the ladies and supported her in the water for fifteen minutes. The doctor in the meantime made two unsuccessful attempts to reach the hole, but the ice gave way under him each time; at last; he so far succeeded in throwing a rope to Mr. Lionel Fraser (who was by this time in a drowning state) and by the rope two were pulled out. Miss Jeannie Barr was rescued by the doctor with the aid of a life-buoy.

At this stage Russell, who was driving his engine down the adjacent line, jumped off, caught hold of a pole, rushed into the hole, and brought Miss Robertson out after supporting her for ten minutes. It appears that the third young lady Miss Wilkie broke through the ice first (some little way from the others) when Mr. Brown gallantly rushed to her rescue, unfortunately the ice again gave way and both were drowned.

The Dam is twenty-seven acres in extent, 300 yards broad, and eight feet deep.

All the salvors incurred extreme risk. An "In Memoriam" testimonial was sent to the relatives of Mr. William Brown M.A.

Mitchell, Hugh, Company Sergt-Major, Royal Engineers.

Case 24821

On the 27th December, 1889, The Rev. C.T. Boyd, Chaplain to the Forces, Colombo, whilst swimming in the sea at Negombo, Ceylon, became exhausted and was unable to regain the shore; for more than a quarter of an hour he struggled against the strong ebb tide, and failing in his endeavours called out for help.

Sergt-Major Mitchell swam out at great personal risk to his assistance, and supported Mr. Boyd for a considerable time; both men in all probability would have drowned, had not a fishing boat gone to their rescue and brought them to shore.

Mr. Boyd is more than an average swimmer, and has on a previous occasion received the Society's Medal for saving life from drowning; but stated that in this case he undoubtedly owes his life to Sergt-Major Mitchell.

Farbrother, Alex James, Vicar's Son.

Case 24838

On the 6th May, 1890, four young gentlemen, named Harry Trewfitt Farbrother, Alex James Farbrother, Thomas Ernest Dickson and Benard John Dickson were in a sailing boat off the Isle of Sheppy, when a sudden shift of wind capsized the boat. The two Farbrothers were good swimmers, and being only 200 yards from shore could have easily saved themselves, but knowing that neither of the Dicksons could swim, each brother took a boy on his back and attempted to swim ashore. Mr. Harold Farbrother appears to have gone down with the elder Dickson, and Mr. Alex J. Farbrother very nearly lost his life in attempting to take the younger boy to the shore, and failed in doing so; a boat, however, came and picked him up. The accident resulted in the loss of three lives, viz H.T. Farbrother, T.E. Dickson, and B.J. Dickson,

An "In Memoriam" testimonial was sent to the nearest relatives of Mr. Harold Farbrother.

Biron, Henry, Third Officer.   Case 24851

On the 10th February, 1890, the ship *Selkirkshire* was off the Coast of New Zealand, and sailing about seven knots, when a man named Whitford jumped overboard in a temporary fit of insanity. Mr. Henry Biron, third officer of the ship, without divesting himself of clothing instantly jumped overboard after the man, and with much difficulty owing to the density of the fog succeeded in finding him. Both men were lost sight of by the ship's crew. A boat was lowered, and it was fully three quarters of an hour later when it returned to the ship with both men on board.

Mathews, Frederick, Police Constable, Metropolitan Police.   Case 24857

At 2.30 a.m. on the 23rd May, 1890, a woman attempted suicide by throwing herself into the Thames at Cleopatra's Needle.

Constable Mathews being on duty near the spot, ran to the place and at once jumped in after her, they were both borne up the river by the strong flood, but the constable succeeded in seizing hold of her, and with great difficulty and considerable personal risk succeeded in bringing her to the steps, where they were assisted out by another man who happened to be passing at the time.

Shortle, Richard, Private, 1st Battalion, Welsh Regiment.   Case 24901

On the 25th May, 1890, a boat with three soldiers in it was upset in Bighi Harbour, Malta. Private Shortle was rowing in another boat near the scene of the accident; he at once pulled to the spot, jumped overboard, and succeeded in rescuing one soldier; he then dived three times for another man who had already sunk, but failing to find him he turned his attention to the third soldier, who appeared unable to keep afloat, and in this instance he was successful in bringing him to the boat, and helping him into it. Shortle afterwards returned to the place where the missing man had sunk and dived again for him, but unfortunately failed in rescuing him. The salvor had eventually to swim to the shore 250 yards distant.

Thomson, Basil H., Private Secretary to Sir W. McGregor.   Case 24956

On the 6th December, 1888, the ship *Hygeia* was at anchor off Port Moresby, New Guinea. At about 7 p.m. a small boat came alongside bringing the steward and another man on board, both under the influence of liquor.

It appears that the cook struck his companion, and in eluding a return blow went backwards through the open gangway into the sea. The night was very dark and a strong tide was running. The man called out for assistance, and Mr. Thomson, then a passenger on board, rushed out of his berth, ran on deck, jumped overboard, and succeeded in catching hold of the drowning man, holding him above water until a boat was lowered and came to their assistance, they were then 150 yards astern of the ship.

The risk incurred was considerable, from the fact that there was no boat in the water at the time, and the night was extremely dark.

Rutherford, Jas. Alex., Gentleman.
McDonnell, Walter, Captain.

Case 25083

On the 26th August, 1890, several gentlemen were bathing in the sea at Kilkee, Co. Clare. One of them (Mr. Tayleur), who had been carried out by the heavy sea, found himself unable to return, and called for help. Captain McDonnell and Mr. Rutherford swam out to his assistance, but failed in bringing him to shore owing to the force of the sea, and it seemed probable that the three gentlemen would all lose their lives; they, however, called out for a boat, and being good swimmers kept afloat and allowed themselves to drift with the tide. Mr. Tayleur, who was much exhausted, begged the others to leave him to his fate, but neither of them would do so. A wicker canoe was launched and three gentlemen, at great personal risk and with considerable skill, got the boat through the heavy surf and finally rescued them. The names of the three gentlemen were Mr. Wm. McDonnell, Mr. Percy Driver, and Mr. Chas. Thompson.

Silver Medals were voted to Captain McDonnell and Mr. Rutherford. Bronze Medals to Wm. McDonnell, Percy Driver and Chas Thompson.

Atkins, Jas., Valet.

Case 25115

On the 5th September, 1890, three young ladies, whilst fishing from a rock in Guernsey, became surrounded by the incoming tide. Mr. Atkins, divesting himself of clothes, swam out to their rescue and brought them ashore one at a time.

The rock was immediately covered by the sea when the last girl was taken off it.

Power, Jas.

Case 25128

On the 16th August, 1890, about 12.30 p.m., two ladies had a narrow escape from drowning whilst bathing at Tramore, Co. Waterford.

Mr. Jas. Power, who ran out from an adjacent hotel, on hearing the alarm, saw a young man with a life-buoy struggling in the sea about 150 yards from shore, further out and fully 250 yards from the beach two ladies appeared to be in imminent danger, being rapidly carried out by the strong ebb tide.

Mr. Power first swam to the young man, but finding that he was unable to swim and could not dispense with the life-buoy, he turned on his back and towed the man with the life-buoy out to where the ladies were, and then with the aid of the buoy he brought the three safely to land.

Connell, John, Boatman, Coastguard Service.

Case 25200

About 4 a.m. on the 19th October, 1890, the sailing vessel *Genesta* of Grimsby became stranded on the Yorkshire coast near Withernsea.

Three of the crew were safely landed in the breeches buoy, after communication had been effected by means of the rocket apparatus, but one man, who had taken refuge in the crosstrees was unable from exhaustion to avail himself of the means afforded. The ship's mate attempted to get him clear of the rigging, but the man seemed powerless to help himself, yet equal to holding on tenaciously at his post. In this position the man was left until John Connell gallantly went off to the vessel and rescued him at considerable personal risk. The ship was bumping, and might have gone to pieces at any moment. The weather was so bad that one man died in the rigging from exhaustion.

Pennett, Wm., Police Constable, Metropolitan Police.

Case 25202

About 1 o'clock a.m. on the 25th November, 1890, constable Pennett being on duty at Tower Hill saw a man throw himself into the Thames, apparently with the intention of committing suicide, he at once divested himself of lamp and belt, and without waiting to take off his uniform, jumped into the river, seized hold of the struggling man, and gallantly rescued him. The night was dark. The magistrate who investigated the case strongly commended the constable's courage and presence of mind.

Waters, Michael, Master Shipwright.   Case 25204

Silver Clasp

On the 3rd October, 1890, at 10 p.m. a man accidentally fell into the floating docks at Limerick. Waters hearing a cry for assistance ran to the dock, and seeing a man drowning at once jumped in and held him above water until a boat came to pick them up.

The salvor is in possession of the Silver and Bronze Medals with clasp for previous acts of gallantry in saving life. See Case 24051 for Silver Medal.

Smith, James, Fisherman.   Case 25292

About 11 p.m. on the 1st March, 1891, the fishing boat *Lady Mathieson* during a gale of wind was driven on the rocks off Scarfskerry, Caithness. Owing to the heavy sea, two of the three men in the boat were unable to land. Smith procured a rope, and leaving one end with the fishermen in the boat, swam ashore, taking the other with him. One of the men was washed off the boat when attempting to fasten the rope round himself. Smith, on hearing his cries, swam back and landed him safely. He then went out to the boat a second time, and finding the remaining man unable to get ashore, he secured himself and the man to the rope, when the first fisherman saved hauled them both to the shore. There was twenty feet of water, and a north-west wind blowing with snow showers. Awarded the Albert Medal for the same act.

Simpson, James Robert, Mate.   Case 25300

At 2 p.m. on the 29th March, 1891, the steamship *Rector*, of Grimsby, was returning home from a fishing voyage, when she shipped a heavy sea, which washed a man named Wicks overboard. The captain immediately ran full speed astern, but owing to the high sea the vessel sheered away from the man overboard, and it was found impossible to get near enough to throw him a line.

Simpson, mate of the ship, picked up a life-buoy with a line fastened on board, and jumped to the man's rescue. Finding the rope too short, he cast it off, swam to Wicks, and placed the buoy over his head, leaving himself to the mercy of the sea, which was then heavy. A gale was blowing, and the ship was under sail as well as steam. A line, however, was at last caught by Simpson, and by this means they were eventually hauled on board.

The salvor has obtained the Board of Trade Silver Medal for this act, and he is in possession of the Society's Bronze Medal for another act of gallantry.

Bjorkander, Swedish Seaman   Case 25328
Werner, Swedish Seaman.

On the occasion of the wreck of the *Utopia* on the 17th March, 1891, in Gibraltar Bay, the two above named sailors jumped overboard from the Swedish war frigate *Freija*, and rendered assistance to several drowning persons. Bjorkander is especially mentioned as having effected a rescue solely by his own exertions. A south-west gale was blowing, with a heavy sea. Distance from shore was half a mile. Both men had to swim back to their ship, about 200 yards off.

Seed, Wm., Chief of Police, Gibraltar.   Case 25329
McQue, Wm., Corpl., 3rd Batt. King's Royal Rifles.

On the occasion of the wreck of the *Utopia* on the 17th March, 1891, in Gibraltar Bay, the above-mentioned men were on duty on the breakwater (a low line of very rough rocks, on which foothold under ordinary circumstances is difficult). A launch with two seamen and eight Italians on board fouled her screw, and in all probability would have been dashed to pieces had not the two men swum out from shore (a distance of eighty yards), taking with them a rope, by which means effective assistance was rendered.

There was a heavy sea and strong current. It was blowing a gale. The night was intensely dark, and the men ran great risk of being dashed against the breakwater. Both also awarded the Albert Medal.

Cundy, George Conway, Seaman.   Case 25350

At 11.30 a.m., in November, 1890, the ship *Pembrokeshire* grounded on a sandbank in the China Sea, about forty miles from Hong Kong. All efforts to get her off were futile. A fierce gale of wind was blowing, with a very high sea. One of the seamen, in securing a boat was swept overboard. A life-buoy was thrown to him, which he caught afterwards, and a rope, which he did not succeed in catching. Seeing this, Mr. Cundy fastened a line around his own waist, jumped overboard, and fought his way to the man; he then succeeded in securing him. Both men were pulled on board by means of the rope. The risk encountered was considerable, owing to the heavy sea.

Girby, Suleiman, Chief Boatman to Thomas Cook & Son, Jaffa.   Case 25356

The Russian steamer *Ichihatchoff* was wrecked on the rocks of Jaffa on the 18th February, 1891.

More than twenty passengers had been swept away before anything was done to save life. At 6.30 a.m., on the 19th February, Girby and his brothers launched a boat, and proceeded to the vessel, from whence they brought off a number of the passengers and landed them. In making a second attempt their boat was smashed against the inner reef, and it was found impossible to launch another.

Girby then swam backwards and forwards to the vessel fifteen times, bringing some one with him to shore each time.

Girby, Suleiman, Chief Boatman to Thomas Cook & Son, Jaffa.   Case 25357

Silver Clasp

At 8 p.m. on the 26th April, 1891, the French frigate *Seignelay* parted anchors and was carried on the rocks at Jaffa.

It was blowing a heavy gale at the time, and none of the natives except Girby would offer the slightest assistance.

Girby volunteered to swim to the ship and deliver a letter to the captain from the Governor. The ship was half a mile from shore, but he accomplished the work after a two hour's swim in a heavy sea. After doing this he dived under the ship and examined the hull, reporting her sound. He then swam ashore, taking a message from the captain. Towards morning, when the sea got higher, the captain signalled and suleiman again swam out, and brought back the captain's wife fastened on his back.

Ovens, G.H., Captain.   Case 25376

At 9 a.m. on the 4th October, 1890, the Ordnance boat *Lady Alice*, under the charge of Sergt. J.H. Dray, 1st Bn. of the "Buffs", arrived at Garden Reach, Calcutta, with ammunition for the s.s. *Pandua*. Sergt. Dray, after delivering his shipment, attempted to step from one vessel to the other, and fell into the river.

Captain Ovens, a saloon passenger on the *Pandua*, seeing the man drowning, at once jumped overboard and made a very gallant attempt to rescue him, without success. A very strong current was running, which carried Captain Ovens a long distance down stream, and an hour elapsed before he was brought on board in an exhausted condition, having been picked up by the magazine boat.

Cow, Robert, a young Indian of Ontario.   Case 25458

On the afternoon of the 16th June, 1891, a sailing boat containing eleven persons was capsized on Rice Lake near Ontario Lake.

The accident resulted in the loss of a gentleman and his two daughters.

A young Indian named Robert Cow by his heroic efforts was the means of saving seven of the persons immersed by getting them on the upturned boat, and keeping them there until another boat came to their relief.

Murray, A.P., Lieutenant, Acting British Consul at Batoum.   Case 25573

On the 19th July, 1891, a Georgian peasant was bathing at the edge of the surf at Batoum, when a wave carried him out to sea. A large crowd collected on the shore, but none of the persons present made any attempt to rescue the man.

Mr. Murray, on coming to the scene of the accident, immediately went into the sea without divesting himself of clothing, and succeeded, after being repeatedly overpowered by the sea, in bringing the man to the shore.

It was blowing a gale at the time, and a heavy surf was breaking on the beach. The rescue occurred sixty yards from shore.

Sinclair, William H. M., B.A. Oxon.   Case 25641

On the 9th September, 1891, about noon, a rescue from drowning was effected at Bonnyglen, Co. Donegal, under great difficulties, and at much personal risk to the rescuer.

At the point of the river where the accident took place there is a small ferry-boat, attached by a chain to a rope stretching across from bank to bank. The river, which is usually six or eight feet deep, had risen to sixteen feet; the rope consequently, instead of being overhead, was on a level with the rushing current. A man named McGroarty, in attempting to cross, capsized the boat, which at once filled, and sank as far as the attached chain would allow it. McGroarty being unable to swim, was left bobbing about in the water, holding the chain and unable to regain his hold of the rope. A considerable crowd collected, but no one attempted a rescue. Mr. Sinclair was sent for, and, grasping the situation at once, divested himself of his coat, ran sixty yards up the bank, plunged in, and swam down stream to the drowning man. The rope impeded his progress, but he surmounted the obstacle, and called to McGroarty to let go his hold of the chain, and that he would save him. Mr. Sinclair then got under the man, and they both sank; but on rising to the surface he succeeded in saving him, but not until they had both been carried down stream for eighty yards.

Wilson, Frederick, Lock Keeper.   Case 25690

At 7.20 a.m. on the 26th October, 1891, a barge in tow of a tug steamer was about to pass through the central arch of Chertsey Bridge, but fouling the buttresses broached to in the strong current and filled, sinking in fifteen minutes after striking. The lock-keeper, F. Wilson, on hearing cries from persons on board, jumped into a skiff, and at considerable risk succeeded in rescuing William Morris, his wife, and three children.

The risk incurred was owing to the nature of the obstruction, a barge in a sinking condition right across the arches, an unusually strong current, and the smallness of the rescuing boat.

Lines, Frank, aged eight.   Case 25742

On the afternoon of the 28th December, 1891, a schoolboy named James Cochran threw his ball on a frozen sheet of ice covering a pond in Brocket Park, Hatfield. The ball rolled out about forty-five yards from the bank, and the lad, in seeking to recover it, ran over the thin ice, and became immersed in five to six feet of water. The boy, however, succeeded in keeping his head partially above water by clinging to the broken ice. Several other lads who witnessed the accident ran off, but Frank Lines, a boy of eight years of age, gallantly effected the rescue of Cochran by crawling out on the dangerous surface and helping him out of the hole. The ice was so extremely brittle that it gave way twice under the weight of the first boy, and in all probability he would have lost his life had not Lines gone to his rescue.

Wylie, M., Works Manager.   Case 25997

On the 2nd May, 1892, at the Pulo Saigon Bridge Works, Singapore, an accident occurred, which might have had a fatal termination had it not been for the gallantry displayed by Mr. M. Wylie, in charge of the works.

Messrs. Riley, Hargreaves, and Co., engineers, were sinking cast iron cylinders for a new bridge, one of them having been sunk thirty-six feet, and having in it about four feet of water. Shortly after the midday meal two Javanese descended to recommence work; they had been put down but a minute or two, when the man at the top in charge of the wire rope called out that the men were suffocating. Mr. Wylie looked down, and saw one man reeling about, and trying to get the other into the bucket. He at once slipped down (the wire peeling his hands in the descent), assisted in putting the more unconscious of the two into the bucket, held him there, and came to the surface with him.

No sooner had the man been taken out of the bucket than it was seen that his companion below had entirely succumbed to the foul gas, and had sunk below the water surface. Mr. Wylie without hesitation, again went down, notwithstanding the fact that his former descent had seriously affected him, groped about in the water, and succeeded in finding the second man, and with the greatest difficulty was he able to put him into the bucket, but not before he himself was reeling from the effects of the gas. The two men were hauled up together, and half an hour elapsed before the Javanese could be restored to consciousness.

Mr. Wylie had to be sent home, so severely was he suffering from his descent. His watch and chain and a dollar were turned perfectly black by the exposure to the deleterious sulphuretted gases in the cylinder.

Bevan, J., Inspector of Police, Burma.   Case 26152

At 11.30 a.m., on the 14th May, 1892, the owner of a fruit-garden near Rangoon had occasion to visit it; and found that his two gardeners had fallen to the bottom of a well sixty feet deep, with about six inches of water in it; their cries had attracted his attention. He at once sent for assistance, and many unsuccessful attempts were made by various persons to rescue them, all failing owing to the foul air generated at the bottom. Mr. Basch, the owner of the property, offered rewards varying from 20 to 500 rupees for rescuing the men, but all efforts proved futile, and the natives, believing that an evil spirit inhabited the well, finally refused to go down. Mr. Basch then went down himself halfway, but becoming insensible had to be hauled up. Another attempt was made by a constable on the arrival of the police, but before he could reach the men he had to be partially hauled up, and letting go of his hold of the rope he was precipitated to the bottom of the well, falling on the two other natives.

At this stage Mr. Bevan, the European inspector, arrived, and at once volunteered to descend; this he did at once, and succeeded in tying a rope around one man and bringing him up - the constable had so far recovered as to be able to ascend by the help of the rope. Mr. Bevan descended a second time, and again succeeded in saving the life of the other native.

It must be noticed, to exemplify the danger incurred by Mr. Bevan, that he became partially unconscious on his first descent, and had to be hauled up for recovery before he finally succeeded in reaching the bottom.

Lee, Patrick, Chief Petty Officer, R.N.   Case 26185

On the afternoon of the 9th August, 1892, Mr. J.W. Booth, engineer, H.M.S. *Audacious*, directed a man named Harris to descend into a water-tight compartment of the ship to execute some duty. After some time Mr. Booth called to the man, and receiving no reply he descended also, when both men became unconscious from the effects of carbonic acid gas.

Chief Petty Officer Lee, on realising their danger, determined to afford them assistance. He at once put on a diving dress and attempted to descend, but finding the man-hole too small to admit him with such an encumbrance, threw the helmet off, unrigged himself, took the end of the air-pipe in his teeth, and descended into the compartment. He then succeeded in attaching a rope's end to the body of Mr. Booth, by which it was pulled up, though unfortunately too late for resuscitation. He then performed the same operation to Harris, and thereby saved his life. Lee was in the compartment fifteen minutes and certainly risked his life.

Long, Margaret, Miss. Case 26273

On the afternoon of the 4th January, 1893, Mr. John R. Patchell was skating with a party of ladies on Simmon's Lake, Dungannon, Ireland. The ice gave way, and Mr. Patchell became immersed in twenty feet of water 150 yards from shore. He remained under the ice for a short time, and finally succeeded in breaking it above him; but on coming to the surface he was unable to do more than keep his head above water, as in every effort he made to assist himself by leaning on the ice, it gave way, and he was continually precipitated under water.

Miss Long seeing how matters stood, courageously skated up to the edge of the hole, threw herself flat on the ice, and, after undoing her cloak, handed the end of it to Mr. Patchell; she managed to retain hold of the other end of the garment, and thus kept the gentleman above water until Messrs. Smith and Hart came to their assistance and took an active part in the rescue. The lady was almost submerged by the overflow of the water on the ice surface, and her position was extremely perilous owing to the treacherous nature of the ice, which was thin and rotten.

The Silver Medal was voted to Miss Long and Bronze Medals to Messrs. Smith and Hart.

Summerfield, Chas., Private, 2nd Bn., Royal Sussex Regiment. Case 26301

At 10.30 a.m. on the 5th October, 1892, a soldier named Burton was bathing in the River Ravi, at Shahpur, Punjab; he appears to have got into a whirlpool, and was being carried under by the current, when Private Summerfield plunged in to his assistance and seized hold of him; he, however, failed to rescue him, as the current carried them both under water, and to save his own life he was obliged to relinquish his grasp, and Burton was drowned. The river at this place is ten feet deep close to the banks, and dangerous. Summerfield risked his own life in the attempt.

Perry, Chas. J. Gunner, Royal Marine Artillery. Case 26337

Two of Her Majesty's ships, the *Philomel* and the *Widgeon*, were anchored at Zanzibar on the 25th December, 1892. About 8.30 p.m. a boat from the latter came alongside the *Philomel*, having for its occupants two men, one of whom, Patrick Kenny, when standing up in the boat, lost his balance and fell over the stern into the water.

Perry, who was doing duty as Corporal of the Gangway, looked over the side and saw something white drifting astern, and was told that a man had fallen overboard. Without waiting to divest himself of any clothing he jumped overboard, and endeavoured to reach the man who was sinking under the ship's bottom. At the first attempt he was not successful, but on diving a second time he reached the man and brought him to the surface, then swam with him to the gangway, supporting him until a rope was passed, which he fastened around Kenny, who was then hoisted on board.

The danger incurred in this rescue was very great owing to the presence of sharks. The night was very dark, and there was a strong tide running at the time with a choppy sea.

Parks, Rufus, Seaman. Case 26434

On the 17th October, 1891, a schooner, during a very heavy gale, was driven ashore near the east end of Nova Scotia. Although the ship grounded at 8 a.m. no communication for several hours could be effected by the efforts of those on shore.

Rufus Parks (one of the men on board) stripped off his clothes and swam on shore, losing the use of one of his legs in so doing; he then obtained some planks, hammer and nails, mended a dory which had been smashed up by the force of the sea, and went to the rescue of his comrades single-handed.

The men on shore helped him to launch the small boat but refused to go with him.

Parks, however, after one unsuccessful attempt, succeeded in rowing out and brought one man to shore, and then returned to the ship, saving three more. He made four successful trips from the shore to the vessel after being twice thrown into the sea by the boat capsizing. He incurred great personal risk.

Halfyard, Robert, A.B., R.N.   Case 26448

At 3.30 p.m. on the 30th April, 1893, an accident occurred in New York Harbour which would probably have resulted in the death of a boy of fourteen had it not been for the bravery of the seaman Robert Halfyard.

H.M.S. *Blake* was moored in the harbour when a boat capsized alongside the ship, and its occupants were thrown into the water. There was a strong tide running, between four and five knots, and there were numerous small steamers, all moving ahead in order to keep abreast of the *Blake*. The seaman Halfyard seeing the boy drowning, at once jumped overboard from the skid deck, a height of some thirty feet, swam to the lad and held him up for a time; but some other person, who had also been an occupant of the capsized boat, caught the man by the leg and pulled him under the surface, causing Halfyard to let go his hold of the boy; he, however, again swam to the boy's assistance, dived and succeeded in saving him.

There was considerable danger incurred by the salvor from the paddle-wheels of the numerous tugs moving around the ship in a tideway.

McDougall, Roderick, Shepherd.   Case 26471

At 1 p.m. on the 3rd June, 1893, two boats were caught in a squall and capsized in the Sound of Vatersay, between Barra and Vatersay, and about thirty yards from shore. The occupants, three fishermen, were unable to swim, but they managed to clamber on to one of the upturned boats.

Roderick McDougall, a lad of nineteen, stripped swam out to them, and attempted to tow the boat and the men to shore; failing to do this, he attempted to get a rope from the boat to his friends on shore, but found it too short for the purpose. He then returned to the boat with a knife, dived under it, and detached a sufficient length of line, which he brought to the shore, leaving one end at the boat. By his directions each man seized hold of the rope, and, supported by McDougall, gained the shore; thus all were successively rescued. There was a strong tide running at the time, and the salvor appears to have incurred considerable personal risk in the rescue of the three men.

Park, Alexander, Labourer.   Case 26484

At 11 a.m. on the 27th May, 1893, at Kinnaird Head, Fraserburgh, a lad of nine years of age fell over a perpendicular cliff into the sea.

Alexander Park's attention was called to the accident; he descended the face of the rock at great personal risk, clinging to tufts of grass, and getting to within ten feet of the water plunged in with all his clothes on, seized hold of the boy, and attempted to swim with him a distance of forty yards to a landing place; he, however, became exhausted after swimming twenty yards, and was obliged to cling to the foot of the cliff, supporting the boy with one hand. In this position they were helped to the shore by two fishermen.

The depth of the water at the place of the accident was ten feet.

Griffin, Cecil P. G., Lieutenant, 1st Bengal Cavalry.   Case 26777

At 4 p.m. on the 18th May, 1893, a sepoy jumped down a well at Saugor, probably with a view to committing suicide. The man's cries awoke Mr. Griffin, who ran out of his bungalow and proceeded to the well. Hearing the man's groans he descended by means of a rope a distance of fifty feet, and dropped a distance of six feet into the water. Not finding the man, he dived , and after a couple of unsuccessful attempts succeeded in bringing the man up from the bottom of the water, which was ten feet deep. Meanwhile Mrs Griffin had been exerting herself in getting together as many servants as she could, obtaining lanterns and procuring ropes of sufficient length to lower a lantern to her husband. Eventually, the original rope having been lowered and a second one let down, both men were drawn to the surface, but owing, unfortunately, to a jerk being given to the rope securing the insensible sepoy, the man's body slipped from its fastening and again fell into the well. Mr. Griffin descended a second time, secured the man's body more effectually, when it was drawn up to the surface, but too late for resuscitation.

The risk in this case was twofold; there was danger in trusting to a well-rope, which may have been of insufficient strength to sustain a man's weight; and a possible risk from the bite of a cobra, as that snake is known to frequent the spaces between the rough stones forming the sides of the well.

Cooke, Henry Arthur, British Vice-Consul at Archangel.   Case 26894

In July, 1890, Mr. Cooke was proceeding across the White Sea in a passenger steamer when he saw a man deliberately jump overboard. Without any hesitation Mr. Cooke jumped after him and supported him for three quarters of an hour before a boat came to pick them up. The rescued man appears to have been suffering from delirium tremens, which added very much to the personal risk incurred by Mr. Cooke in effecting the rescue.

Cumming, W. W., Secretary, Woollen Mill.   Case 26901

About 6.50 p.m. on the 29th May, 1893, three young ladies namely Miss Sheppard, Miss Harcourt and Miss Hardange, were in a boat on the River Trent near Cambellford, Ontario. The strong current carried the boat rapidly down the river towards the dam, where an immense volume of water passes over a boom. Before arriving at this part of the river the boat struck an old railway pier, and as it swung round Miss Hardange managed to jump out on to the pier and thereby saved herself.

The other two ladies in trying to do the same thing upset the boat, and were swept onwards by the rapid current. Miss Sheppard was carried under a bridge and over the dam, and nothing more was seen of her for four days after, when her body was found four miles below.

Miss Harcourt was also carried under the bridge, but just at that moment Mr. Cumming seizing a small rope jumped off the bridge, telling a man to retain the other end of it. The rope, however, parted, and was useless. Mr. Cumming then seized hold of the lady, and both were carried towards the boom, where their death seemed inevitable, but Mr. Cumming fortunately was enabled to cling to a piece of projecting board a few feet above it and supporting the lady until assistance arrived, when both were rescued from their perilous position.

Addison, Albert Percy, Midshipman. R.N.   Case 26994

On the 17th January, 1894, when H.M.S. *Garnet* was lying in Esquimault Harbour, an accident occurred which would probably have had a fatal result had it not been for the promptness and bravery of the above-named officer. At 7.15 a.m. a seaman of the watch fell from the lower boom into the water; he was heavily clad in waterproof and sea boots; the tide was setting away from the ship, the weather exceedingly cold, with a bitter south-east wind blowing and a choppy sea.

Mr. Addison, who was on watch at the time, seeing the helpless state of the man, at once jumped overboard, swam after him, and succeeded in holding him up until a boat could be lowered, and by which they were finally picked up.

Mr. Addison encountered considerable personal risk, as it was almost dark at the time, and it was a difficult matter for a swimmer to make headway against the wind and the tide.

McCabe, George, Fisherman.   Case 27062

About 6 p.m. on the 26th May, 1894, the North Shields Fishing Boat *Teal Duck* was proceeding to the Fishing Ground in the North Sea, when the master, William Crumbie, accidentally fell overboard whilst drawing a bucket of water. The weather was very tempestuous, and there was too much sea on to allow a boat to be launched. One of the crew, George McCabe, with a line fastened around his body, gallantly jumped overboard and succeeded in reaching the drowning man after a swim of fifty yards; he was just in time to seize hold of Crumbie, and with difficulty brought him alongside the vessel, when they were hauled on board.

At the time of the accident the vessel was going nine and a half knots. There was a heavy sea running, and the salvor ran great personal risk in effecting the rescue.

Thomas, James, Police Constable, Gloucestershire Constabulary.   Case 27252

On the 2nd August, 1894, a labourer named Penny went down a newly made well which had been sunk at Redwich in Gloucestershire. He appears to have been overcome by the foul air, and unable to ascend. Another man named Roach gallantly went down to help, and also succumbed. No other person having attempted a rescue police constable Thomas was sent for, and he at once volunteered to go down the well. Tying a rope around his waist he attempted the descent, and when halfway down found Penny hanging head downwards with his foot entangled in the ladder, and quite unconscious. Thomas then brought him to the surface, and descended a second time, when he found Roach at the bottom in a state of collapse; he also managed to bring him to the surface, but unfortunately too late for recovery.

Webster, John S., Fourth Mate.   Case 27291
Mackenzie, John, Boatswain.

On the 1st February, 1894, the British India Steamship *Dorunda* was at sea in lat. 8.15 S. and lon. 127.19 E. when a passenger was seen to jump overboard. Mr. Webster immediately sprang over after him, followed by Mr. Mackenzie, and both officers diligently sought for him, but unfortunately were unable to find him. The night was very dark, and great personal risk was incurred, as sharks abound in that part of the ocean.

Turner, A.H., H.M. Solicitor General for Jersey.   Case 27379
Hamilton A.R., Landed Proprietor.
Hardyman, W.H., Lieut., West India Regiment.

About 3 p.m. on the 29th September, 1894, two young ladies had wandered over some rocks, under high cliffs, at Plemont, Jersey. They were cut off from the shore by the incoming tide, which rose very rapidly, it being the second highest during the year.

The above named gentlemen realizing their danger quickly undressed, crossed through several channels of water, climbed over several rough rocks, and eventually rescued the girls at great personal risk. The gentlemen had to swim across three distinct channels, and as the tide was rapidly running in with great strength, the salvors had great difficulty in swimming with the girls to shore. One gentleman took the younger girl on his back, the others supported the elder, who could swim a little. The rocks from which the girls were rescued were soon after under water.

Morris, John, Commissioned Boatman, Coast Guard.   Case 27498

At 7 p.m. on the 13th January, 1895, the ship *Northern Belle* was wrecked near the sea wall at Sandgate, having stranded about 120 yards from shore in ten feet of water.

Communication was effected by means of the rocket apparatus, but the crew did not seem to understand the working of the small line, which they made fast to their vessel. Finding that the whip would not work, John Morris volunteered to go on board by the small line, which feat he accomplished partly by swimming, and partly by hauling himself on board. This was done at great personal risk, as a heavy sea was breaking over the vessel. On getting aboard he righted the entangled gear, and sent three persons ashore, landing afterwards in a most exhausted state. Awarded the Sea Gallantry Medal for the same act.

Dodd, Wm., Miner. Case 27571
Watts, John, Miner.

On the 14th January, 1895, the Diglake Colliery at Audley, Staffordshire, was flooded with water from the old workings of an adjoining mine. About 240 men were at work in various parts of the pit. Mr. Wm. Dodd and Mr. John Watts, hearing the sound and seeing the water rushing in, started off in different directions to warn the men of the imminence of the danger; they took a leading part in the rescue of thirty-five men.

Another miner named Sproston, also behaved very gallantly, and nearly lost his life in his humane efforts. Thirteen men were distinguished for their gallant conduct in saving and attempting to save life on the occasion. Their names are as follows:

Wm. Dodd	John Watts	John Sproston	John Johnson
Thos Langshaw	John Bolton	John Carter	Amos Hinckley
Joseph Bateman	Moses Barlow	George Rowley	Jas. Maddock
Richd. Hoole			

Silver Medals were voted to Dodd and Watts and Bronze Medals to the others. William Dodd was also awarded the Albert Medal, 1st Class.

Whitehead, F.P., R.N.R., Chief Officer of the *Norham Castle*. Case 27584
Ferris, R.G., Apprentice, of the ship *Fascadale*.

On the 7th February, 1895, the ship *Fascadale* went ashore near the mouth of the Impenjali River on the Natal coast. There was a heavy swell breaking over the wrecked vessel, and the crew were clinging to the rigging when the ship was first sighted.

The Chief Officer of the *Norham Castle* (Mr. Whitehead) proceeded in a lifeboat to the stranded vessel, taking with him a lifeboat's crew, but he found it impracticable to get near enough to effect communication, and when about 100 yards from the wreck plunged overboard from his boat, taking a line with him, and swimming towards the other ship. An apprentice named Ferris, belonging to the wrecked vessel also jumped overboard from the wreck, and met the officer with another line, by which means a junction was effected, and the survivors of the *Fascadale* were rescued. Extreme risk was incurred, as sharks are numerous on the coast. Each also awarded the Sea Gallantry Medal in Silver.

Slater, James, Ship Engineer. Case 27593

At 2 p.m. on the 1st September, 1894, the Union Steamship *Natal* ran aground in crossing a sand-bank at Chinde, East Coast of Africa. The ship bumped upon one of the anchors of a buoy, and in doing so knocked a hole in her bottom and soon after settled, leaving only a part of the mast and funnel above water. All the crew and passengers took refuge on the funnel in a most dangerous position, with a heavy surf breaking over them.

Mr. Slater seeing that the tide was rising, and that darkness would soon set in, asked for volunteers to accompany him in a swim to shore (eight miles off) for the purpose of getting assistance to those unable to make the land.

Messrs. Scott and Millett, each having a cork jacket, went with him. The tide was in their favour. Mr. Slater soon found that his companions were unable to get to the shore, therefore he assisted them in turns. After they had both become unconscious, and were only kept afloat by the corks, Mr. Slater continued his heroic exertions, first moving one, then the other, until he finally reached the river opposite to the town, where they were picked up by a boat after being above four hours in the water, Slater alone being conscious.

Morrison, Roderick, Chief Engineer.   Case 27637

At 3 a.m. on the 1st December, 1894, a man fell into the Thames off the Albert Dock between the river wall and a ship. Mr. Morrison, Chief engineer of the steamship *Celtic King*, jumped overboard, seized the man, and had him pulled on deck. The night was very dark and bitterly cold, and a strong tide running. The salvor had to jump a height of 17 to 18 feet, and he had great difficulty in getting on board again, as his hands were badly cut.

Traill, Wm. Acheson, C.E.   Case 27662

In the afternoon of the 6th May, 1895, a pleasure boat having for its occupants a gentleman and his wife, son, daughter, and niece, with two boatmen, capsized off the Antrim coast two miles from Portrush. The accident took place about 300 yards from shore. Just after the accident happened an electric car train passed along the cliff road, and Mr. Traill, who was travelling by it, seeing the state of affairs, stopped the train and dashed down the steep slope to the shore, then throwing off some clothing, swam out towards the drowning persons. He succeeded in saving two of the party; three of the others were drowned.

Evans, M.L., Miss.   Case 27693

At 8 p.m., 2nd June, 1895, a boat, having for its occupants one man and two women, capsized close to the Hythe Pier, Southampton. Miss Evans, who was on the pier at the time, hearing cries of distress, ran to the landing steps, and, without divesting herself of any clothing, jumped into the water, seized the man and one of the women, and succeeded in pushing them near enough to the steps for them to be assisted out. The second girl was then sinking. Miss Evans went to her assistance also, and brought her safely to the steps. There was a strong ebb tide, and the depth of the water was 12 to 14 feet.

Worman, Herbert, Watchman.   Case 27801
Wheal, Robt., Turncock.   See also case 27880

At 7.30 a.m. on the 1st July, 1895, a workman named Digby proceeded down a manhole in the East Ham Sewer. Whilst returning to the surface he was overcome by the foul gas and fell off the ladder to the bottom of the shaft. Five men then rushed to the mouth of the shaft and descended, whereupon they were also affected by the foul air, and unable to return.

More men then came on the scene, and two of them, Worman and Wheal, at once went down to the rescue. They found four men dead and one insensible, whom they brought to the surface, but who afterwards died, never having regained consciousness.

Four In Memoriam Testimonials were sent to the relatives of the deceased men.

Fielden, R.M., Lieut., 2nd Battalion, Oxford Light Infantry.   Case 27876

At 2.30 p.m. on the 23rd July, 1895, a boat capsized about 100 yards from the rocks bounding the shore at Hayburn Wyke, Yorkshire. The occupants of the boat were Mr. Fielden and two ladies. The former on coming to the surface managed to seize the boat's painter, and was then enabled to place both the ladies on the upturned boat, which he commenced to push towards shore. After having gone several yards one of the ladies was washed off the boat by a roller, when Mr. Fielden left the boat and swam to her assistance, finally succeeding on getting her to the rocks and landing her. The other lady managed also to gain land as the rollers carried the boat inshore. The depth of water was twenty feet where the accident occurred.

Cole, George, Labourer.   Case 27880
See also Case 27801

At 7.30 a.m. on the 1st July, 1895, at the East Ham Sewage Works, George Cole gallantly descended to the sewer by the manhole, and attempted to rescue several men who unfortunately succumbed to the noxious gas. He had to be drawn up in a dazed state, and nearly lost his life. The manhole was 27 feet deep, with five feet of sewage in it. Five men lost their lives in the sewer. George Cole's name was inadvertently omitted in Case 27801, and, being since reported, a similar reward was voted, namely, a Silver Medal.

Belfon, David, Boat Owner.   Case 28038

On the 25th June, 1895, between the hours of 5 and 9 p.m., a boat having on board, besides the owner and two men, two women and two children, capsized in a heavy sea about eight miles off the coast of Grenada, West Indies.

While the two seamen were endeavouring to right the boat, the owner, David Belfon, looked after the women and children. He dived and found both women and the younger child under the boat, and succeeded in extricating them. The boat was then righted, and he made the women hold on to it, but the boat again turned over, and Belfon had to dive again for the women and one child, the other having gone down in the first instance. The women were repeatedly washed away from the boat, and as often brought back to it by Belfon. The second child was lost, but the boat having again been righted, both women were got into it and their lives saved by the gallant exertions of Belfon.

Nutman, William John, Captain.   Case 28185

About daybreak on the 19th January, 1896, the British steamer *Adair* foundered in the Mediterranean near Messina. When first sighted by the steamship *Staffordshire* she was on her beam ends, and to all appearances sinking fast. Two boats from the *Staffordshire* rescued all the officers and crew with the exception of Captain Nutman and an injured fireman, whom he had dragged from his berth as the ship went down, and was supporting him on the bottom of an upturned boat. The captain insisted on the last boat's crew seeing to the safety of those they had rescued, and return for him if possible. This they succeeded in doing, and both men were saved after half an hour on the overturned boat. There was a very high sea running at the time.

The Albert Medal was afterwards awarded by the Board of Trade to Captain Nutman for the same action.

Hannah, David, Pit Manager.   Case 28210
Morris, T.H., Colliery Surgeon.
Williams, Roderick, Fireman.

At 5.40 a.m. on the 27th January, 1896, an explosion occurred at the Ferndale Colliery, Tylorstown, Glamorganshire, whereby fifty-seven lives were lost, and the mine left in a wrecked condition. On reaching the pit Mr. David Hannah, the manager, distinguished himself by his bravery, and literally carried his life in his hands, as without any companion he thoroughly examined one part of the pit and satisfied himself that no one there needed his help.

Dr. T. H. Morris, the colliery surgeon, also displayed great energy and disregard for danger, as he ventured into the midst of the noxious gases and succeeded in saving many lives. Roderick Williams, a fireman, also behaved in a very praiseworthy manner, and ran great risk in his efforts to save life.

Eleven men in all were distinguished for their gallant conduct in saving and attempting to save life on the occasion;

David Hannah	Dr. T.H. Morris	Roderick Williams	Thos. Williams
Moses Williams	Thomas John	Lewis Lewis	Joseph Evans
Evan Morris	Evan Jones	Rees Howells	

Silver Medals were voted to Hannah, Morris and Roderick Williams, and Bronze Medals to the others.

Butt, Charles, J.P.   Case 28247

About 7 a.m. on the 6th March, 1896, the Norwegian barque *Volo*, of Arundal, went ashore at the mouth of the Bushman's River, South Africa. There was a thick mist at the time, and the sea was breaking over the vessel, the crew having taken to the rigging. On discerning the wreck Mr. Butt at once swam out, and at the third attempt succeeded in reaching the ship, which was lying about one hundred yards from the land. He obtained a rope, and with it swam to shore, and in a short time the crew of twelve men were landed.

Mr. Butt was quite benumbed, having been in the water, which was extremely cold, for more than an hour.

M'Kellar, John, Seaman.   Case 28257

At 2 a.m. on the 19th April, 1896, a collision occurred, near the Kish light on the coast of Wicklow, between the barque *Firth of Clyde* and the steamer *Marsden*. The vessels collided with great force, and the barque being nearly cut in two sank almost immediately. Those of the crew who were on deck along with the captain jumped overboard, several of them having no time to provide themselves with life-belts. M'Kellar, a seaman, was fortunately able to swim, and when in the sea kicked off his sea-boots to lighten himself, and transferred his life-belt to a comrade. After being in the water for about thirty minutes they were picked up by a boat belonging to the *Marsden*. The night was bitterly cold, and the water like ice.

James, David John, Mason.   Case 28614

At 1.30 p.m. on the 24th August, 1896, a young man named Thomas Phillips descended a well which he had been sinking, adjacent to his house at Dafen, near Llanelly, and was overcome by foul gas which had accumulated.

Rosser Rosser attempted to rescue him, but became unconscious and fell down before he reached the bottom of the ladder. An experienced collier, Wm. Williams, now went down, but he also became unconscious when within a few feet of the bottom. Efforts were now made to dispel the deadly gas, and in about forty-five minutes David John James with a rope tied round him descended and succeeded in bringing the bodies of the unconscious men to the surface. Rosser and Williams recovered, but Phillips was dead.

The Silver Medal was voted to David J. James, and Bronze Medals to R. Rosser and Wm. Williams.

Frend, Matthew, Sapper, 36th Coy., Royal Engineers.   Case 28651

Between 8 and 9 p.m. on the 26th September, 1896, a rowing boat with five men on board was capsized in Mangrove Bay, Bermuda, throwing its occupants in the water. Four of the men caught hold of the upturned boat, but the fifth man being unable to swim was carried away. Sapper Frend left the boat and went to his assistance, and succeeded in bringing him back to the boat, where he held on to the rudder until it became unshipped, and he sank. Frend then dived, brought him to the surface, and placed him alongside the other three men on the keel of the boat. He then undressed, and seizing the painter towed the boat, on the bottom of which were the four men, to the nearest land, a distance of about half a mile, the time occupied being two hours, all being then in an exhausted state.

The night was somewhat dark and the weather unusually cold and boisterous. One of the men has since died from the effects of the exposure.

Forman, A.B.,	Second Lieut.	Royal Artillery	Case 28742
Gosling, C.,	Lieut.,	1st Battalion King's Royal Rifles	
Down, R.,	Sergt.	"	
Allen, J.,	Sergt.	"	
Newby, R.,	Lance-Corpl.	"	
Howes, G.,	Private	"	
McNamara, N.,	Private	"	
Carr, E.,	Private	"	
Arrowsmith, M.	Private	"	
Grisley, W.J.,	Private	"	
Croft, C.,	Private	"	
Wootton, L.A.,	Private	"	
Selous, R.,	Second Lieut.	2nd Battalion. York and Lancaster	
Bayley, G.E.	Second Lieut.	"	
Roe, J.N.,	Private	"	
Flannery, T.,	Private	"	
Windham, W.G.,	Lieut.	Royal Indian Marine.	
Huddleston, E.W.,	Sub-Lieut.	"	

At 2.20 a.m. on the 14th January, 1897, the Royal Indian Marine troopship *Warren Hastings*, conveying troops from the Cape to Mauritius, was wrecked on the Island of Reunion.

The night was so intensely dark that it was impossible to distinguish anything more than a few feet away, and the rain falling in torrents. The sea at the time was calm, with a moderate swell, the backwash being sufficient to prevent anyone landing without assistance. Perfect discipline was maintained, and the obedience, good order, and coolness displayed by the men was remarkable. Even when it was expected that the vessel would heel over, the men stood quietly aside to allow the women and children to be taken to shore. The total number of persons on board was 1246, and all were safely landed with the exception of two natives, who were drowned in endeavouring to swim to land.

There were numerous acts of devotion and gallantry in saving life, and Lieut. Colonel M. Forestier-Walker, commanding the troops on board, named the above mentioned eighteen men as having specially distinguished themselves under the trying circumstances in which they were placed.

Serjt Allen received the Meritorious Service Medal.

Lloyd's Silver Medals were also awarded to 2nd Lieut Forman, Lieut Gosling and 2nd Lieut Selous. Lloyd's Bronze Medals awarded to Serjt Down and Private Wootton.

The following has been extracted from Public Record Office file - MT9.1267/M1000/1919.

McNamara, N., 7679, Private, 1st Bn. Kings Royal Rifles, was the first man to attempt to swim to the shore on the port side, carrying a light line, by means of which ropes were carried over and made fast, thus enabling many men to escape.

Carr, N., 6168, Private, 1st Bn. Kings Royal Rifles, swam out some distance to the assistance of Mr. Gadsden, R.I.M., Chief Engineer of the ship, and brought him ashore.

Howes, G., 4221, Private, 1st Bn. Kings Royal Rifles, at the time a patient in hospital, dived in and attempted to save a native cook, who drowned. He had afterwards to be helped out of the water.

Newby, R., 7291, Lance Corporal, 1st Bn. Kings Royal Rifles, dived from the ship and assisted a man of the York and Lancaster Regiment (name unknown) to a rope by which he was got ashore.

Grisley, W. J., 5680, Private, 1st Bn. Kings Royal Rifles, swam out with a buoy to the assistance of Private J. Brown, 1st Bn. Kings Royal Rifles, by which he was saved.

Arrowsmith, M., 6131, Private, 1st Bn. Kings Royal Rifles, was on the rocks near the bow of the ship, when a child of one of the York and Lancaster Regiment, was being brought down the ladder, slipped and fell into the sea, Private Arrowsmith although unable to swim, jumped in with a rope and was pulled out again with the child in his arms.

Wootton, L.A., 1st Bn. Kings Royal Rifles, swam out to the assistance of Private G. Taylor, 1st Bn. Kings Royal Rifles, and after bringing him ashore, went in again with a buoy to Private Danner, 1st Bn. Kings Royal Rifles, who was getting exhausted. Private Danner missed the buoy and Private Wootton then supported him to the rocks.

Windham, W. G., Lieut., Royal Indian Marine. and **Huddleston, E. W.**, Royal Indian Marine were instrumental in saving several lives, but I have been unable to get particulars, except in the case of Lance Corporal Robinson, 1st Bn. Kings Royal Rifles, who could not possibly have got ashore but for their assistance, and was saved by them both; and Private Diamond, 1st Bn. Kings Royal Rifles, whom Sub-Lieut Huddleston saved, being afterwards himself dashed insensible against the rocks, and picked out of the surf by Serjeant **J. Allen** and 7030, Private **C. Croft**, both of the 1st Bn. Kings Royal Rifles, at great risk to themselves.

Mr. Tyler, Bandmaster, 1st Bn. Kings Royal Rifles, was in the water, on the starboard side, and unable to make any headway against the backwash of the waves, or to get near the shore; Lieut **C. Gosling**, 1st Bn Kings Royal Rifles, endeavoured to reach him, but after going some twenty yards was washed back, thrown on the rocks and injured.

Forman, A.B., 2nd Lieut., Royal Artillery, at once went in with a rope and a life-buoy. When, however, the men on the shore began to haul the rope, it parted. 2nd Lieut. Forman stayed with Mr. Tyler, and Lieut. Gosling then made a second attempt to reach him, failed and was brought ashore.

Bayley, G.E., York and Lancaster Regiment, then swam out with a rope, and the three were then brought in close to shore, where Forman and Bayley were hauled up on to the rocks, over which then sea was washing. In endeavouring to pull Mr Tyler in the buoy slipped, and the backwash carried him out at once. At this time one of the boats belonging to the ship, which had washed loose, was drifted sufficiently near the rocks to be got hold of, but was all the time being dashed against them, and actually, being broken up. It was caught and manned by Colour-Serjeant Jones, who was at the time a hospital patient, Serjeants H. Howarth and **R. Down**, Corporals R. Hodgson and C. Young, and Privates 6206, W. Parkinson, 6040, G. Kaley, 6064, T. Jones, 5756, J. Connell, 7441, T. Steele, 8094, P. Pickersgill, all of the Kings Royal Rifles, and an attempt was made to row out to Mr Tyler, who was much exhausted.

Not being able to get the boat out, Serjeant Down dived from the stern and swam to him, supporting him till he could be got on board; but the sea afterwards swept him out of the boat and he was pulled in again by Corporal C. Young and 6231, Private C. B. Jones, and eventually landed in safety, though insensible, together with the crew of the boat.

Selous, R., 2nd Lieut., 2nd Bn York and Lancaster Regiment, jumped overboard on the starboard side and assisted a man to shore who at that time was sinking, and would most certainly have drowned if not so assisted; this officer also saved another man on the port side, who was sinking, by jumping into the sea, catching hold of him and holding him up till a rope was thrown to them, by means of which they were both pulled to shore.

Roe J. N., Private, A Company, 2nd Bn York and Lancaster Regiment, who was on guard at the time of the wreck as a sentry on the lower deck, stood to his post till the water was up to his knees, and would not leave until ordered to do so by 2nd Lieut Bayley, after he had reported that everyone had left that part of the ship.

Flannery, T., Private, A Company, 2nd Bn York and Lancaster Regiment. Who was on guard and on sentry over the fresh water tanks, also remained at his post till the water was over his knees.

Swann, Alfred J., British Central African Administration. Case 28810

On the evening of the 7th July, 1896, Alfred J. Swann, of the British Central African Administration, hired an open boat for the purpose of conveying a wounded European across Lake Nyassa to enable medical advice to be obtained. There was great danger in undertaking this voyage during the night, the aspect of the weather being threatening. Nothing daunted, Mr. Swann determined to make the attempt, and taking with him a native crew and his wounded friend, set out. During the night a strong south-westerly gale sprang up, and his black crew became cold and frightened and lay down under their mats to die. About 2 a.m. on the morning of the 8th, the sea being exceedingly rough, he was unable to keep enough sail on the boat to run away from it, and a huge wave came over the quarter, washing one of the boatmen overboard. Instantly catching hold of the main-sheet, Mr. Swann jumped after him, and being a good swimmer caught the man as he rose to the surface, and by means of the rope attached to the main-sheet succeeded in reaching the boat, into which, without assistance from any of the crew, he hauled the man, who was so thoroughly prostrated as to be unable to render his rescuer the least help. The night was dark, a heavy sea running, and the distance from land about fifteen miles, so that considerable risk was incurred.

Clifford, William T., 4th Officer.   Case 28887

At 3.10 p.m. on the 14th June, 1897, while the Royal Mail Steamer *Scot* was in lat 30 8 N. lon 17 13 W., on a voyage from the Cape to Southampton, a first-class passenger named Barnett Isaacs Barnato jumped overboard. Immediately the cry "Man overboard!" rang through the ship, and Mr. William T Clifford, fourth officer of the *Scot*, who was on the deck at that time, at once ran to the rail and plunged in after him. Owing to the heavy sea running he found it impossible to reach the drowning man, and was obliged to support himself on a life-buoy which had been thrown from the ship. The steamer had now been brought round, and a boat lowered, which picked up Mr. Clifford after he had been twenty-five minutes in the water, the body of Mr. Barnato being recovered soon after. Efforts which were at once made to restore animation proved unsuccessful.

There was a north-east wind with heavy sea, the speed of the vessel being fifteen knots, and there was a great danger of being struck by the propellers, which are well out on the quarter of the *Scot*.

Fullerton, Edith, Miss.   Case 29055

At 8 a.m. on the 7th August, 1897, Mr. J.M. Turner, a manufacturer of Alloa, was bathing from the beach at Carnoustie, on the Forfarshire coast. Mr. Turner, who is about fifty years of age and a practised swimmer, had gone out about 300 yards so as to be beyond the broken water, when he was seized with cramp, and was being rapidly carried out to sea.

An alarm was raised, and Miss Fullerton, who was also bathing, courageously swam to his assistance, and succeeded in supporting him till both were picked up by a boat which had put out from the beach.

Great risk was incurred, the place being described as exceedingly dangerous, there being a heavy sea with an ebb tide aided by a strong current from the Barry Burn, which enters the sea here.

Brown, John, Miner.   Case 29087
Brand, Reginald, Miner.

On the 1st June, 1897, a rush of mud took place in a tunnel at the 1000 feet level of the De Beers mine, Kimberley, South Africa, resulting in two native miners being imprisoned in a rise above the tunnel. A rescue party was at once formed, but as between 150 and 200 yards of mud had to be removed, it was considered almost hopeless that the two men would be taken out alive. At 3.15 p.m. on the 2nd it was discovered that there was a space of about six inches between the mud and the top of the tunnel, through which it might be possible to squeeze, and thereby reach the bottom of the rise in which the men were entombed. Fully recognising the danger to which they would be exposed, Brown and Brand decided to make the attempt, and half crawling, half swimming on top of the mud for a distance of 200 yards, succeeded in reaching the men and eventually releasing them from their perilous position.

The work of rescue occupied two hours, everything being in total darkness, with very little air, and great risk of any movement of the mud, there being actually a second rush on the following day, filling up all tunnels in the locality.

Walker, Thomas Bertie, Apprentice.　　　　　　　　　　　　　　　　　　　　　　　　　　　　　　　Case 29247

At 9 p.m. on the 24th October, 1897, it was discovered that there was an escape of gas in a chamber underneath the purifying house at the Gas Works, Wrexham. Mr. S. B. Hesketh, the assistant manager, went down through a manhole into this underground chamber, and found the gas escaping in great volume from a three-inch pipe. He returned for a plug, and although warned of the danger again went down and endeavoured to stop the leak, but was struck down by the noxious fumes.

A stoker named Henry Perrin at once went down to attempt the rescue, and succeeded in dragging the unconscious man several yards nearer to the entrance, when he to was overcome, and was with difficulty got out by his fellow workmen. Thomas Bertie Walker, an apprentice, now had a rope tied round him, and descended four times before he was able to fix a rope around Hesketh, by which he was drawn up; unfortunately it was too late, as life was found to be extinct. Walker was severely affected, and lost consciousness the last time he went down, being drawn up by the rope he had taken the precaution to fix round his body. Both men ran great risk of suffocation from the sulphuretted hydrogen gas, the place being in total darkness.

The Silver Medal was voted to T.B.Walker and Bronze Medal to H.Perrin.

D'Alton, Bertram J., Agent.　　　　　　　　　　　　　　　　　　　　　　　　　　　　　　　　　　　　Case 29261

At 2.30 a.m. on the morning of the 5th of May, 1897, the three-masted ship *Cambusnethan*, 1368 tons, commanded by Capt. Hughes, failing to battle with the terrific gale, went ashore at Spring Mount, about thirty-five miles to the eastward of Port Elizabeth, on the South African coast. Signals of distress were at once made, in response to which Mr. D'Alton and a number of farm hands hastened to the beach opposite to where the ship was lying on a reef about 500 yards from shore, there being a deep and rapid current running between the wreck and the land.

At about 9 a.m. a boat was lowered from the ship, only to be capsized immediately on reaching the water. A second boat was then launched from the port side of the ship in which eight of the crew seated themselves, but was also capsized, throwing the men into the sea, but with the aid of ropes and assistance from shore all of them were safely landed. Two other boats were now lowered, but were at once dashed to pieces, the occupants being swept away by the current. D'Alton now plunged into the fearful surf, and, being a powerful swimmer, rescued three men, the others succeeding in reaching land unaided.

The remaining boat was now lowered, only to share the fate of the others, leaving the sailors struggling in the water, only an occasional glimpse of whom could be had from shore.

Regardless of danger D'Alton swam out, and with his assistance all were saved, although in an exhausted and helpless state.

Only the captain now remained on board, he having resolutely refused to leave his ship. Night was fast approaching, and the storm showed no sign of abatement, it not being possible for a boat to live in such a sea, D'Alton decided to swim out with a rope and try and induce the captain to leave; but when within twenty yards of the ship became so exhausted that he had to abandon the attempt and turn towards shore, which he reached thoroughly exhausted.

Extreme risk was incurred there being a winter gale blowing, with torrents of rain, heavy sea, and dangerous surf. There was also danger from sharks, which abound in these waters.

Indar Singh, Gunner, No 3 Peshawar Mountain Battery, Tochi Field Force.　　　　　　　　　Case 29320

In connection with the operations being carried out by the Tochi Field Force several men of the No 3 Peshawar Mountain Battery, were about 4 p.m. on the 13th September, 1897, returning down the Surtoi Nullah, on their way to camp at Pirakai, when owing to a violent storm among the hills the defile they were traversing was suddenly transformed into a mountain torrent, the water rushing along with terrific force. Four men and eight mules were at once swept away. Two of the men managed to reach a rock in the middle of the stream, only one of whom was able to retain his hold, the other being carried away by the force of the water. The man on the rock was in a most dangerous position, and rapidly becoming numbed with the intense cold.

The water having gone down slightly, Gunner Indar Singh stripped, and entering the torrent from the opposite side, succeeded in reaching the rock, where he remained supporting the now almost insensible man, for some considerable time, when, the water having gone down a little lower, he was enabled to reach a place of safety.

Considerable risk was incurred, as large stones were being carried down by the stream, which was composed of freshly thawed hail, the depth being about breast high, and the width sixty feet.

Blyth, Robert, Miner. Case 29337

At 9 a.m. on the 11th March, 1898, the Auldhouseburn Colliery, Muirkirk, Ayrshire, became inundated, owing to a sudden inrush of water from an old working, which flooded the mine until it rose four feet above the door-heads, the main road to the pit bottom being full to the roof for a distance of about fifty feet.

There were forty-five men down the pit at the time. Of these three were drowned, twenty-six got out in safety, and the remaining sixteen were rescued the following morning, mainly through the self-sacrifice and heroism of Robert Blyth, who refused to ascend and leave his comrades to perish. With great presence of mind he turned back from the pit bottom, and having forced his way through the rising water, reached these men, who were attempting the impossible task of gaining the bottom of the shaft, and from his intimate knowledge of the workings kept them at a point above the level of the flood, where he cheered them on, and encouraged them to hope for deliverance. After being in this critical position for twenty-four hours, the water began to yield to the constant working of the pumps, which had been kept going, and all were enabled to reach the pit bottom, whence they were drawn to the surface.

Robert Gibson remained at his post at the pit bottom till the water reached his neck, and just before leaving a boy named John McGladrie floated forward on some wreckage; Gibson at once sprang forward, and at great risk caught the lad and dragged him to a higher level, eventually reaching the pit head safely.

The Silver Medal was voted to R. Blyth, and the Bronze Medal to R. Gibson.

Joynes, John James, Miner. Case 29338

At 9 a.m. on the 20th December, 1897, the Wimberry Colliery, Forest of Dean, became flooded, owing to the bursting of the barriers of an old working. So quickly did the water rise that within seven minutes it had risen over six feet in the main shaft. There were about forty men and boys at work at the time, all of whom escaped with the exception of six, whose retreat had been cut off.

Joynes at once called for volunteers to try and effect a rescue. Several men at once came forward, and Joynes selected John Davis, Philip Watson, and Samuel Mansfield.

They descended by a travelling way at an incline of 1 in 2, through which the water was rushing at a terrific rate, breast high. After going some distance, clinging to the timbers on the sides and roof, at times being carried off their feet, they lost their lights and proceeded in darkness, until by shouting they ascertained that the men were alive, and eventually found them all huddled together by the side of the road unable to face the water and debris that was being washed down against them. With great difficulty and much danger, all were got up through the water to the shaft, the last man being rescued about two hours after the accident.

The Silver Medal was voted to J.J. Joynes, and Bronze Medals to J. Davis, P. Watson and S. Mansfield.

Benjamin, Alfred, Ferryman. Case 29360

About noon on the 25th February, 1898, the *Viking*, a small steam launch of twenty-five tons, in endeavouring to cross the bar at the entrance to Port Natal harbour, was struck by a sea, capsized, and sank.

Thirteen persons were on board at the time; of these, eight were drowned, two were picked up by the boat from a tug which had put out to render assistance. Of the remaining three, two secured a life-buoy and the other a spar with the idea of reaching the shore.

An attempt to launch the lifeboat having failed, a small raft was quickly made, with which Alfred Benjamin, ferryman, and Francis Cox, constable, water police, swam out through the surf, taking a line with them. Before reaching the men it was found necessary to leave the raft and swim the remaining distance; this Benjamin did, and the line being made fast, all were pulled to the beach. The men were about 300 yards out when picked up by Benjamin.

The remaining man with the spar was now seen floating with the current about 150 yards out. Benjamin and Cox again swam out, and with considerable difficulty brought him in. The weather was squally with a rough sea and heavy surf, making the rescue one of much danger, which was increased by the presence of sharks, which abound in these waters.

The Silver Medal was voted to A. Benjamin, and the Bronze Medal to Constable Cox.

Gray, Andrew, Electrician, Telegraph Steamer *Faraday*. Case 29554
Payne, Ralph Lavington, aged eleven.

At 11.30 a.m. on the 10th July, 1898, Andrew Gray, A. E. Hickmott, W. Good, A.E. Davidson, and two boys, Ralph and Jocelyn Payne, aged ten and eleven years respectively, went for a sail in a small boat called the *Intrepid*, from St George's, Grenada, West Indies. After going to the last point on the south, and finding the sea too rough, they tacked back, and anchored the boat near to Point Salines. After bathing, they were returning home about 2 p.m., when a heavy squall struck the boat, and the jib being tied, she capsized and sank. Mr. Andrew Gray, who is an electrician belonging to the telegraph steamer *Faraday*, at once took charge of the younger boy Payne, and started for shore, distant about two miles. This arduous task he succeeded in accomplishing, after being in the water about three hours.

Meanwhile the elder lad Payne had divested himself of his clothing, and knowing that Mr. Good could not swim, stayed to help him. Seizing an oar which had floated, he, with its aid, supported him for some time, and when he could hold on no longer, but began to sink, caught hold of him by the neck and also by the hair in his endeavour to keep him afloat, the rough sea washing over them every minute. At last becoming exhausted, he had to release his hold, and Good sank. After swimming some time he saw Hickmott go down, but could not help him.

About an hour afterwards he met Davidson, who had his clothes on, and tried to help him undress, but could not manage it, and he also sank. After swimming and floating for three hours, and being much exhausted, he saw the schooner *Ocean King*, of Trinidad, bound for Grenada, and the crew in response to his shouts, picked him up, he being then about three miles from land.

It is well known that these waters are infested with sharks.

McField, Wilson, Seaman. Case 29639

At 2 a.m. on the morning of the 2nd December, 1897, while the schooner *Dolphin* was on a voyage from the coast port of Prinzapulca to Bluefields, Nicaragua, she was struck by a sudden squall, and capsized. The crew, who were on deck at the time, managed to reach the bottom of the upturned vessel. Two passengers who were in their cabin were not so fortunate, and were imprisoned there when the vessel went over. In response to the repeated knocking of these men, it was decided by the crew to try and rescue them from their perilous position, and Wilson McField volunteered to make the attempt. Taking a rope, he dived from the bottom of the schooner and found his way into the cabin where the men were, and giving them the rope, induced them to enter the water, when they were pulled on to the bottom of the *Dolphin* by the remainder of the crew, whence they were rescued by the s.s. *Yulu*. The two men had been in the cabin about six hours before being liberated. Great risk was incurred, the rescue being effected in total darkness.

Phillips, James Arthur, Petty Officer 2nd Class, R.N. Case 29724

At 10.50 p.m. on the 25th September, 1898, a shore boat, having on board four liberty men, and two boatmen named Murray and Jacobs, capsized alongside H.M.S. *Champion* in the Thames at Sheerness, by the swell from the Flushing steamer. A boat belonging to the ship was at once lowered, and the four sailors were picked up, but the two boatmen had been carried away by the current. James Arthur Phillips was below in his hammock at the time, and hearing the cry for help rushed on deck, and at once plunged overboard, succeeded in finding the men and taking them one at a time to the ship's boat, whence they were taken on board. When found by Phillips the men had drifted 200 yards from the ship.

Great risk was incurred, the night being dark, and the depth fourteen fathoms, with a strong ebb tide running.

Macklin, George, Ship's Steward.   Case 29822

At 2.15 p.m. on the 27th October, 1898, Timothy McCarthy, A.B., H.M.S. *Columbine*, accidentally fell overboard off Louisberg, Cape Breton Island. Life-buoys were at once thrown, but being confused by the spray he failed to reach them. On a volunteer being called for to effect the rescue, George Macklin, ship's steward, took a life-buoy, and jumping overboard swam to McCarthy, whom he placed in the buoy, and supported till they were picked up by a boat. There was a heavy sea running, with the wind blowing the tops off the waves into blinding spray, and the ship making eight knots under steam and sail.

Juddery, J.W.H., Quartermaster.   Case 29884

About 6.30 p.m. on the 24th October, 1898, the s.s. *Mohegan* went ashore on the dangerous Manacle rocks on the Cornish coast, when 106 lives were lost, and only 53 saved. The wind was from the south-east, blowing half a gale, and there was a high sea running. Thirteen of the survivors, including Mr. Juddery, took refuge in the mizzen rigging, where they remained exposed to the full force of the gale for some six hours. When the lifeboat at length arrived it was deemed unsafe to approach too close to the wreck.

Quartermaster Juddery then plunged into the raging sea and swam to the lifeboat, where a line was given him, with which he returned to the wreck, thus establishing communication by which he and his twelve comrades were rescued, reaching the shore about 5 a.m. the following morning.

The court of inquiry into the cause of the wreck expressed its approbation of his noble and gallant conduct in thus exposing himself to great personal risk in order to save others. Awarded the Sea Gallantry Medal.

Rotch, Sydney F.S., Lieut., R.N.   Case 29942

At midnight on the 29th November, 1898, the dinghy belonging to H.M.S. *Onyx* left Harwich pier for the purpose of returning to the ship, there being on board Lieut Rotch, of the *Onyx*, Mr. R. Johnson, Chief Officer of H.M. Cruiser *Beaver*, A.Pope, armourer's mate of the *Onyx*, and two seamen. When some fifteen yards from the ship the boat capsized, throwing all into the water. The two seamen managed to save themselves. Mr. Johnson, who is unable to swim, at once called for help, and Lieut. Rotch swam with him to the quarter boom, leaving him there in safety. He then swam out to Pope, who was in a critical position, and also took him to the boom.

Meanwhile the alarm had been given on board, but it took twenty minutes to lower the whale-boat, the falls being frozen.

Eventually all were saved, after being in the water nearly half an hour.

The tide was flowing strong, and there was great danger of being numbed by the cold, there being three degrees of frost at the time.

Baron, Charles, Miner.   Case 30089

About 10.30 a.m. on the 5th June, 1899, three men who had been instructed to clean out certain parts of the Wigan Corporation main sewer, descended a manhole in the township of Pemberton for the purpose of carrying out the work, and were at once struck down and rendered unconscious by an accumulation of foul gas. A fourth man who was present gave the alarm, and Charles Baron, a miner, volunteered to go down and endeavour to effect their rescue; but he, on entering the manhole, also fell down insensible from the effects of the gas.

A boathook was procured, by the aid of which Baron was drawn to the surface, where artificial respiration was resorted to, but one hour and twenty minutes elapsed before he regained consciousness.

The bodies of the three men were recovered later, but they had succumbed to the effects of the deadly gas.

Great risk was incurred, as had there been no other assistance at hand Baron must also have lost his life.

Swanger, Arthur, Ordinary Seaman.   Case 30130

At 10.5 a.m. on the 29th April, 1899, the Orient Line Royal Mail Steamer *Oroya*, on a voyage from London to Sydney, was in the Red Sea, When W. Inglis, an A.B., while attending to the third-class sun-screens, missed his footing and fell overboard.

Arthur Swanger, an O.S., immediately jumped after him and succeeded in keeping him afloat. The *Oroya* was steaming fourteen and a half knots, but was stopped as quickly as possible, and a boat lowered, which picked both men up, Inglis being unconscious. On being taken on board artificial respiration was resorted to, and continued for one hour and a half without success.

Great risk was incurred not only in jumping from the moving vessel, but from the numerous sharks which infest the waters of the Red Sea. Awarded the Sea Gallantry Medal.

Green, Walter, Boatman.   Case 30357

At 10 p.m. on August 5th, 1899, a boat in charge of Walter Green, Lakeside, Lurgan, and having on board three other men, was capsized at the entrance to Kinnego Bay, Lough Neagh, throwing all into the water. One of the men managed to cling to the boat, the other two being assisted to her by Green. The accident took place about three quarters of a mile from shore in about thirty to forty feet of water., and the night being dark the chance of rescue was remote. Finding there was no response to their calls for help, Green volunteered to swim to land. The others though much exhausted, tried to dissuade him, but to no purpose, and he started. His clothing and boots hampered him greatly, and in trying to get rid of his jacket it caught his arm, and he was nearly overcome. Nothing daunted, he continued swimming until his knees touched the stones in shallow water, as he feared if he lowered his legs to test the depth he might not be able to raise them. On landing he soon found a boat, which he rowed out to the relief of his companions, reaching them at the same time as another boat which had put off in answer to shouts heard from the Lough. All were then taken on board and landed in safety.

Charlton, E.F.B., Commander, R.N.   Case 30422

At 5 p.m. on the 29th June, 1899, the steam cutter belonging to H.M.S. *Orlando* grounded on a sand bank in Muda River one mile below Sumatal, near Penang. The river is some eighty yards wide, with a depth of twelve to sixteen feet, and flows with a strong current. In order to get the cutter afloat, Commander Charlton, Lieut. Hyde, and Edward C. Holloway, petty officer carried out an anchor as far as the depth of water would allow, when dropping the anchor all three were swept off their feet by the current. Lieutenant Hyde succeeded in reaching the stranded boat, but Mr. Holloway was unable to do this, and was directed by Commander Charlton to try and gain the opposite bank, about thirty yards distant, he himself accompanying him. When about five yards from the bank Holloway suddenly threw up his arms and sank. Commander Charlton at once dived and caught him by the hair, but this being short he slipped from his grasp, and although the Commander dived again several times he did not succeed in finding him, and he drowned. Meanwhile Lieut. Hyde left the cutter and swam to the place, but was too late to render any assistance, although he remained by Commander Charlton till a landing was effected about fifty yards lower down.

Great risk was incurred, the river being infested with crocodiles.

The Silver Medal was voted to Commander Charlton, and a Testimonial on Vellum to Lieut. Richard Hyde.

McGregor, John, Wood Merchant.   Case 30424

Between 4 and 5 p.m. on the 24th October, 1899, James Donald in the course of his duty descended a lime kiln at the Newton Lime Works, Ayr, for the purpose of spreading some coke over the limestone, when he was overcome and rendered unconscious by the gas or other fumes. The depth of the kiln is fourteen and a half feet, and the diameter at the top seven feet. On his condition being discovered, Joseph Irvin, the lessee of the works went down by the ladder and attempted to raise Donald, but was also overcome, and became unconscious.

An alarm was raised, and a number of men gathered round the top of the kiln, amongst them being John McGregor, wood merchant, who at once volunteered to go down and endeavour to effect the rescue; and this he did, having first fastened a rope round his waist, the end of which was held by those at the top. He first raised the body of Donald, who was dead, and took it to the surface, and again going down he was successful in taking Irvin to the top, who remained unconscious for about two hours.

Great risk was incurred, as the combined gases rising from the slowly burning limestone are known to be very deadly.

The Silver Medal was voted to John McGregor and Bronze Medal to Joseph Irwin.

Williams, John.   Case 30454

At 5.30 p.m. on the 29th October, 1899, the brigantine *Rob the Ranter*, of Fowey, was driven on shore on the Carnarvonshire coast during a heavy gale. Her crew of six men got into their small boat and endeavoured to reach the shore, but shortly after leaving the wreck the boat was swamped, throwing all into the sea, where they were at the mercy of the breakers. Two of them were soon overcome and drowned, a fate that would in a short time have overtaken the others had not John Williams, of Trefalluyn Farm, Llanengan, dashed into the surf and dragged them one after the other to a place of safety. When landed the men were much too exhausted to be able to stand.

Great risk was incurred, the wash after each wave rushing back with fearful force.

Thomas, David, Miner.   Case 30484
Francis, Thomas, Miner.

At 8 a.m. on the 9th December, 1899, the Glanmwrwg Pit, Llangennech, Carmarthenshire, was flooded, owing to the tapping of an old working. David Thomas, in whose headway the inrush took place, instead of seeking his own safety went into the lower part of the workings to warn the miners employed there, and on returning had to contend with a heavy rush of water. By this action four men were warned in time to escape with their lives. These men on reaching a place of safety went home, but returning later to the pit found that two men were missing. Hearing a moaning sound proceeding from the workings, Thomas Francis and William John Hunns volunteered to swim in and try to effect a rescue. At about 1 p.m. they made the attempt, but after going some ten yards were forced to return, as the water was nearly touching the roof. At 3.30 p.m. Francis made a second attempt alone, and the water being slightly lower he managed to get within ten feet of a miner named Lloyd, who was clinging to a beam in the roof. It was, however, impossible to reach Lloyd, owing to a cross beam which blocked the way. A third attempt was made, Francis and Hunns being joined by David Jones, and the three men taking a rope succeeded in reaching Lloyd and rescuing him, after hanging in the cold water for ten hours. The second man, named Williams, was drowned.

Extreme risk was incurred by all these men, the rescue of Lloyd being effected in ten feet of water and with no light.

Silver Medals were voted to David Thomas and Thomas Francis, and Bronze Medals to William John Hunns and David Jones.

Clements, Francis G., Farmer, Palling, Norfolk   Case 30526
Hubbard, Samuel, Labourer.

About 7.15 a.m. on the 14th February, 1900, the brigantine *Lizzie and Edith*, of West Hartlepool, while on a voyage from Sunderland to Southampton with coals, was driven on shore at Palling on the Norfolk coast. A strong easterly gale with blinding snow storms prevailed at the time, and there was a heavy surf running. On striking, the vessel at once began to break up, and her crew of eight men took to the sea in the hope that by some remote chance they might reach land.

Clements and Hubbard were on shore, and seeing the struggles of the fast-drowning sailors, rushed into the surf and succeeded in landing four of them, the other four despite their utmost endeavours, being swept away and drowned.

Great risk was incurred, not only from the fearful surf, but from the floating timbers which were driven ashore from the wreck.

Hale, Joseph, Colliery Under Manager, Drybrook, Forest of Dean. Case 30549

At 4.30 a.m. on the 1st March, 1900, a fire broke out in the timbers of a roadway at the Trafalgar Colliery, Drybrook, Forest of Dean. This occurred about a mile from the bottom of the shaft. Two miners named Knight and Jones were at work in this roadway, and were rendered unconscious by the smoke. Charles Black, who was acting as night inspector, knowing that these men were there, attempted to reach them, but was driven back by the fumes.

Joseph Hale under manager of the Colliery, had now reached the scene, and going down the roadway found both men lying insensible some 200 yards from the entrance. He at once returned for further help, and four men named Joseph Powell, William Wall, Llewellyn Whittington, and Frederick Bennett, taking with them a horse and empty tram, went with him. On reaching the place Knight and Jones were put into the tram and taken to pure air.

Great risk was incurred by all, Hale being quite prostrate through inhaling the poisonous fumes, the others being affected in a lesser degree.

The Silver Medal was voted to Joseph Hale, and Bronze Medals to Charles Black, Joseph Powell, William Wall, Llewellyn Whittington and Frederick Bennett.

Parnaby, Christopher, Miner, Chester-le-Street, Co. Durham. Case 30559

On the forenoon of the 20th February, 1900, two miners named Robson and Stenlake were engaged in constructing a staple or upward shaft from the mine level of the Craighead Colliery near Chester-le-Street, Co. Durham. The mine is 240 feet deep, and the staple was intended to reach a seam of coal sixty feet above. This staple or shaft is eleven feet by seven and is cut out from below, being divided into two sections - one, nine feet by seven for the stone as it is taken down, the other two feet by seven for a manway. The manway is partitioned off from the stone section by sleepers held in place by cross pieces of timber, called buntings, three feet apart. These buntings are used as a ladder by which the top of the shaft is reached.

On the day in question the shaft had been driven to a height of 54 feet. About 10 a.m. two shots were fired, and at 10.50 Robson and Stenlake went up to begin work, Stenlake being shortly after struck down by a combination of foul air and gas. Robson called for help, when a miner named Sydney Cooper went up taking a rope with him, which Robson tried to put round Stenlake; but he became unconscious before being able to fasten it. Cooper now became giddy and went back to pure air, calling for further help. Another man named Laurence Wilson, went up, but could not reach the platform where the men were. A third man, Christopher Parnaby, then went up and passing Wilson reached the platform, and finding Stenlake got him over into the manway, and with Wilson's help lowered him to the bottom. The rope was then pulled up and Robson was lowered in like manner. Parnaby now came down and with some help from Wilson reached the bottom, where he became unconscious. All three men were then removed to the engine-house, where police constable Johnson used the Sylvester method of treatment, resulting in Stenlake recovering in twenty minutes, Robson in one hour, and Parnaby in an hour and a half.

Great risk was incurred not only from the foul gas, but from the confined space in which the men were, with real danger of falling down the manway. Robson fell down dead three days after from the effects of the gas.

The Silver Medal was voted to Christopher Parnaby, Bronze Medals to Wilson and Cooper, and a Resuscitation Certificate to Constable Johnson.

Sclanders, D.G., Trooper, Natal Carabineers.　　　　　　　　　　　　　　　　　　　　　　　Case 30567

About 2 p.m. on the 17th January, 1900, the 13th Hussars were crossing the River Tugela at Trichard's Drift in face of the enemy. The Tugela is some seventy-five yards wide at this point, the depth varying from six to twenty-five feet, and the current strong. Some of the cavalry horses became nervous in crossing, a number of them being swept down with the stream. Trooper G. Roddy, Natal Mounted Police, attempted to save one man, who had got separated from his horse, but failed, and had to be assisted to land. Captain J. H. Tremayne, of the 13th Hussars, also went to the man's help; but failing to reach him got into difficulty himself, and was only saved by Trooper D. G. Sclanders, Natal Carabineers, swimming out, and with the assistance of Major F. E. Cooper, R.A., and Captain L. Parke, Durham Light Infantry, bringing him to the bank in an unconscious state. At the same time and place Lieutenant F.H. Wise, 13th Hussars, saved Private Prince, who was among those who had been carried away.

Great risk was incurred by all the above named, especially by Trooper Sclanders, who was breathless and exhausted from his efforts in saving other men when he went to the rescue of Captain Tremayne.

The Silver Medal was voted to Trooper Sclanders, and Bronze Medals to Major F.E. Cooper, Captain J.H. Tremayne, Captain L. Parke, Lieutenant F.H. Wise, and Trooper G. Roddy.

Haig, N. W., Lieutenant, 6th (Inniskilling) Dragoons.　　　　　　　　　　　　　　　　　　　Case 30586
Harris, J., Lieutenant.
Williams, Sergeant.

On the 15th of March, 1900, a squadron of the 6th (Iniskilling) Dragoons was ordered to cross the Orange River at Allemans Drift. Finding it impossible owing to the flooded state of the river to cross with their horses, the above named, with Lieut. A.J.G. Meek and Second Lieut. F.N. Dent swam across, and after resting some time were returning, when about halfway back Lieut. Meek became exhausted and called for help. Lieut. Haig, who had reached the bank, at once returned to his assistance, and was successful in landing him.

About the same time Second Lieut. Dent was in difficulties in midstream, and Sergt. Williams, seeing his danger, went to his help, reaching him after he had gone under twice. Finding that he could not in his exhausted state take him to the bank, Williams called for further help, and Lieut. Harris, who had got across, again plunged in, but failed to reach Dent, who was carried away and drowned; Sergt. Williams had great difficulty in reaching the bank.

Extreme risk was incurred, the river being in flood and full of eddies and dangerous whirlpools.

Tinney, Louis H. J., 4th Officer, S.S. *Tagus*.　　　　　　　　　　　　　　　　　　　　　　　　Case 30715
Hamilton, R., Private, 2nd Bn., West Yorkshire Regiment.

At 3.30 p.m. on the 19th June, 1900, the hired Transport *Tagus*, carrying troops from England to South Africa, was in lat. 4, lon. 15, when one of the crew, named Dawkins, accidentally fell overboard. Instantly the cry "man overboard" was raised, and a lifebuoy was thrown to him, while a boat in charge of the fourth officer was got ready for lowering as soon as the propeller ceased working. When this was done and the boat in the water, the propeller suddenly started working, and the boat being drawn under, was smashed to pieces, one of the crew named Nixon being badly cut, and, owing to loss of blood, unable to retain his hold of the wreckage of the boat.

The officer in charge, Louis H.J. Tinney, at once swam to his help, and Private Robert Hamilton, 2nd Battalion West Yorkshire Regiment, jumped overboard and assisted in supporting him till they were picked up by another boat which put off from the ship.

Extreme risk was incurred, not only from the rough sea and moving propeller, but from sharks, which infest the locality.

Samuels, Charles, Captain, British Steamship *Virginia*.   Case 30945

At 5.30 p.m. on the 2nd May, 1900, the British Steamship *Virginia*, belonging to the Port of London, whilst on a voyage from Cuba to Baltimore with a cargo of iron ore went ashore on the Diamond Shoal, eight miles from Cape Hatteras, on the American coast. The weather was thick and rainy with a heavy sea running. When the vessel struck she broke in two almost at once, the after part going down stern first. The last boat which had been launched was capsized to leeward by the seas breaking over the vessel, and six men were drowned. The remainder of the crew took to the rigging, where they were for sixteen hours, after which they got down to the bridge and chart-house, which were above water, and remained there all day.

The fore part of the vessel had sunk at an angle leaving the forecastle head out of the water, and Captain Samuels decided to try and get there to obtain oil to burn as a signal of distress. Being successful in his endeavour, he then assisted his chief officer to join him, and together they managed to build a raft capable of holding all, at the same time burning flares which eventually attracted the attention of the lighthouse-keepers at Cape Hatteras, and two lifeboats being sent out all who remained on board were saved, after being forty-six hours on the wreck. The lifeboats experienced much difficulty in taking them off, owing to the heavy seas and strong eddy currents prevalent on the shoals, and these Captain Samuels had to contend with when swimming from one part of the wreck to the other.

Morris, George Henry, Sergeant, Royal Garrison Artillery.   Case 31070

At 12 noon on the 26th October, 1900, a small sailing boat, having on board Lieutenant W.H. Cox, Indian Medical Service, Sergeant G.H. Morris, No 7 Company, Eastern Division, Royal Garrison Artillery, and a native bullock-driver named Beni Mati, was struck by a sudden squall and capsized about half a mile from shore, at Lai-chi-Koh, near Hong Kong, China. Lieutenant Cox and the native were unable to swim, and Sergeant Morris succeeded in getting them on the keel of the upturned boat, when finding that this was unable to support all three of them, he started for shore, swimming in his heavy boots and clothing.

The accident having been seen from the beach, Sergeant Watson, of the Commissariat Transport Department, put off in a boat to render assistance. Sergeant Morris, seeing this boat approaching, turned back, and assisted in transferring Lieutenant Cox and the native from the sunken craft to the rescuing boat, which ultimately landed them all in safety.

Sergeant Morris incurred great risk, as he had to swim in his heavy clothing and boots.

Sparks, Albert Edward, P.O.1., R.N., H.M.S. *Terrible*.   Case 31127

At 8 a.m. on the 31st October, 1900, H.M.S. *Terrible* was at anchor off Wei-hai-Wei, China. It was blowing a gale and there was a heavy sea running. The steam picket-boat which was riding by hawser 100 feet astern of the ship foundered, her crew of nine men being thrown into the water. Eight of the men, including Albert E. Sparks, Petty Officer 1st Class, managed to reach the sailing launch, which was riding still further astern, but the ninth man, an able seaman, named Hawkins, being unable to swim, was carried rapidly away. Seeing his danger Sparks left the launch, and going after him was successful in bringing him back to safety. Great risk was incurred, not only from the heavy sea, but from the close proximity of a precipitous lee shore.

Miller, G.H., Private, Imperial Yeomanry.   Case 31214

On the 12th March, 1901, the hired transport *Tagus* was on her way to the Cape with troops on board. Four days after leaving St. Vincent, while steaming at fifteen knots, one of the crew either fell or jumped overboard. Private G.H. Miller 19th (Lothian) Squadron, Imperial Yeomanry, without any hesitation sprang after him, but did not succeed in overtaking him. The transport was quickly brought round, and a boat being lowered both men were picked up, after being fifteen minutes in the water. Although he did not reach his man Trooper Miller incurred great risk, three sharks being seen close to the boat as the men were being hauled in.

Nairn, Adam, Pilot
Weller, Samuel, Seaman.
Gray, Tennant, Seaman.
McLaren, A., Seaman.
McDowell, Wm., Seaman.
Brooke, R., Seaman, R.N.R.
Adams, L.B., Seaman.
McCarthy, E., Seaman.
Bradley, J., Seaman.
Hansen, J., Seaman.
Bowman, N., Seaman.
Petersen, C., Seaman.

Case 31232

On the morning of the 22nd March, 1901, the s.s. *Taher* in trying to enter the harbour at Port Louis, Mauritius, struck the reef on the outer side of Barkly Island. There was a heavy ground swell at the time, with the surf setting on to the reef. From the moment of striking the seas broke clean over the fated ship. There were in all eighty-eight persons on board, a number of whom jumped overboard, or tried to save themselves in a boat which was carried away from the davits.

It being practically impossible to approach the wreck from the island owing to the tremendous surf, it was decided to attempt the rescue from the seaward side. Volunteers were accordingly called for from English ships in the harbour, and fourteen men were selected from those responding to the call, two lifeboats were manned, and under the guidance of an experienced pilot endeavoured to reach the vessel. Unfortunately both boats were capsized in the surf and three of the brave occupants drowned, the other twelve, including the pilot, being washed on shore, all of them suffering severe injuries. Seventeen of those on board the *Taher* were lost.

In Memorium testimonials were voted to the relatives of W. Cawsey, W. Hutchinson and C. Hansen, who lost their lives in the surf.

Yame, Boatman, Fiji.

Case 31250

About midnight on the 13th March, 1901, the cutter *Aggie*, a small vessel of twelve tons, was at anchor on the north side of the Island of Ovalau, Fiji, when she was capsized during a hurricane. Those on board consisted of Mr. E. Wilkinson and four natives, Ratu Mele, Yame, Osea, and Elia. Elia being a local man and knowing the coast got ashore early in the morning. When the cutter went down Mr. Wilkinson, Ratu Mele, and Osea each got hold of a hatch, and Yame the topmast. The night was most tempestuous, the wind blowing with hurricane force and a heavy sea running. When daylight came Mr. Wilkinson was much exhausted, and the three natives rendered him assistance alternately. By midday Ratu Mele became exhausted and Yame went to his help, bringing him up to the others. The three hatches were now fastened together, Osea tearing up his loin cloth for this purpose. On this frail raft Mr. Wilkinson and Ratu Mele were placed until they somewhat recovered, when the hatches were unloosed and all swam on again. In the afternoon the roar of the reef was heard and Osea swam on ahead in the hope of landing and procuring help, but it was midnight before he managed to reach the shore, being hardly able to stand and almost unable to speak, so that no boat was sent out until morning. After Osea left Mr. Wilkinson and Ratu Mele became very exhausted and Yame assisted them in turn, but just before dusk Ratu Mele slipped from his hatch and sank. Yame now assisted Mr. Wilkinson till about midnight, when he also slipped from his hatch. Yame dived and got him back, but he was now in the last stage of exhaustion, and finally Yame became weak and unable to render further aid, and seeing that Mr. Wilkinson had ceased breathing, left him and got on to the reef whence he was taken in the morning by the boat which had put out. Osea was in the water twenty-four hours and Yame over thirty hours, having also six square inches of skin rubbed from his stomach through dragging Mr. Wilkinson on to the raft.

The Silver Medal was voted to Yame, and the Bronze Medal to Osea.

Swan, W. Charles, Chief Officer, S.S. *Trigona*. Case 31251

On the morning of the 12th April, 1901, four Malay seamen were engaged in washing down an oil tank, from which benzine had been discharged, on board the steamer *Trigona* at Singapore. The men were standing on a stringer plate about seven feet from the top of the tank and nineteen feet from the bottom, when they were suddenly overcome by vapour given off by the oil. Two of the men fell on the plate on which they were standing and were got out unconscious, but recovered some three quarters of an hour later, the other two men falling to the bottom of the tank. W. Charles Swan, chief officer of the steamer, volunteered to try and rescue them. On descending he passed a rope round one man, who was hauled up, but found to be dead, the fall having killed him. Owing to the density of the vapour, Mr. Swan could not secure the second man, but had to come on deck much affected. On recovering he again went down and succeeded in sending the man up, but he had succumbed to the effect of the gas. Great risk was incurred, as when Mr. Swan first came up he was so exhausted that he could not stand for some time.

Cholmondeley, C.E., Sergeant, 3rd New Zealand Contingent. Case 31342

On a date between the 22nd March and 6th April, 1900, a number of men belonging to the Third New Zealand Contingent, after giving their horses a wash in the sea at East London, went out themselves for a swim, when one of them named Franks, was unable to get back. Lieutenant Walker and Trooper Harper went to his assistance, but Lieutenant Walker himself got into difficulty, while Harper, with the aid of a rope, got Franks in. Sergeant O'Farrell and Trooper Cross then went to Walker's help. Sergeant Cholmondeley seeing them some distance out, went towards them and assisted O'Farrell into shallow water, and then going back he caught Lieutenant Walker and brought him to shore in an unconscious state. The beach where the accident took place is sandy, on which heavy seas were breaking, there being a rapid current of which the men were unaware.

Lecky, H.S., Sub-Lieutenant, R.N., H.M.S. *Widgeon*. Case 31365

On the 25th August, 1900, H.M.S. *Widgeon* was anchored at Kosi Bay, some fifty miles south of Delagoa Bay, for the purpose of landing troops and stores, the work being accomplished by means of surf boats. Heavy breakers rolling in about fifty yards apart made the work exceedingly dangerous. One boat loaded with stores and having eight men on board was capsized about 300 yards from shore. By dint of hard swimming and with the help of the oars six of the men managed to reach land. The other two men clung to the boat, which drifted keel upwards in a line almost parallel with the shore, being constantly swept by huge breakers, and the men had great difficulty in retaining their hold. When about 150 yards from the beach Sub-Lieutenant Lecky threw off his clothing and plunging into the surf endeavoured to swim to their help. He was twice thrown back on the beach by the heavy seas, but ultimately succeeded in bringing first one and then the other safe to land. Both men were quite unconscious, having been nearly half an hour in the water, but recovered on application of the usual method of treatment.

Extreme risk was incurred, not only from the sea, but from sharks, which were observed both before and after the accident.

Heath, Ida Ethel, Miss., Bigbury Bay, South Devon. Case 31502

About 4 p.m. on the 6th August, 1901, Miss B. Cornish-Bowden, Miss E.M. Hare, and Mrs. Colley were bathing from the beach in Bigbury Bay, South Devon. Miss Cornish-Bowden, who is unable to swim, soon got out of her depth, and being carried seaward called for help. Miss Hare at once went to her assistance, but also got into difficulty, when Mrs. Colley went in but could not effect the rescue, and was also in danger. Mr. Thomas Heath and his daughter now came up, and seeing the three ladies struggling in the water, at once plunged in without removing any of their clothing, and by their united efforts were successful in bringing all three safely to land. There was a strong seaward current, the distance from shore being twenty yards, so that considerable risk was incurred.

The Silver Medal was voted to Miss Ida E. Heath and the Bronze Medal to Thomas Heath.

Maynard, J.F., Sergeant, Royal Marine Artillery. Case 31567

At 3 p.m. on the 13th December, 1900, the Egyptian gunboat *El-hafir* got aground on a sand-bank in the Bahr-el-Seraf, a branch of the White Nile, about twenty miles north of Shambi. A large number of the crew at once got out on the bank and were pushing the steamer off when she suddenly swung round, leaving two men on the bank, from which they were soon swept away by the strong current. One of the men managed to gain a foothold about 300 yards from the steamer, the other being carried into deeper water about 700 yards from the steamer. Sergeant Maynard jumped from the top deck and succeeded in reaching the furthest man, but was greatly hampered owing to his pants slipping down and getting entangled round his feet. He, however, managed to support the man until several sailors followed with planks, on which he was placed, and they were towed back by means of a line, the second man being picked up by them in passing. The place where the accident happened is very dangerous, the current running five knots and the depth from three to nine feet, in addition to which crocodiles and hippopotami are very numerous. The man was half an hour in the water, being unconscious when rescued.

M'Donald, James, Boatman, Malling Bay, Inverness-shire. Case 31689

At 1 p.m. on the 8th May, 1901, a small sailing boat was capsized by a sudden squall in Malling Bay, Inverness-shire. The accident took place some 400 yards in a westerly direction from the pier at Mallaig and about seven yards from a small island known as Anchorage Island, the depth of water being thirty feet. There were four persons on board - James M'Donald, the boatman, Jessie and Nellie Cameron, and Helen Norman, these three girls having hired the boat for a sail. On the boat going over, M'Donald got all three girls on the keel, and the anchor breaking loose kept the boat from drifting. He then swam to the island and removed his heavy boots and some of his clothing, and returning to the boat he took off Nellie Cameron and conveyed her to the island. On the second trip he took Helen Norman to land, and after resting to recover from exhaustion, he again entered the water and rescued Jessie Cameron, who had been about half an hour on the upturned boat. Shortly afterwards they were seen on the island, and a boat put out and landed them on the mainland.

Francis, Andrew W., False Bay, Cape Colony. Case 31788
Borez, Antony, Fisherman.

On the 20th November, 1901, a fearful storm suddenly sprang up in False Bay, Cape Colony. An inner section of the bay is known as Kalk Bay, from which several fishing-boats were out at the time. With one exception all these boats managed to reach the land in safety. By the aid of a telescope the missing boat was discovered in distress, being apparently waterlogged or upset, and some men were seen clinging to her. In spite of the tremendous sea running it was decided to make an effort to reach her, Andrew W Francis and six others volunteering to make the attempt. Putting off in an ordinary boat, they, after a terrible struggle, reached the wrecked craft, to which two men were clinging, the other five members of the crew having been lost. The two men proved to be Antony Borez and his brother, and it was found that the younger Borez had been swept away from the boat no less than six times, and had on each occasion been brought back by his brother Antony. Having got the two men into their boat, Francis with his gallant crew, with the utmost difficulty and danger, gradually worked their way back to the beach, which was eventually reached in safety.

Silver Medals to A.W. Francis and Antony Borez. Bronze Medals to Thos. Eustaquio, Charles Ward, Indilla, jnr., Charles Flatwell, A. Diedricks, and A. Mathieson.

Wallis, Charles B., Lieutenant, Scottish Rifles., A.D.C. Sierra Leone Protectorate. Case 31809

About 4 p.m. on the 4th December, 1901, Lieut. C.B. Wallis, Scottish Rifles, Assistant District Commissioner, Sierra Leone Protectorate, with two soldiers of the West African Frontier Force and a boy, were in a canoe on the Big Bum River at Bahol, Sierra Leone. The river is here some 500 yards wide, and flowing with a strong current. When about midstream, in making a turn the canoe upset and turned bottom up. The boy swam to land, while one of the soldiers held on to the canoe, which drifted away, and was picked up some time after and taken to the bank. Lieut. Wallis started for land, but finding that the second soldier was unable to swim, and was drowning, turned back to his assistance, but on reaching him was clutched and repeatedly dragged under; but, being a powerful swimmer, he stuck to his man, and eventually landed him after being half an hour in the water. Extreme risk was incurred, not only from the strong current running, but from the numerous crocodiles which infest the river.

Lynch, Michael, Fisherman, Dublin.   Case 31826

About 1 a.m. on the 9th February, 1902, Christopher Gore, an old man of 72 years, by some means fell into the Liffey, near to Rogerson's Quay, Dublin. The river at this point is some 600 feet wide, the depth at the time about 30 feet, and the tide running out. The night was very cold, the temperature being 10 degrees below freezing.

Hearing cries from the river, Michael Lynch, fisherman, who was then on his way home, ran to the quay, and seeing the man in the water at once plunged in and, swimming out about thirty yards, succeeded after a hard struggle in taking the man to the ferry steps and landing him.

Great risk was incurred in going into the river, with no other person near to render assistance.

The Silver Medal was voted to Michael Lynch, and being in poor circumstances, the Committee added some pecuniary assistance.

Duckworth, Edward, Insurance Agent, Blackburn.   Case 31896

At 10.30 a.m. on the 22nd February, 1902, a lad named Alexander A. Baldwin, was sliding on the ice on a disused stone quarry at Blackburn, when a breakage took place and he fell through, sinking in from twenty to thirty feet of water.

An alarm being raised, Edward Duckworth, insurance agent, came up and, at once throwing off his coat, dived in and tried to find the lad, but in vain. The break extended about four yards from the bank, and Duckworth, on going down right under the ice, found it was too dark to see anything, and on rising to the surface nearly missed the opening through which he had dived, and had thus a narrow escape with his own life.

Baldwin's body was recovered some time after by means of a drag.

Pitman, Richard G., Commissioned Boatman, Coast Guard, St Ives.   Case 31935

At 3 p.m. on the 10th April, 1902, Arthur Mottram, a youth of 16, removed the cover of an old mine shaft at Treylon, near St. Ives, Cornwall, and began to descend an iron ladder inside, which had been there for many years. When his full weight came on the ladder it gave way, and he was precipitated down the shaft. His companions raised an alarm, and the coastguards hurried to the place, Richard G. Pitman volunteering to go down. With a rope around him he was lowered into the inky darkness of the shaft, and at the depth of one hundred feet found the lad on some timbers which in their fall had jammed in the opening, which varies in width from five to seven feet. Trusting to this frail and insecure support, Pitman took the rope from his own body and fastened it round the lad, who was then carefully got to the surface, when he was found to have his arm broken and suffering from various cuts and bruises. Meantime another rope was sent down, and by this his rescuer also reached the top, but in an exhausted state. Twenty feet below the obstacle in the shaft there was a depth of sixty feet of water; also the danger from impure air and from falling stones and timbers from the lining of the shaft.

Ahmed El Shamy, Able Seaman, Egyptian Coastguard Cruiser *Teyr-el-Bahr*.   Case 31963

About 4.30 p.m. on the 14th May, 1902, four sailors put off in a small boat from the Egyptian Coastguard cruiser *Teyr-el-Bahr*, then at the anchorage at Mersa Matamer, in the Red Sea, for the purpose of picking up a water-keg which had broken adrift and floated away. While attempting to lift the keg from the water the boat capsized, three of the men remaining underneath her. Able seaman Ahmed El Shamey, on coming to the surface, missed his comrades and at once dived under the boat three times, each time bringing out one of the sailors and placing them on the boat. Immediately this was done the boat again went over, throwing the men into the water, and El Shamy then gave two oars to one of the men and placed the other two on the boat, whence they were taken in an exhausted state by the cruiser. The sailor to whom the oars were given sank, and was drowned.

Petersen, Christian, Able Seaman, Barque *Dalblair*.　　　　　　　　　　　　　　　　　　　　　　　　　　　　　　　Case 31966

On the morning of the 4th February, 1902, the Glasgow barque *Dalblair*, when off the island of Mauritius, was caught in a cyclone, and eventually was driven on the reefs a little to the south and west of Mahebourg Harbour on the morning of the 5th. After the vessel struck tremendous seas continued to break over her, sweeping the decks and smashing three out of the four boats she carried. On the afternoon of the same day the remaining boat was launched, but soon after capsized, and of the ten men on board, seven only succeeded in reaching land. The following morning (February 6th) Christian Petersen, A.B., volunteered to swim to the reef with a line, and succeeding in his endeavour, communication was established, the captain and the remainder of the crew being safely landed.

Great risk was incurred from the heavy surf on the reef.

Irving, David, Chief Officer, S.S. *British Empire*.　　　　　　　　　　　　　　　　　　　　　　　　　　　　　　　Case 31989

About 3 p.m. on the 17th May, 1902, the Liverpool steamer *British Empire* was unloading at the port of Antwerp. When the hatches of No. 3 hold were removed a number of labourers went down to sling the cargo, and six of them were at once overpowered by the noxious fumes which had generated in that part of the ship. The remainder of the hatches were then taken off, and Mr. David Irving, chief officer of the steamer, having bound a handkerchief over his mouth, and a rope round him, went down, and, placing a second rope round the nearest victim, rushed up the ladder, the man being quickly pulled up after him. This he did five times, when Mr. Clifford Roberts took his place, and, in like manner, brought up the sixth man. Medical aid had been summoned, and three of the unconscious men were revived, but the other three had unfortunately succumbed to the effects of the foul gas.

The Silver Medal was voted to Irving, and the Bronze Medal to Roberts.

Freyone, Arthur, Calpe Rowing Club, Gibraltar.　　　　　　　　　　　　　　　　　　　　　　　　　　　　　　　Case 32030

On the morning of the 18th May, 1902, several members of the Calpe Rowing Club left Gibraltar in two boats to spend a day at Los Barrios, a village in Andalusia, fourteen miles distant. All went well during the day, but on the return journey a north-west wind set in and a rough sea was encountered. About 8 p.m. darkness came on and the boats became separated, one of them (the *Swallow*), with six persons on board, capsizing about two miles from land. The second boat reached the port in safety. When the *Swallow* went over three of the occupants managed to cling to her, two others being swept away, but Mr. Arthur Freyone, who was the sixth person on board, succeeded in bringing them back to the upturned boat, to which he exhorted them to cling, he himself starting to swim to shore for help. Owing to the darkness and strong current this was a most difficult task, but he kept on. Meanwhile the repeated shouts of those on the wrecked boat had been heard by the Spanish guard, and some fishermen being told they at once put off in their boat and picked up the five men. This rescue boat was heard by Mr. Freyone, but he kept silent as it passed near him so as not to delay the rescue of his comrades. Eventually he reached land, and tried to get further help before falling unconscious on the beach.

Extreme risk was incurred from the rough sea, the jagged rocks fringing the shore, and the darkness of the night.

Herr Bongard, Secretary to the German Government, Dar-es-Salam.　　　　　　　　　　　　　　　　　　　　　　　　　　　　Case 32044

On the 22nd July, 1901, a Zanzibar dhow left the harbour of Dar-es-Salam, there being a strong wind blowing at the time. When the vessel was about 300 yards from shore, the sail broke loose and knocked an Indian child overboard. It was impossible to reach it from the dhow, and none of the natives lining the shore would venture out for fear of the sharks, which are numerous in these waters. At this juncture Herr Bongard, Secretary to the German Government, chanced to come up, and on being told what had occurred, gallantly plunged in, and swimming to where the child was, picked it up and restored it to its mother on board the dhow, then starting to swim to land. When within about 100 yards from shore his strength failed him, and as no one would go to his assistance, he threw himself on his back, and, as the tide was coming in, he in this way floated in, reaching the shore in a most exhausted state.

Great risk was incurred, not only from drowning, but from the sharks which here abound.

Webster, R.V., Captain, Cape District Mounted Troops Port Elizabeth. Case 32379

On the morning of the 1st September, 1902, a terrific gale, which had lasted all the previous night, was raging along the South African coast. In the vicinity of Port Elizabeth twelve sailing ships were driven on shore and wrecked, more than fifty lives being lost. About 10 a.m. eight or nine men were seen clinging to the rigging of one of these vessels, and it being evident that they could not for long maintain their hold, being nearly frozen by the intense cold and bitter wind, Captain Webster volunteered to try and take a line out and thus effect their rescue. Four times did he make the attempt, but was on each occasion driven back by the tremendous seas. Later in the day, when the storm had considerably abated, three other men who attempted a similar rescue were swept out to sea and drowned.

Extreme risk was incurred, the sea being exceedingly rough and full of floating wreckage, while the locality abounds with sharks.

Robson, William, Farmer, Carlisle. Case 32385

On the 3rd November, 1902, James Thomas Turner, a labourer, was engaged in cleaning out a tar still at the Grimsdale Bridge Tar Distillery, near Carlisle. During the dinner hour foul gas had accumulated in the still, and on returning to his work at 1.30 p.m. Turner was struck down unconscious. The still is circular, seven feet ten inches deep, seven to eight feet in diameter, and is entered by a manhole at the top, the bottom being reached by a ladder.

George Walker, a fellow workman, on discovering the accident, at once went to his assistance, but was also rendered unconscious. Efforts to reach the men with a rake failed, and none of the other workmen would venture down. About twenty minutes after William Robson, a neighbouring farmer, came on the scene, and learning the state of affairs, volunteered to go down. With a rope round him and a wet cloth over his mouth he entered the still twice, each time getting a rope round one of the men, by which they were drawn up, but all efforts at restoration failed, they having succumbed to the effects of the noxious fumes.

The Silver Medal was voted to Robson and an In Memoriam, to relatives of George Walker.

Senior, William, Foreman Moulder, Dewsbury. Case 32400

On the forenoon of the 15th November, 1902, an outbreak of fire occurred in the oil store at the Victoria Foundry, Dewsbury. The store is situated under the main offices, and is reached by going down a flight of steps, at the bottom of which the door opens inwards. Dense black smoke laden with poisonous fumes was issuing from the cellar, in which a man and boy were employed when the outbreak took place. The man, named Pickard, had evidently made for the door, but, being overcome, his body fell against it preventing it being opened. William Senior, foreman moulder, determined to try and effect the rescue of the two men. He succeeded in partially opening the door and was able to get Pickard's body round it, when he had to retire, being nearly overcome by the fumes. A man named Thompson then attempted to enter, but was struck down, when Senior again rushed in and dragged him out, both being assisted up the steps.

Pickard unfortunately did not recover, and the boy also lost his life.

French, Herbert C., Captain, Royal Army Medical Corps. Case 32417

On the 17th November, 1902, H.M. transport *Wakool*, on a voyage from Singapore to Calcutta with troops on board, was off the south-west point of the Malay Peninsula, steaming at the rate of twelve knots, the weather being fine and the sea smooth. About 5.15 p.m. a coloured stoker, evidently intent on suicide, threw himself from the ship. Hearing the cry "man overboard," Capt. Herbert C. French, who was on the promenade deck, at once jumped after him from a height of thirty-six feet, but the man went under before he could reach him.

Meanwhile the transport had stopped and a boat launched, which picked up Capt. French and also the body of the unconscious stoker, who was eventually restored by means of the treatment usual in such cases.

There was great risk from the sharks which abound in these waters.

Pett, George, Cement Worker, Rochester.   Case 32424

Between 2 and 3 p.m. on the 27th November, 1902, W.J.Hermitage and Richard J. Bigg were at work in a kiln at the Borstal Cement Works, Rochester, when Hermitage was overcome by fumes from an adjoining kiln. Bigg at once called for help, and endeavoured to carry his comrade to the ladder, but himself lost consciousness. George Pett then called Henry Hill, the foreman, and went down in the kiln, followed by Hill, and as they were dragging Hermitage to the ladder Hill was overcome by the fumes, but Pett managed to get his head through the eyelet-hole and call for help before he himself lost consciousness, being eventually dragged out by another workman named Payne. Ropes were now procured and a rescue party formed, Ernest Godden, with a rope round his waist, being the first to go down, taking with him a spare rope with a noose, which he was able to fasten round Hermitage, and both men were then dragged out, Godden being nearly exhausted. John Tong then went down with a rope in like manner, which he fastened round Hill, and both were got out, Tong being unconscious. Edwin Harmer now went down, and in the same way got a rope round Bigg, and was also unconscious when drawn up. Artificial respiration was then used, but Hermitage, Bigg, and Hill did not recover. Tong and Harmer recovered soon after being got out.

Extreme risk was incurred owing to the deadly nature of the fumes.

The Silver Medal was voted to George Pett, Bronze Medals to Godden, Tong, and Harmer and "In Memoriams" to the relatives of Hill and Bigg.

Main, Andrew, Seaman. Schooner *Benmore*.   Case 32506

About 1.30 p.m. on the 4th March, 1903, the schooner *Benmore* was capsized by a sudden squall some two and a half miles outside the harbour at Stonehaven, and foundered. The catastrophe was noticed by a man at the village of Cowie, about a mile from Stonehaven, to which he hastened and alarmed the fishermen, who at once got a boat ready and proceeded to the scene of the wreck, in the hope of picking up any of the survivors. When the place was reached two men, Andrew Nain and James Pirrie, were found on some floating wreckage and taken on board the boat. When found Pirrie was lashed to a spar and unconscious. It transpired that when the schooner went down Main, finding that Pirrie was exhausted, got a rope round him, and thus managed to keep him afloat, the sea at times breaking clean over them, making it extremely difficult for a man to retain his hold, much less to give help to a comrade. These two men were the only survivors.

Brooke, R.G., Major, D.S.O., 7th Hussars.   Case 32536

On the 16th February, 1903, in connection with the recent operations in Somaliland, a party consisting of Bombay Sappers and Miners and 2nd. Sikhs arrived at Belambeli to sink and clean out wells. Those wells which required cleaning contained a quantity of decayed vegetable matter and putrid filth, which gave off poisonous gases. A man of the Sappers and Miners, went to the bottom of one of the wells, became unconscious from this cause, and Sepoy Ratan Singh, of the 2nd Sikhs, went down and managed to get a rope round him, when he himself was overcome. As the first man was being hauled up his body caught under an overhanging ledge, and remained fast. Major Brooke, seeing what had happened, at once went down and cleared the body from the ledge, and going on to the bottom got a rope round Ratan Singh, who was then drawn up. Another rope was lowered to Major Brooke, who was brought up just in time, as he was on the verge of fainting. Ratan Singh was unconscious for four hours after rescue.

Again in Wargallo, on February 28th Major Brooke went down a well and rescued a man after two others had failed in an attempt to reach him.

Great risk from inhaling the poisonous fumes.

The Silver Medal was voted to Major Brooke, and the Bronze Medal to Sepoy Ratan Singh.

Barnes, Philip, Pottery Worker, Reading.　　　　　　　　　　　　　　　　　　　　　　　　　　　　　　　　　　　　Case 32557

At 12.30 noon on the 8th May, 1903, John Chapman, employed at the Groveland Pottery Works, Reading, was altering the weights on a machine, and had occasion to go into a pit below it, the entrance being by a manhole, when he was overcome by foul gas which had accumulated in the pit. Alfred Watts, who was assisting in the work, saw him fall, and on going to his assistance was also struck down. Geo. A. Clarke, another workman, seeing the position of his comrades, was then lowered down by a rope, but was immediately overcome by the poisonous gases and was drawn up. Efforts were then made to reach the men with rakes, but without success. Philip Barnes then volunteered to go down, and was lowered into the pit, where he succeeded in fastening a rope round Watts. Barnes was quickly drawn up and Watts after him. Barnes again went down to try and rescue Chapman, but became partially overcome before being able to get the rope round him, and was drawn up. After resting he again went down, and this time managed to get the rope round Chapman, who was then got to the surface. Both men were removed to hospital in a critical state, and Chapman did not recover consciousness for twenty-four hours after.

Extreme risk was incurred owing to the deadly nature of the gas.

The Silver Medal was voted to Philip Barnes, and Bronze Medals to Watts and Clarke.

Kiddle, Edward B., Commander, R.N., H.M.S. *Albion*.　　　　　　　　　　　　　　　　　　　　　　　　　　　Case 32608

At 11 a.m. on the 4th December, 1902, while H.M.S. *Albion* was in lat. 4 29 N., lon. 106 11 E., steaming at the rate of eight knots, and not under full control owing to the steering position being shifted from the fore to the after conning tower, there being a slight swell on at the time, Charles F. Stubbs, Petty Officer Second Class, fell overboard from the net-shelf. A lifebuoy was at once let go, and Commander Kiddle jumped from the quarterdeck, and, securing the lifebuoy, towed it to where Stubbs was, and eventually both were got on board.

The danger incurred was considerably enhanced owing to the existence of sharks in these latitudes.

Marshall, John, Iron Worker, Chesterfield.　　　　　　　　　　　　　　　　　　　　　　　　　　　　　　　　　Case 32653

At 3 p.m. on the 15th June, 1903, John Brassington descended a well or sump at the works of the Stavely Coal and Iron Company, near Chesterfield, for the purpose of attending to the suction-pipe of the pump, when he was overcome by foul gas, and fell into 3 to 4 feet of water at the bottom. The sump is about 17 feet deep, the manhole being formed by a 42 inch pipe, in which a ladder is placed for the purpose of reaching the suction-pipe. On seeing Brassington fall from the ladder, George Henstock, a fellow workman, went to his help, but was also overcome, and fell to the bottom. Fred Booth, another workman, now went down with a rope round him, but being overcome was hauled up.

The outer covering of the sump was then removed, and Marshall, with cloth over his mouth and nostrils and a rope round him, went down and managed to secure Henstock with another rope, by which he was pulled up. Marshall then performed a like service for Brassington, when he himself was overcome and drawn to the surface. Booth and Henstock recovered under restorative treatment, but Brassington was dead. Great risk was incurred from the deadly nature of the gas.

The Silver Medal was voted to John Marshall, and Bronze Medals to George Henstock and Fred Booth.

Noble, Alfred Robert, Mossel Bay.　　　　　　　　　　　　　　　　　　　　　　　　　　　　　　　　　　　　　Case 32682

On the morning of Friday, the 13th March, 1903, Mrs R.C. Ferris (wife of the Civil Commissioner, Mossel Bay) and baby. Accompanied by her daughters Maud and Gladys, with Mr. Noble and a native driver, went on a visit to George, Cape Colony, in a cart drawn by four horses. On reaching Cook's Drift the water was very high owing to previous rain, and the driver was advised not to risk passing, but he replied there was no danger, and immediately went in.

The current being very strong turned the leaders down stream, and the driver, loosing all control of the horses, flung away the reins and sought to save himself, the cart and horses meantime drifting down the river. Mr. Noble threw out the front seat for more room, and the cart tilting over on one side was gradually filling when the two girls were washed out and carried under the cart. Leaving Mrs. Ferris and the baby in the cart, Mr. Noble dived and brought both to the surface, when they held on to the cart. Noble then took the baby and swam with it to the bank. Returning, he got hold of Mrs. Ferris and Maud, and succeeded in landing them also. Meanwhile the cart, with Gladys, had been carried a considerable distance down the stream, but running along the bank until he headed the floating mass, he swam out and called on the girl to let go, which she did, and having caught her he landed her in safety.

All four horses were drowned, the depth of the river being about 14 feet. Great risk was incurred, not only of drowning, but of being kicked by one of the struggling horses, Mr. Noble being once struck on the leg and knocked under water.

Lambart, Ford A.O., Electrician, East London, South Africa.   Case 32911

At 11 a.m. on the 8th March, 1903, John C. Wilson was bathing from the beach at East London, South Africa, and being ignorant of the coast, got into the under-current, and was carried out about 120 yards, the depth being 15 to 18 feet. There was an off-shore wind blowing, with heavy backwash and surf. Mr. Lambart, who was also bathing, swam out to his assistance, and after a severe struggle succeeded in landing him in an unconscious state.

Maung Kynn Bin, Coolie, Burma   Case 32947

At 11 a.m. on the 12th June, 1903, an Indian boy named Bukread, aged about ten, in trying to jump on to the landing stage from a steamer, fell into the Irrawaddy river at Prome, Burma. There was a very strong current running at the time, and the depth about 30 feet. Maung Kyun Bin, a Burman coolie seeing the boy being rapidly carried away, snatched up a small metal anchor buoy, and plunging in, caught him after swimming about 100 yards, and lashed him to the buoy. He then swam towards the bank, pushing and pulling the buoy with him, and eventually reached land after covering a distance of 250 yards, having been in the water some twenty minutes.

Booker, Henry, Labourer, Hornsey.   Case 33036

At 3.30 p.m. on the 5th August, 1903, three workmen in the employ of the Hornsey District Council opened a manhole in Woodside Avenue, Muswell Hill Road, for the purpose of removing some stoppage in a drain which enters the sewer near the manhole. The sewer is here some 23 feet below the level of the roadway. After the obstruction had been removed one of the men went down to see that everything was clear, and he was overcome with sewer gas. The other two men going to his assistance were overcome, and all three rendered unconscious. On this becoming known Henry Booker volunteered to go down, and with a wet cloth over his mouth and a rope round his waist, he descended the manhole and succeeded in fastening ropes round each of the men, who were then hauled to the surface, two of them being taken to the hospital and the third to his home.

The risk incurred was suffocation by sewer gas, the deadly nature of which is well known.

Watkins, William, Sewer Flusher, Hornsey.   Case 33078

At 3.50 p.m. on the 5th August, 1903, two workmen in the employ of the Hornsey District Council descended a manhole in Woodside Avenue, Muswell Hill, for the purpose of removing some obstruction in a drain which here enters a sewer. After a clearance had been effected the men were overcome by sewer gas and fell down unconscious some 23 feet below the surface. On this becoming known William Watkins at once volunteered to go down to their help, and this he did without ropes or any other requisite for ensuring his own safety. On reaching the bottom he at once succumbed to the effects of the gas, and fell down near the men he was trying to help. All three were finally rescued by Henry Booker, who received the Silver Medal in Case 33036, the claim of Watkins for recognition not being put forward till a later date.

The risk incurred was suffocation by sewer gas, the deadly nature of which is well known

Blackett, William C. Mining Engineer, Sacriston Colliery, Durham. Case 33080
Tate, Simon, Colliery Worker.
Walker, William, Colliery Worker.
Brass, John, Colliery Worker.
Hall, John, Colliery Worker.
Blackburn, Henry, Colliery Worker.

At about 11.30 a.m. on the 16th November, 1903, a sudden inrush of water took place at the Sacriston Colliery, Durham, which flooded the workings, and by which three men were imprisoned. In the intervening part of the colliery the water reached the roof, necessitating pumping operations on a large scale before it was at all possible to reach them, and it was not until a lapse of ninety-two hours that this was accomplished. Throughout the whole of this period constant attempts were being made to penetrate to where it was known the men must be. William C. Blackett, mining engineer, took the lead in directing these operations, others who specially distinguished themselves being Simon Tate, William Walker, John Brass, John Hall, and Henry Blackburn. Continual risk was incurred by all these men, not only of drowning, but by sudden falls from the roof, the supporting timbers having been washed away, the presence of fire damp and foul gases making it impossible to use the ordinary miner's safety lamp, resort being had to the use of electric hand-lamps.

Ultimately, on the 20th November, the water level was so far reduced as to render it possible to swim to where the men were, and one of them, Robert Richardson, was got out alive, the other two, John Whittaker and T. McCormick, having succumbed.

Groombridge, William, Works Manager, Birmingham Cold Storage Company. Case 33091

At 9.10 a.m. on the 11th January, 1904, John Henry Carter, electrical engineer, employed at the works of the Birmingham Cold Storage Company, was engaged in the engine-room, where one of the pipes connected with the refrigerating apparatus burst. The engine-room was immediately filled with ammonia vapour, by which Carter's throat and respiratory organs were badly scalded, causing him to fall down on the floor. Hearing the noise of the explosion, William Groombridge, manager at the works, at once went to the engine-room, which was full of ammonia fumes. Hearing that Carter was still alive, he crawled in on his hands and knees, and, finding him about six yards from the door, he with considerable difficulty dragged him out, but he died in hospital on the following day. Great risk was incurred, Mr. Groombridge himself being in a fainting condition when he got Carter out.

Owen, William P., Lance Corpl. 2nd Batt. Royal Welsh Fusiliers. Case 33102

At noon on the 2nd November, 1903, while the 2nd Batt. Royal Welsh Fusiliers, on the march from Chakrata to Meerut, were fording the river Jumna at Kalsi, Private W. Fermalon was swept away and carried over a rapid below the ford. Between this, and a second rapid some forty yards lower down, the river ran very fast, smooth, and deep. Lance Corpl. W.P. Owen had run along the bank, and without a moment's hesitation dashed into the torrent and caught the drowning soldier. It now appeared that both would be swept over the second rapid, which was of a dangerous nature, but when within a couple of yards of this Owen managed to reach the bank and gain a footing, when both were assisted to land.

Frogley, Henry, Petty Officer 1st Class, R.N., H.M.S. *St. Vincent*. Case 33120

At 7.15 p.m. on the 10th February, 1904, Arthur J. Elkins and Harry Mitchell, boys on board H.M.S. *St. Vincent*, at Portsmouth, were being hoisted in a gig, when the foremost fall carried away, precipitating both into the water. The night was cold and dark, with a strong flood-tide and a gale of wind blowing, the depth being six fathoms. Henry Frogley, 1st class petty officer, who was supervising the hoisting of the boat, seeing the danger, at once dived off the platform alongside the ship and swam to their help. He caught Elkins, who was about five yards away, and brought him back to the boat, which was hanging with her bows in the water. Leaving him clinging there, Frogley then went to the assistance of Mitchell, and kept him afloat till they were picked up by a boat from the ship.

Frogley ran considerable risk of being washed against the ship's side and thus injured.

Gunner, George W., Police Constable, City Police.   Case 33121

At 1.20 a.m. on the 28th February, 1904, an unknown woman was seen to mount the parapet of the Blackfriars Bridge, between the second and third arches, and throw herself into the Thames. The night was cold and frosty, with the tide running out at about nine miles an hour. George W. Gunner, Constable, City Police, who was on duty on the bridge and saw the woman jump off, at once threw off his greatcoat, lamp, belt, and helmet, and sprang after her from a height of 45 feet. On coming to the surface he swam towards her, but when about six yards away she sank and was not seen again. Gunner then swam towards a small boat near the Steamboat Pier, where he held on till picked up by two firemen, who put off from the Fire Float Station in a boat. He was then in a most exhausted state, having been in the water for ten minutes. Great risk was incurred, not only by leaping from the bridge, but from the dangerous undercurrent at this particular place.

Mansell, Charles, Able Seaman, R.N., H.M.S. *Tauranga*.   Case 33317

At 10 p.m. on the 13th October, 1904, while H.M.S. *Tauranga* was in Cook Strait, off Wellington, New Zealand, the sea being rough, with a heavy gale blowing, Lieutenant A.J. Payne was washed overboard. A lifebuoy was thrown and the ship's way stopped. It being impossible to lower a boat owing to the rolling of the ship, Charles Mansell, A.B., had a grass line made fast round his waist, and jumping in, succeeded in reaching the officer; but the bight of the line having become foul in a gun-port, the next roll of the ship parted them with a jerk, and Lieut. Payne was drowned, Mansell being with great difficulty pulled on board in an exhausted state.

Milman, Daphne E.D.Hart, Miss., Lake Windermere.   Case 33636

At 12.30 p.m. on the 20th September, 1904, Miss Milman, with her sister, Miss R. Milman, and Miss D.F. Richmond, took a boat and went some distance out on Lake Windermere with the intention of bathing. Miss D. Milman dived in from the boat, Miss Richmond, who was a poor swimmer, going in from the opposite side, while Miss R. Milman remained in the boat. Suddenly Miss Richmond got into difficulty, and on Miss D. Milman going to her assistance she was clutched and dragged under water. An oar was now thrown to them from the boat, but was insufficient to support both, and they again went under. The boat had now drifted some distance away, and with only one oar Miss R. Milman was unable to reach them owing to the rough water and current, and she therefore paddled to the nearest land, and running to the boat-house, got another boat, with two oars, with which she returned. Meantime the boat she had left drifted some way out, and Miss D. Milman, being much exhausted, made a supreme effort, and reaching it got in and paddled back to where the body was. Finding it impossible to get Miss Richmond from the water, she being now apparently dead, Miss D. Milman again jumped in, and the sisters, by their united efforts, got the body into the boat which Miss R. Milman had rowed out. Both then began artificial respiration, but it was half an hour before any sign of life appeared. They were now noticed and assisted to land, where the treatment was continued until Miss Richmond recovered.

Great risk was incurred by Miss D. Milman from her prolonged efforts in deep water.

The Silver Medal was voted to Miss D. Milman, and the Resuscitation Certificate to Miss R. Milman.

Pearce, Dan., Steward, R.M.S. *Rimutaka*.   Case 33824

At 10.50 a.m. on the 16th April, 1905, while the R.M.S. *Rimutaka* on a voyage to London was in lat. 9 N., lon. 26 W., and steaming at twelve and a half knots, a lady passenger in a fit of insanity leapt overboard. Pearce who is a steward on board the steamer, was below at the time, but hearing the cry "some one overboard!" he ran on deck and jumped from the stern of the vessel, fully clothed, and swam to a lifebuoy which had been thrown. Not seeing the lady, he swam away in the ship's wake, and after going some three hundred yards found her, and after a hard struggle got her into the buoy, and with difficulty kept her afloat till they were picked up by a boat after being thirty minutes in the water.

Danger from sharks and from the violence of the insane lady.

Eussoof Nobo, Lascar Coal Trimmer, P. & O. *Moldavia*.　　　　　　　　　　　　　　　　　　　　　　　　Case 33845

At 8.40 a.m. on the 14th April, 1905, while the P. and O. steamship *Moldavia* on the voyage from Sydney to Hobart was off Cape Deliverance, steaming at 16 knots, a native coal trimmer, Moossa Nassib, accidentally fell overboard. Instantly the cry "Man Overboard!" was raised, and Eussof Nobo, also a lascar coal trimmer, knowing he was only a poor swimmer, sprang after him, and succeeded in getting his heavy clothing off and supporting him till they were picked up by a boat which was lowered from the steamer. Moossa was much exhausted, and had to be lifted from the boat and carried on board. Great risk was incurred, the weather being cold and the locality abounding with sharks.

Large, Arthur G., Chief Officer, S.S. *Nicaraguan*.　　　　　　　　　　　　　　　　　　　　　　　　Case 33892

On the 19th March, 1905, the Leyland Line steamer *Nicaraguan*, on a voyage from Jamaica to Vera Cruz, ran ashore at the mouth of the Palma River, on the Mexican coast. The steamer was in a critical position, there being a heavy surf beating on the rocky shore, which was some three miles distant from where the vessel struck. The captain determined to communicate with Vera Cruz and ask for assistance. It being impossible to land owing to the heavy surf, Arthur G. Large, chief officer, was pulled as near as it was deemed safe for the boat to go, and divesting himself of his clothing, swam to land, a distance of about half a mile, sent off his message, and then returned the same way to the boat. The steamer, after being ashore for twelve hours, came off and resumed her voyage. Great risk was incurred from the numerous sharks which infest the locality.

Narrish, Edwin, Oxton, Notts.　　　　　　　　　　　　　　　　　　　　　　　　　　　　　　　　　　　Case 34002

At 6 p.m. on the 8th July, 1905, Alfred Foulds, a little boy aged two years, accidentally fell down a well at Oxton, Notts. The well was sixty feet deep, with two feet of water at the bottom. William Foulds, the father, then got another boy, and placing him in the bucket he was lowered down, but before reaching the bottom he called out that he was suffocating from the foul air, and was pulled up. Narrish was cycling through the village, and hearing what had taken place, he at once volunteered to go down, which he did, and brought up the child, but life was extinct. Great risk was incurred, not only from the foul air but from the rotten state of the windlass and chain by which he went down.

Shaik Mahomed Shaik Ally, Police Constable, Bombay.　　　　　　　　　　　　　　　　　　　　　Case 34155

At 10 p.m. on the 23rd April, 1905, a man named Kasum Jamal, when under the influence of liquor, lost his balance and fell down a well on Cruickshank Road, Bombay. The depth of water in the well was fifteen feet, and the distance from the top of the parapet wall whence the man fell to the surface of the water thirty feet. It was pitch dark at the time and Jamal could not swim. An alarm was raised, Police Constable Shaik Mahomed Shaik Ally, who was in plain clothes at the time, at once ran to the place, and jumping in, kept the man's head above water till ropes were brought and they were pulled out. Great risk of being clutched by the intoxicated person in the well.

Llewelyn, L.W., Miner, Cambrian Collieries, Clydach Vale.　　　　　　　　　　　　　　　　　　Case 34296
Price, Trevor, Miner.
Davies, David, Miner.
Davies, Morgan, Miner.
Davies, Daniel, Miner.
Williams, W.M., Miner.
Jones, William, Miner.

On the evening of Friday, the 10th March, 1905, a disastrous explosion took place in the No.1 pit, Cambrian Collieries, Clydach Vale, the general conditions connected with the explosion being more than usually dangerous; for not only was there deadly after-damp and other poisonous gases present in great quantities, but the fire which raged also was such as to render the work of rescue most difficult, the fact of thirty persons being killed and fourteen being injured testify to this. Forty-five men were at work in the six-foot seam, which is 410 yards below the surface, and seventy men in the lower seam when the explosion occurred.

A rescue party consisting of the above mentioned men, descended the No.2 pit, and after reaching the bottom made their way to No.1 shaft, and after releasing the cage, a work of two and a half hours, the seventy men here at work were sent to the surface.

The rescue party then ascended, and, changing cages, descended to the six-foot landing, and eventually, after penetrating as far as possible into the workings, succeeded in saving fifteen of the men in the upper seam.

Great risk was incurred by all from the terrific heat, after-damp, and danger from falls of roof, etc.

Keymer, A.E., Chief Engineer, S.S. *Fitzpatrick*.   Case 34343

On the 21st March, 1905, while the steamer *Fitzpatrick* was on a voyage from Rangoon to Penang, a lascar, while employed in washing the rails, accidentally fell overboard. A lifebuoy was thrown, but the man did not reach it. A.E. Keymer, chief engineer, then jumped in fully clothed, and securing the buoy, swam to the man, and supported him for thirty-five minutes, when they were picked up in an exhausted state.

Great risk incurred, these waters being infested with sharks.

Woolfield, Ernest, Police Constable, East Sussex Constabulary.   Case 34357

At 10.30 a.m. on the 10th October, 1905, a man named Wood was at work in a well which was being sunk at Plumpton, in Sussex. He had reached a depth of fifty feet when he felt himself being overcome by foul air, and called on his assistants to lower the bucket, but before this reached him he fell down unconscious. No one present would venture down the well to his assistance and further help was sent for. A short time after, Ernest Woolfield, constable, East Sussex Constabulary, reached the place, and at once volunteered to go down. He was lowered by a rope, and having secured Wood, both were drawn to the surface, and the constable at once used means for restoring the man to consciousness, in which he was successful.

Tuff, John, Iron Worker, Wansbeck Ironworks, Morpeth.   Case 34361
Hunter, John, Iron Worker.

At 1.30 p.m. on the 16th October, 1905, William Grey, after being warned of the danger, went into a furnace at the Wansbeck Ironworks, Morpeth, for the purpose of doing some slight repairs. The furnace had been recently charged and lighted, the level of the charge being some six feet below the charging doors. Before Grey completed the work he was struck down by the rising fumes. George Blackhall then went in with a rope, which he fastened round Grey, who was pulled out, he himself falling down in an unconscious state. John Tuff then went in to try and save Blackhall, but before he could get a rope round him he himself collapsed. Various methods were now tried to reach the men, and Tuff was got out without his rescuers actually entering the furnace. John Hunter, with a handkerchief over his mouth, then went in with a rope, and although seriously affected succeeded in fastening this round Blackhall, who was drawn up along with him. Artificial respiration was at once used, but Blackhall and Grey did not recover.

The Silver Medal was voted to John Tuff and John Hunter and an "In Memoriam" to the relatives of Blackhall.

Harvey, Joseph, Orton Elgin.   Case 34370

On the morning of the 5th October, 1905, Harvey and six other men who were engaged in reconstructing the railway bridge crossing the Spey at Orton Elgin were in a boat which was capsized in the river, this being at the time in flood. A raft was being used, and this was moored to the banks by ropes at various angles, the moorings being made insecure by the wrecked boat which had fouled them, and it was for the purpose of removing this boat that Harvey and his men went out. On the boat capsizing three men were swept away and drowned; two others clung to the bottom of the up-turned boat. Harvey caught hold of a small wire rope, and by hauling on this hand over hand he reached the bank in an exhausted state. On landing he saw the last man, Alexander Mitchell, in mid-river holding on to the same rope. He at once let down a lifebuoy to him, but it was then seen that Mitchell was becoming weak. Harvey then determined to go out along the rope, and on reaching Mitchell after a hard struggle found that one of his legs was fast under water. On his liberating this Mitchell was at once swept away and drowned, and Harvey got to the bank, where he became unconscious, in which state he remained for three quarters of an hour. The two men who were swept away on the up-turned boat were rescued by Alexander Cowie, who overtook them in another boat nearly two miles down the river.

The Silver Medal was voted to Joseph Harvey, a Testimonial on Vellum and pecuniary to Alexander Cowie.

Clinch, Robert D., Apprentice.   Case 34506

About 9.30 a.m. on the 11th March, 1906, five apprentices belonging to R.M.S. *Port Kingston* and one from the s.s. *Delta*, left the former vessel in the gig for a sail in Kingston Harbour, Jamaica. All went well until about 10.30, when the main sheet accidentally slipped and blew out to leeward, and in trying to secure this the boat was capsized, throwing all into the water.

Clinch, who was one of the party, being a strong swimmer succeeded in righting the boat, and then for two hours devoted himself to saving his companions, some of whom were unable to swim. Unfortunately, one of the youths named Wade became exhausted and sank, although Clinch tried hard to save him. Eventually a rescuing boat reached them, and they were picked up after being two and a quarter hours in their perilous position.

Great risk was incurred not only from the rising sea but also from sharks which abound in Kingston Harbour.

Davidson, Christopher, Second Hand, Steam Trawler *Southcoates*.   Case 34558

At 8.30 a.m. on the 14th February, 1906, the steam trawler *Southcoates* of Hull ran ashore on the south coast of Iceland. There was a strong south-east gale blowing with snow showers, the thermometer registering fifteen degrees of frost. It was impossible to launch a boat, as heavy seas were making a clean breach over the vessel where she lay about sixty yards from shore. Christopher Davidson, second hand on the vessel, volunteered to try to swim ashore with a line, and there being no other hope of saving the crew, the captain consented. Davidson then went over the side, and after a hard struggle succeeded in reaching land, and communication thus being established, the crew of eleven men were hauled through the surf and landed in safety.

Great risk was incurred, not only from the heavy seas and extreme cold, but also from the want of lifebelts, there being none on board.

Wilson, William, Works Manager, Maryhill Oil Works, Glasgow.   Case 34559
Munro, William, Works Boy.

At 7.30 a.m. on the 12th April, 1906, a man named Mathew, employed at the Maryhill Oil Works, Glasgow, entered a naphtha tank for the purpose of cleaning it and was overcome by the fumes, falling down unconscious on the bottom of the tank. William Wilson, works manager, went down to try to save him, and succeeded in raising him sufficiently to be reached from the manhole, and he was got out. Meanwhile Wilson had himself succumbed to the noxious fumes and fallen down unconscious. William Munro, works boy, volunteered to go down to his assistance, and a rope being fastened round him, he was lowered down and managed to fasten a rope round Wilson, and both were then drawn up. Medical aid being at hand, both men were at once treated, and afterwards recovered.

Jockie Bar, Fisherman, Steam Trawler *Linnet*.　　　　　　　　　　　　　　　　　　　　　　　　　Case 34898

At 8.40 p.m. on the 25th February, 1906, the steam trawler *Linnet*, of East London, was driven ashore about five miles from Fish Point, near Chalumna, about twenty miles eastward of East London, grounding about 200 yards from the beach. The lifeboat was at once got out, but broke away with a native boy on board, and was driven ashore. Jockie Bar, a Portuguese coloured fisherman, then tried to reach land with a line, but this broke, he himself, however, reaching the beach, where he remained all night. About 9 a.m. on the morning of February 26th Captain Oswald jumped overboard and swam towards shore, when Jockie, taking a plank, went out, and meeting him half way, gave him the plank, and then assisted him to land. A rope having now been got from a farm near by, Jockie swam out with it, and after five or six ineffectual attempts succeeded in taking it on board. A lifebuoy was then fixed to the rope, and in this way he brought two men ashore. With the help of several farmers who had come up, a rough raft was now constructed, and with this he made four journeys out to the wreck, and in spite of the heavy sea still running brought the remainder of the crew to land.

Extreme risk incurred from the heavy seas and from the sharp rocks on shore, the man being almost continually in the water for over six hours.

Fairtlough, James W., Lieut., R.N., Gun Vessel *Landrail*.　　　　　　　　　　　　　　　　　　　Case 35041

About 3.30 p.m. on the 4th October, 1906, the gun vessel *Landrail*, which had been used as a target for firing practice, was being towed back to Portland, when she began to heel over to starboard, and soon went down. The tug boat took off as many men as possible, the remainder being ordered to jump overboard just before she sank. One of these men named Wardley, a signalman, could not swim, and Lieut. Fairtlough, the officer in charge, kept him afloat for some minutes, the lop of the sea rendering the task very difficult, and eventually Wardley slipped from his grasp and was drowned, Lieut. Fairtlough and the other men shortly after being picked up by a boat.

Connell, G.D., Chief Officer, S.S. *Chupra*.　　　　　　　　　　　　　　　　　　　　　　　　　　　Case 35095
Webster, A.W., Fourth Officer.

On the afternoon of the 31st October, 1906, the British Indian Steam Navigation Company's steamer *Chupra* arrived in Bombay harbour with a fire burning in the hold. After anchoring, she was ordered out into deeper water, and the anchor had thus to be hove up, two of the native crew being sent down to the chain locker to stow the chain. On their going down they were struck down by foul gas which had accumulated as a result of the fire. This being observed, a third man went down, but was also overcome. The chief officer, Mr. G.D. Connell, then went down, and as the result of his efforts the third man was got on deck. Again Mr. Connell went down, and succeeded in sending up another man, who recovered, but has since died in hospital.

Mr. Connell being now joined by Mr. Webster, fourth officer on the steamer, these two went down, but the first officer being overcome, had to be got out. Mr. Webster now went down by himself, and succeeded in bringing up the third man, who was dead.

Great risk was incurred, both officers being much affected by the deadly gas which had penetrated from the burning hold.

Leverett, Sydney, Shipwright Diver.　　　　　　　　　　　　　　　　　　　　　　　　　　　　　　Case 35433

About 7.30 p.m. on the 12th July, 1907, Walter Trapnell, a shipwright diver, had gone down to the wreck of Torpedo Boat No.99 which had sunk at sea about four and a half miles E.S.E. from Berry Head, when his breast-rope and air-pipe became foul of some part of the wreck.

In order to effect his release Sydney Leverett went down, and after three hours work under water succeeded in liberating Trapnell and bringing him to the surface after being five hours under, but he died twenty-four hours later.

Although Leverett went down as part of his duty, there was extreme risk incurred, the depth being 25 fathoms, the state of the tide, the darkness of the night, the short supply of air, and the possibility of fouling some part of the wreck.

Neaber, Ernest W., Stoker, 1st Class, R.N., H.M.S. *Eclipse.*   Case 35669

At 8.45 p.m. on the 1st October, 1907, Richard Greening, petty officer 2nd class, was returning in the pulling cutter to H.M.S. *Eclipse* which was anchored at Yarmouth, Isle of Wight, when in stepping from the boat to the gangway he fell overboard and was being rapidly carried astern by the tide.

A lifebuoy was thrown, which he got hold of, and at the same time Ernest W. Neaber, stoker 1st class, jumped from the boat and helped to support him. About half a minute later John D. Bradley, A.B., also jumped from the cutter and swam to their assistance. A patent lifebuoy was let go and another boat lowered, the searchlight being brought into use in order to locate the men. Eventually all three men were picked up by the cutter about 200 yards astern of the ship.

The night was very dark, the current running three knots, with a strong wind and choppy sea.

The Silver Medal as voted to Ernest W. Neaber and the Bronze Medal to John D. Bradley.

Moores, James, Furnace Labourer, Derby Ironworks, Bolton.   Case 35813

At 1.20 p.m. on the 22nd January, 1908, John Thomas Shuttleworth entered a cupola or furnace at the Derby Ironworks, to chip off some clinker which he had previously forgotten to do. The furnace is about twenty-three feet high, the charge-hole, which is two feet six inches wide and three feet high, being about eleven feet from the bottom. The furnace was charged to within five feet of the charge-hole, and the fire had been lit about two hours. In about one minute of entering through the charge-hole Shuttleworth was struck down by the deadly fumes. John Naylor, a fellow workman, at once went in with a rope, which he got round him, but when being pulled out the rope slipped and he fell back. Meantime Naylor had himself been assisted out. James Moores then went in and again got the rope round him and steadied the body until it was got out, after which he himself was assisted from the furnace. Artificial respiration was tried for about three hours, but Shuttleworth did not recover. Both men were affected by inhaling the noxious fumes.

The Silver Medal was voted to James Moores, and the Bronze Medal to J. Naylor.

Gater, James, Miner, Brereton Collieries, Staffs.   Case 35847

About 4.40 a.m. on the 15th February, 1908, a sudden inrush of water occurred in the Coppice Pit at Brereton Collieries, Staffs, there being about forty men at work at the time. Instantly the miners dropped their tools and made their way towards the shaft through the quickly rising flood, some of them being at times washed off their feet by the rushing stream.

Daniel Ball, aged eighteen, was one of those working nearest to the fracture and experienced the full force of the inrush, being, with horses, coal tubs, and great pieces of timber, swept away headlong. Fortunately he was carried in the right direction towards higher ground, two others who were working with him being carried in another direction and drowned. In a bruised half-dazed state he kept scrambling along in total darkness, not knowing exactly where he was. In this condition he was found by James Gater, who at once went to his help and got him to his feet, and then with almost superhuman effort succeeded in taking him along the roadway, the water at times being up to their chins. Eventually safety was reached, and Gater then went to warn some other men of the impending danger, thus saving their lives. Three men in all were drowned.

Stenning G.J.F., Corporal, Royal Engineers.   Case 36027

About 2.30 p.m. on the 25th April, 1908, the American liner *St. Paul*, then on her outward voyage, came into collision with H.M. cruiser *Gladiator* in the Solent off Yarmouth, Isle of Wight. It was snowing hard at the time, the wind being fresh with a rough sea. The *Gladiator* was so badly damaged that she was run on shore, where she turned over on her side. On the alarm being given, all the men belonging to the 22nd Company, R.E., who were in Fort Victoria at the time, turned out and engaged in the work of rescue. The following men specially distinguished themselves in saving life.

Stenning, G.F.J.,	Corporal.	Silver Medal
Poole, B.,	Lance Corpl.	Bronze Medal
Creeth, G.W.,	Sergt-Major.	Bronze Medal
Griffith, H.D.,	Corporal.	Testimonial on Vellum
Ballard, C.G.,	Bugler.	"
Wiltshire, J.,	Corporal.	"
Peacock, J.,	Sapper.	"
Hill, C.,	Sapper.	"
Crisp, R.,	Lance Corpl.	"
Peacock, R.,	Sapper.	"
Turner, R.G.,	Lance Corpl.	"
Southern, J.H.,	Sapper.	"

Corporal Stenning swam out into deep water seven times and brought out seven men, he being then so much exhausted that he fell down on the beach.

Smith, Jeremiah, Millwright, Brymbo Steel Works, Wrexham.   Case 36405

At 7 a.m. on the 5th August, 1908, John Hallam, in the course of his usual employment, entered a flue at the Brymbo Steel Works, near Wrexham, for the purpose of cleaning it, and was overcome by an accumulation of gas. These flues or tubes are two feet three inches in diameter, and are used to convey gas from the coke ovens to the washer, there being manholes or openings about every sixteen feet. Hallam was midway between two of these openings when he became unconscious. On the alarm being given a fellow workman named Jeremiah Smith entered the flue and dragged him to one of the openings, when he also became unconscious, but it being now possible to reach them without going into the flue they were both pulled out.

Smith remained unconscious for two hours after being got out, but Hallam did not recover, and died about six hours after, in spite of all the efforts made to restore him.

Freeman, Henry, Ordinary Seaman., R.N., H.M.S. *Glory*.   Case 36479

At 11.30 a.m. on the 25th November, 1908, the s.s. *Sardinia*, which was on fire and burning fiercely, was run ashore off Ricasoli, Malta. The ship took the ground about seventy yards from the rocks, on which a heavy surf was breaking, the sea being very rough. At the moment of striking an explosion occurred on board which littered the sea with long entangling strips of cotton fabric. Several of the passengers at once jumped overboard and endeavoured to swim ashore.

Acting on his own initiative Henry Freeman, O.S., H.M.S.*Glory*, though fully clothed, took a lifebuoy and attempted to swim through the surf to one of these who was seen to be too exhausted to reach the rocks. Twice he was beaten back, but on the third attempt he reached the man and then made a signal to be hauled in, when it was found the rope had become detached from the buoy. He then towed the man towards the shore where he was eventually washed up alive, being the only one who jumped from the ship who escaped.

Freeman himself was ordered not to attempt to land but to swim seaward, and being carried round the bows of the *Sardinia* he managed to get far enough out to enable a launch to pick him up after being twenty minutes in the water.

Great risk incurred not only of being dashed on the rocks or against the burning vessel but also from entanglement in the cotton strips, which were very numerous.

Jones, William, Workman, St. Philip's Marsh, Bristol.   Case 36648

At 7.30 a.m. on the 8th April, 1909, two workmen in the employ of the Corporation were engaged in a sewer manhole at the end of Small Street, St. Philip's Marsh, Bristol. One of the men Samuel Lever, was below at the foot of the ladder examining the valve regulating the flow of tidal water, the other man John Gane, watching at the top. Suddenly there came a rush of sewer gas, and Lever fell down unconscious. Gane at once raised a cry for help and descended the ladder to the assistance of his comrade, but on reaching the bottom he also was struck down, falling across the body of Lever. At this time two other workmen named Jones and Carter were at a point some sixty-eight yards distant and hearing the cry for help they ran to the place. Jones, seeing what had happened, at once went down to the assistance of his fellow workmen, while Carter obtained a rope and lowered it to Jones, who although only partially conscious, got it round Lever, who was then hauled up. Again the rope was let down, and Jones with much difficulty got it round Gane who was also drawn up. Jones then made his way up unaided, and although suffering much from inhaling the deadly gas he at once began endeavouring to restore the unconscious men, and this, with the help of others, was successfully accomplished.

The Silver Medal was voted to William Jones and the Bronze Medal to John Gane.

Taylor, E.A., Commander, R.N., H.M.S. *Brittania*. Case 36649

At 11 a.m. on the 25th May 1909, Walter T. Toomer, shipwright, while securing a gun-port accidentally fell overboard from H.M.S. *Brittania* at sea in lat. 55 23 N., lon. 0 17 W. The ship was steaming twelve knots at the time, there being a lumpy breaking sea. The night type lifebuoy aft was at once let go but dropped about sixty yards from the man, who failed to see it owing to the lumpy sea. The lifeboat was now got away, but was some 300 yards from the buoy. Seeing that the boat was making slow progress the ship was brought round near to the man, who was now so exhausted that he failed to reach a circular lifebuoy which was dropped close to him, and Commander E.A. Taylor jumped overboard and took this buoy towards him, but before he could be reached he began to sink. Commander Taylor then let go the buoy and succeeded in bringing him to the surface and keeping him there until they were taken into the boat, which was close at hand.

When the Commander let go the buoy John Tucker, A.B., jumped from the forecastle and took it back to him thus rendering useful service.

The Silver Medal was voted to Commander E.A. Taylor and the Bronze Medal to John Tucker, A.B.

Maloney, James C., Police Constable, Barbados. Case 36763

At 12.30 p.m. on the 31st May, 1909, six men and three girls left Challenor's Jetty, Speightstown, Barbados, in a fishing boat, intending to sail to Holetown. When the boat reached Fort Shoal she was suddenly struck by a squall, and before anything could be done to save her she filled up and sank some 300 to 400 yards from shore. The men, with the exception of James C. Maloney, police constable, did nothing to save the girls, who were unable to swim, and as they held on to him he had great difficulty in keeping himself afloat. Finding he could not possibly support them all he called to a man named Wilson for help. Wilson then took one of the girls named McClean, but he lost his hold of her and she was drowned. Maloney then attempted to reach shore with the other two, and had nearly succeeded when a man named Earle took one of the girls and landed her, Maloney himself bringing in the third. There can be no doubt that but for the gallant efforts of Maloney the three women would have been drowned

Schembri, Rocco, Sewer Worker, Malta. Case 36803

At Malta on the morning of the 26th July, 1909, Rocco Schembri, Giovanni Azzopardi, Salvatore Mifsud and Guiseppe Grech were at work in the Marsamascetto sewer some 250 feet distant from the shaft, but had to give up work owing to the exhalation of foul gases.

On reaching the top, the pit being forty feet deep, Azzopardi found that he had forgotten his cap, and with R. Schembri went back to fetch it. On reaching the place where they had been working Azzopardi fainted, and Schembri also feeling the effect of the foul air ran back and called for help. Grech and Mifsud then went down together to save Azzopardi, but on reaching him they fainted.

As these men in the sewer did not answer his calls Schembri then went down again and found all three lying senseless in the sewage. He got hold of the nearest man and pulled him to the bottom of the shaft, tied him to a rope and helped him up.

He then returned for Azzopardi and carried him on his shoulders to the pit and he was hauled up, Schembri himself coming up also, as he was all but overcome. However, he again went down and tried to reach the third man, but could not effect this and came back for fresh help. Police-constable Guiseppe Spiteri and Salvatore Bugeja, a labourer, then volunteered to go down, and directed by Schembri reached the third man and carried him to the shaft, where he was hauled up. With medical assistance Mifsud and Grech recovered, but Azzopardi died some six hours later in hospital.

The subway in which the men were lying is about four feet high, and the width allows only one man to pass at a time. R. Schembri showed conspicuous bravery throughout the affair.

The Silver Medal was voted to R. Schembri; Bronze Medals to G. Spiteri and S. Bugeja; and Testimonials on Vellum to S. Mifsud and G. Grech.

Lee, Percy R., Beaumont Works, St. Albans.   Case 36827

On the 5th August, 1909, three men employed by the Urban District Council were engaged in emptying a dumb well or cesspool at the Beaumont Works St Albans. The well is used for the disposal of liquid chemical refuse from the Raincoat Factory, and is forty-one feet deep, the manhole at the top being only large enough to admit one person at a time, a rope and cross-bar being used for going down. About 12 noon William Pugh, who was working at the bottom, became affected by the gas, which was liberated when the sediment was disturbed, and called for the bucket to be sent down. On this being done he got in, but while being pulled up he became unconscious and fell to the bottom into the chemical refuse, injuring his head in the fall. Arthur Payne, a fellow workman, then went down by the cross-bar but was unable to fasten a rope round him, and feeling himself being overcome he was hauled up. Percy R. Lee then volunteered to go down and succeeded in fastening a rope round Pugh, who was then pulled up, Lee having remained at the bottom until the rope was let down and he was then drawn up.

Great risk was incurred from the deadly nature of the gas.

The Silver Medal was voted to Percy R. Lee and the Bronze Medal to Arthur Payne.

Birrell, Adam, Gentleman, Solway, Kirkcudbrightshire.   Case 37127

On the 6th August, 1909, a pleasure party consisting of four gentleman and one lady were in a motor boat on the Solway. When off Rascarrel Point, Kirkcudbrightshire, and about two miles from shore a spirit lamp was being used for preparing tea, when some petrol vapour, which had collected in the cabin, exploded blowing off the roof and setting fire to the boat, which in a few minutes was burned to the water's edge.

One of the party, Adam Birrell, showed marvellous courage and resource, seeing that each of the others was supplied with a lifebelt, in addition to which he unshipped the mast and put it overboard as a further means of support. When all were in the water Birrell placed the mast underneath the lady's arms, one of the others who could not swim also holding on to it, and after giving each member of the party instructions as what was best to be done he started to swim to shore, then about one and a half miles off, for help. Owing to the strong tide he was carried a considerable distance out of his course, and as darkness had set in it was only with the greatest difficulty that he eventually reached land, but in such an exhausted state that he had to crawl part of the way to the nearest farm-house, where an alarm was given.

On the rescuing boat, which at once put out, reaching those in the water it was found that two men had drowned, one man and the lady being picked up alive, but she succumbed a few minutes after being got into the boat.

Hallowes, Frederick H., Lieutenant, R.N., H.M.S. *Antrim*.   Case 37137

At 10.30 a.m. on the 24th October, 1909, Gerald A. Barnes and George Piggott, able seamen, were washed overboard from the picket boat belonging to H.M.S. *Antrim* during the passage from the gunwarf to Spithead.

Seeing that Barnes was sinking Lieut F.H. Hallowes jumped overboard into the heavy sea running and just succeeded in getting hold of him

Two lifebuoys were then thrown, but both fell short, and Sub-Lieut. Robert L.F. Hubbard at once jumped in and took one buoy to Lieut. Hallowes and Barnes; Theodore Joughin, Petty Officer, also jumped overboard and took the second buoy to Piggott. Frederick Fisher, A.B., then jumped in and assisted Lieut. Hallowes in taking Barnes back to the boat.

The Silver Medal was voted to Lieut. F.H. Hallowes and Bronze Medals to the others.

Drummond, George Richard, Electrical Engineer to the Maharaja of Bikaner, Rajputana, India. Case 37357

At 6 p.m. on the 4th January, 1909, the oilman at the Jail Well Engine Pumping Station at Bikaner, Rajputana, India, while oiling his pump near the bottom of the well, dropped his lamp on the platform, which caught fire, the well being 336 feet deep and 9 feet wide, with 10 feet of water at the bottom. The man came up, and water was thrown down in an attempt to extinguish the fire. Four men then went down, but on reaching the bottom two of these became unconscious, the other two returning to the top. Later another man went down to try to save his comrades, but was overcome about 40 feet from the bottom. The well was now filled with smoke and fumes, so that respiration was difficult.

Mr. G.R. Drummond, Electrical Engineer to the Maharaja of Bikaner, was sent for, and on reaching the place he at once descended by the ladder to the place where the last man to go down was lying, but, there being some delay in lowering the box which he signalled for, he was rendered so powerless that he could not lift the man into it when it arrived, and he returned to the surface, which he reached with difficulty. When somewhat recovered he again went down, this time in the bucket, taking one man with him, and another going by the ladder, and they were successful in getting the man into the bucket, all then returning to the surface. Knowing that the two unconscious men were about 40 feet below the point he had previously reached he descended for the third time, going by the ladder, two men at the same time going by the bucket, but when some 50 feet from the water Mr. Drummond became exhausted, and allowed these men to proceed alone, which they did, and reaching the unconscious men, got them into the bucket, and they were drawn up, they themselves returning to where Mr. Drummond was, and all then climbed up, and with difficulty reached the top. The first man got out recovered, but the other two were dead. There was great risk of being overcome by the smoke and poisonous fumes in addition to the excessive heat which prevailed in the lower part of the well.

Williams, R.R., Headmaster, Clydach Vale Council School, Rhondda Valley. Case 37557

About 4 p.m. on the 11th March, 1910, a reservoir or natural dam formed by some old colliery workings high up on the hillside above Clydach Vale, in the Rhondda Valley, burst, and the torrent of water, together with masses of earth and stone, rushed down the hillside with terrific force, sweeping away everything it encountered in its mad career. Following the conformation of the ground, it soon reached the village, the first house in its path being completely wrecked and the occupants drowned. Soon the Clydach Vale Council School, containing some 900 children, was reached, and the playground was flooded to a depth of 6 or 7 feet, the water rushing through the main corridor of the school into the yard. Realising the extent of the danger, the headmaster, Mr. R.R. Williams made his way to the girls and infants departments, directing what should be done to get the children out in safety. Often waist-deep in water, Mr. Williams passed from place to place, at one time being carried off his feet and with the greatest difficulty saving himself. In all this he was splendidly seconded by the assistant teachers and by some colliers who came to their help, so that in the end only two of the children lost their lives.

Cook, Thomas, Third Hand, Trawler *Thankful*. Case 37636

At 11.30 p.m. on the 6th August, 1910, F. Wilson, a fisherman belonging to the trawler *John Alfred*, in attempting to go on board his vessel in the Fish Dock at North Shields, slipped and fell in between the piles under the quay. A lifebuoy was at once thrown, but owing to the darkness was not seen. Thomas Cook, third hand on the trawler *Thankful*, who was on his vessel in the dock, at once jumped overboard fully clothed and swam to the drowning man, who three times dragged him under, but retaining his hold, he succeeded in supporting him until a flare-light was got, when both men were seen and help given in getting them on board, after being half an hour in the water, Wilson being in an unconscious state.

Chandler, Harold Victor, Able Seaman, Steamer *Holgate*.   Case 37756

At 4 p.m. on the 29th January, 1910, the London steamer *Holgate*, being in mid-Atlantic in lat 40 15 N., lon. 10 49 W., there being a high sea and the ship steaming at 8 knots, John Brien, a seaman, in a sudden fit of insanity threw himself overboard.

Harold V. Chandler, A.B. who was in the forecastle at the time, rushed on deck and at once sprang after him and, succeeded in reaching him, supported him until he became unconscious, when he became a dead weight, and Chandler becoming exhausted had to reluctantly let go and was himself picked up by the ship's lifeboat after being twenty minutes in the water.

Extreme risk was incurred, not only from the high sea, or of being pulled under by the drowning man, but from sharks, which are numerous in that locality.

Denham, Richard Charles, Sergeant, Royal Marine Artillery, H.M.S. *Duncan*.   Case 37861

At 4.15 p.m. on the 18th September, 1910, H.M.S. *Duncan* was in the Mediterranean in lat. 37 5 N., lon. 5 8 E., steaming at twelve knots, the sky being overcast and a considerable sea running, when Frank Pye, musician of the Royal Marine Band, deliberately jumped overboard with the intention of committing suicide. Sergt. Richard C. Denham, without removing any of his clothing, at once sprang from the quarter-deck and swam in the direction of Pye, who was then about fifty yards astern of the ship, but in spite of his utmost endeavour he was unable to reach him before he sank. Meanwhile the ship's lifeboat had been got out and Denham was picked up, a further search being then made for Pye but without success.

Great risk was incurred owing to the state of the sea, the speed of the ship, and the fact that the man was intent on suicide.

Hughes, Dunbar B.B., M.B., C.M. (Edin.), Grenada, West Indies.   Case 37927

At 2 p.m. on the 29th November, 1909, two men named Clouden and De Lisle, after landing a boat-load of provisions at the jetty at Carriacou, Grenada, W.I., were returning to their vessel when a heavy sea caught the boat, carrying it under the jetty and smashing it to pieces. Clouden clung to the iron-work of the jetty, while De Lisle was wedged in among the piles.

Dr. Hughes at once went in fully clothed and assisted Clouden from between the piles and succeeded in landing him. He then returned under the jetty and succeeded in liberating De Lisle, who was under water and unconscious, and further help now arriving he was got ashore but did not recover.

Great risk incurred, as had another wave broken while he was under the jetty he must have lost his life.

Richardson, Jesse, Police Constable, City Police, London.   Case 37935

At 9.20 p.m. on the 18th October, 1910, a man named McClintock was seen to throw himself from the centre of Blackfriars Bridge into the Thames. The tide was low, running at the rate of two and a quarter miles per hour through the arches and one and an eighth miles per hour in the open stream, the height from the water to the parapet being fifty-one feet, and the depth eight feet, the night being wet, cold, and very dark.

On an alarm being raised, Jesse Richardson, constable, City Police at once ran to the place, and throwing off his helmet and cape climbed over the parapet, and diving into the river swam after the man, but he sank before Richardson could reach him. The constable then swam to the columns of the railway bridge, where he was picked up by a boat from the fire-float *Alpha*, the body of the man being recovered the following day.

Great risk incurred owing to the tide being low, the darkness of the night, and the treacherous nature of the river at the point.

Tonge, Alfred Joseph, Pit Manager, Pretoria Pit, Over Hulton, Bolton. Case 37996

At 7.50 a.m. on the 21st December, 1910, a disastrous explosion took place at the Pretoria Pit, Over Hulton, near Bolton, by which some three hundred miners unfortunately lost their lives. Mr. Tonge, the manager, with a number of men acquainted with the mine, descended in the hope of being able to save some of those who were below. From the moment they reached the pit bottom they were in an atmosphere of noxious gases liable to ignite at any moment, rendering the work not only difficult, but exceedingly dangerous. For several hours they continued their exertions, no effort being spared by any of the men in their self imposed task of saving or attempting to save their less fortunate fellow workmen.

The Silver Medal was voted to Alfred J. Tonge and Bronze Medals to the following twenty-five men :-

Polley, Jas. H.	Hilton, John	Moss, Jas.	Hardman, John	Markland, Wm.	Williams, L.
Hartley, Jas.	Mangnall, Ben.	Greenhalgh, R.	Bullough, J.	Williams, John	Marsh, Wm.
Leigh, W.H. MRCS	Stott, Abraham	Russell, J.C., MB	Herring J.	Roberts, R.	Dixon, H.O.
Bullough, E.	Gerrard, J.	Corner, W.	Holliday, C.	Dixon, G.W.	Turton, J.
Schofield, W.					

An In Memoriam being sent to the relatives of W. Turton, who succumbed to the effects of the foul gas met with.

Thomas, A.W., Third Engineer, Steamer *Memnon*. Case 38100

At 2.45 on the morning of the 3rd March, 1911, W. Culley, a seaman on the Liverpool steamer *Memnon*, who had been sleeping on deck, accidentally rolled overboard at Winnebah, on the West African Coast. The vessel was at anchor one and a half miles from shore in six fathoms of water, there being a two and a half knot current running and the locality frequented by sharks. Ropes were thrown but Cully made no effort to secure them.

A.W. Thomas, third engineer on the steamer, then plunged in and having caught the man, supported him until a boat which had been got out reached them and picked them up. Cully being unconscious for two hours after rescue.

Risk of drowning and attack by sharks, several having been seen the previous day.

Davies, J.L., Third Engineer, Steamer *Konakry*. Case 38537

At 5.45 p.m. on the 4th July, 1911, while the Liverpool steamer *Konakry* was at Forcados, on the West African Coast, P.J.J. Morris, deck-boy, accidentally fell overboard and was being carried away by the strong ebb-tide then running. Although he was fully aware that the river is infested with sharks, J.L. Davies, third engineer on the steamer, sprang in from the taffrail, a height of thirty feet, and swam after the boy, but failed to reach him before he sank.

Davies who is not a strong swimmer, incurred risk of being swept away by the current and also from sharks.

Thomas, Charles John, Insurance Clerk. Case 38685

At 1.30 p.m. on the 6th August, 1911, the fishing boat *Honour* with a pleasure party on board was off the Nore lightship when the boat which was making twelve knots, jibbed, and the main-sail, swinging round, caught Harry Saunders, who was at the tiller, knocking him overboard. A heavy sea was running, which quickly carried him 200 yards astern, and being heavily clothed his position was most dangerous. Charles John Thomas, insurance clerk, plunged in from the boat, and swimming against the tide reached Saunders and succeeded in keeping him afloat for nearly a quarter of an hour, when they were picked up in a most exhausted state by the dinghy of the fishing boat.

Corbett, Noel M.F., Lieutenant, R.N., H.M.S. *London*. Case 38838

At 10 p.m. on the 13th December, 1911, while a cutter was proceeding from H.M.S. *London* to endeavour to rescue passengers from the P. & O. s.s. *Delhi*, which had gone ashore three miles south of Cape Spartel, on the Morocco coast, a big sea broke on board, half filling the boat and washing Geo. H. Luxton, A.B., overboard. Luxton is unable to swim well and had no lifebelt on, but managed to reach an oar, to which he clung. This occurred about a quarter of a mile from shore, in a depth of two and a half fathoms, with heavy breakers and a strong current, the weather being overcast with heavy rain squalls.

Lieut. Corbett undressed, and, taking a life jacket, jumped in and swam after him for about fifty yards and caught him, and after forty minutes exertion succeeded in getting Luxton ashore, both being in a very exhausted state. Also awarded the Sea Gallantry Medal.

Marsden, Arthur, Lieutenant, R.N., H.M.S. *Erne*. Case 38961

At 10 p.m. on the 25th March 1912, James Cameron, A.B. on H.M.S. *Erne*, was employed on a target which was being got ready for towing by H.M.S. *Exe* at sea off Parkeston. Before he got clear of the target the *Exe* went ahead, and the bowline he was wearing got round the mast of the target which was now being dragged away from the *Erne*'s side. Cameron succeeded in clearing himself, and jumping from the target attempted to swim back to the *Erne*, but became exhausted and called for help before reaching the buoy which had been thrown. Seeing that he was on the point of sinking, Lieut. Marsden plunged in from the bridge, fully clothed, and supported him for some five minutes, when they were picked up by a boat.

Great risk incurred, the night being dark and bitterly cold, with a choppy sea and strong rippling tide.

Hamilton, Guy, Lieut., R.N., H.M.S. *Invincible*. Case 38970

At 11.45 p.m. on the 9th April, 1912, John E. Mahoney, an A.B. on H.M.S. *Invincible*, fell overboard from the picket boat in the North Ship Channel entrance to Portland Harbour, the night being very dark with a nasty sea running. The boat was at once turned, and as soon as possible a lifebuoy was thrown close to the man, but he appeared unable to reach it.

Lieut. Guy Hamilton at once jumped in, fully clothed, and towed the buoy to Mahoney, and then swam back to the boat with him, he being in an unconscious state when got on board.

Williams, John Francis, Sub-Lieut., R.N. Case 39100
Cumberlege, Claude Lionel, Commander, R.N.

Shortly after midnight on the 28th May, 1912, the Harbour Service Launch *Dragon* was returning from Parkeston Quay, Harwich, to the collecting Torpedo Boat Destroyers, and when off H.M.S. *Swale* Alfred Castle, 1st class stoker, in attempting to leave the launch, fell overboard, and was quickly swept astern by the strong tide.

Seeing Castle struggling with his head under water, Sub-Lieut. J.F. Williams at once plunged in, fully clothed, and having caught Castle swam with him to the side of the *Swale*, when Commander Cumberlege, seeing their difficulty in the strong tide running, also went overboard and assisted in supporting Castle until the *Dragon* dropped astern and picked them up. The night was fine but pitch dark, with a strong ebb-tide.

Davies, Frederick Bryan, Clerk. Case 39124

At 1 p.m. on the 16th June, 1912, Frederick B. Davies and Thomas J. Holt were in a small sailing boat off Canvey Island at the mouth of the Thames, when a sudden squall struck the boat, nearly capsizing her, and throwing Mr. Holt overboard.

Mr. Davies at once dropped anchor and lowered the sail, then seeing that his companion could not regain the boat and was becoming exhausted, he jumped in to his assistance and supported him for some eight minutes, he being then in an unconscious state, when another boat came on the scene and picked them up. The sea was very rough, with driving rain, and Mr. Davies knew that there was little chance of regaining the anchored boat, wind and tide being both against him, and he was unaware of any other boat being in the vicinity.

Woolley, William D., Miner, Hollybush, Monmouthshire.   Case 39195
Winborn, Arthur T., Miner.
Leach, James, Miner.
Howells, Llewellin, Miner.

At 1.40 p.m. on the 18th May, 1912, an explosion occurred at the Markham Colliery, Hollybush, Monmouthshire, cause by an ignition of gas at a depth of about 350 yards. Four men standing on the top of the pit were blown considerable distances and killed, the shaft being much damaged, the air-pipes being wrenched from their fastenings and hanging in very dangerous positions. Only one man was down the shaft at the time a sinker named Snashall, and in order to save him a rescue party, consisting of W.D. Woolley, A.T. Winborn, Jas. Leach, and L. Howells, was formed, and these descended the shaft, each man wearing the Draeger breathing apparatus, and succeeded in bringing Snashall to the surface alive.

Considerable risk incurred, not only from the after-damp with which the shaft was filled, but from the dangerous position of the debris and loose hanging material through which they had to pass.

Thompson, Frederick G., Cellarman, Lion Brewery, Lambeth.   Case 39667
Jenner, George, Cellarman.

At 2.15 p.m. on the 5th November, 1912, John Weaver went into a vat at the Lion Brewery, Lambeth, for the purpose of cleaning it, and was overcome by carbonic acid gas which had accumulated. The vat is 9 feet 8 inches deep, entrance being gained by a manhole, 18 inches square, at the top. George Jenner, cellar-man, went down, but feeling the effect of the gas came out without being able to assist Weaver. Ropes had now been procured, and he went down again with a rope round him, and got the spare rope which he carried round Weaver, but could not fasten it properly, when he collapsed and was drawn out in an unconscious state. An attempt was made to pull the man up, but he slipped from the rope back to the bottom of the tank. Thompson, with a rope round him, now went down, and succeeded in getting a spare rope round Weaver, who was then drawn up after being fifteen minutes in the vat. He was at once removed to hospital and recovered.

Tallant, John, Mate of the Dublin Corporation s.s. *Shamrock*   Case 39732

At 9.30 a.m. on the 4th January, 1913, a gang of men were engaged cleaning out the sludge culvert and pit at the Pigeon House Sewage Outfall Works, Dublin.

Having finished their work the men ascended to the top, but a ducklight which was used in the course of their work was left behind, and one of the men, Christopher Leonard, went back for this and was seen to collapse. The depth of the shaft or manhole, which is entered from the pump-room, is about 21 feet.

Bartholomew O'Connor, with a handkerchief over his mouth went down, but also became affected and lost consciousness. Henry O'Brien was then lowered down by a rope, but also became unconscious and was drawn up. John Tallant, mate of the Corporation s.s. *Shamrock*, was then lowered down with a rope which he placed round O'Connor and both were drawn up. After seeing that proper means were being used to restore O'Connor, he went back down the shaft and got a rope round Leonard, but on reaching the top he was found to be dead. Several other men who assisted were considerably affected but soon recovered.

The Silver Medal was voted to John Tallant, and Bronze Medals to Bartholomew O'Connor and Henry O'Brien.

Todd, Albert, Carpenter, West India Dock, London. Case 39759

At 2.15 p.m. on the 19th December, 1912, Herbert Adams, while engaged in assisting to repair the lock gates at the Blackwall entrance to the West India Docks, had occasion to go down the manhole to hold the bolts and prevent them turning while the nuts were taken off, and was overcome by foul air which had accumulated. The manhole is 21 inches by 14 inches, the rungs which are let into the wall reducing this space to 21 by 10.

Albert Todd, carpenter, at once got a rope and attempted to reach Adams, but had to return owing to the foul atmosphere in the manhole. On recovering he again went down and succeeded in making the rope fast round one leg, but it was impossible to pull the man up in this way. He went down a third time and fastened the rope round both legs and Adams was then drawn up, but life was found to be extinct.

Luter, Frederick, Seaman, Steamer *Dunelm*. Case 39769

At 10.30 a.m. on the 11th January, 1913, the Sunderland steamer *Dunelm* in endeavouring to make the port of Blyth was driven broadside on amongst the dangerous rocks a little to the north of the harbour. There was no chance of getting the lifeboat out, and as tremendous seas constantly swept the decks of the vessel the position of those on board was perilous in the extreme. The Volunteer Life-saving Brigade were able to get within 150 yards, it being low tide at the time, but could not establish a connection with the ship, which was fast breaking up, and without which it seemed impossible to save the crew. Frederick Luter, a young seaman, then volunteered to swim ashore with a line, and with sea boots and heavy clothing on a lifebelt was fastened round him, and going overboard he succeeded in carrying a light line to the rocks, which he reached in a thoroughly exhausted state. Communication was thus established with the vessel, and the crew, fourteen in number, successfully landed.

The rescue was effected in a raging tempest of wind and snow, with the sea exceedingly rough, so that the greatest possible risk was incurred.

Washington, Charles, Gas Worker, Kensington Borough Council. Case 40009

On the afternoon of the 18th March, 1913, three sewer flushers in the employ of the Kensington Borough Council entered the sewer in Pembridge Place, Notting Hill, in search of an escape of coal-gas and were overcome and rendered unconscious. Charles Washington, who with a companion, was at work in another direction, was passing the entrance to the Pembridge Place sewer when he heard a call for help and at once went to the rescue of his comrades, but was also overcome by the gas and became unconscious. Meanwhile a number of firemen belonging to the London Fire Brigade had been summoned, and protected by smoke helmets, went down and succeeded in bringing up Washington and others, but the last man, named Parry, could not be found. After being treated at the hospital Washington volunteered to again go down and show two firemen where Parry was at work. These two men, who were provided with oxygen and smoke helmets, were unfortunately overcome and lost their lives, and Washington, although much exhausted and seriously feeling the effects of the gas, assisted in recovering their bodies and bringing them to the surface. Subsequently the body of Parry was got out by making an excavation in the road.

The greatest courage was displayed by the firemen, and especially by Washington, who was aware of the dangerous conditions existing.

The Silver Medal was voted to Charles Washington and Bronze Medals to the following men of the Fire Brigade :-

Dyer, A.R., Divisional Officer. Barber, A.E., Fireman. Pittaway, J., Superintendent.
Newberry, W.F., Fireman. Peck, A.G., Sub-Officer. Gordon, A.W., Sub-Officer.

In Memoriam Testimonials being given to the relatives of Firemen R.F. Libby and W. McLaren, who succumbed to the effects of the gas.

Murdoch, Allan, Weigher, United Grain Elevator Company, Liverpool. Case 40102

At 7 a.m. on the 12th May, 1913, two men named William Brown and John Weedell were employed in unloading damaged grain from the hold of the barge *Arctic* in the Harrington Dock, Liverpool. On the hatches being removed Weedell went down the ladder and was overcome by fumes from the damp grain. This was seen by John F. Blower, captain of the barge, who first called for further help, and going down, dragged Weedell to the foot of the ladder, but was so much affected he could do no more and only just managed to reascend the ladder, Allan Murdoch, a weigher in the employ of the United Grain Elevator Company, and W. Brown then went down, but Murdoch feeling the effect of the fumes reascended while Brown collapsed. On recovering Murdoch again went down with a rope, which he placed round Weedell, who was pulled up and recovered; the rope being again lowered, Brown was drawn out, but he had succumbed to the deadly fumes. Murdoch himself was then pulled up in an exhausted state.

The Silver Medal was voted to Allan Murdoch; the Bronze Medal to John F. Blower; and an In Memoriam Testimonial to the relatives of John Brown.

Young, George Ellis, Mine Manager, Benwell Pit, Newcastle. Case 40194

At 12.40 p.m. on the 6th June, 1913, Captain W.H. Ramsay of the Northumberland and Durham Collieries Rescue Brigade, with two assistants, went down the Benwell Pit, Newcastle, for the purpose of experimenting with a breathing dress in an old disused drift in the colliery. Accompanied by Mr. Young, the manager of the mine, they made their way into the drift until they began to meet with foul air. Captain Ramsay and his assistants then fitted on their dresses and proceeded, leaving Mr. Young to await their return. After going some distance Captain Ramsay intimated to his assistants that he would go on alone, and after being away for a short time he returned in a state of utter collapse and fell unconscious to the ground. His assistants tried to drag him out but failed, and as they themselves were beginning to be affected one of them returned for Mr. Young, who without hesitation, and knowing the risk, at once went in without any breathing dress, and reaching the place where Captain Ramsay lay, succeeded with the help of the second assistant in bringing him to the mouth of the drift, but he unfortunately succumbed to the effects of the foul gas encountered in the drift.

Heighway, Edward J, Seaman, S.S. *Carmania*. Case 40567

At 11 p.m. on the 9th October, 1913 the s.s. *Volturno* was on fire in the Atlantic, and a number of vessels were standing by for the purpose of saving life, among them being the s.s. *Carmania*, of the Cunard Line. About 11 p.m. a cry was heard from the darkness, and on the searchlight being turned in the direction of the sound a man was observed struggling in the water on the starboard bow. An endeavour was made by manoeuvring the ship to bring the man alongside, and lines were thrown, which were of no avail.

Edward J. Heighway, seaman, then threw off his clothes and lowered himself into the sea from the B deck, letting go the line. He swam out and, getting hold of the man, succeeded in bringing him to the lower door amidships. After considerable buffeting against the ship's side he managed to secure a line which was thrown, and both were safely got on board.

There was a fresh gale blowing, with a heavy sea and swell, so that great risk was incurred.

Connor, Alexander G., Chief Officer, S.S. *Sanui*. Case 40631

At 3 a.m. on the 17th March, 1913, a disabled motor-boat, named *Rosette*, was in tow of the s.s. *Sanui* off Kwang Lee Island, in the West River, China, when Carey J. Pirie, chief engineer on the *Sanui*, who had gone on board the motor-boat to effect some repairs, accidentally stepped overboard.

The cry "man overboard" was heard on the *Sanui*, and the commotion awoke Mr. Connor, the chief officer, who, thinking the disabled craft had broken adrift, at once went on deck. Finding that Mr. Pirie was in the river, he got into the dinghy with a couple of Chinese and proceeded to search for the missing man. In the intense darkness he faintly discerned some object in the water, and instantly jumped in, to find that it was only a piece of driftwood. Swimming about in the strong current a light was flashed from the dinghy which enabled him to locate Mr. Pirie in a sinking condition. A few strokes brought him alongside and, though weighed down by his sea-boots, he managed to keep him afloat until the dinghy arrived, but this being now waterlogged he was compelled to remain in the river till a lifebuoy thrown from the *Sanui* reached them, and they were got on board.

The West River is very treacherous and runs with a strong current, the night being very dark.

Oddy, Arthur, Chief Petty Officer.
Sworn, Sydney, Leading Boatman, H.M. Coast Guard, Sennen's Cove, Land's End.

Case 40668

At 6.40 a.m. on the 15th March, 1914, the sailing ship *Trifolium* was driven on shore off Sennen's Cove, Land's End, in an exceedingly dangerous position among the rocks, where she was rapidly breaking up. Arthur Oddy, Chief Petty Officer, and Sydney Sworn, Leading Boatman, H.M. Coast Guard, who were on duty, exerted themselves to the utmost in saving or attempting to save life. Oddy plunged into the violent surf and was successful in saving two of the crew who were vainly endeavouring to reach the shore. Sworn also swam out and caught a man belonging to the ship, but after landing him he was found to be dead. He again rushed into the surf and saved a local fisherman who in attempting to give help was in danger of being swept away.

Both men incurred great risk of being carried away by the undertow, and of being dashed on the rocks by the heavy sea running.

Howlett, James F., Skipper, Trawler *Datum*.

Case 40720

At 12.45 p.m. on the 9th May, 1914, two steam trawlers, the *Achievable* and the *Datum*, which had left Lowestoft on their way to the northern fishing grounds, were off Gorleston, the weather being squally, with a high wind, sharp showers, and the sea exceedingly rough. The *Achievable* was leading, and when she rolled in the heavy seaway Alfred J. Turrell, a fireman, who had come on deck, was accidentally knocked overboard. Two lifebuoys were at once thrown, but failed to reach him. The accident was seen from the *Datum*, and on that vessel coming up James F. Howlett, the skipper who was at the wheel, instantly plunged overboard, and reaching Turrell, who was now completely exhausted, succeeded in bringing him to the trawler, and they were eventually got on board.

Heap, Arthur, Works Manager, Cumberland By-Products Company, Flimby, Maryport.

Case 40737

At 9.30 a.m. on the 25th February, 1914, two men named Graham and McArthur, while engaged repairing a tar still at the works of the West Cumberland By-Products Company, Flimby, near Maryport, detected a smell of gas and decided to leave. The still is 12 feet deep and 9 feet wide, being entered from the top by a manhole 16 inches in diameter. Graham succeeded in getting his head out of the manhole and was pulled out, but McArthur was overcome by the gas and became unconscious. William Frankland, works foreman, on reaching the place at once went down to try and help McArthur, but was also overcome by the gas. Ernest Shaw, with a rope round him, then descended but was struck down and was pulled out with the rope. Arthur Heap, works manager, with a rope round him and taking with him a spare rope, was lowered into the still, and getting the rope round Frankland he was pulled up. Again Mr. Heap was lowered into the still, and McArthur was got out the same way. Both men were unconscious for about three hours after rescue, but eventually recovered.

Great risk was incurred owing to the deadly nature of the gas.

The Silver Medal was voted to Arthur Heap and Bronze Medals to Frankland and Shaw.

Barne, Michael, Acting Commander, R.N., H.M.S. *Majestic*.

Case 41249

At 4.15 p.m. on the 6th October, 1914, William Moran, an able seaman, was washed overboard from the starboard torpedo net shelf of H.M.S. *Majestic* in the North Sea. The speed of the ship at the time was 4 knots, the sea being very rough with a heavy swell. A lifebuoy was at once let go, but in the heavy sea running it appeared improbable that he would be able to reach it. Seeing this Commander Barne threw off his coat and jumping from the quarter-deck swam towards the man, who was now about 100 yards from the ship, and succeeded in getting within 20 yards of him when he threw up his arms and sank. Commander Barne then swam round the place but he did not again come to the surface, and was himself picked up by a boat from the ship. Considering the state of the sea Commander Barne ran great personal risk.

Renouf, Edward de Faye, Lieut., R.N., H.M.S. *Conqueror*. Case 41279

At 8.30 a.m. on the 14th October, 1914, the *Orion, Conqueror*, and *Thunderer*, belonging to the Second Battle Squadron, were steaming in single line ahead 500 yards apart, the *Orion* leading, when Sydney L. Robertson, signal boy, accidentally fell overboard. He was seen in the water by Lieut. Renouf of the *Conqueror*, the next ship in line, who at once went overboard to his help. A lifebuoy was also let go, which Robertson reached while Lieut. Renouf was still some distance away. As the *Thunderer*, the third ship in the line, passed a second lifebuoy was thrown which Lieut. Renouf took, he having seen that Robertson was already at the buoy thrown from the *Conqueror*. Eventually both were picked up and taken on board the *Orion*.

Lieut. Renouf ran extreme risk owing to the peculiar circumstances under which he went overboard. The ships were steaming 13 knots and being cleared for action, all boats were inboard and the davits down, while owing to the danger from submarines it was a question whether any ship was justified in stopping to pick them up.

Brooks, Percy, Second Hand, Trawler *Eric Stroud*. Case 41318

At 9 p.m. on the 7th December, 1914, the steam trawler *Eric Stroud* was at sea about 65 miles east by north of Aberdeen, the night being dark with high wind and an exceedingly rough sea running. The crew were engaged repairing a net before placing their gear in the water, the vessel being hove to at the time. Suddenly a heavy sea broke on board, sweeping the deck and carrying the whole of the fishing gear over the side, together with William Mckenzie, fireman of the vessel. Ropes were at once thrown which he failed to grasp, and a lifebuoy was then thrown, which he succeeded in reaching. The lights were burning brightly, and McKenzie was seen in the water about 30 yards away. Percy Brooks second hand on the trawler, at once threw off his sea boots and oilskins and, plunging overboard, reached McKenzie, who at once grasped him round the neck, nearly choking him, but Brookes stuck to his task and at last succeeded in reaching the side of the vessel, where both were hauled on board in an exhausted state, after being 15 minutes in the water.

Cockburn, J.B., Lieut.-Col., Royal Welsh Fusiliers. Case 41324

On the afternoon of the 9th November, 1914, the steam launch *Keka* was in the Wori River, West Africa, having a lighter full of carriers attached to her starboard side. The launch was steaming 10 knots, the depth being about 14 feet and the current running 3 to 4 knots, the river being in flood. Able seaman Morgan was in charge of the tiller of the lighter, and, this giving way, he fell backwards into the river.

Lieut.-Col Cockburn, Royal Welsh Fusiliers, serving with the 1st Nigeria Regiment, who was on board the launch, at once jumped after him, but owing to the swift current and having his clothes and heavy boots on, failed to reach him and becoming exhausted was forced to return to the launch, where he was got on board, Morgan being drowned. The river is infested with crocodiles.

Leech, Herbert, Fisherman, Trawler *Fraternal*. Case 41328

At 7 a.m. on the 3rd November, 1914, the steam trawler *Fraternal* on her way back from the fishing ground was some 20 miles east by north of Lowestoft, steaming about 8 miles an hour, the sea being choppy, when she struck a German mine and sank in three minutes, three of the crew being killed by the explosion, the remainder being thrown into the water. On coming to the surface Herbert Leech found himself clear of the wreckage, but saw his captain come up entangled in the nets, which were over his head holding him down. Leech at once went to his assistance and, getting him clear, swam with him to some wreckage to which the cabin boy was clinging, and remained by them until they were picked up by the trawler *Launch Out*, which brought them into port.

Ebden-Currey, Charles N., Lieut., R.N. Case 41337

At 10.30 a.m. on the 26th December, 1914, H.M. Trawler *Tom Tit* was driven on the rocks at the entrance to Peterhead harbour. It was blowing a gale from the south-east, and the sea was breaking heavily on the rocks. It was at once evident that the vessel would be a complete wreck and that no time should be lost in getting the crew on shore. The vessel was on a rock about fifty yards from land with deep water between, there being a smaller rock close to the vessel over which the heavy seas were continually breaking.

Taking a line with him Lieut. Ebden-Currey swam out through the surf to this rock, and, although several times washed off, he eventually succeeded in throwing his line to the *Tom Tit* and then made his way back to shore, where he was hauled up the rocks in an exhausted state. A stronger rope was then got on board by which the crew were landed in safety. Lieut. Ebden-Currey incurred great risk of being smothered in the breakers, his hands being bruised and cut by the rocks.

Wodehouse, Norman A., Lieut., R.N., H.M.S. *Warrior*. Case 41386

At 7 a.m. on the 19th December, 1914, Charles W. Crisp, A.B., accidentally fell overboard from H.M.S. *Lowestoft* when entering the harbour at Cromarty. It was pitch dark at the time, there being a slight swell on, the weather very cold, and the ship steaming 7 to 8 knots. A lifebuoy was thrown, which Crisp failed to see. Hearing the man's cries for help, Lieut. Wodehouse jumped from H.M.S. *Warrior*, the next vessel in line, and finding Crisp kept him afloat until he reached the lifebuoy, after which they were both picked up by a boat and taken on board the *Warrior*. As the ships were under war conditions, Lieut. Wodehouse knew that no boat would be available to pick him up for some time.

Rafter, Stephen, Steeplejack, Leeds. Case 41449

Between 3 and 3.30 p.m. on the 22nd December, 1914, Stephen Rafter and Esau Mayall were engaged demolishing a large chimney at the Corporation Electricity Works, Leeds. The men were laddering the chimney, which is 180 feet in height, and had nearly reached the top, Rafter being on the ladder at the height of 160 feet and Mayall 30 feet lower down. A hammer which Rafter had been using slipped from his belt and struck Mayall on the head, stunning him, but in falling his left leg caught in the rungs of the ladder and he hung suspended head downwards. Rafter at once got down the under side of the ladder and getting underneath him raised him into a prone position. To do this he had practically to hang on to the ladder with one leg and support Mayall till further assistance came. A rope was now passed up to him which he fastened round Mayall's body and then round his own shoulders and neck. He had then to raise the body into an upright position to enable him to get the leg clear of the ladder. When this was done the whole weight was borne by Rafter, from whose neck and shoulders the man was suspended, and in this way the descent was made and the bottom reached in safety. Had Rafter made a single false movement or missed his foothold it meant instant death for both.

		Case 41502
Lotbiniere, H.G. Joly de,	Major, Royal Engineers.	
Lynam, C.G.J.,	2nd. Lieut.	
Senior, Gavin,	Sergt.	
Blythe, Walter,	Cpl.	
Waugh, John,	Cpl.	

The Royal Engineers were practising trench warfare at Colchester, and on the afternoon of 29th April, 1915, a mine was exploded. The earth was broken up, but no crater was formed, and on the morning of the 30th April a party of men were sent to clear away the loose earth so that the mine chamber could be inspected, but with orders not to enter the gallery. Contrary to instructions Sapper Williams entered the gallery and did not return, and Sappers Scott, Simpson, Bullock, and Lichfield went in to try to get him out, but they failed in their object and were all more or less affected. Cpl. Blythe then went in and got these four men out unaided; 2nd Lieut. E.J. Darton then went in to try and reach Williams, but did not return. Cpl. Blythe made a heroic effort to reach Lieut. Darton, but failed and had to be removed to hospital. Maj. de Lotbiniere, 2nd Lieut. Lynam, and several other men made gallant efforts to reach Lieut. Darton and Williams, and eventually they were got out, but both had succumbed to the carbon monoxide gas present in the gallery after the mine was exploded.

Silver Medals were awarded to the four men listed above and Bronze Medals to the following (all Royal Engineers):--

Blake, Frank	Sergt.	Scott, William	Sapper	Simpson, David	Sapper
Sclater, Robert	Sapper	Dowler, Robert	Sapper	Williams, George	Sapper
Bullock, Henry J.	Sapper	Lichfield, William	Sapper		

An In Memoriam Testimonial was awarded to the relatives of 2nd Lieut. E.J. Darton.

Kennedy, Hugh M., Boy Scout, aged 15, Durban, Natal.   Case 41503

On the 5th of October, 1914, two boy scouts named Kennedy and Trafford left the esplanade at Durban, Natal, in a boat, intending to bring back Mr. S.M. Goldsmith, the scoutmaster, and several scouts who were on the Bluff side of the Bay. About 7.30 p.m. the boat grounded on an island about 100 yards from the Bluff, and the boys could not move it. The channel between the island and the Bluff is some 20 feet deep, there being a strong current running through, and these waters are infested with sharks. The boys shouted across to Mr. Goldsmith, and, being a good swimmer, he started to swim across in the hope of moving the boat. When about half way across he called for help two or three times and then went under water. Hugh M. Kennedy, aged 15, who was one of the boys on the island, on hearing the call at once entered the water and swam out to where Mr. Goldsmith was last seen, but although he dived several times could find no trace of him.

The place where the accident occurred was very dark and gloomy.

Muscat, Angelo, Stoker, Malta R.N.R.   Case 41541

On the 21st March, 1915, one of H.M. Torpedo Boats had been driven ashore on the Island of Lemnos by a fierce gale. Between 6 and 7 p.m., the wind being of hurricane force and the boat on a lee shore about 200 yards from land, a volunteer was asked for to take a line ashore. Angelo Muscat, stoker, Malta R.N.R., at once volunteered, and nothing lighter being available he made fast the end of a two and a half inch grass line to his life-belt and went overboard with it. Although known as a powerful swimmer he had a desperate struggle in reaching the shore, owing to the weight of the line he was towing. This line was the means of saving the lives of three of the crew.

Moyes, William E., A.B.   Case 41845

On the night of the 18th of May, 1915, the Canadian Government Steamer *Christine* was run into and sunk by one of H.M. ships in the St. Lawrence River about 15 miles below Quebec. The collision took place about half a mile from land, the depth being 11 fathoms with a strong tide, the water being very cold and the night dark.

William E. Moyes went overboard from the ship with a line and succeeded in saving Lieut. Brander, R.N.V.R., and the signalman of the *Christine*, bringing them to the ship, where they were got on board.

Hore, Percy H., Writer, R.N., Hospital Ship *Soudan*.   Case 41950

At 11 a.m. on the 13th August, 1915, the transport *Royal Edward* was sunk in the Mediterranean near the Dardenelles. The Hospital ship *Soudan* being near engaged in the work of picking up survivors and succeeded in saving 442 persons. On two occasions Percy H. Hore, writer on the *Soudan*, slid down a wire stay and swam to two soldiers who were in difficulty and succeeded in bringing them to the ship, where he put a rope round them and they were hauled on board. One of the men was almost exhausted and clutched Hore, who had great difficulty in bringing him alongside.

On three other occasions Hore went down the ship's side to the water and put ropes round men by which they were got on board.

Hore ran great risk, there being a heavy sea running, into which he went fully clothed.

D'Oyly-Hughes, Guy, Lieut., R.N., H.M. Submarine.   Case 41986

At 6.30 a.m. on the 20th July, 1915, one of H.M. Submarines was in the Mediterranean about 130 miles from Malta. The vessel was going slow under power, the sea being choppy, when a stoker named Maine was washed from the casing by a wave. Lieut. D'Oyly-Hughes at once jumped after him but failed to reach him before he sank.

Croly, William C., Major, Royal Army Medical Corps.   Case 41995

At 6.30 p.m. on the 13th June, 1915, a motor launch was conveying a number of sick officers and men up the Shatt-el-Arab in Mesopotamia to the general hospital. The launch was going full speed when one of the patients, Private Jarmy, Norfolk Regiment, suddenly jumped into the river and, making no attempt to struggle or swim, remained for a short time on the surface, head downwards.

Major Croly at once plunged in after him fully clothed and wearing boots, but before he could reach him the man sank and did not rise again. As the launch could not be brought round in time a native boat put out from the bank and picked Major Croly up in an exhausted state. The Shatt-el-Arab is here about 800 yards wide, 25 feet deep, with a swift current and full of treacherous eddies, the attempted rescue taking place about 100 yards from the bank.

Landry, Richard, Farmer, Porthtowan, Cornwall.   Case 42058

About midday on the 7th September, 1915, a youth of 18, named William C. Greet, made an attempt to climb the cliff at Porthtowan, Cornwall. The cliff is about 300 feet in height, and when about a third of the way up he found he could neither go forward nor yet return, having only a very insecure foothold and a small tuft of grass to hold on to. A rope was obtained about a quarter of a mile away and this was lowered over, but from the overhanging nature of the cliff failed to reach the lad.

Richard Landry, a farmer who was at work near, volunteered to try and effect the rescue; going down the rope he was successful in reaching the lad, and by almost superhuman strength got him in front of him and with his burden climbed up hand over hand until he reached the top.

For clasp see Case 43507.

Creasy, John H., A.B.   Case 42124

At about 7 a.m. on the 27th May, 1915, H.M.S. *Majestic* was torpedoed and sunk of Cape Helles. A trawler proceeded to the scene of the disaster, and the skiff was lowered in the hope of saving life, Creasy and another man going away in her. As the ship went down great quantities of oil came to the surface. One of the engine-room suctions was still pumping, and in endeavouring to bring the skiff to the rescue of some men who were being drawn into this suction one of the thole-pins broke, leaving the boat helpless.

Creasy then jumped overboard and succeeded in bringing one man who could swim a little and then another who could not swim and was exhausted to the boat through the oil and against the undertow a distance of 50 feet. There was great risk of being sucked under.

Adamson, W., Private, Royal Army Medical Corps.   Case 42133

At 9.15 a.m. on the 13th August, 1915, the transport *Royal Edward* was torpedoed and sunk in the Mediterranean, there being a rough sea running at the time. On coming to the surface Private Adamson swam to a boat which was stove in and floating bottom up. From this he swam out three times and succeeded in taking three men back to the boat. One of these men was suffering from a compound fracture of the ankle, another being almost unconscious.

West, A.H., Captain, Royal Horse Artillery.   Case 42237

On the morning of the 26th October, 1915, during the voyage of the Indian Expeditionary Force from Bombay to Marseilles, a stoker from the transport *Clan M'Phee* threw himself overboard in the Red Sea, the speed of the vessel being about 10 knots. A lifebuoy was thrown from the following ship but did not reach him, and seeing this Captain West at once jumped overboard, swam to him, and took him to the lifebuoy. Under the impression that Captain West was in difficulty Gunner H. Nunn, R.H.A., jumped from the ship and swam to them. A boat was now got out and all three were picked up and taken on board, Captain West having been about fifteen minutes in the water.

There was a slight swell at the time, and this part of the Red Sea is infested with sharks.

The Silver Medal was voted to Captain A.H. West and the Bronze Medal to Gunner H. Nunn.

Oldershaw, George, Kibworth, Leicestershire. — Case 42252

At 8.30 a.m. on the 7th January, 1916, a man named Fred Oldershaw, in order to prepare for the work of the day, entered a bucket and was lowered down a well which had been sunk to a depth of 30 feet at Kibworth in Leicestershire. When some 6 feet from the bottom he was overcome by foul gas and fell from the bucket. Percy Burnham then went down by the bucket in order to effect his rescue, but when near the bottom he also was overcome and fell from the bucket. With a rope tied round him, George Oldershaw then went down but feeling the effect of the gas was drawn up. On recovering he fastened a wet Handkerchief over his mouth and again went down. This time he succeeded in placing a rope round Burnham, and he was pulled up. Going down a third time, he got a rope round Oldershaw, and he also was drawn up. Burnham recovered in about fifteen minutes, but Oldershaw remained unconscious for four hours after the rescue.

The Silver Medal was voted to George Oldershaw and the Bronze Medal to Percy Burnham.

Bird, James C., Lieut., R.N., H.M. Mine-sweeper *185*. — Case 42272

At 3.50 p.m. on the 21st December, 1915, H.M. Mine-sweeper *186* was struck by a mine and blown up about one mile N.W. of the Longsand Light Vessel. Mine-sweeper *185*, commanded by Lieut. James C. Bird, approached as near as possible to pick up survivors, but she had lowered her boats two to three hundred yards away so that if she herself struck a mine they would be ready in the water to give help. While thus a considerable distance ahead of her boats two men named Baines and Patterson were seen struggling and trying to hold on to small pieces of wreckage. Lieut. Bird left the bridge and diving off the forecastle head swam to the two men. A lifebelt was floating about 10 yards away, and this he secured and tied to Patterson, whom he then assisted to a larger piece of wreckage. Baines was now very much exhausted, and Lieut. Bird supported him with one hand and with the other held on to the wreckage on which Patterson was until all were picked up by the boats after being about fifteen minutes in the water.

Rowley, Martin, Collier, Long Lane Colliery, Ashton-in-Makerfield. — Case 42628

At 1 a.m. on the 1st July, 1916, four men named Gallagher, Lynch, McLoughlan and Ashurst were at work repairing the roof in the four-foot seam at Long Lane Colliery, Ashton-in-Makerfield, when a fall took place, burying all four men. A rescue party, consisting of Martin Rowley, Patrick Regan, Thomas Eden, and Thomas Kelly; at once went to their assistance, it being found that the fall, which was estimated at about 14 tons of stone and earth, had completely buried McLoughlan and partly buried Lynch, with iron girders on top of both. Ashurst and Gallagher were easily liberated, but it was only after one and a quarter hours arduous work that Lynch was reached and got out, and a quarter of an hour later when McLoughlan was also freed, but he was then dead. Owing to the confined space in which the rescuers had to work it was necessary for one man to lead, this post being taken by Rowley. There was constant fear of another fall, which might have taken place at any moment, so that great risk was incurred.

The Silver Medal was voted to Martin Rowley and Bronze Medals to Patrick Regan, Thomas Eden and Thomas Kelly.

Wright, Richard K, Clerk. — Case 42839

Soon after noon on the 20th August, 1916, a sailing boat with eight persons on board was capsized near the mouth of the River Lune, all the occupants being thrown into the water; but eventually they managed to get on the bottom of the capsized boat. Wright volunteered to endeavour to swim to shore for help, and, taking an oar with him, started, but the tide was running fast, and the wind had risen, making the water choppy, and he had also to contend with cross currents from the estuary of the Conder, so that his progress was much impeded. After being over an hour in the water and swimming about two miles he reached land, but was so exhausted that he had difficulty in climbing the bank to summon help. Before the rescuing boat could reach them all the seven left behind were drowned.

Hilson, D.N., Storekeeper, Quagga, Cape Colony.   Case 42992

About 10 a.m. on the 5th May, 1916, the Gamtoos River in Cape Colony was in high flood, inundating the whole valley for a width of two miles, the river being some 48 feet above its normal level.

At the township of Quagga ten adult natives and three children were marooned on some high ground about 300 yards from the edge of the flood. As the water was still rising their position was fast becoming hopeless. W.H. Hilson, a storekeeper, swam out to them and taking one child returned with it to the side. He again went out, but the water on the rising ground was now shoulder high. Two boys had also gone out on horseback, and to these he gave the two remaining children and they were safely landed, but the horses would not again enter the water. Hilson then decided to get as many of the adult natives as possible to some tall trees 50 to 100 yards away, and succeeded in taking one woman and two men to them, when having been two hours in the water he took cramp and had to abandon the others in order to save himself, having to be assisted from the water when he reached the side. The seven natives left were all drowned. Great risk was incurred, as the rushing flood was bringing down trees and other debris.

Tuckfield, H.R., Acting Sergeant, A.I.F.   Case 43024
Mills, R., Acting Sergeant, A.I.F.

At 2.30 p.m. on the 5th November, 1916, the transport *Nestor*, bringing troops from Australia, was steaming at Fourteen and a half knots off the West African Coast, when Private F.W. Ryland accidentally fell overboard.

Acting-Sergeant Mills saw the accident, and without a moment's hesitation sprang after him without a lifebelt or buoy, and succeeded in reaching him.

Mills was immediately followed by Acting-Sergeant Tuckfield, but the latter after swimming some distance returned for a lifebuoy which had been thrown, and with the help of this Ryland was kept afloat until all three were picked up by a boat which had been quickly got out from the ship.

There was great risk, not only from jumping from the fast-moving vessel, but from the sharks which infest these waters.

Hockey, Edward, Lance Corporal, Tyne Royal Engineers.   Case 43033

At 11.15 a.m. on the 25th November, 1916, Irene McDonnell, aged 4, was walking along the street at West Hetton, Durham, when the ground suddenly gave way and she disappeared. It was found that she had fallen down a new pit crack, and could not be seen, but was heard crying. A pit lamp was let down and it was found that she was wedged between the sides of the fissure 45 to 50 feet below the surface.

Coporal Hockey at once volunteered to go to her help, and with a lamp and rope attached to him he was lowered down; but in order to avoid the danger of loose stones falling on the girl the descent was made some distance away. After an hour's hard work he got within a few feet of her and then stuck fast. He was, however, able to lower a rope to her and draw her up till he got hold of her hand, and both were then pulled to the surface. The child was fortunately little the worse, but Corporal Hockey was completely exhausted by his efforts.

There was great risk from falling stones or from the fissure closing up.

Gregory, C., 2nd Lieut., 3rd Batt. Lancashire Fusiliers.   Case 43102

At 10.15 p.m. on the 18th November, 1916, the s.s. *Oakwell*, on a voyage from Seaham to London, went ashore on the Yorkshire coast near Withernsea. There was a heavy easterly wind blowing, the night being very dark, and the vessel grounded broadside on about 30 yards from shore with the waves breaking over her.

2nd Lieut. Gregory, wearing full equipment, swam out to the vessel and not knowing whether it was an enemy ship or not carried a revolver and electric lamp with him. He managed to get on board and found the captain and crew of nine in an exhausted state. Returning to shore, he organised a rescue party to assist, and forming a chain of men standing in the surf, again swam out to the wreck accompanied by Sergeant R. Dawson, and together they assisted the crew down the ship's side and passed them on to the chain of men who then got them safely to land.

The Silver Medal was voted to 2nd Lieut. C. Gregory and the Bronze Medal to Sergeant R. Dawson both of the 3rd Batt., Lancashire Fusiliers.

Reynolds, Philip John William, A.B., H.M.S. *Paris*.   Case 43120

At 6 p.m. on the 26th December, 1916, a steam launch with liberty men on board was coming alongside H.M.S. *Paris*, in Sheerness harbour, when Trimmer James Allen, in trying to jump from the boat to the gangway, fell overboard. The night was pitch dark and foggy with no moon, and Allen who was unable to swim, was immediately swept along the ship's side by the three-knot tide then running.

Reynolds, who was on board the launch, without any hesitation jumped overboard, and endeavoured to reach him, an extremely difficult undertaking, owing to the strength of the tide. Eventually, he succeeded in overtaking his man about ten yards astern of the ship but was at once clutched and both went under water. Reynolds succeeded in freeing himself, and both men came to the surface, when, in attempting to get hold of Allen from behind, he was again clutched and dragged under.

A second time he managed to free himself, and then after a severe struggle, succeeded in keeping the man afloat until both were picked up by the launch about 200 yards astern of the ship after being fifteen minutes in the water. A searchlight had been turned on but failed to locate the position of the men.

Cross, Henry, Miner, Long Lane Collieries, Ashton-in-Makerfield.   Case 43199
Mather, Levi, Miner.
Ashall, James, Miner.
Yeates, George F, Miner.
Taylor, John T, Miner.

At 8.30 a.m. on the 24th February, 1917, three men named John Webb, Benjamin Morris, and Thomas Jones, were engaged in repairing the main haulage in No.1 Pit, Long Lane Collieries, Ashton-in-Makerfield, when a fall of roof, estimated at forty tons took place, completely burying Morris and Jones and partially burying Webb.

A rescue party consisting of Cross, Mather, Ashall, Yeates, and Taylor, was at once formed and began the hazardous task of attempting to extricate the three men. After some forty minutes work Webb was liberated, and continuing their efforts they were successful in reaching and rescuing Morris after four hours work, but it was not until a further four hours had elapsed that the body of Jones was reached and brought out. These five men worked unceasingly for eight hours without food, and in constant danger of a further fall of roof, portions of which were continually falling while they were at work.

Craven, Arthur Henry, Petty Officer, R.N.   Case 43224

On the occasion of the loss of H.M.S. *Triumph*, in the Eastern Mediterranean, on the 25th of May, 1915, Craven who was on a trawler, dived overboard, and by his sustained exertions was instrumental in saving the lives of about twenty-five men. He remained in the water for over half an hour, giving the men belts and planks to support them until they were picked up by boats, and was successful in rescuing five men who had gone under water, being himself finally taken on board H.M.S. *Newmarket*.

Innes, Francis A., Lieut., R.N.R. Case 43273

At about 11 a.m. on the 10th April, 1917, the Hospital Ship *Salta* struck a mine about a mile from Whistle Buoy, Le Havre, and sank in five minutes. Two swamped boats floated away and one of H.M. ships was steered so as to lay her alongside these two boats. The after boat was furthest from the ship and to assure that she would not drift astern Lieut. Innes jumped overboard with a line and made her fast and then getting into the boat proceeded to pass bowlines round the survivors, all of whom were exhausted and some entirely helpless. Once he fell out of the boat but managed to scramble back and went on with his work. In this way he succeeded in saving about twenty persons including two Hospital Nursing Sisters.

The wind had blown the ship broadside on to the sea and she was rolling between 20 and 30 degrees each side of the vertical, there being danger of crushing between the boat and the ship three lives being lost in this way.

Wilson, Frank, Telegraphist, R.N.V.R. Case 43435

At 9.30 p.m. on the 30th May, 1917, one of H.M. ships was blown up at sea, which was rough, with rain, a number of men being left struggling in the water.

Wilson swam from one to another of these men bringing them planks and pieces of wreckage. Two of the men thus assisted were unfortunately drowned, but two others Trimmer L.C. Chalmers and Lieut. C.D. Nettlingham, were picked up by another ship about half an hour afterwards, Lieut. Nettlingham having been assisted by Wilson during the whole of this period.

Roberts, William Charles, Miner, Minaes Geraes, Brazil. Case 43489

At 8.45 p.m. on the 13th December, 1916, a round of holes was being blasted in the Mine of the St. John del Rey Mining Coy., at Minaes Geraes, Brazil, when one of them missed fire and the explosion gave off noxious fumes. The ventilating fan being temporarily stopped for some slight adjustment it was not safe for anyone to venture in until sufficient time had been allowed for the fumes to be cleared away. One man, however, persisted in going in although strongly advised by his fellow workmen not to do so, and when nearing the face he fell down overcome by the poisonous fumes.

After a short interval two of his companions attempted to reach him, but failed, and returned saying that he was dead. Roberts then went in and succeeded in reaching him, and carrying him out a distance of some 250 feet, and he was restored to consciousness after thirty minutes work; Roberts himself was so overcome that it was necessary to use artificial respiration for some twenty minutes before he recovered.

Pearson, Frank Edom, Third Officer, S.S. *Tycho*. Case 43490

At 6.0 p.m. on the 20th May, 1917, the s.s. *Tycho*, of Hull, was torpedoed in the English Channel by an enemy submarine, sinking in about half an hour. The two boats were safely lowered and all hands left the ship before she sank. The s.s. *Porthkerry*, which was about a quarter of a mile away, turned round to pick up the boats, and when these were safely alongside she also was torpedoed, one of the boats being shattered, all the crew except one man being killed. The second boat was capsized, throwing all the crew into the water. On coming to the surface Mr. Pearson, 3rd officer s.s. *Tycho*, swam to the upturned boat and climbing on the keel assisted the remainder of the crew to also get on the keel. When in this position a knocking was heard from inside the boat, and Mr. Pearson then stretched down under the water and managed to get hold of the ship's cook who was underneath the boat. This man he laid across the keel of the boat and was successful in keeping him and some fourteen others there until they were picked up by another steamer about an hour afterwards.

Landry, Richard, Farmer, Chapel Porth, Cornwall.   Case 43507

Silver Clasp

About 7 p.m. on the 7th July, 1917, a man named Willesford and his sister were on the rocks at the base of the cliff at Chapel Porth, Cornwall, when their return was cut off by the incoming tide. The cliff is some 300 feet high and almost perpendicular. A number of persons went to the place, and Richard Landry a farmer, fastened a rope to an iron peg which he drove into the ground, throwing the other end over the cliff. Descending, he found the people were further out than he had estimated, and he reclimbed the rope. A second rope was now fixed, but on going down he found he was out too far. Returning to the top he refixed the second rope, and going down for the third time he managed to reach them and get them to a part of the cliff which is not quite so steep, and where with his help they were able to reach the top.

Received Silver Medal in 1915, see case 42058.

Evelegh, Markham H., Sub-Lieut., R.N.   Case 43510
Scotcher, Cyril G., Midshipman R.N.R.

At 11 a.m. on the 1st January, 1917, a steamer was torpedoed by the enemy and sank at sea. There was a strong wind and heavy sea running, which caused one of H.M. ships which came up to roll violently. The surgeon of the steamer was seen in the water, where he was struck by the bilge keel of the rescuing ship and rendered unconscious. Sub-Lieut. Evelegh jumped in with a line, but this proving too short, he returned for a longer one, which he got round the body of the surgeon, but when pulled on board life was extinct.

Meanwhile, Midshipman Scotcher had also jumped overboard, but failed to reach the surgeon in time. He then went to the help of a military officer, who was too weak to hold on to a rope, and getting a line round his body he was hauled on board.

Guido, Marinaio Lanternari, Italian Air Service.   Case 43543

At 11.45 a.m. on the 17th July, 1917, a British seaplane containing Flight Sub-Lieut. R.G. Begg and Observer Sub-Lieut. E.A. Planterose crashed from a height of about 150 feet into the sea at Otranto. The machine was completely wrecked, only a small portion remaining above the water, which was 20 feet deep, the distance from shore being about 320 yards, both occupants being held fast in the wreckage under water. Guido, who was on an Italian seaplane about 200 yards from the scene of the accident, at once went to the spot, and throwing off his coat dived repeatedly under water, but failed in his efforts to reach either of the men, whose bodies were recovered later.

There was considerable danger of becoming entangled in the wires and other parts of the wrecked machine.

Thornton, Edward C., Lieut., R.N.   Case 43713

At 4.20 a.m. on the 2nd May, 1917, one of H.M. ships struck a mine and sank. Lieut. Thornton and Mr. Frank Ellis, Gunner, who were on the bridge at the time, were blown into the sea about 20 yards from the ship, both being injured. Lieut. Thornton got hold of a lifebuoy, but seeing that Ellis was severely hurt and unable to keep afloat he gave up the buoy to him, and having secured a second buoy he endeavoured to keep the man afloat but failed, and was himself picked up about 10 minutes later in a state of collapse.

Moon, Edwin R., Flight-Commander, D.S.O., Royal Naval Air Service.   Case 43992

On the morning of the 6th January, 1917, Commander Moon, and Commander the Hon. R.O.B. Bridgeman, D.S.O., R.N., were in a seaplane over the Delta of the Rufidji River, East Africa, and were forced to descend owing to engine trouble.

Finding it impossible to repair the damage these officers proceeded to burn the machine, and then attempted to make their way up the bank of the river towards Betya. As they had nothing to eat or drink and as night was coming on Commander Moon swam across the river in the hope of finding some food or some sort of boat, but being unsuccessful he remained on the north bank of the river for the night. On the morning of the 7th both officers moved along their respective banks of the river, managing to keep in touch with one another until opposite Betya, when Moon again swam the river and rejoined his companion. In this neighbourhood they got hold of some cocoanuts, but afterwards were without food or drink.

On the night of the 7th they found an empty house, and removing a window-frame, constructed a frail raft by fastening some planks to it, and in the early morning of the 8th commenced their journey, but could only make slow progress. It was Moon's intention to make for the Kimboni mouth of the river on the chance of finding some guards or watchers, but both officers now being very much exhausted and unable to stem the tide the raft was, during the night, carried out to sea through the Simba Uranga mouth of the river. On this day, January 9th Bridgeman being practically unconscious, Moon spent thirteen hours on the raft, at least nine of which were in the open sea. Again and again Bridgeman was washed off the raft, each time being rescued and put back by Moon, until about noon when he either died from exhaustion or was washed away, and Moon could not recover him. In the course of the afternoon the raft was brought back by the tide to within a short distance from the shore, and Moon managed to reach land, where, although he fell into German hands, he ultimately recovered.

The Rufidji River is from three quarters to one and a half miles wide, seven to ten fathoms deep, with a stream running 3 to 5 knots, and is infested with crocodiles and sharks.

Bristow, Charles J.W., Engine Man, R.N.R., H.M. P.M.S. *Queen of the North*.   Case 44024

At 1.38 p.m. on the 20th July, 1917, H.M. P.M.S. *Queen of the North* was blown up by an enemy mine in the North Sea and sank in 50 seconds. Charles J.W. Bristow, who with others of the crew was thrown into the water, seeing T.H. Dawson being taken under by the suction of the sinking vessel, at once dived and brought him to the surface, where he placed him on an upturned boat. He then saw James Bray, another of the crew, in difficulty, and finding a life-belt he put this on him. After this he saw a life-raft about 100 feet away, and swimming to this he managed to bring it back, and got Dawson and Bray safely on to it, whence they were ultimately picked up.

There was great risk from the suction of the sinking vessel, and afterwards from the floating wreckage.

Kay, Isaac, Miner, Lea Green Colliery, St. Helen's   Case 44171

About 1.15 a.m. on the 23rd May, 1918, William Griffiths, employed as a fireman at the King Pit, Lea Green Colliery, St. Helen's, was seen going in the direction of No. 13 Level. About six o'clock the same morning it was discovered that he was missing, and an alarm was raised. On a search being made his lamp was found hanging from a prop at No. 1 Brow, which had been fenced off owing to the presence of coal gas, and moaning could be heard coming from the Brow, which is 800 yards from the Pit Eye.

Isaac Kay, Ford, Scragg and Richard Davies, then entered the Brow, but after going a short distance the latter three turned back, as they felt themselves being overcome. Kay, however, kept on, and finding Griffiths, dragged him a little way, and then himself became unconscious. Ford, Scragg and Richard Davies, finding that Kay did not return again, entered the Brow, and three times tried to reach him, but failed.

Various attempts on the part of Jones, William Davies, Richard Davies and Ford to reach Kay were unsuccessful.

After an interval of some ten minutes Jones, Richard Davies and Ford made a final effort, and reaching Kay, dragged him back to the entrance, and he was eventually restored by artificial respiration.

The body of Griffiths, who had been dead for some time, was recovered later. All the men were aware of the danger incurred in entering the Brow.

The Silver Medal was voted to Isaac Kay, and Bronze Medals to :-

Jones, Ellis J.   Ford, James   Davies, Richard   Scragg, Joseph   Davies, William

Murphy, Patrick J., Lower Umfolozi District, Zululand.
Hammar, Augustus, jun.
Thomas, Beatrice, Mrs.

Case 44283

On the 15th February, 1918, the whole of the Lower Umfolozi District in Zululand was inundated by the rising of the Umfolozi and Umsinduzi Rivers.

There had been two days rain but no imminent danger was apprehended, as although the Umfolozi had risen considerably it was confined within its banks, until about 2.15 a.m. on the morning of the 15th February the flood broke forth in all its fury, giving practically no warning and catching everyone in bed. Most of the people living within the area broke through the ceilings of their houses and got on to their roofs, to find that they had not escaped the peril - brick buildings collapsed before the torrent, and wood and iron buildings were torn from their foundations and washed downstream, breaking up as they went. The hotel, bank, store and railway station were carried away, the mill factory, where some natives and Indians had taken refuge, being the only building left intact. The current rushing along at a terrific rate, variously estimated at from 12 to 20 miles an hour, carried with it trees, logs, grass cane and huge masses of papyrus, which came tearing down, sometimes two or more together, threatening to crush or engulf whatever came in their way, in addition to which the waters are infested with crocodiles and many snakes, which attach themselves to the trees and logs.

It was under the foregoing appalling and disastrous conditions that efforts were made to save, or attempt to save life, and it speaks well for the heroism of those engaged in this work that in some instances rescues were effected. The sixteen persons named, with the greatest gallantry, courage and devotion, exerted themselves in the arduous work, which extended over a period of several days, the efforts put forth by Patrick J. Murphy, Augustus Hammar, jun., and Mrs Beatrice Thomas being specially distinguished. Mr. Alfred W. Upton unfortunately lost his life owing to the capsizing of a boat with which he was endeavouring to render assistance.

Bronze Medals were voted to :-

Brook, William H., jun.	Johansson, Martin.	Nilsen, Gottfred M.
Moran, Richard.	Nel, Daniel A.	Stewart, Cecil T.
Fowler, R.W.	Workman, Philip C.	Hibberd, Charles F.M.
Green, Henry.	Addison, Lewis P.	Perry, Martin J.F.

An In Memoriam to the relatives of Alfred W. Upton.

Parker, H.L., Captain, Cameron Highlanders.

Case 44628

About 9.50 a.m. on the 10th October, 1918, the Royal Mail steamer *Leinster* was torpedoed by an enemy submarine in the Irish Channel about two miles from the Kish Lightship.

Mrs M.M. Rae and her husband were passengers on the ship, and when the second torpedo was fired both were thrown into the sea and parted, the lady being unable to swim. Capt. Parker, who had practically only the use of one arm, owing to wounds received in France, swam to her assistance, and, in spite of the rough sea, kept her afloat for nearly two hours, when they were picked up by a boat from the destroyer *Mallard* in a very exhausted condition.

Of 777 persons on board the *Leinster* only 164 were eventually saved.

Hopper, Humphrey G., Sub-Lieut., R.N., H.M.S. *Mallow*.

Case 44656

On the night of the 14th July, 1918, the French steamship *Djemnah*, with troops on board, was torpedoed in the Mediterranean, and sank in two minutes. H.M.S. *Mallow*, which was in the vicinity, lowered and sent away all her boats to pick up survivors, there being nothing left in the ship in the early morning except the Carley rafts. These, when put overboard were found to be slow and unhandy in the choppy sea when picking up isolated survivors, and were finally abandoned.

Seeing this, Sub-Lieut. Hopper stripped and went overboard several times, swimming out to the men who were supporting themselves on small pieces of wreckage in the last stage of exhaustion and bringing them to the ship, where they were got on board. In this way at least six lives were saved whom it would otherwise have been impossible to reach.

See Case 46560A for Silver Clasp.

Maher, William, Stoker, R.M.S. *Leinster*.   Case 44724

About 9.50 a.m. on the 10th October, 1918, the Royal Mail steamer *Leinster* was torpedoed by an enemy submarine in the Irish Channel about two miles from the Kish Lightship.

On being thrown into the sea, Maher, who was a stoker on the *Leinster*, succeeded in reaching a raft to which others were clinging, and two of these, a mother and daughter, would without doubt have been washed away but for the help he was able to give them. Some two and a half hours after, a motor launch came up, and Maher managed to get the life-line round the mother and she was pulled on board. During this operation the raft capsized and the daughter was washed away, but in spite of his exhausted condition Maher swam after her and succeeded in getting her on board the launch.

Maher at the same time rendered material assistance to Private Duffin, of the Suffolk Regiment, who was also rescued.

Wright, Walter J., Skipper, R.N.R., H.M.T. *Candidate*.   Case 44725

About 8.45 a.m. on the 6th January, 1919, H.M. Trawler *Candidate* was engaged in sweeping operations about 14 miles from land, off Ellie Ness, at the entrance to the Firth of Forth, there being a heavy sea running and the weather very bad. Benjamin Williams, a seaman, was preparing the sweep wire when a sudden lurch of the vessel threw him overboard.

The skipper, Walter J. Wright, at once jumped after him, and supported him in the water for an hour, it being exceedingly difficult to bring the ship into a favourable position for picking them up, but this was eventually done, Williams being then unconscious and Wright in a very exhausted state.

Macleod, John Findlay, R.N.R. (T.), H.M. Yacht *Iolaire*.   Case 44766

About 2 a.m. on the 1st January, 1919, H.M. Yacht *Iolaire* with 280 officers and men on board ran on the rocks at the entrance to Stornoway Harbour.

Macleod, who was on board, swam from the yacht to shore with a line, and after being twice swept off his feet by the waves succeeded in placing it round a rock, and by holding on prevented it from slipping.

Subsequently a hawser was hauled ashore by the line and Macleod attended at the shore end until overcome by numbness due to his immersion. He thus materially assisted in saving a number of lives. In addition to the risk of drowning there was a great danger of being dashed against the rocks when attempting to land. Two hundred and one of those on board were unfortunately lost.

Hartle, J. Crossley, Lieut., Machine Gun Corps.   Case 45189

At 10 a.m. on the 29th September, 1919, the Ambulance Transport *Ellora* on a voyage from Bombay to Marseilles, was in the Gulf of Aden steaming at a speed of 14 knots. One of the passengers, Capt. H.V. Burt, 37th Lancers, who was a mental patient, in some way escaped from his guard and threw himself overboard.

Fully aware of the grave risk he ran, Lieut. Hartle, who was being invalided home after service in Palestine and Egypt and was far from well at the time, at once jumped after him fully clothed and attempted to hold him up, but being grappled with, released his hold and allowed him to sink. The same procedure was adopted by the rescuer until Capt. Burt ceased to resist, and Lieut. Hartle then supported him until they were picked up by a boat from a ship after being about ten minutes in the water.

Extreme risk incurred not only from drowning, but from the numerous sharks which infest the locality.

Belcher, Thomas H.P., Boy 1st Class, R.N., H.M.S. *Renown*.   Case 45233

About 10 a.m. on the 10th November, 1919, a man fell overboard from H.M.S. *Renown*, then on passage from Trinidad to New York, and one of the cutters which was being used as a lifeboat to pick the man up was capsized, throwing her crew into the water.

Belcher was one of the crew, and he first swam to Lieut. Oliver, but finding he was able to keep afloat devoted his attention to seaman Light, who was in a dazed condition, and without a lifebelt. He procured some spars, to which Light held on for some time, and then letting go grabbed the boy by the collar.
In this position Belcher supported him for about twelve minutes when he was clutched round the waist, and after managing to free himself Light drifted away and went down, Belcher being too exhausted with his previous effort to do more.

The ship had been stopped in order to get the boat out, there being a heavy sea at the time.

Toy, John Lyle, Fisherman, Fishing Boat *Our Boys*.   Case 45675

About 1 a.m. on the morning of the 22nd September, 1920, the fishing boat *Our Boys* went ashore on a submerged rock off the Longships, Cornwall, and was in immediate danger of sinking. The nearest point of safety was a high rock about forty yards distant, the intervening channel being a seething cauldron of broken water.

John Lyle Toy, who was one of the crew, took a rope and volunteered to try and swim to the rock, which he succeeded in doing, and by means of the rope the remainder of the crew, consisting of the skipper and three fishermen, were enabled to reach the rock, where they managed to hold on for five hours, being eventually rescued from their perilous position by the Sennen life-boat.

Dolan, Francis S., A.B., S.S. *Montana*.   Case 46200

At 1.30 a.m. on the 19th October, 1921, Gordon Gillard, mess-boy and F.S. Dolan, A.B., were going on board their vessel the s.s. *Montana*, then lying in Tilbury Dock, and Gillard fell from the gangway into the water between the ship and the quay, the distance to the water being some twenty feet.

Dolan ran down the gangway to the quay, and taking off some of his clothing jumped into the water, seized Gillard and held him up. Feeling the ship heeling towards the quay he called to a watchman, but nothing could be done, and both men were pinned by the ship, but not seriously injured. A rope was then lowered and with assistance Dolan got on to the quay.

The ship having moved off again Dolan jumped in, and with help Gillard was brought up. Dolan then started artificial respiration, and when breathing commenced carried Gillard to his bunk and left him in charge of the surgeon, who later ordered his removal to the Cottage Hospital, where he died at 4.30 a.m.

By his action Dolan incurred grave risk. He entered the water twice, the depth of which was 32 feet between the ship and the quay. The vessel was moored fast to the quay without fenders and laid about two feet from the dock wall, and being light stood high up in the water. A brisk wind was blowing, and at the time the water in the dock was increasing in depth through the tide flowing in through the lock gates causing the vessel to roll heavily.

Griffin, John, Fisherman.

Case 46225

At about 9 a.m. on the 27th September, 1921, three men were in a canoe close to the cliffs of Moher Aran Islands, where they were setting their nets. The sea was exceedingly rough and a huge wave broke over the bow of the canoe, sinking her immediately. One of the men, Patrick Flaherty, went down with the canoe, being evidently entangled in the nets. John Griffin succeeded in swimming to shore, and the third man, Michael Faherty, was washed on to a ledge of rock under the perpendicular cliff, from which the succeeding wave swept him away, and he was being carried seaward. Seeing this Griffin plunged in and succeeded in bringing him back to the ledge, where they managed to hold on until another boat came and took them off. There was a strong wind blowing from shore with a dangerous sea running, and no person unacquainted with the locality can have any conception of the risk incurred when he swam out to the rescue of Faherty.

Hopper, Humfrey G., Lieut., R.N., H.M.S. *Raleigh*.

Case 46560A

Silver Clasp

About 3.30 p.m. on the 8th August, 1922, H.M.S. *Raleigh* stranded near Armour Point, Forteau Bay, on the coast of Labrador, a dense fog prevailing at the time. With a view to saving those on board, a cutter was lowered in order to get a line ashore and thus establish communication with the ship. Lieut. Hopper, went into the cutter, but seeing that they might be unable to get ashore owing to the reefs, over which heavy seas were breaking, he took a line, and leaping into the sea near the ship swam to the reefs and succeeded in getting through the breakers, and then made his way through the surf to the rocks and landing the line by which over 700 officers and men with the aid of rafts were safely landed. There was a strong wind with heavy sea and thick fog, the water being very cold.

For award of Silver Medal see Case 44656.

See also Case 46560B, Stanhope Medal 1922, to Midshipman Hutton.

Walmsley, Richard, Under Manager, Littleton Collieries, Huntington, Stafford.

Case 46688

At 11 a.m. on the 18th November, 1922, a fall of roof took place in No 2 Pit, Littleton Collieries, Huntington, Stafford, the fall extending over a length of 20 yards, bringing down many tons of rock and debris, pinning down a miner named Ronald Leckie under the mass. A rescue party was at once organized, directed by Richard Walmsley, under-manager, but their work was rendered exceedingly difficult and dangerous by the continually falling roof and sides. It was found that Leckie, who was still alive, could be reached by crawling under the broken timbers, but it was impossible to reach him until a road had been dug down to him from the top of the fall. While this was being done Walmsley several times crawled in to where the man was, and gave him refreshment, and did his best to keep the debris from smothering him. Some thirty-five to forty men were actually engaged in the work of rescue, under the direction and constant leadership of Walmsley; and eventually after eleven hours heroic work the man was released and brought out alive.

Watkinson, William J., Skipper, Stem Drifter *Silver Line*.

Case 46696

At 3.30 a.m. on the 17th February, 1923, the Steam Drifter *Silver Line* was driven on a submerged rock under the cliff at Ravenscar, about ten miles north of Scarborough on the Yorkshire coast, the rock on which she struck being about 20 yards from shore. It was almost dark at the time, a fierce gale blowing with heavy rain, the sea being exceedingly rough and the water icy cold. It was found impossible to launch the small boat as the seas were breaking right over the vessel. The skipper, Mr. Watkinson, issued life-belts, and there being no response to the flares which had been lit, decided to try to reach shore with a line. Lowering himself over the side he was caught by a heavy sea and hurled against a rock, to which he clung. He then waited for the next sea, by which he was fortunately washed ashore.

Communication being thus established, the crew, seven in number, were successfully landed, two of them being so badly bruised that Watkinson had to go in and assist them to shore, where unaware of their situation, they remained drenched and terribly cold until daylight came some four hours later.

Treagus, Tom Henry, A.B., R.N., H,M.S. *Tamar*.   Case 47132

On the 18th August, 1923, a severe typhoon swept over Hong Kong, during the progress of which H.M. Submarine L9 broke adrift from a buoy to which she was moored, and Lieut. Thomas H. Dickson, H.M.S. *Titania*, jumped on board to try to secure her, but failing in this was unable to get back ashore. There was a heavy sea running, the wind being of typhoon force, with a tide of 4 to 5 knots, and the submarine sank about 100 yards from the west end of the dockyard wall, Lieut. Dickson being able to reach the buoy, to which he clung with the utmost difficulty, the seas constantly breaking over him. Tom H. Treagus, A.B., H.M.S. *Tamar*, went overboard from the s.s. *Ginyo Maru*, which was moored to the dockyard wall, taking a line with him, and after a severe struggle succeeded in reaching Lieut. Dickson, who still clung to the buoy, and both were then hauled back and hoisted on board.

Pryor, Wilfred S., Chinwangtao, North China.   Case 47133

On the 13th August, 1923, the Russian Band belonging to the Kailan Mining Company, which had been taken to Chinwangtao, a seaside resort in North China, for a short holiday, was encamped on a piece of land separated from the rest of the place by a creek or arm of the sea, the approach being across a dam with sluice gates. Owing to continual heavy rains the surrounding country was flooded, the dam being swept away and the water rushing seaward with terrific force. Under these conditions five of the men attempted to swim across the creek, but only two succeeded in doing this, two turned back, but the fifth, Mr. Winogradoff, was carried down to the mouth of the creek. Seeing his danger, Mr. Pryor undressed, and going in succeeded in reaching him, and after a hard struggle lasting nearly half an hour was able to bring him to land.

The waters meeting the incoming tide caused a sea of tumbling water, five feet high, extending a quarter of a mile seaward from the mouth of the creek, and the tide being too strong to swim against, Mr. Pryor could only keep on his back and support the man, until they were eventually swept round and carried to shore.

Ryan, Victor, Schoolboy, Camps Bay, Cape Colony.   Case 47678

About 5.15 p.m. on the 1st March, 1925, a man named Albert Keyser was bathing from the beach in Camps Bay, Cape Colony. In a short time he got out of his depth and was rapidly carried seaward for a distance of 200 yards or more, the depth being at least 12 feet. Victor Ryan, who was well acquainted with the conditions, swam out fully clothed, and reaching him, succeeded with the utmost difficulty in bringing him within 50 yards of the beach, when several people with a rope assisted him in landing them, both being in a very distressed state. This particular place is well known to be very dangerous owing to the extremely strong under-current and backwash.

Hughes, Francis E.C., Capt., 4th P.W.O. Gurkha Rifles.   Case 47697
Lalbahadur Mal, Rifleman.   Posthumous Award

The battalion transport was crossing the Beas river at Mirthal in the Punjab. The river, owing to heavy floods in Northern India, being much swollen, had left its usual channel and was running in several sections with a strong and dangerous current. When crossing the last arm or section a number of camels were forced off the ford by the strength of the stream, and three men, who lost their hold on the camel ropes, were rapidly swept down stream into deep water, and were eventually drowned.

Captain Hughes who had crossed the river on horseback at the head of the camels, was standing on the bank, and he at once called on Rifleman Lalbahadur to help him try and rescue these men. Both then ran down the stream to a point below, where one man was struggling, and jumping in, endeavoured to reach him, but he was swept past them and carried away, they themselves being also swept downstream. After a hard struggle, lasting about five minutes, Captain Hughes managed to reach the further bank in an exhausted condition, Rifleman Lalbahadur being carried away and drowned.

Captain Hughes well knew the dangerous and treacherous nature of the Punjab rivers when in a state of flood.

The Silver Medal was voted to Captain Francis E.C. Hughes and a Posthumous Silver Medal to the relatives of Rifleman Lalbahadur Mal.

Wintle, Mary C.A., Miss., Student, Clifton-on-Sea, Capetown.   Case 47720

About 4 p.m. on the 20th January, 1925, a lady, Mrs. Elisabeth Van der Velde, on entering the water at Clifton-on-Sea, Capetown, for her usual swim, was seized with cramp and quickly carried seaward for a distance of fully 250 yards. There was a strong wind blowing, with rough sea, heavy backwash, and strong current running out. Three men put on lifebelts and swam out, but owing to the current were unable to reach her, and were themselves for some time in a position of the utmost difficulty.
Miss Wintle, a young student of 18, entered the water without a lifebelt and succeeded in reaching Mrs. Van der Velde, whom she managed to bring back to the breakers, where help was given in actually landing her.

Miss Wintle ran great risk of being carried out to sea, and from cramp, the water being very cold.

Couper, John V.H., Biarritz, France.   Case 48058
Krassilstchikoff, Antoine.
Fourquet, Paul.   Posthumous Award
Jemmett, William B.   Posthumous Award

At 11 a.m. on the 23rd July, 1925, two ladies, Mrs. and Miss Williams, were bathing in the sea at Biarritz, France, and got into difficulty owing to the rough sea and strong current, which was carrying them towards the barrier of rocks.

Seeing their danger, the four gentlemen named swam out, Monsieur Fourquet having the life-line with him, but this was of no use as it broke when those on shore were hauling it in. They succeeded in reaching the ladies, but the current was so strong that all were being carried towards the rocks, and ultimately were separated, Mr. Jemmett, M. Fourquet and Mrs. Williams being drowned, Mr. Couper, M. Krassilstchikoff and Miss Williams being thrown on the rocks, cut and bruised, and in a most exhausted state, whence they were taken to a safe situation.

Silver Medals were voted to J.V.H. Couper and A. Krassilstchikoff, and Posthumous Silver Medals to the relatives of W.B. Jemmett an Paul Fourquet.

Cawood, Richard J., Electrical Engineer, Sydney-on-Vaal, South Africa.   Case 48112

About 3 o'clock on the afternoon of the 26th June, 1925, two native children aged about 11 years were returning to their home at Sydney-on-Vaal, South Africa, and in trying to take a short cut across the Vaal river were swept away by the current, but managed to scramble on to a rock in midstream, some distance further down. Some natives tried to rescue the children, but failed. About 8 o'clock in the evening an organized effort was made by the police and others, in order to reach them.

Richard J. Cawood, an electrical engineer, hearing their piteous cries, undressed and although the night was bitterly cold and freezing, swam out to the rock, where he found them in a state of extreme exhaustion, and as the current was too strong for him to swim back with them, he decided, naked as he was, to stay on the rock and support them until further help arrived. Meanwhile Sergeant O'Reilly and Lekobo had found a home-made pontoon about half a mile up river, and on this frail and dangerous craft, which they guided with shovels, they came down stream and managed to reach the rock and take the children on board, after which they themselves entered the water and succeeded in pushing the pontoon to the bank, which they reached after being swept a long way down stream. On the children being taken on to the pontoon, Cawood swam to the bank, which he reached so cold and exhausted that he was unable to dress himself.

The Silver Medal was voted to Richard J. Cawood, and Testimonials on Vellum to Police Sergt Anthony R.C. O'Reilly and David Lekobo.

de Verteuil, Henri, Mrs., Tobago.   Case 48123

Mrs. Henri de Verteuil, while bathing with others in the sea at Tobago on the 3rd August, 1925, heard shouts of "shark" raised, and saw a commotion among the bathers nearer the shore, who were leaving the water as speedily as possible. She herself and her companions then swam back towards the shore, but before leaving the water she turned and saw Bandsman Guy swimming alone and in great difficulty and surrounded by blood.

Calling to those on the beach to hand her a bamboo, she went out towards the man, telling him to hold on that she might pull him in. He then held up his arms, showing that he had lost both hands.
She then went further out till the water reached her neck, and taking him under the chin, helped him towards the shore, where others came to her assistance, and they carried him in and sent for medical aid.

Mrs de Verteuil's act was one of great bravery attended by grave risk to herself, as a shark was following the man when she first reached him.

Mackinnon, Thomas D., aged 14, Tannoch Loch, Milngavie.   Case 48756

At 7.45 p.m. on the 19th January, 1927, a number of young people, estimated at above 30, were skating and sliding on Tannoch Loch, Milngavie, when a break took place, and eight persons were immersed.

Major George MacFarlane, who is only a poor swimmer, and Mackinnon went on the ice and succeeded in dragging out four persons, when the ice on which they were standing collapsed, throwing them into the water. MacFarlane succeeded in scrambling back on to the ice, while Mackinnon searched to see if he could find anyone under water, and came out saying that he had felt a body. A rope was then procured, and with one end round his waist, the other end being tied round Major MacFarlane, Mackinnon again went in, and after surface diving found the body of a girl and brought her out, on whom artificial respiration was tried without success, one other person also being drowned. The break took place about 15 yards from the side, the depth being 8 feet and the night dark.

Mackinnon is a delicate lad, who three months previously severed some of the arteries of one arm, and was forbidden to enter the water for at least six months.

The Silver Medal was voted to Thomas D. Mackinnon, and the Bronze Medal to Major George MacFarlane.

Hopkins, Frank, Labourer, Newport, Mon.   Case 49048

At 9.20 p.m. on the 18th August, 1927, the s.s. *Cambrian Baroness*, ready for sea, was in the lock entrance to the dock at Newport, Mon., when J.A. Lilygreen, a seaman, in attempting to go on board slipped from the pilot ladder and fell into the lock between the ship and the quay, a distance of some 15 feet. The ladder with a line was then let down to the water surface, and Lilygreen got hold of it, but on being hauled up he lost his hold and fell back into the lock. The vessel was now gradually closing in, and was now about 3 feet from the quay wall. Hopkins knowing the risk, then volunteered to go down the ladder, which he did, and having caught the man they were both pulled to the top of the lock, the vessel a few seconds later closing in on the wall. When it was seen that the ship was nearing the wall one of the onlookers advised Hopkins to come up quickly and save himself, to which he replied, "I have got him now and will bring him up." The distance from the coping to the water level was 17 feet, and the depth of water 36 feet.

Great risk was incurred not only of drowning, but of being crushed between the ship and quay. Also awarded the Albert Medal for the same act

Duckworth, Thomas W, Engine-Room Artificer, R.N., H.M. Submarine *L4*.   Case 49157
Paterson, Harry P., Able Seaman, R.N.
Wright, Edward, Stoker 1st Class, R.N.

At 8.10 p.m. on the 20th October, 1927, H.M. Submarine *L4* sighted the s.s. *Irene* entering Bias Bay, South China, and suspecting that she was in the hands of pirates, ordered her to stop, and as she did not do so, shells had to be used. She was on fire, and when she was burning the submarine went alongside to take off passengers and crew. This was difficult on account of the swell, and four passengers lost their lives.

The three above-named men repeatedly dived from the submarine into the sea, and rescued drowning Chinese who had jumped overboard. Each man saved about ten who would, without doubt, have been drowned otherwise, as there was considerable swell, the night was very dark, and there was only one small light to illuminate the scene. The men rescued were up to 200 yards from the submarine, and the ships were two miles from shore.

The submarine returned to Hong Kong with 6 European officers and 226 Chinese from s.s. *Irene*.

Wind S.E.; force 3. No lifebelts were worn. Some of the men saved were pirates and resisted.

McFarlane, C., Chief Officer, S.S. *Chakla*.   Case 49160

On the 12th November, 1927, the s.s. *Chakla* on voyage from Bombay to Karachi, sighted a native boat flying a distress signal and in a derelict condition. A heavy gale was blowing at the time and the light failing; nearing her, figures were seen clinging to the bottom of the vessel, ropes were thrown and the crew were told to jump for their lives; in this way five reached safety. During this time the dhow was being heavily dashed against the sides of the steamer and was breaking up, it being miraculous that any of the crew were rescued without being crushed. At the last moment a man was seen crouching in the stern of the dhow. A rope was thrown, but he was too frightened and exhausted to help himself.

Then Mr. McFarlane, the chief officer, climbed over the rails, down the rope ladder, and jumping on to the dhow, seized the man, swung him on to the ladder and brought him to safety. In view of the mountainous seas and the practical certainty of the officer being either swept off the ladder or crushed between the two vessels, it was a very gallant action.

The dhow was then cast adrift and almost at once turned turtle and broke up.

Bowman, James P.S., Bettws-y-Coed Falls.   Case 49624

On the afternoon of the 25th August, 1928, two young men from Southampton, Mr. R.H. Rogers and Mr. G.H. Windsor, while viewing the falls at Bettws-y-Coed slipped into the foaming turmoil of whirlpools and rapids below the upper part of the Swallow Falls, and were swept over the lower falls and lost to sight amid the deep pools and rocks in the gorge some 50 feet below.

Mr. James P.S. Bowman, age 21, was at that moment on the rock which juts out just below the first fall, and saw one man being carried away. Throwing off his coat he jumped in, and was at once hurled on his back by the force of the water, and driven back on to the boulders at the head of the second falls. He succeeded, however, in clutching the hair of one man, but in a moment they disappeared and were all carried out of sight down the second fall. Ultimately Mr. Bowman managed, after a desperate struggle, to scramble to the bank of the river about half a mile lower down, much bruised, the two other men being drowned.

Tomlinson, John W., Master, Trawler *Ben Ardna*.   Case 49881

The vessel was fishing about 136 miles east from the Tyne on the night of Sunday, the 7th July, 1929, at 10 p.m., with a strong wind and nasty sea. The gear had just been hauled in and preparations were being made to shoot the trawl again, when a heavy sea came along; the vessel gave a quick lurch and the net went over into the sea, taking Andrew Burgon with it, and in his struggles he became entangled in the netting and was drawn under water.

Orders were at once given for the hauling of the gear, and when near the surface Burgon's body was seen beneath the net.

Mr. Tomlinson at once plunged in fully clad, and by diving got underneath the gear and seized Burgon, and managed to get him to the surface and hold him there. A line was then thrown in; Tomlinson caught it and they were both hauled alongside and Burgon recovered after treatment.

Great risk was incurred by diving beneath the net, and then having to swim with the man till clear of the gear.

Lord, Walter P., Foreman Engineer, Liverpool.
Barrow, Frederick, Workman.

Case 49925

On the 22nd April, 1929, Henry Saul and another man were at work on a well in the premises of J. Bibby & Sons, Waterloo Road, Liverpool, and Saul going down first in the chair was in difficulties shortly after reaching the bottom.

His workmate went to his assistance, but was quickly drawn up again, as it had become apparent to those at the top that he was overcome by the fumes.

Then Mr. Lord, foreman engineer, went down in the chair, found Saul unconscious, fastened him in the chair and sent him to the top. While waiting for the chair to descend he himself lost consciousness, and another workman, F. Barrow, promptly went down, and remaining in the chair secured Lord, and holding him across his knees they were drawn up, and in spite of Lord's struggling under the effect of the gas, succeeded in retaining his hold till they reached the surface. Both recovered after treatment.

Well 120 feet deep and 12 feet in diameter. Risk incurred was of suffocation or asphyxia owing to the presence of petrol fumes in the well, caused by a leak in a naptha tank near by.

Tyler, Albert, Labourer, Burnham Green, Herts.

Case 50100

Men were engaged in the work of cleaning out a cesspool at the Skin Factory, Burnham Green, Herts. on the 18th October, 1929. Ernest Tyler was lowered down the well in a wooden bucket attached to a wire rope, and on reaching the bottom he shouted out "Pull me up!" This was being done, when some 14 feet from the bottom he fell out of the bucket, being overcome by foul gas.

William Tyler (aged 67) then slid down the wire rope to help his son, but was at once overcome.

Albert Tyler then went down and got within some 12 feet of them, but was dazed on account of the gas and had to be pulled up. After a little while he made another attempt and was able to touch his father, then felt powerless and had to be pulled up. With a wet handkerchief round his mouth he went down again a third time, taking a spare rope with a hook attached. This he placed round the body of his father and they were drawn up.

Again, going down the fourth time, he placed the rope round his brother, who was then brought to the surface. Artificial respiration was used on both men, but without success.

The cesspool was 34 feet deep and 43 x 46 inches wide at the top, which was oval in shape.

The Silver Medal was awarded to Albert Tyler and the In Memoriam Bronze Medal to the relatives of William G. Tyler.

Varcoe, Vivian, St. Margaret's Bay, Kent.

Case 50427

About 7 p.m. on the evening of the 3rd August, 1930, Mr. J.M. Troughton while bathing in a rough sea at St. Margaret's Bay, Kent, found he could make no headway and was quickly being carried away.

Mr. Vivian Varcoe heard his cries for help and throwing off his coat, plunged in and swam out some 200 yards to where Mr. Troughton was in difficulty, and attempted to push him towards the shore, but in failing in this he caught him under the arms and succeeded in dragging him in.

The sea was rough, half a gale blowing and current running out from the shore. Mr. Troughton is a heavy man and Mr. Varcoe undoubtedly incurred great risk himself in effecting the rescue.

Martin C.F., Clerk of the Ship, S.S. *Vita*.

Case 50560
Posthumous ward

About 10.30 a.m. on the 11th August, 1930, a child fell overboard from the British India Steam Navigation Co. s.s. *Vita* then on voyage from Bombay to Basra.

When he realised that the child was in the water, Mr. Martin, Clerk of the ship, went over after him without giving warning to anyone. A cook gave the alarm on seeing a man in the water and four lifebuoys were thrown in; the vessel was turned short round and hands were sent aloft and a boat held in readiness for lowering. The vessel was back on the position of the buoys in about nine minutes from the time of the alarm, but the child's body was not sighted till 40 minutes later and a boat lowered, but the swell was too heavy for the boat to be of any use, and the ship was manoeuvred alongside the body, which was secured with life lines.

Artificial respiration was tried for over an hour with no effect. Mr. Martin was not seen, and it is presumed he was struck by the propeller and sank immediately.

Posthumous Silver Medal awarded 28th October, 1930.

Farthing, M., Police-Sergeant, Hook, Wiltshire.
King, George W., Contractor.

Case 50709

At 2 p.m. on the 13th February, 1931, at Hook, Wiltshire, Alfred Butler and Leslie A. Hunt were working near the bottom of a well, which was being excavated, and were standing on a ledge of rock 25 feet from the surface, when the timbering and several tons of clay behind collapsed, burying the two men; the board fell across the well and prevented the men being suffocated.

Ash was the first to go down; he slid down a rope and began to shovel clay into buckets, which were pulled up by others; after some minutes he collapsed and had to be hauled to the surface.

A ladder was then lowered and G. King went down and carried on the work with William Cole.

Then P.C. England came on the scene and relieved King, and was in turn relieved by P.S. Farthing, and eventually both the buried men were set free and sent up to the surface. There was danger all the time of the sides of the well caving in, as the hoops had fallen in.

P.S. Farthing in particular rendered good help, and Mr. King the contractor, whose men were sinking the well, states that he is doubtful if the men would have been got out alive if the police officers had not arrived, as nobody had sufficient nerve to go down the well to assist him.

Silver Medals awarded to Police-Sergeant Farthing and G.W. King, Bronze Medal to Police Constable E.E. England, and Testimonials on Vellum to Albert E. Ash and William Cole.

Falzon, Paul, Tigne, Malta.
Parsons Victor G.A., Petty Officer, R.N.
Webb, Alexander H.W., Able Seaman, R.N.
Picton, Sydney E., Driver, Royal Artillery.

Case 50710

Posthumous award.

At 4 p.m. on the 6th February, 1931, at Tigne, Malta, Mrs. A. Palmer Cohen was washed from the steps leading to the foreshore at the bathing place near Tigne Barracks, a heavy sea running at the time.

Falzon alone witnessed the accident and plunged in. He managed to reach her 30 or 40 yards out, and bring her close to the shore, but they were carried out again and again by the backwash, and eventually he was thrown on the rocks alone, and hauled out by means of a rope.

Meanwhile the alarm had been given in Tigne Barracks, and Driver Picton and another man ran down, and Picton plunged in fully dressed, Mrs Cohen being seen floating some way out.

Then Petty Officer Parsons and Able Seaman Webb came up and both plunged in, Driver Picton disappearing about the same time or just after they swam out. They reached Mrs. Cohen, and between them brought her near the shore (some ten yards or so), but owing to the heavy seas and backwash off the rocks, could not effect a landing, became separated, and were with difficulty helped out themselves.

At this stage Gunner Clarke went in, swam out and got within a few yards of the lady, but was then compelled to return, and was helped out in a battered condition.

Heavy sea and backwash. All these attempts were made at great personal risk. Mrs. Cohen's body was not recovered.

Silver Medals awarded to Falzon, Parsons and Webb, In Memoriam Silver Medal to the relatives of Driver Picton, Bronze Medal to Gunner Dennis Clarke, R.A.

Davies, John, Cadgwith Cove, Ruan Minor, Cornwall.   Case 51381

About 6.30 p.m. On the afternoon of 25th August, 1932, Lieut. J.B. Howes, of the Royal Warwickshire Regiment, while bathing in Cadgwith Cove, Ruan Minor, Cornwall, became entangled in a mass of seaweed floating in the centre of the Pool and was quite helpless.

Two girls and a man tried to help him, but were unable to do so, and had to give up from exhaustion.

Their calls attracted the attention of Mr. Davies, who had just come in from a long swim and was dressing on the beach. He at once plunged in and swam out, and after a hard struggle, during which he had to dive underneath to disentangle Mr. Howes, succeeded in freeing him and then towed him to shore, both then being thoroughly exhausted.

Danger of being dashed against the rocks. A rough sea and strong wind, and some 100 yards from shore. Too rough to launch a boat.

Mant, Herbert, 2nd Officer S.S. *Watford*.   Case 51475

At 9.30 a.m. on the 10th September, 1932, while bound for Sydney, Nova Scotia, from Quebec, the vessel was driven on the rocks at Cape Percy, two miles from Glace Bay, Cape Briton Island. Heavy seas breaking over her made it impossible to launch the lifeboats. S.O.S. signals were sent out, but help was not available, and the ship was breaking up rapidly.

Their only hope being to get a line on shore, Mr. Mant, the 2nd Officer, volunteered for this, and plunged in, battled his way through heavy breakers and reached shore, though the line was swept from the ship. Contact was made by a rocket apparatus fired from the ship, which was secured by Mr. Mant with the assistance of some shore men working under his supervision, and all the crew, some 37 persons, with the exception of the Chief Officer and a fireman, were saved.

Heavy N.E. gale with squalls of hurricane force and high seas.

Olsen, Ernst M.O., Mate, Danish S.S. *Rota*.   Case 51503

About 10 p.m. on the 9th October, 1932, at Newcastle-upon-Tyne, a member of the crew of the Fishing Cruiser H.M.S. *Harebell* fell into the water between the vessel and the quay. Without hesitation Olsen slid down a rope over the ship's side, and holding on with one hand, succeeded in reaching the drowning man and holding him till both were hauled to safety.

With the incoming tide and a strong current running there was a very grave risk of the vessel moving and crushing both the drowning man and the mate.

Foy, Harold Basil, Mount Lavinia, Ceylon. Case 51547

About 9.45 a.m. on Sunday, 30th October, 1932, several parties of people were bathing from a sandy beach about half a mile north of Mount Lavinia, Ceylon. For most of the year this spot is considered safe for bathers, but between the monsoons a strong current runs either north or south, and on this occasion three persons found themselves in difficulties and could not regain the shore.

G. Chambers, aged 26, finding he could not stand against the undertow, asked Foy, who was near, to help him. This he did, but could not make much headway until Pound came up, and then they reached the shore. Then Algar, aged 54, was seen in difficulties. He also was swept off his feet and carried out of his depth. Foy and Edmunds and Pound swam out and reached him, and with Foy holding him up and the others towing them to shore, they reached a chain of hands and were pulled in. Then C. Emmerson, aged 53, was seen floating face downwards beyond the breakers, and Foy and Edmunds again swam out, and brought the man in, in the same way, but he did not recover.

Some 40 to 60 yards out, 8 feet deep. Sea rough and strong current down the coast. Mr. Foy took the principal part in all the rescues.

Silver Medal awarded to H.B. Foy, and Bronze Medals to Lieut. Eric Edmunds and Leonard D. Pound.

Ifereimi Raqoneqone, Macuata Coast, Fiji. Case 51590

On the morning of the 11th April, 1932, four Fijians, three men and one woman, named Sulueti Ganake, were diving for sici shell on the Macuata Coast, when the woman was attacked by a shark while swimming in deep water.

On hearing her cry for help Ifereimi, who was some 20 yards distant, at once swam to her, and diving down saw, with the aid of his submarine glasses, that a shark had attacked her and was pulling her down, so seizing her arm he pulled her up, and in the struggle her leg was lacerated. Reaching the surface he then swam, supporting the woman and repeatedly fighting off the shark with his spear, until he reached shallow water and got her into the dinghy which had now been brought up by the other men, and into which she was placed, having fainted, having been bitten on the thigh and calf of the leg.

Later she was attended by a Native Medical Practitioner and spent a month in the hospital at Labasa, where she made a complete recovery.

Adams, John, River Isioha, Kenya. Case 51871

About 6.30 p.m. on the 17th March, 1933, John Adams, Basil Cochrane and Benjamin P. Fayle went to bathe in the River Isioha, 6 miles west of Kakmega, Kenya Colony. Adams and Fayle swam upstream through a deep pool, and stood up in shallow water reaching to the thigh. Cochrane was then undressing on the bank.

Suddenly Fayle's right arm was seized by a crocodile, which shook his arm and tried to drag him under water. He shouted out and Adams at once gripped the crocodile by the head, and by pulling and shaking it made it release its grip. He pulled Fayle to his feet, then helped him out of the water. His arm was broken in two places and Adams attended to it, then with Cochrane got him back to their camp.

Danger of being dragged into deep water. Mr. Adams showed exemplary initiative, courage and tenacity, and at great personal risk saved Mr. Fayle's life.

Ali Akbar, River Ichbar, North West Provinces, India. Case 52181

On the 14th August, 1933, the Ichbar River, North-West Provinces, India, was in full flood owing to heavy rains, the depth being 5-6 feet, with large boulders being swept along by the torrent. Communication between the opposite banks was impossible, with the result that over 100 people, with several motor cars and lorries, were held up until the water subsided. About 5 p.m., the water having fallen a little, a coolie in the Public Works Department attempted to cross the nullah about 300 yards above the stone causeway. He was swept off his feet and carried downstream until he was luckily washed against the iron water gauge post on the edge of the causeway, to which he clung.

Ali Akbar and two other men attempted to reach him along the causeway, but the strength of the torrent, was still too great. A rope was obtained to float across to him, but proved too short. Ali Akbar then attached his turban to the rope and floated it past the man, who tied it round his wrist and then let go of the post, while the rope was hauled upon. The knot between the rope and turban parted, with the result that the man was swept downstream again. Ali Akbar at once jumped in, swam after him, and finally reached him about 200 yards below the causeway, both being luckily swept ashore at a bend and rescued. It was over an hour later before the cars and lorries were able to cross the nullah by the causeway.

Juma Kalanzi, retired pensionless, Government Servant.   Case 52287

In July, 1933, a small native boy, whilst walking on an unoccupied seasonal steamer-landing on the Nile, fell into the water and was seized by a waiting crocodile.

Some distance off, a retired pensionless Government servant named Juma Kalanzi heard the shouting, and in spite of being unable to swim, jumped high and out beyond the Papyrus-sudd, landing on a weed and mud bottom, with water up to his chin. The crocodile had seized the boy by both legs above the knee, and was swimming off, trying to submerge. The child's arm only being visible above the water, Juma seized the arm and tried to pull the child back and up to the surface to get breath. Little by little he did so, whilst the infuriated crocodile lashed the water into foam with his tail. The boy, who had lost a lot of blood and was half drowned, was unable to assist Juma in any way. Juma's small son seized a spear from an onlooker and hurled it to his father, who, whilst retaining his hold of the boy, stabbed the reptile with the spear. The crocodile tore his teeth clear of the child's legs and then turned to attack Juma, seizing him by the hand and wrist, crushing the bone and permanently damaging the arm. Juma pushed the child behind him into shallow water, whilst he continued to stab the reptile underneath the plating on its back. The crocodile finally released Juma's arm and made off, whilst Juma returned with the boy ashore. Juma was injured intestinally, and had to find his way to a hospital over 100 miles away to undergo a serious operation. Neither the boy nor his family was known to Juma Kalanzi, and it was only by a chance remark that the rescue was ever brought to the Society's notice.

Richards, Jack, Ironmonger's Assistant, Lee Bay, Devon.   Case 52499

On 19th August, 1934, whilst bathing in a heavy sea at Lee Bay, Devon, a man was swept 150 yards seawards and was unable to return. Three other men swam out to his assistance, but two returned when they encountered the full force of the tide and seas.

Jack Richards, hearing shouts for help, dived off some rocks at the end of the bay, swam out to the two now exhausted men, whom he encouraged and advised to swim with him seaward, with a view to being swept by the current into the next bay. A large wave separated the two men, so that each thought the other had drowned. Richards and one of the men eventually managed to land on some rocks in the next bay, after being swept back into the sea on at least eight or nine occasions. The other man had been swept on to a submerged rock some 25 yards off the cliffs, to which he clung in spite of the pounding of the waves. Richards on getting ashore, saw his situation, and in spite of the difficulties in getting over the rocks and gullies, finally managed to bring him ashore, both being in a very exhausted condition. The waves were so high that people ashore were unable to see what was happening, and the surf boat had been smashed to pieces earlier in the day. The rescue took over an hour to effect.

Johnson, Frederick W, Labourer.   Case 52561
Withers, Wilfred R, Labourer.

About 9.35 a.m. on the 11th September, 1934, F. Eales, a Council roadman, descended a 20 ft. deep manhole to clear some waste surface water there. Finding a pipe choked he fetched his broom, and on clearing the obstruction released carbon dioxide gas, and fell unconscious into the water. Griffith Griffiths descended to his rescue and was also overcome. Frederick W. Johnson was fetched from a nearby house, descended, hauled Eales up out of the water, shouted for a rope, but was overcome by the gas and not rescued until three-quarters of an hour later. James McCarthy, a roadman, then arrived, and seeing the three men at the bottom, descended but smelling gas and becoming giddy, returned and warned others of its presence. Wilfred R. Withers was driving up the street, stopped and descended with a rope round his waist, and endeavoured to hook a rope on to Griffiths, before, he, too, was overcome and had to be hauled to the surface. Withers and Wood then each descended twice, with hook ropes which they attached to the men's clothing, but failed to rescue them before being hauled up for treatment. Gas masks and ropes had now arrived from an adjacent colliery. Withers donned one and descended again, fastened ropes round each of the three men in turn to enable them to be hauled to the surface, he, owing to the narrowness of the manhole, having to ascend each time to permit the body to be recovered. Eales and Griffiths were dead on arrival at the surface, but Johnson recovered under artificial respiration.

Silver Medals were awarded to Withers and Johnson, Bronze Medals to P.C. Wood and Griffiths, Vellum Testimonial to McCarthy.

Jagannathrao Krishnarao Bhonsle, Lieut., 5th Mahratta Light Infantry.   Case 52973

About 5.30 p.m. on 13th January, 1935, Capt. and Mrs. Horsley and two friends got into difficulties whilst bathing in a rough sea and strong wind at Cannanore, Malabar, S. India, and being visitors, were unaware of the strong undercurrents set up under these conditions. Mrs Horsley, on finding herself being swept seaward, called to her husband for assistance, but he was unable to tow her back owing to the adverse current. Mr. Aitken grasping the situation, stayed with Mrs. Horsley and encouraged her to float, whilst her husband and other friend were washed ashore on the rocks in a semi-conscious condition. An officer on the cliff top, seeing the four persons in difficulty, procured a rope, which was too short to reach them from the beach.

Lieut Bhonsle volunteered to swim out to their aid, but owing to the conditions being such that he would in all probability have sacrificed his own life also, he was forbidden to do so by a senior officer present. The two persons were now observed being swept inshore round the promontory into the next bay. Lieut. Bhonsle took the rope, scaled the jagged cliff of the promontory, finally reaching a high isolated rock at the extremity. Seeing that the two persons were again being swept seawards, he tied the rope around his waist, left the other end to be tended by some men who had just arrived, dived in, swam out 40-50 yards, tied the rope around Mrs Horsley, who was then pulled back to the rock, whilst he himself assisted Mr. Atkins to swim there. Great difficulty was experienced in hauling the three persons up the 10-15 ft. high rock. Lieut. Bhonsle had to remain clinging to the jagged rock under these dangerous conditions until the others had reached safety, when he, too, was hauled up, completely exhausted.

Jone Draunimasi, Fiji.   Case 53112

On 22nd March, 1934, Jone Draunimasi, his nephew Williame Uate, and two other Fijians set out in a punt to collect Trochas shell. On arrival at the reef, Williame, followed by Jone, jumped in and commenced their search for shells, but finding the current too strong, Jone decided they ought to return, and informed Williame accordingly. Williame then discovered two shells and was left diving for them whilst Jone continued his search en route for the reef. On one of his arrivals at the surface he was informed by one of the other natives that Williame was being attacked by a large barracuda. Jone turned and swam unarmed at once in that direction, and saw his nephew swerve past the fish, and then when about 3 fathoms away, saw him attacked again and seized by the arm, which was severed at the shoulder, tearing away part of the lung also. Jone thereupon dived, seized his nephew in his arms, and using his legs only swam for the reef, being followed by the fish. The other natives brought over the punt as quickly as possible, but Williame died in a few minutes.

The Governor of Fiji, in reporting the case, states that the natives fear the barracuda more than the shark, owing to its fierceness and directness and rapidity of its attack.

Collins, Frederick George, Baker, Whitsands Bay, Plymouth.   Case 53175

About 3.30 p.m. on 23rd June, 1935, Collins and a party of friends were playing at Whitsands Bay, near Plymouth, with a beach ball, which was accidentally kicked into the breakers and carried seaward by a strong ebb tide. Rendle a good swimmer and about to bathe, said he would recover it, was warned of the dangerous nature of this part of the coast, swam out to it and tried to return. Finding he was being swept rapidly seawards in spite of all his efforts, he called out for help. Collins fully aware of the danger that the current would be too much for the strongest swimmer, swam out, found Rendle blue in the face and practically exhausted, encouraged him to keep afloat, and succeeded, after a great struggle, in towing him back to the edge of the breakers, where a number of persons, who had formed a human chain, hauled them both ashore to safety.

Rescue 250 yards out in deep water. Strong ebb tide and undertow. No life-saving appliances on the beach, or any boats in the vicinity.

Webster, Clarence G., Captain, Motor Vessel *C.M. Laura*.   Case 53232

The wooden Motor Vessel *C.M. Laura*, 75 tons net register, left Belize, British Honduras, on 14th March, 1935, with passengers, mostly women and children, and a crew of eight, bound for Utilla Island, Republic of Honduras.

A strong north-westerly wind, accompanied by heavy rain squalls, sprang up during the night. Whilst running before the heavy following seas, the vessel grounded on the north coast of the island about 3.30 a.m. and in pitch darkness. The engines were reversed, but without result, the vessel remaining fast on the rocks with heavy seas breaking over her, causing her to pound heavily, with every likelihood of breaking up quickly.

The searchlight was switched on and it was then discovered that her bows were about 60 feet off the low and rock bound coast and that there was considerable backwash of the 10 ft. high and jagged rocks. The lifeboat was smashed to splinters by the seas breaking over the vessel, and it was evident that the persons on board must be got ashore with despatch.

Capt. Webster who was in the Chart Room when the vessel grounded, tried to quieten the frenzied passengers, and, seeing that none of the crew in the bows were making any attempt to get a line ashore, secured a line around his waist, dived overboard from the poop, swam amongst the rocks until able to reach the shore, where he experienced great difficulty in landing, due to the backwash and heavy seas, secured the line and then returned along it to supervise the landing of his passengers and crew.

None of the passengers could be induced to make the attempt until Mr. McPherson Miller, himself a passenger, joined the Captain in the water, and between them the two men managed to land safely the whole of the passengers and crew, remaining in the water until the last was safely landed at daybreak. Capt. Webster was badly cut and bruised by contact with jagged rocks whilst swimming ashore. The vessel became a total wreck.

Capt. Webster was awarded the Society's Silver Medal and Mr. McPherson Miller the Bronze Medal.

Cross, Henry, Engineer, M.V. *Derek*.   Case 53371

On 14th February, 1936, during a two days cyclone, the Fiji Government Workboat, m.v. *Derek*, was driven ashore on Komo Island, being stranded broadside on the rocks and swept by the tremendous seas. Owing to her position it was impossible to launch a boat on either side, and it was therefore decided to try and reach the shore by swimming before the vessel either broke up or rolled over to windward and sank.

Capt. Twentyman had gone down the gangway so as to get a good shove off with the next incoming wave, when a sudden lurch of the ship caused his feet to slip on the copper sheathing, resulting in his being sucked under the vessel by the backwash from the rocks under her lee.

Mr. Cross, the engineer of the *Derek*, seeing Twentyman's predicament and realizing that he would probably be crushed on the rocks when the vessel swung back, held on to a rock, groped under the bottom of the ship, seized him and succeeded in drawing him clear before the vessel did so. Twentyman was completely exhausted by now and was therefore unable to assist Cross in any way during their 30 yards swim for the shore, where both were helped ashore by others, who had previously landed.

Camp, Harold Hugh, Municipal Beach Guard, East London, South Africa.   Case 54139

At 4.30 p.m. on 7th February, 1937, a native youth, Messisa, whilst bathing from the Native Area at Eastern Beach, East London, South Africa, was caught by the current and carried 300 yards out to sea, through huge breakers and two reefs of rocks. A native boy ran 450 yards over to the European Bathing Area and informed the Municipal Beach Guards Camp and Moffat, who at once proceeded to the rescue. Camp entered the water between the two beaches, swam out to the native, who struggled violently, mastered and supported him until the arrival of Moffat, who after procuring the Surf Life-saving Reel, had donned the harness and swum out with the line.

The rescue was effected at considerable risk, due to the distance out, the state of the sea, and the danger from the reefs of rocks.

Silver Medal to Camp and Bronze Medal to John Moffat.

Littledale, Charles Edgar, Manager, Iraq Petroleum.　　　　　　　　　　　　　　　　　　　　　　　Case 54402

About 6.30 p.m. on the 25th July, 1937, Littledale attempted to enter Mudeford Harbour, Christchurch, Hants, in a motor-boat, but found he was unable to do so owing to the 6 knots ebb tide in "The Run". After the boat had grounded on the Bar, been swept stern first through a row of piles near the pier, it was anchored in the pool to seaward of them, to wait for the tide to slacken.

Shortly afterwards, five visitors (two fathers and their three young children) attempted to cross the River Stour in a boat, were caught by the strong tide in "The Run", and swept broadside onto the piles, the boat being capsized and all on board being thrown into the water. One man and his daughter were swept against the piles, to which they clung, until rescued, whilst the others were swept seaward past the anchored motor-boat. A buoy was thrown in their direction but it failed to reach them.

Littledale, knowing the danger of the strong undertow at the edge of the pool, then dived in fully clothed, swam after and supported the two children, whilst the father swam after and retrieved the lifebuoy, by means of which they were all enabled to land safely on some rocks further out to seaward. Littledale then ran back along the shore, saw that the other two were becoming exhausted and liable to be swept away from the piles, dived in, seized a lifebuoy from the motor-boat thrown within reach, and was thus able to bring the man and his daughter back to the boat. All three were taken on board the motor-boat and subsequently landed.

But for Littledale and the anchored boat, all five persons would have been swept out to sea and probably drowned.

Ryle, Iris Mary, Miss. (now Princess Wittgenstein)　　　　　　　　　　　　　　　　　　　　　　　Case 54406

About 4 p.m. on 5th September, 1937, a party of four persons (consisting of a husband and wife, his brother and friend) were surf-bathing in Constantine Bay, Cornwall, and after a time became separated by the tide. The wife and her friend, being furthest out, suddenly discovered that they were in a strong current, and in spite of swimming hard towards the shore found they were unable to make progress. The husband, later realizing that his wife and friend were in difficulties, swam to their aid accompanied by his brother, and on reaching them they assisted the wife and friend respectively, both of whom now being exhausted by their efforts to get out of the current. The flood tide had commenced to make by now, thereby increasing the size of the breakers, which not only separated the two pairs of bathers, but also prevented them seeing one another except when on the crest of a wave. The people ashore had by now realized the danger, and the buoy and line (kept on the beach for that purpose) had been fetched for use. Henry Harvey got the buoy, and with others attending the line, started to swim out to their aid, but found himself being swept southward. He then attempted to stem the current, but without success.

Miss Ryle, who was sun-bathing in a relative's garden on the cliff-top, realized the danger, ran 150 yards down to the beach and on to some rocks towards which she knew the tide set, waded out waist deep, and called to Harvey to swim in her direction, which he did. After taking the buoy from him she swam out across the current in the direction of the two men furthest out, leaving Harvey to unravel and attend to the line. This he was unable to do in time, and so swam out after her, eventually losing his hold on the line, thus leaving Miss Ryle to swim out unattended. Harvey then followed after her, was caught by the current and swept out towards the husband and wife. On her way out Miss Ryle passed one of the men, who said he was all right and told her to go on to his friend who was further seaward. This she did, and found him to be very exhausted by now. With the man holding on to the buoy Miss Ryle turned and made for the shore, swimming diagonally across the current due to its strength. Eventually she managed to reach the rocks, and whilst the line was being hauled ready for the next attempt, it was discovered that the other man, seeing a rope dragged past him, had held on to it, and was thus saved also.

Miss Ryle's aunt then arrived with her personal belt with line attached, and the two women then set out to attempt the rescue of the husband and wife, who had by now been over one and a half hours in the water, with the waves continuously washing over them. As Miss Ryle's line was not long enough, two men swam out and attached another length to it. On reaching the persons in danger, she discovered that Harvey had been swept close to them, and that he was very exhausted indeed. With the wife and Harvey holding on to the buoy, and the husband on to Harvey's shoulder, she made for the shore, being assisted by persons ashore hauling in on the line. The aunt was also hauled ashore, as due to the drag on the line she had been unable to get out through the breakers

The rescue was at least 100 yards out from the shore, and took over one hour in all to effect. The heavy ground swell and breakers added considerably to the risk, and all the persons saved state they owe their lives entirely to Miss Ryle's courage and resources under very difficult conditions.

Miss Ryle was awarded a Silver Medal and Henry George Lewarne Harvey a Bronze Medal.

Meston, Robert Alexander, Captain, Zand River, New Pietersburg, South Africa.   Case 54522

At 5 p.m. on 5th February, 1937, two native girls, aged 10 and 8 years, were playing in the Zand River near their home at New Pietersburg, Transvaal, and when on a rock in midstream were trapped by a sudden rush of flood waters from up river.

Their mother, on being informed of their plight, attempted to go to their aid, likewise their uncle, but the strength of the current was too strong to allow them to do so. Their mother then tried to get some of the numerous natives present, who knew the river well to attempt the rescue, but none would risk it. An European resident then phoned the Police at Pietersburg who arrived shortly afterwards in cars. The two children were still marooned on the rock in midstream, but were now up to their knees in water, with the river still rising and darkness impending. An immediate attempt at rescue was therefore necessary if the girls were not to be swept off the rock and drowned.

Seeing that a direct attempt at rescue at this spot was impracticable, due to the numerous rocks and boulders Meston and the Police proceeded upstream to where the river divided round an island, which looked to be near enough to enable them to wade down to the children, provided the raging torrent in between could be crossed.

A rock about 1 foot above the water level and near the head of the island was then discovered, which looked as if a rope could be made fast and thus help them to cross the flooded river.

Gobedi a strong swimmer, then volunteered to try to get a rope across to the rock, refused to have it tied around him, took it in his hand, entered the river further upstream, was at once swept off his feet, but managed to cling on to a submerged rock near to the one for which he was making. Meston seeing him in difficulties, at once entered the water to go to his aid, saw him scramble out on to the rock, and after securing the rope temporarily, Meston made his way out to him, being followed by Mandala after the rope had been properly secured by Meston. The three men then made their way on to the island and down to its tail, where Meston waded downstream, waist deep, to the rock where the children were marooned, and brought each in turn back to the island on his back. They then all returned to the head of the island to attempt to re-cross the river before darkness set in completely.

The two Native Constables holding on to the rope close to the rock, Meston took one of the children on his back across to the bank, and then returned for the other. During his passage across with the second child, the rope broke and submerged both him and the child, but luckily the two Constables were able to seize the end of the rope in time to prevent Meston and the girl being swept downstream.

Meston in spite of his exhaustion, then returned to the island again to see the Constables across, was swept off the rope, but managed to get on to a submerged rock, being helped out by one of the Native Constables. After a short rest, Meston ordered Mandala to regain the bank whilst he and Gobedi held on to the rope. This he was able to do at the second attempt. Meston then sent Gobedi across whilst he remained holding on to the rope alone. In midstream Gobedi was sucked under, dragging Meston off his feet also, and both men were swept downstream holding on to the rope. The Police on the bank then hauled in on their end of the rope, and got both men ashore completely exhausted.

The rescue took over an hour to effect and was witnessed by hundreds of natives on the one bank and by numerous Europeans on the other. The river actually did rise higher during the night, and but for this rescue, the children would certainly have been swept off the rocks and drowned.

A Silver Medal to Captain Robert Alexander Meston and Bronze Medals to Native Constables Frans Gobedi and Joseph Mandala, South African Police.

Bowden, Clifford, Miner.   Case 54523

About 4.30 p.m. on 23rd January, 1937, the wall of rock separating the old Wheal Boys Shaft from the Wheel Reeth Mine caved in resulting in thousands of tons of water pouring into the levels and down the shafts until the whole mine was flooded.

Being a Saturday, most of the men had already come up, and all those below managed to escape with the exception of three men who were imprisoned in a level, due to the water rising up to the roof in a V-shaped sump between their stope and the shaft. It was necessary, therefore, to extricate these trapped men before the water rose still higher along the level and drowned them.

Bowden, who was working in his stope on the 220-ft. level, felt a rush of air, thought an air-pipe had burst, stopped his machine and went to investigate. While going along the level he heard a roaring sound and saw a wall of water rushing along the level towards him. Realizing that there were two men working in the 310-ft. level below him, he ran back, worked his way round and down to them, and got them back and up to his stope as the water was already chest-deep in his level. After three hours they were located from a level above, and a rope lowered down the shaft to them, of which they eventually got hold, in spite of the water still pouring down the shaft and flooding the lower levels. Ultimately, all three men were hauled up through the pouring water to safety.

On Sunday, 24th January, it was found that with all the pumps going, the water level was only being lowered about three inches per hour. Additional pumps were therefore obtained from other mines nearby, and deep-sea divers asked for from Plymouth and Penzance. Attempts were also made to bore down to where the three men were trapped, in case the water rose any higher, owing to a further break.

On Monday, 25th January, men had been working all the day, as the water level fell slowly, to try and get through or round the sump to the level where the three men were trapped. Kemp had made several attempts, but the water was still too deep, with dynamite lockers, baulks of timber and other obstructions floating about. Bowden then arrived and, on being informed that the water level in the sump had fallen below the roof level, volunteered to try to get through. A thermos of hot coffee was strapped to his waist, and with a torch tied round his neck so that his movements could be followed, he waded down the level past Kemp, until he had to swim across the deepest part of the sump (about 30 feet). He then touched bottom, was able to wade out the rest of the distance, found the now very exhausted men, and gave them the coffee. Kemp then arrived, was asked to go back for more coffee, which he did. The water then suddenly dropped, other rescuers were now able to wade across and assisted the entombed men to the shaft, up which they were sent to safety after 56 hours below ground, 53 of which they had been trapped.

To effect the rescue, Bowden had to wade about 200 feet and swim 30 feet through icy cold water through the flooded level, with the water only a few inches below the roof level. On reaching the surface he collapsed from exhaustion, due to the extreme coldness of the water.

A Silver Medal to Clifford Bowden and a Bronze Medal to James Kemp.

Carmichael, Hugh, Mate, Steam Trawler *Cape Cheyuskin*. Case 54540

The steam trawler *Cape Cheyuskin*, while crossing the Spitzbergen Sea, on her return to the Norwegian Coast from the Bear Island Fishing Grounds, encountered a strong north-westerly gale (force 7/8) with heavy seas and freezing hard. The crew had been ordered to remain below decks (except for duty) and life-lines had been rigged fore and aft.
At 12.40 p.m. on 15th February, 1938, when in lat. 73 40 N., lon. 18 E., Poskett, a learner deck-hand, who had been battened down below in the forecastle since the previous day, came up on deck for some reason unknown, was washed overboard when the vessel gave a heavy lurch, and was seen floating astern by the Bo-sun, who was in the wheelhouse at the time.

Carmichael, the Mate of the Trawler, was having his dinner, heard the cry of "Man overboard", ran up on deck, and as the vessel was manoeuvred by the Skipper to pick up Poskett, threw a heaving-line over the man's shoulders, but he made no attempt to get hold of it. Carmichael then secured the end of the line around his waist, discarded his sea-boots, jumped overboard fully clothed, swam to Poskett, but was unable to retain his hold, due to the extreme coldness of the water, and, becoming unconscious himself, was hauled back on board by the line. The Trawler was again manoeuvred alongside Poskett's body, which was still floating, his oil-frock was seized with a boat-hook, but this tore away the material, causing the body to sink and not come to the surface again.

Kent, Ernest William, Labourer, Hackney Wick Stadium, London. Case 55004

Boring operations for the erection of a totalizator in the Hackney Wick Stadium at Hackney, were in progress, and steel tubes of 14 1/2 inch internal diameter were being sunk in connection with the foundation piles.

At 3 a.m. on 25th October, 1938, an obstruction took place in one of these tubes, which had been sunk 18 feet into the ground. Baker who was in charge of the gang, descended feet first on the winch cable to try and clear the tube, and when about 12 feet down was heard to be gasping for breath. The winch was reversed and Baker was hauled up to within 4 feet of the top, when he released his hold and fell to the bottom of the tube in an upright position, with his arms about his head.

Kent, in spite of being warned of the gas he would encounter, at once volunteered to go down. Had his feet tied to the winch cable and was lowered head first into the tube, with instructions to keep talking all the way down. On hearing Kent also gasping for breath, the winch was reversed and he was hauled up quickly in a semi-conscious state and bleeding from the mouth. First aid was rendered to him and, on the arrival of the fire brigade and ambulance, an oxygen bottle, partly opened, was lowered down the tube close to Baker's mouth in the hope of dispersing the gas and keeping the man alive until rescued.

Attempts were then made to dig out the tube, and after unscrewing the top section (3 1/2 feet) it was realized that it would take too long to save Baker by this means. As the gas should have been partly dispersed by now, it was decided to send another man down. Kent though not fully recovered, again volunteered, but Davlin was sent first. His shoulders caught in an obstruction in the tube when he too, had been lowered head first into the tube, and he had therefore to be hauled up again.

Though there were numerous volunteers to go down the tube, no one was small enough to do so. Kent, fully realizing the risk he would incur, was again lowered into the tube head first, caught Baker's wrists, was again heard gasping for breath, and calling "Quick, quick", was hauled up and managed to retain his hold of the man's wrists, until others were able to get hold of Baker's arms and take the weight. Kent then collapsed (and was again bleeding from the mouth), but was quickly restored with oxygen and removed to hospital.

All attempts to restore Baker failed, due to the tube being full of gas, as, in spite of a partly-opened oxygen cylinder, it only contained 3.1% of oxygen instead of the usual 21%.

A Silver Medal was awarded to Ernest William Kent, and a Vellum Testimonial to Frank Davlin.

Faram, Ernest Arthur Charles, Police-Sergeant, Wellingborough, Northants.   Case 55020

Owing to the wind being in an unfavourable direction, it had been impossible to clean out the effluent pit at Messrs. Nicholson, Sons & Daniels Tannery Works at Wellingborough, Northants, prior to the August Bank Holiday, and it was not until the 9th August, 1938, that the wind veered and enabled work to be commenced on it.

The pit dredger was started at 4 p.m. and at about 5.40 p.m., when the residue was about 3 feet deep, the first pair of men, Alwyn Sharp and William Smart, both wearing thigh boots, descended to clear out the sludge. Apparently, the two men were overcome by the fumes on reaching the bottom by the time the next pair, George Smart and Alfred Gayton, were ready to descend.

Smart, seeing his brother in a collapsed state at the bottom, at once descended to his aid, being followed by Gayton, whose shouts for help, before descending, brought Linnell and Clow running to the pit. On their arrival, Gayton was seen to be slumped at the bottom of the ladder. William Smart was lying in the sludge with only the back of his head visible, George Smart was lying face downwards over his brother as if attempting to hold him up, and no trace of Sharp was visible.

Linnell at once descended the ladder, followed by Clow, who told Linnell to go back and put on waders, the two men crossing one another on the ladder. Linnell then returned to the surface, called for help and collapsed. On coming to again, he found four men from the works on the opposite side of the road attending him. Linnell then obtained two ropes, secured one round his waist, made a loop in the other, descended the ladder again, passed the loop in the other rope under Gayton's arms, and remembers nothing further until he regained consciousness in hospital.

Wood, who was leaving his works (on the opposite side of the road to the Tannery about 6.5 p.m., was informed of the accident, obtained a rope and first aid outfit, ran across to the pit, and on looking down, saw two bodies lying close together at the foot of the ladder. Securing the rope around his waist and with a handkerchief over his nose and mouth, he descended with a spare rope, which he tied around one of the bodies, and then remembers nothing further.

Howe, who was driving his lorry along the street, was informed of the accident, stopped and went inside the Tannery and saw one man (presumably Gayton) lying on the ground and being attended to by others. On being told that there were other men still down the pit, he secured a rope around his body, held his breath and descended the ladder with a spare rope, which he tied round a man (presumably Clow), and then remembers nothing further.

Sergeant Faram then arrived with the Police car and saw two men (presumably Gayton and Clow) with Dr. Evans attending to one of them. He then started resuscitation on the other man until informed that there were others still down the pit. Running to the pit, he discarded his helmet and tunic, put on a respirator that a man had got, tied a rope around his waist, and taking a spare rope, descended the ladder and found he was thigh deep in sludge. Tying the rope around the nearest man, he signalled to haul up and then assisted to get the body up, as it had to be swung out and over a large row of pipes half way up. The respirator was too large and not functioning properly, and he was now beginning to feel the effects of the gas.

Faram again descended the ladder and assisted to get the second man up and, on being told that there was a third man, descended again. The respirator now slipped outwards and the canister fell into the sludge, causing misting of the eye-pieces. Groping in the sludge, he found a third man and got him up also. He was then informed that all had been recovered, was washed down with a hose and then carried on with the attempted restoration, though feeling dizzy. Later he was sent to hospital and detained for the night.

The pit is 20 feet deep, lit by electric light, and 10,000 to 12,000 gallons of water pass through it hourly. The presence of gas has never been known previously, and it is thought that the heavy thunderstorm about 4 p.m., which flooded the yard, must have washed some hydrochloric acid from the carboys stored there into the drain which runs into the pit.

Silver Medal awarded to E.A.C. Faram, Bronze Medals to Linnell, Wood, Howe, and In Memoriam Testimonials to the relatives of George Smart, Alfred Gayton and Clow.

Sinclair, John MacLachlan Harvey, Flying Officer, Royal Air Force.   Case 55088

At 10 p.m. on the 20th September, 1938, the Sunderland Flying Boat L.2162, of No. 210 (GR) Squadron, R.A.F., while on night-flying practise, crashed at 75 knots when landing on the surface in Milford Haven, throwing six of the crew of eight into the water, but two men were trapped in the interior.

When the boat capsized and broke in two, Sinclair, with the Squadron Leader, were thrown through the broken coupe. They swam to the broken hull, which was upside down with the wings awash.

Sinclair clambered on the starboard wing. All the crew were injured except one man, and those in the water clung to the wreckage. They were picked up by the R.A.F. Tender which arrived on the scene, A/C.1 Reed, with a broken pelvis, being assisted by Sinclair, who entered the water and tied a rope round him with which he was hauled aboard.

Sinclair, on being picked up by the Tender, discovered that two men were trapped inside the wrecked hull. Undressing, he dived into the hull, endeavouring to locate the men amongst the broken debris of the interior, which was 3 ft. to 6 ft. deep in water, getting deeper as time elapsed. He entered at the break in the hull, which was not jammed, but opening and closing its jagged edge in a dangerous manner. There was danger from fire should the petrol tanks explode, also the possibility of the hull sinking at any time. Sinclair failed to find the men who drowned.

Gibson, George, Driver, Royal Army Service Corps.   Case 55137

At 11.30 a.m. on 28th September, 1938, a party of twelve men were bathing in the Mediterranean Sea, at Burg-el-Arib, Egypt, when one of them got caught in an outgoing strong current, and was swept out through the breakers, being unable to return owing to the roughness of the sea and the strength of the current.

Gibson and three others went to his aid, and Gibson brought the man ashore in an unconscious state. Meantime, the other three would-be rescuers had themselves got into difficulties.

Gibson swam out again, bringing in two of the others in succession, the third man being swept out through the breakers for about a quarter of a mile. He got into another current which swept shorewards again. In spite of his exhaustion, Gibson again swam out into the breakers and helped the now very exhausted man ashore. The first two rescued men were unconscious, and were restored by artificial respiration after 15 and 30 minutes respectively. There was a strong onshore breeze, and rough sea with breakers, the rescue taking place 200 yards out, with water 12 ft. deep.

Silver Medal to Driver G. Gibson, and Vellum Testimonials to Drivers William G.E. Reeves, William King, and Albert V. Haseldine.

John, Roy Powell, Installation Manager, Asiatic Petroleum Co., China.　　　　　　　　　　　　　　Case 55151

At 11 a.m. on 20th July, 1938, when foreigners and their staffs had been evacuated from Kiukiang, on the River Yangtsekiang, to a place four miles upstream, a man on the Asiatic Petroleum Company's Tug *Kiangsi*, which was alongside H.M.S. *Cockchafer*, slipped on the wet decks and fell overboard, being swept away by a five and a half knot current (due to the summer spate - i.e. melting of the snow up country).

John jumped in after him, supporting him until picked up by the Tug 200 yards downstream. A minefield had been laid off the town, one line of which was surface mines, which added to the risk of picking up persons in the water by means of boats.

The river is one mile wide, and 12 fathoms deep, the rescue taking place 800-900 feet from shore. Very confused water, due to curve in the river, and the confluence of Lung Kai Creek.

Watson, Edna L., Mrs.　　　　　　　　　　　　　　Case 55254

At 1.12 p.m. on 21st January, 1939, in the North Atlantic Ocean, the R.M.A. *Cavalier*, whilst operating on the New York - Bermuda service, was forced to alight in the sea some 280 miles off Cape May (U.S.A.) and sank after 20 minutes.

Mrs Watson, who was one of the eight passengers, was given his own lifebelt by Captain Alderson, and on the aircraft breaking up he was struck by the fin, and was supported by Mrs. Watson, the only person near. The crew of four, Alderson and the passengers joined one another, linked together and formed a ring, Alderson who had no lifebelt, being supported mainly by Mrs Watson during approximately the whole period of ten hours during which the passengers and crew were in the water before being picked up by the s.s. *Esso Baytown*. During the latter part of this period Capt. Alderson was thoroughly exhausted, and had not the strength to hold on to Mrs. Watson, so that it became necessary for her to support him entirely.

Reports of the circumstances of the accident show that it was largely due to Mrs Watson's fortitude and presence of mind that the morale of the survivors as a whole was sustained during the ordeal which followed the accident, so preventing panic. The unselfish efforts of Mrs Watson in supporting Capt. Alderson were calculated to have taxed her powers of endurance to the utmost, and so reduced her own chances of surviving.

Swell running. Slight wind. Moderate temperature of sea. The aircraft, luckily, was clear of the cold Davis Strait current, but the water was only about 60 degrees at the time and the survivors were all numbed before long. Mrs Watson had a badly-cut hand, of which no one was aware until after rescued.

Fowlow, Samuel, Anglican Teacher, Harbour Le Cou, Newfoundland.　　　　　　　　　　　　　　Case 55412

At 1.15 p.m. on 13th March, 1939, at Harbour Le Cou, Newfoundland, the harbour had frozen over owing to the very cold weather, a thing which seldom happened because of the tides and current. The water at the head of the bay had frozen first, and after a couple of nights afforded a safe skating surface of about 100 by 15 yards, but there was only one place where one could land, there being a strip of unfrozen water along the shore. The outer waters had frozen over the previous night, but the ice was very thin and not safe to walk on.

After school Fowlow had gone skating on the safe ice, no other men being left in the village, as they had gone to the woods. While skating, he heard shouts ashore, and was pointed out three boys near the wharf on thin ice, one of whom was in the water. As the water was unfrozen near the shore, it was impossible for the boy to be rescued from the shore. Fowlow skated diagonally across to the boy (nearly 100 yards), the ice sagging as he skated across it. When about 15 feet off, he lay down, and crawled over the ice, with one of the other boys holding on to his skates (he let go quickly when the water seeped over the edge of the ice). The ice bent down until there was nearly a foot of water over it, necessitating Fowlow keeping his head well up. Telling the boy to paddle towards him, he managed to get hold of his hands and gradually drew himself backwards by means of his skate tips. The edge of the ice broke several times, but eventually Clarke was drawn out on to firmer ice. Fowlow then hurried the half-frozen lad towards the wharf, found it impossible to land him there, took him back to the only safe spot at the bottom of the harbour, and landed him.

Very considerable risk indeed, as Fowlow weighs nearly 15 stone. It was a bitterly cold day and no boats were available to launch at a moment's notice. To the spectators ashore, it looked as though Fowlow was lying in the water when the edge of the ice bent down under his weight. He pulled the boy backwards about 8 - 10 feet before it was safe to stand on the ice again.

King, William, Corporal, C.R.M.P.
Bensley, Denis, Lance Bombardier, R.H.A.

Case 55519

Between 2 p.m. and 3 p.m. on the 13th August, 1939, at Khayat Beach, Haifa, Palestine, a group of men were bathing in a rough sea with a dangerous undertow, this being an unauthorized place for bathing.

About 2.10 p.m. one man got into difficulties and called for help. King, swimming 100 yards out, swam out a further 300 yards and brought the man to shore.

At 2.45 p.m. five or six men were seen in difficulties and being carried out to sea. King again swam out and brought in one man who was suffering from cramp. Bensley, meantime had brought back two men to shallow water. King and Bensley once again swam out, bringing two others to shore.

Their attention being directed to another man, they swam out, but he disappeared when they were within ten yards of him. King was now exhausted, and Bensley, who is a very good swimmer, assisted him ashore.

Sea very rough, with stronger undertow than usual. Normally 100 yards out before one is out of depth. Rescue took place 300 - 400 yards out in deep water.

Robbins, James., Fitter, Flathouse Quay, Portsmouth.

Case 56112

At 9.20 a.m. on the 26th September, 1940, at Flathouse Quay, Portsmouth, a Motor Torpedo Boat was lying alongside with some 1,500 gallons of petrol on board, when an explosion occurred, followed by a very serious fire on board, and many petrol fires started in the sea. Fitter James Robbins, badly injured in the head, together with Thomas A. Wilkins, Leslie Jones and T. Harrison, were blown into the sea. Two other persons lost their lives, and eighteen were seriously injured.

Robbins, in spite of scalp wounds, burns and shock sustained by himself, seized and supported Wilkins, who was seriously injured, until relieved by Percy le Clercq.

Apprentice Fitter Percy le Clercq dived 20 feet from the quay fully clad, swam about 20 yards to the burning Motor Torpedo Boat, and taking the injured Wilkins from Robbins, brought him to the launch. He then swam to where Jones, also injured, was clinging to the Motor Torpedo Boat and took him to a dinghy.

Aircraftsman Charles W. Gard, Royal Air Force, who also dived from the quay fully clad, swam to the spot where it was believed Harrison had sunk. He dived repeatedly in the water covered with burning petrol in an effort to find Harrison, but without success. Harrison's body was found in tangled wreckage later.
Both rescued men were non-swimmers. Danger of further explosions.

Silver Medal awarded to James Robbins, and Bronze Medals to Percy le Clercq and Aircraftsman Charles W. Gard.

Lackie, John, Diver, Methil Docks, Methil, Fife.

Case 56582

At 8.45 a.m. on the 26th August, 1941, David G. Grieve, diver, wearing diving suit descended into No. 2 Dock, Methil Docks, Methil, Fife, to clean up the refuse on the dock bottom near the gates. Ten minutes later his lifeline became taut, indicating that he was caught in some obstruction.

Lackie, wearing diving suit, descended, and found that Grieve had been caught in an open sluice and was being held there by the pressure of water. Coming up he obtained a rope and again going down tied the end round Grieve's legs. Men on the quay pulled on the rope but failed to release Grieve.

Stewart, who had not done any diving for about two years, arrived and, donning a suit, went down with Lackie. After going down several times Stewart was warned by the doctor to take a rest. He persisted in rescue efforts, however, and, after a weighted tarpaulin had been sunk over Grieve's body, Stewart again went down with Lackie. They tried to cut a hole through the tarpaulin to release Grieve when Stewart was drawn into the sluice beside Grieve, being dead when released by Lackie, assisted from the top by others, who pulled the body to the surface half an hour later.

Lackie was ordered to give up any further attempt at 12 noon, and the body of Grieve came to the surface later. Both men were aware of the great danger of being drawn into the sluice.

The area of the dock is six and a half acres, being 355 ft. wide and 27 ft. deep.

The Silver Medal was awarded to John Lackie and the In Memoriam Testimonial to the relatives of the late William S. Stewart.

Kirkup, Kenneth P., Lieut., Royal Naval Reserve.

Case 56191
Posthumous Award

During the night of the 11/12th October, 1940, one of H.M. ships, of which the late Lieut. Kirkup was in command, was sunk at sea by enemy action.

Lieut. Kirkup, wounded in both legs, was the last to leave the ship, and, on reaching the water, found Seaman A. Armour, suffering from a dislocated jaw, in difficulties. He managed to get the man on his back, then swam 200 yards to a Carley float, on to which they were taken, although it was carrying over its full capacity.

Later Lieut. Kirkup lost consciousness through wounds and exhaustion, fell overboard and was lost. Four others were lost from the float during the night.

The sea was smooth with hazy weather, and it was dark at the time.

Bengough, Arthur, Miner, Craigwen, Pontypridd.
Brown, Bryn, Colliery Overman.

Case 57007

At 3.45 p.m. the 6th June 1942, Wendy Williams, an evacuee, with her aunt and other children was walking across the farm land at Llan Farm, Craigwen, Pontypridd. The child, playing, jumped into a small trench, where the ground gave way due to a colliery subsidence and she disappeared. The Police and Fire Services were called to the scene with ropes and ladders.

The hole in the trench was examined and found to be just wide enough to allow a very thin man or a small boy to get in. The earth was soft and loose, and there was definite danger of another subsidence if the hole was tampered with.
Leslie Richards, aged 14, volunteered to try and locate the child, whose cries could be heard. A rope was tied round his feet and he was lowered head first into the hole, but was unable to see anything and was hauled out. After a few minutes he was provided with a torch and was again lowered some seven feet, and when brought out said that he could not get any further.

Brown then volunteered and was lowered in the same way, but could not get very far and reported that the child was some way down. He suggested that an excavation should be made a few yards from the hole and after sufficient depth had been reached a tunnel to the position of the child should be made. This was started, Brown taking charge. Brown made another descent, later assisting in the final rescue.

Hazell, a youth, was then lowered head first, but failed to locate the child. He also descended later, assisting in the final rescue.

Digging was being continued through the night, with the aid of miner's lamps, and reaching rock it was smashed partly with sledge hammers. The ground under the workmen caved in, but they carried on. About 6.30 a.m. next day they were 18 ft. down and had to exercise great care to prevent a further fall of earth. Jones now volunteered and was tied by the feet and lowered head first. When brought out he said the child was some 12 ft. below and near another crevice.

The child's cries could still be heard. Archer was then lowered head first, going down nine feet. He shouted that he had got hold of the child and asked to be raised. He lifted the child about two feet. but, owing to an overlapping piece of rock, could not get her through and had to leave go. He was brought up, and at once made another attempt. The same thing happened again and Archer was brought up completely exhausted. The child was now silent.

Christopher was now lowered, and getting no reply to his shouts it was feared that the child had fallen further down. Bengough and others, who had just finished night-shift in the colliery, arrived, and, though the workings were now definitely unsafe, Bengough volunteered to go down. He was tied by his feet and lowered seven feet, then asking for a walking stick. With this he chipped away some earth and shouted to be lowered further. He was lowered another five feet. He then shouted that he had found the child dead or unconscious. When he grasped her she began to cry, and taking off his vest he wrapped it round her feet and called for a length of rope, which was lowered. Tying it round her feet he shouted for a pull to be given. Not being able to get the child past his body he asked for a thin boy to be lowered. Hazell was again lowered, and, after doing as Bengough directed, he was hauled out absolutely exhausted.

Bengough then gave instructions for the child to be raised slowly, but when she reached the position of his feet near rock it was impossible to get her head past. He then directed the men on top to lower him further. This was done, but the child was still jammed. Brown now again went down head first and with difficulty pulled her clear and she was hauled to the surface.

Bengough, still head first down the hole, was in a dangerous position. He was raised a few feet and his body became jammed, and it was only after a difficult struggle by the men on top and much wriggling by Bengough that he was finally raised to the surface. He was a mass of cuts, scratches and bruises, and though the pressure of the rope on his ankles caused agonizing pain he stuck to his task.

The child, taken to hospital, recovered.

Crevice: Mountain district. Subsidence 25 ft. deep; 2 ft. wide at the top narrowing downwards.
Rescue : 12 ft. down. Bengough head down in hole for half an hour. Child in hole 16 hours - throughout the night.

Silver Medals awarded to:-	Arthur Bengough and Bryn Brown.
Bronze Medals awarded to:-	Malcolm Hazell and George Archer.
Testimonials on Vellum awarded to:-	Leslie Richards, Emlyn Jones and Thomas Christopher.

Arthur Benbough was also awarded the Stanhope Gold Medal for the year 1942.

Meyers, Sidney A., Police Sergeant, South African Police. Case 57026

Between 2 p.m. and 3 p.m. on the 16th November, 1941, Police-Sergeant Meyers with his family, together with Lance-Sergeant Snyman and his family, were viewing the Debengeni Waterfalls in the Letaba District, Transvaal, South Africa, when Lance-Sergeant Snyman's daughter, Martha, aged 8, crossing a stream between the upper and lower fall, lost her balance and was swept down the steep slope of granite towards the waterfall.

Myers grabbed at her, but missed, and the girl was being swept at considerable speed down the 50 ft. slope towards a fall of 20 ft. to the rocks or pool below.

Myers at once dived down the slope in an effort to push her clear but, unable to do so, lifted her clear and threw her on to the side. Unable to stop himself he was swept over the fall, striking a rock just as he fell into a deep pool. Unconscious when he hit the water, the shock restored him sufficiently to enable him to tread water and keep himself up. It was impossible to get out, the sides being of granite.

Sergeant Snyman broke off a large branch of a tree and holding it out, was able to get Myers out.

Myers sustained injuries to the right side of his face, chest and left knee.

Sibson, James N., Volunteer Mate of Harbour Launch, Solent.   Case 58522

In the afternoon of the 31st August, 1944, a Harbour Launch manned by a volunteer crew of emergency yachtsmen was engaged in placing Pilots on Merchant Ships anchored in the Solent with a gale blowing at between "seven" and "eight" and a strong ebb tide.

The gale increased when the last ship was reached, and on the fourth attempt to approach the ship the Launch rose on top of a wave and the Pilot grasped the ladder, but failed to secure a foothold, being thrown with his back to the side of the ship. Before he could recover the Launch was thrown violently against the side of the ship, crushing the Pilot, who fell into the sea.

Sibson at once dived overboard into the angry sea between the vessels. He reached the Pilot, whom he supported, and in spite of the sea continually breaking over them secured a rope round the man, who was hoisted on board and found to be dead.

There was a strong ebb tide and rough sea with wind of gale force, the rescue taking place between the anchored ship and the Launch in deep water.

Reed, Raymond T., Leading Motor Mechanic, R.N.   Case 58688

At sea, 4.5 miles from Teignmouth, South Devon. At 3.40 a.m. on the morning of the 8th December, 1944, an Admiralty craft (special) 34 ft. long of 11 tons was proceeding in the dark at a speed of 4-5 knots when she developed a heavy list and, shipping a heavy sea, sank, trapping Lieutenant Leonard G. Ardell in the after hold.

Leading Motor Mechanic Reed, deliberately holding on to the binnacle, went down 18-20 ft. with the craft, the engine still going full speed ahead, and forcing open the hatch against the pressure of water, pulled the unconscious Lieutenant out by the hair. Reaching the surface he held on to the flotsam with one hand and supported Lieutenant Ardell until he regained consciousness.

They were both picked up by H.M.T. *Tirade* escort ship. Dark and cold. Wind N.W. force 7. Heavy short seas.

Day, Henry James, Warrant Officer II, Royal Engineers.   Case 59511

On the evening of the 11th June, 1944, (5 days after D-Day) orders were given to send 3 gangs of men to unload the M.T. Ship No. 19 then laying at anchor off Arromanches, Normandy. Owing to the gale, rough seas and heavy swell, the officer in charge decided that it was not safe to send the whole party off in one trip in the launch provided, and consequently only two gangs consisting of 2 officers and 45 other ranks embarked at 5 p.m. The bulk of the party were able to find accommodation between decks, but 10 persons had to remain on deck, and found considerable difficulty in holding on, due to the heavy rolling of the launch in the big swell then running. When about one mile off shore, the launch nearly capsized due to an extra large wave and a Lance-Corporal (a non-swimmer) lost his hold and fell overboard. A lifebuoy was thrown from the launch in his direction, but failed to reach him and was swept away by the wind and sea.

Lt.-Col. A.C. Lusty, R.A.O.C. and W.O. Day, seeing the Lance-Corporal in difficulties, had immediately dived overboard fully clothed and held him up while the launch endeavoured to put about to pick them up. Seeing the time it would take for the launch to turn round in the heavy swell, W.O. Day swam after the lifebuoy and with great difficulty managed to tow it back against the wind and sea to where Lt.-Col. Lusty was still supporting the semi-conscious Lance-Corporal.

The U.S.A. Launch which had been hailed then turned and picked up the three men and had great difficulty in getting them on board due to the state of the sea. W.O. Day was the last to be picked up.

His action in collecting the lifebuoy undoubtedly ensured the safety of his officer and saved the life of the Lance-Corporal. The rescue took place about one mile off shore in deep water. The weather conditions were bad, viz. rough sea, heavy swell, wind - gale force 7-8 - and with the ever present possibility of an enemy air attack.

W.O.II Henry James Day, R.E, was awarded the Silver Medal of the Society and Lieut.-Col. Alan Charles Lusty, R.A.O.C., the Bronze Medal.

Edwards, Leslie Alan, Lieut. (A), R.N.   Case 60171

At Treyarnon Bay, near Padstow, Cornwall.

About 2.30 p.m. on the 12th October, 1947, Air Artificer 4th Class Derrick G. Belcher, R.N., from the R.N. Air Station at St. Merryn, went for a bathe at Treyarnon Bay, and was seen swimming outside the breakers and in no apparent difficulty. A little later he must have realized that the current was carrying him towards some dangerous rocks on the right-hand side of the Bay with seas breaking violently over them. His calls for help were heard by Lieut. Edwards, who happened to be on the beach at the time, who instructed him to try and keep clear of the rocks while help was being sent for. Seeing Belcher was then in difficulties. Edwards swam out through the breakers into the swell (a distance of about 300 yards), the breakers being heavy and considerable effort required to get through and beyond them. Edwards eventually reached Belcher, and encouraging him to make further efforts, assisted on two separate occasions the now exhausted man to make for the shore, but only able to gain ground over short distances. All the time the waves were breaking heavily over them, and both men were being swept rapidly towards the rocks and were in great peril.

Some time had now elapsed and it was obvious to spectators that though Edwards was very exhausted himself, he continued to assist Belcher either by a rescue method or swimming alongside, but Belcher seemed unable to make any headway. Finally, Lieut. Edwards became so exhausted it became imperative for him to look for his own safety. He therefore made for the beach and, after battling with the waves with great difficulty, arrived having been in the water about 40 minutes.

It was observed on one occasion when the waves had widened the distance between them that Edwards turned back and could be seen exhorting Belcher to make further efforts. This he did although he himself felt doubtful of his own ability to reach the shore.

Belcher had been in the water one hour before he submerged, and when reached by Edwards had little to say but understood and reacted to encouragement, but appeared to make little headway.

Rescue: 300 yards out in deep water. Heavy swell and breakers near the rocks. Edwards had to swim out through them with no life-saving appliances on or handy. Other rescuers attempted to swim out with a life jacket and line, but were unable to negotiate the breakers.

Ditty, Margaret Elizabeth, Mrs., Housewife, Cushendall Bay, Co. Antrim, Northern Ireland.   Case 60173

About 2.0 p.m. on the 20th August, 1947, four members of the Transport Drivers Annual Excursion went out in a boat, and when one of them dived overboard he capsized the boat with three of them, non-swimmers, in difficulties.

Mrs. Ditty, who was outside her caravan, swam out alone to their aid followed shortly afterwards by Harold Winter and Miss Mona Ryan, and between them they brought one of the men ashore. Mrs. Ditty then returned with Miss Margaret Campbell to the scene of the accident and found that a second boat, which had gone out to the rescue, had also capsized and one of the occupants was trapped underneath with his foot jammed in the bottom boards. Finding an unconscious man floating face downwards she and Miss Campbell supported his head above water until another boat arrived on the scene and assisted to get him on board. Mrs. Ditty then dived under the second upturned boat, released the man's foot and assisted him to the boat and on board it. Harold Winter and Miss Ryan had then swam out again with Miss Ryan's air dinghy and supported the remaining two men while all were either rowed or towed ashore by the rescue boat.

Rescue: 200 yards out in deep water, the strong ebb tide making conditions difficult to reach the shore from seaward.

The Silver Medal was awarded to Mrs Ditty and Bronze Medals to Harold Winter, Miss Mona Ryan, and Miss Margaret Campbell.

Thomas, Edward Arthur, Technical Assistant, Cable and Wireless. Porthcurno Bay.   Case 60176

About 7.45 p.m. on 27th June, 1947, Hewitson, who was spending a caravan holiday with the Smith family, while swimming with his R.A.F. rubber dinghy, got caught by the surf and was unable to return. Frank Smith (son) went to his aid but was unable to assist. William Smith (father of Frank Smith) then went out and all three persons were now holding on to the dinghy, being washed down by the heavy surf and unable to get ashore.

Thomas was walking on the cliff top prior to going on night duty at the Cable and Wireless Office at Porthcurno, heard a woman calling for help (Mrs. Smith), ran to the spot and saw three men hanging on to the dinghy 100 yards out. He climbed down the perpendicular cliff to a ledge about 30-50 feet up, stripped off his clothes, realized he could do nothing without a lifebuoy and line, re-climbed the cliff and met Roberts coming down with one. The two men climbed down to the ledge, and decided Thomas should swim out while Roberts should throw the lifebuoy out as soon as Thomas was clear of the surf at the foot of the cliff, Thomas then dived in, swam through the surf at the foot, the buoy was thrown but fouled the cliff. Thomas then swam back through the surf and after several attempts collected the buoy, pushed it ahead of him through the surf and took it out to the three men hanging on to the rubber dinghy. Smith (father) was then either unconscious or dead, and was being supported by one of the others. Seeing that all had a good hold on the lifebuoy they made for the cliff rocks, Roberts hauling in on the line. Thomas then decided to land at the foot of the cliffs ready to receive the others, and after great difficulty did so (washed back by the undertow four times) and was very exhausted. After recovering, seeing the other three men a few yards out, he pulled on the buoy rope until the dinghy got close enough to seize one of the men by the arm. A heavy swell then broke and washed the three men and Thomas off the rocks and caused the man supporting Smith (father) to lose his hold. (Smith was swept away and his body only seen one and a half hours later when a coastguard climbed down to recover it, but was unable to do so.) Seeing there was no hope of recovering Smith (father) Thomas concentrated on landing Smith (son) and Hewitson, and after several attempts managed to get them on to the rocks, where he held them until Roberts climbed down and assisted to get them up to the ledge. A quarter of an hour later the Coastguards arrived with stretchers, cliff lines, etc., and after attention all four men were got to the top of the cliff. Thomas then changed and reported for night duty at the Cable and Wireless Office, Porthcurno.

Rescue: In slight sea and swell but heavy surf breaking on the cliffs due to a sand bar half a mile out. The cliff is a sheer 240 feet drop with a shallow ledge 30-50 feet up from bottom. Sea always washes bottom of cliff and is 2 fathoms deep at low tide. 70-100 yards out in heavy surf. Thomas made four attempts to land on rocks, being swept off each time by the heavy undertow.

Coastguard report states: "It is considered the most difficult cliff rescue that has taken place in this area for some years."

The Silver Medal awarded to Edward A. Thomas. Testimonials on Parchment to F. Smith and S.A. Roberts, also In Memoriam Testimonials to relatives of W. Smith.

Steytler, John M., Architectural Student Draughtsman, Margate, South Coast, Natal.   Case 60396

At 10.45 a.m. on 22nd April, 1948, about 100 persons were bathing off the beach which is reasonably safe at the actual bathing point itself, but which is fringed with dangerous rocks. An exceptionally high sea was running with a strong current. The waters beyond the breakers were shark infested.

While bathing one man got cramp and a strong current drifted him towards rocks at edge of beach. His plight being perceived a professional life-saver went out with life-line, but was forced to give up rescue attempt on account of current and the fact that the man with cramp was now close to the rocks on which the breakers were pounding with terrific force.

The man in difficulties drifted parallel to the rocks for a distance of over half a mile and reached a spot where a chance of rescue appeared possible. Again a local life-saver made the attempt, but was forced to abandon it. Finally John M. Steytler, a citizen of Johannesburg, went through the surf with a line which was not part of life-saving equipment and reached the man in danger. When despite the danger from breakers which threatened to batter both of them to death, he brought the man to safety. The rescue occupied about one hour. Salvor swam 150 yards in tremendous seas.

Horne, Robert Sutherland, Chartered Architect, Portsmouth Harbour, Hants.   Case 60580

At 5.30 p.m. on 5th September, 1948, Horne was sailing in Portsmouth Harbour in his converted naval whaler when he, with other competitors of a race of the Portsmouth Sailing Club, saw two men in difficulties. The two men were fishing in a prahm dinghy which, while changing ground, was capsized by the strong tide. The men were caught in the tide and flung against the mooring buoy of the *Foudroyant* and *Implacable* which are moored alongside one another in the harbour. The two men managed to cling to the mooring cable.

Conditions were unfavourable for rescue. The tide was 14 foot spring at full ebb strength of 8-10 knots, and the overhang of the sterns of the two ships prevented any possibility of getting a boat near the buoy. Horne, with his boat, and a number of others of the Club tried to get alongside of the *Foudroyant*, but the tide swept them past. Horn then saw a power-driven fishing boat and went on board. The boat proceeded up tide and thus astern of the *Foudroyant* and *Implacable* and Horne with a line and bowline on him was streamed down the tide to the mooring buoy. He grasped one man, but owing to the indifferent power of the fishing boat both men were swept on the wrong side of the rudder. After a struggle Horne got the man round to the port side of the rudder on which the fishing boat had a straight pull. Both men were submerged with the tide, but Horne held fast and both men were hauled to the boat of H.M.S. *Mauritius* which had come to assist.

Noticing that the motor boat of H.M.S. *Mauritius* was more powerful than the fishing boat Horne determined to make his second rescue from this. He was again streamed down tide and reached the second man, who was wearing raincoat and sea boots. Horne got hold of the man and with great difficulty held on to him. Both were hauled clear to a mud bank from which they were transferred to the motor boat.

Horne suffered laceration of the arms and legs from the ship's rudder.

Booth, Cicely, Miss, Schoolgirl, aged 15 years 10 months, Barmston, Bridlington, Yorkshire.   Case 60588

At Barmston, near Bridlington, Yorkshire.

At 3.30 p.m. on 1st September, 1948, a man aged 48 was paddling a canoe off the beach, some 200 to 300 yards out in deep water, swamped his canoe and took to the water. Miss Booth, who was swimming, saw his plight and swam towards him. When his canoe sank the man tried to swim towards Miss Booth, but owing to the wind and tide could make little headway. There was a strong offshore wind, ebbing tide, and slight swell at the time.

The man, after some efforts at swimming against the current, became exhausted, Miss Booth got hold of him, turned him on his back, and tried to tow him to the shore. In view of his weight and the prevailing conditions of sea and tide, however, she was unable to make progress, and for thirty minutes remained floating with the man, who became unconscious.

A boat was manned by two men and put off from the shore, but as it had no proper fittings the men rowed with their hands, so progress was slow. When the boat was about 10 yards away Miss Booth said she could not last out any longer, so one of the men went over the side and helped Miss Booth and the unconscious man rescued by her into the boat.

The second salvor was awarded the Testimonial on Vellum.

Prince, Ashborne, Carpenter, Kingston, Jamaica.   Case 60599

At Regent Street Gully, Kingston, Jamaica, British West Indies.

About 4 p.m. on 2nd June, 1948, very heavy rain was falling and the Regent Street Gully was a roaring torrent with the full force of a river in spate. A boy aged 11, was standing on a bridge when he overbalanced and fell in, being swept away by the torrent. In the course of his transit he went under swallowing a quantity of water.

Prince saw his plight, went in, and got the boy under his arm. He thus had only his right hand free to fend off both against walls and gully and try to grasp any objects which would arrest their downward progress. Both were swept fully a mile in a seaward direction in the course of which Prince sustained injuries from being dashed against concrete walls of the gully. When 100 yards from the sea Prince secured hold of a branch overhanging the gully and held this with one hand and the boy with the other until spectators pulled them both out.

Fincham, Alfred David, Trader, Pitsani, Bechuanaland Protectorate.   Case 60833

In a disused well at Pitsani, Bechuanaland Protectorate.

Alexander Fincham, aged two and a half, nephew of Mr. Alfred Fincham, was trying to secure a bird which another boy had shot at 5.45 p.m. on the 18th December, 1948, in the land surrounding his parents house. While thus occupied he trod on the cover of a well, which gave way and he fell to the bottom. The well had been disused for twenty years, is 96 feet deep with 43 feet of water in it, and the drop into the water is thus 53 feet. There is an under-water channel feeding the well. The sides are very slippery, and there is considerable danger from snakes.

The alarm was given by a native servant. Mr. Fincham got a pulley chain from the store nearby and ran to the scene. He made fast one end of the chain at the top and sent the chain down. He then went down hand-over-hand, stripping his hands of skin on the thin chain. In the meantime other persons had arrived at the top of the well to assist. Mr. Fincham found the boy floating unconscious on the top of the water. He decided to send the boy up as the chain was not strong enough to support two people. This was a difficult operation, as Mr. Fincham cannot swim. He is 6 feet 3 inches tall, however, and managed to wedge himself against the slippery sides of the well while he made the chain fast to the boy, who was sent up. This left Mr. Fincham braced against the sides of the well in danger from snakes.

The boy having been hauled to safety the chain was again lowered, and Fincham was hauled up completely exhausted.

Gray, Robert, Second Engineer, Steam Trawler *Avondale*. Case 61121

In a steam filled engine-room at sea.

At 4 p.m. on the 20th July, 1949, the Steam Trawler *Avondale* was at sea on the fishing grounds 60 miles East of Tynemouth when the steam check valve fractured, and the engine room filled with steam.

Second Engineer Gray was turned in, in his bunk, but hearing the explosion, and fearing for the safety of the Chief Engineer, he ran to the engine room, which was full of steam, and entered it to search for his Chief. Although he did not know it, the Chief Engineer had extricated himself. Second Engineer Gray, however, continued to search in the scalding steam until exhaustion and burns forced him to give up.

The ship was put about and returned to harbour. The Chief Engineer escaped with slight scalds, but Second Engineer Gray's condition was so serious that he had to be removed to hospital for prolonged treatment.

Saunders, Harold Wright, Auxiliary Coastguard, Bindon Hill, West Lulworth, Dorset. Case 61288

At "Cockpit" Cliff, Bindon Hill, West Lulworth, Dorset.

At 6 p.m. on 11th September, 1949, three young soldiers were walking along the beach under the cliffs when they found themselves being cut off by the tide. Two climbed up the cliff face but stuck, one falling 40 feet, and the third climbed up to assist the first two. Eventually, as darkness fell, all three were stuck 150 feet up the cliff, a sheer precipice 530 feet high, and were faced with dangerous crumbling rock.

The alarm was given by the Army authorities, and the Volunteer Auxiliary Coastguard called out. They were transported to the cliff top in tanks, arriving at 6.40 p.m. From the top of the cliff one man could be seen so Mr. Saunders was lowered with a spare line. He attached this to the man who was then lowered to the beach, 150 feet below. The first man rescued cast off the line which Mr. Saunders had hauled up for the rescue of the second man.

The second man rescued gave most trouble as he had lost his nerve. Mr. Saunders Lowered him until he disappeared out of sight, but then the line went slack and Mr. Saunders had him hauled up again. The man said that he could not face the descent, so, with this consideration in mind and also knowing that the rising tide was covering what was left of the beach, Mr. Saunders decided to have him hauled up to the cliff top, Mr. Saunders accompanying him. During the ascent loose rocks fell down on the climbers. Mr. Saunders was saved from injury by the helmet he wore, but his lanyard and whistle were carried away.

The rescue of the third man had now to be attempted. It was completely dark and a searchlight had been sent for but, as it would be some time before this arrived, Mr. Saunders decided to go down with a spare line and hurricane lamp. Owing to the crumbling nature of the cliff, Mr. Saunders decided to be lowered to the side of the stranded man not from directly above him. He got to the estimated distance down and traversed right calling to the man without reply. He then traversed left, and, after a while, found himself below the third man. He was then hauled up and, at 11.25 p.m., secured the third man and both were hauled to safety. The whole rescue took nearly six hours, and Mr. Saunders had been on the cliff face for four hours in rescuing the three men.

Fox, Harold, Constable, Bristol Constabulary, Avon Gorge, Bristol. Case 61303

On the night of the 24th October, 1949, at about 9.20 p.m., a woman fell into the Gorge near Observatory Hill and opposite the Suspension Bridge. The Gorge is almost precipitous and 250 feet in depth. The night was dark and it had rained during the day, making the cliff slippery.

The woman, having fallen from the top, was caught on a ledge 100 feet down. Her cries were heard and an Inspector with four constables came to the scene. The Inspector sent for rescue apparatus and then decided to go down himself. He would have preferred another man to accompany him but no volunteers were available, so he went down alone. Just as he was starting his descent another car with more Police arrived and Constable Fox volunteered to go down. The Inspector went down on a bowline while Constable Fox went down with rescue harness, but they could not locate the woman in the darkness.

The fire brigade now arrived with flares enabling the woman to be seen but the two Police Officers in the Gorge could not reach her. They were then hauled up. The inspector, the eldest of the party, was tired after his gallant and resolute efforts at rescue and, in any case, as senior, his work of supervision could best be carried out from the cliff top. Constable Fox, accompanied by a fireman, now went down, the fireman in the only set of harness available and Constable Fox on a line. Constable Fox reached the woman but could not move her, so he and the fireman returned to the top of the cliff.

Constable Fox now went down in the harness with a stretcher on a line. He again reached the woman. She was injured, and the Constable realized that moving her was going to be a matter of great difficulty. He would have preferred to have had an assistant in putting the woman on the stretcher but, as only one set of harness was available, he considered the risk to another man would be too great by his coming down on a line. He accordingly accomplished the amazing feat of removing the harness from himself while standing on a narrow ledge and securing the line of the stretcher round his chest. He then waited until the harness was hauled to the cliff top and the fireman again sent down in the harness. The woman could now be placed on the stretcher by the efforts of both men and hauled up, the fireman being hauled up with the stretcher, the constable coming up last. The rescue was not completed until 11.50 p.m.

Constable Harold Fox was awarded the Silver Medal, Inspector Edward Twitt and Leading Fireman Edward Parsons were awarded the Bronze Medal.

* * * * *

INDEX TO STANHOPE AND SILVER AWARDS

Adams, J. 152
Adams, L.B. 104
Adamson, W. 134
Addison, A.P. 86
Agassiz, R.L. 48
Ahmed El Shamy 107
Aitken, F.M. 52
Aitken, J. 34
Alexander, H. McC. 35
Alexander, J. 26
Ali Akbar 152
Allen, J. 92
Allen, W. 10
Andrews, A. 70
Apper, A. 37
Arrowsmith, M. 92
Arscott, J. 50
Ashall, J. 137
Atkins, J. 79
Baboo Kristo Chunder Chuckerbutty 3
Barne, M. 130
Barnes, F. 46
Barnes, P. 111
Baron, C. 98
Barrow, F. 149
Bartlett, A.E. 45
Battison, A. 6
Bayley, C.H. 52
Bayley, G.E. 92
Bayley, S.B. 31
Bean, H.R. 32
Beazor, E. 53
Beith, W. 45
Belcher, T.H.P. 143
Belfon, D. 90
Bell, A.L. 74
Bell, T.W. 59
Bengough, A. 24, 163
Benjamin, A. 96
Bennett, G. 58
Bensley, D. 162
Betts, P. 61
Bevan, J. 83
Bird, J.C. 135

Biron, H. 78
Birrell, A. 122
Bjorkander, 80
Blackburn, H. 113
Blackett, W.C. 113
Blyth, R. 96
Blythe, W. 132
Bongard, 108
Booker, H. 112
Booth, C. 168
Borez, A. 106
Bouttell, T. 13
Bowden, C. 157
Bower, H. 66
Bowman, J.P.S. 148
Bowman, N. 104
Boyer, F.H. 47
Brace, H. 62
Bradley, J. 104
Bradley, W. 70
Brand, R. 94
Brannon, T. 16
Brant, J. 45
Brass, J. 113
Brassey, T.A. 61
Breadalbane, 73
Brenton, R.O.B.C. 35, 42
Brimelow, W. 59
Bristow, C.J.W. 140
Brooke, R. 104
Brooke, R.G. 110
Brooks, P. 131
Brown, B. 163
Brown, C.G.L. 26
Brown, J. 94
Brownbill, J.H. 40
Browne, W.L.H. 32
Bulteaux, R. 29
Bussell, G.V. 46
Butt, C. 91
Butterfield, J. 33
Buttle, R. 37
Camp, H.H. 155
Carmichael, H. 158

Carr, E. 92
Carus-Wilson, E.J. 57
Cawood, R.J. 146
Chainey, G.B. 9
Chambers, W. 51
Chandler, H.V. 124
Chappell, H. 72
Charlton, E.F.B. 99
Chatfield, C.K. 69
Cholmondeley, C.E. 105
Christian, G.H.P. 38
Clayton, H. 17
Clements, F.G. 100
Cleverley, W. 5
Clifford, W.T. 94
Clinch, R.D. 117
Coates, J. 53
Cochrane, C.H. 58
Cockburn, J.B. 131
Cole, G. 90
Coleman, M. 53
Collin, J.H. 8
Collins, A. 5
Collins, F.G. 154
Colville, B. 51
Connell, G.D. 118
Connell, J. 79
Connolly, P. 58
Connor, A.G. 129
Cook, T. 123
Cooke, H.A. 86
Cooling, J.F. 72
Cooper, A.J. 7
Corbett, N.M.F. 126
Corry, E. 73
Couper, J.V.H. 146
Cow, R. 82
Cox, W. 44
Craig, J. 75
Craven, A.H. 137
Creasy, J.H. 134
Croft, C. 92
Croly, W.C. 134
Cronch, H.J. 55
Crook, J. 63
Cross, H. 137

Cross, H. 155
Cumberlege, C.L. 126
Cumming, W.W. 86
Cundy, G.C. 81
Cunningham, H.W. 50
Cunningham, J. 55
Cusack, J.W.H. 54, 65
D'Alton, B.J. 95
D'Oyly-Hughes, G. 133
Davidson, C. 117
Davies, Daniel 115
Davies, David 115
Davies, F.B. 126
Davies, J. 151
Davies, J.L. 125
Davies, M. 115
Day, H.J. 165
de Verteuil, H. 146
Denham, R.C. 124
Ditty, M.E. 166
Dodd, J. 36
Dodd, W. 88
Dolan, F.S. 143
Donald, 58
Donner, C.S. 48
Dornin, A. 44
Dowdney, J. 35
Down, R. 92
Dowson, P. 39
Drake, C. 71
Drake, C.E. 43
Drake, F.C. 25
Drummond, G.R. 123
Duckworth, E. 107
Duckworth, T.W 147
Duggan, R.J. 49
Dutton, S. 63
Dykes, W. 50
Eade, H.H. 47
Eales, G. 68
Ebden-Currey, C.N. 131
Eccles, R. 53
Edwards, L.A. 166
Ellis, J. 40
Ellul, A. 76
Eussoof Nobo 115

Evans, M.L. 89
Evelegh, M.H. 139
Eyre, G.S. 45
Fairley, D.S. 24
Fairtlough, J.W. 118
Falconer, J. 49
Falzon, P. 150
Faram, E.A.C. 159
Farbrother, A.J. 77
Farthing, M. 150
Ferguson, P. 27
Ferris, R.G. 88
Fielden, R.M. 89
Fincham, A.D. 168
Flannery, T. 92
Fleet, E.J. 67
Ford, W.H. 44
Forman, A.B. 92
Fourquet, P. 146
Fowlow, S. 161
Fox, H. 170
Foy, H.B. 152
Francis, A.W. 106
Francis, T. 100
Fraser, A.D. 77
Fraser, D.L. 77
Fraser, F. 13
Freeman, H. 120
Fremantle, E.R. 4
French, H.C. 109
Frend, M. 91
Freyone, A. 108
Frogley, H. 113
Fry, J.W. 49
Fudge, J. 38
Fullerton, E. 94
Gater, J. 119
Gibbons, W. 31
Gibson, G. 160
Girby, Suleiman 81, 81
Goodwyn, J.E. 60
Gosling, C. 92
Graham, E.F.C. 51
Grainger, E. 61
Gray, A. 97
Gray, R. 169

Gray, T. 104
Green, W. 99
Gregory, C. 136
Grey, A.A.D. 16
Griffin, C.P.G. 86
Griffin, J. 144
Grimston, W. 60
Grisley, W.J. 92
Groombridge, W. 113
Guido, M.L. 139
Gunner, G.W. 114
Hackett, S.M. 76
Haig, N.W. 102
Hale, J. 101
Hales, E.J. 14
Halfyard, R. 85
Hall, J. 113
Hall, W. 9
Halliday, C.C. 14
Hallowes, F.H. 122
Hamilton, A.R. 87
Hamilton, G. 126
Hamilton, R. 102
Hammar, A. 141
Hannah, D. 90
Hansen, J. 104
Harding, W. 57
Hardyman, W.H. 87
Harris, J. 102
Harrison, J. 31
Hart, R.C. 62
Hartle, J.C. 142
Harvey, C.L. 41
Harvey, J. 116
Hatton, E.A. 8
Haveron, J. 63
Hawkes, T. 47
Heap, A. 130
Heath, I.E. 105
Heathcote, W.C.P. 72
Heaton, H.W. 38
Heighway, E.J. 129
Henderson, A. 74
Henderson, A.C. 11
Hetherington, C. 15
Hewetson, J.B. 67

Heyland, W.O.L. 44
Heyns, A.H. 19
Hill, E. 22
Hill, H. 6
Hilson, D.N. 136
Hockey, E. 136
Hodge, C.H. 48
Hoghton, J. de. 2
Holt, H.W.L. 47
Hookum, Ali 32
Hopkins, F. 147
Hopper, H.G. 141, 144
Hore, P.H. 133
Horne, R.S. 167
Howarth, H. 70
Howell, J.W. 45
Howells, L. 127
Howes, G. 92
Howlett, J.F. 130
Hubbard, S. 100
Huddleston, E.W. 92
Huddleston, W.B. 7
Hughes, D.B.B. 124
Hughes, F.E.C. 145
Hunt, D. 73
Hunter, J. 116
Hutton, P.C. 17
Ifereimi Raqoneqone 152
Indar Singh 95
Ingham, G. 17
Innes, F.A. 138
Irons, E.G. 21
Irving, D. 108
Isaac, F.V. 42
Ishar Das 75
Jablouski, P. 65
Jagannathrao Krishnarao Bhonsle 154
James, D.J. 91
Jemmett, W.B. 146
Jenkin, G. 20
Jenkins, J. 4
Jenner, G. 127
Jockie Bar 118
Johansson, J. 56
John, R.P. 161
Johnson, E.T. 18

Johnson, F.W. 153
Jone Draunimasi 154
Jones, D. 76
Jones, H.E.B. 20
Jones, J.G. 54
Jones, W. 115
Jones, W. 120
Joste, 58
Joynes, J.J. 96
Juddery, J.W.H. 98
Juma Kalanzi 153
Kay, I. 140
Kennedy, H.M. 133
Kennett, B. 39
Kent, E.W. 158
Keymer, A.E. 116
Kiddle, E.B. 111
Kinch, N.A. 22
King, G.W. 150
King, P. 61
King, W. 162
Kirby, H. 44
Kirk, J. 57
Kirkup, K.P. 163
Knight, F. 49
Kough, P. 59
Krassilstchikoff, A. 146
Labat, F. 46
Lackie, J. 162
Lalbahadur Mal 145
Lambart, F.A.O. 112
Landry, R. 134, 139
Lang, W.M. 49
Large, A.G. 115
Lawrence, R. 45
Le Fleming, S.H. 37
Le Mesurier, C.J.R. 62
Leach, J. 127
Lecky, H.S. 105
Lee, M. 23
Lee, P. 83
Lee, P.R. 122
Lee, R.J. 54
Leech, H. 131
Lemmi, G.M. 75
Leonard, E. 56

Leverett, S. 118
Lewin, F.H.L. 15
Lewis, J.W. 51
Lines, F. 82
Littledale, C.E. 156
Llewelyn, L.W. 115
Long, M. 84
Lord, W.P. 149
Lotbiniere, H.G.J. de 132
Lowrey, A. 31
Lowry, A.C. 10
Lucas, H. 23
Luter, F. 128
Lynam, C.G.J. 132
Lynch, M. 107
M'Donald, J. 106
M'Kellar, J. 91
Mackenzie, J. 87
Mackenzie, T.C. 11
Mackin, J. 77
Mackinnon, T.D. 147
Macklin, G. 98
Macleod, J.F. 142
Macmeikan, C.H. 41
Maddox, J. 50
Maguire, J.A. 71
Maher, W. 142
Main, A. 110
Maloney, J.C. 121
Mansell, C. 114
Mant, H. 151
Margary, A.R. 36
Marsden, A. 126
Marshall, J. 111
Martin C.F. 150
Marx, J.L. 44
Mather, L. 137
Mathews, F. 78
Maung Kynn Bin 112
Maynard, J.F. 106
McCabe, G. 87
McCalmont, J.M. 32
McCarthy, E. 104
McCarthy, P.K. 33
McCluskey, J. 60
McCoy, H. 40

McCulloch, D. 59
McDermott, T. 7
McDonnell, W. 79
McDougall, R. 85
McDowell, W. 104
McFarlane, C. 148
McField, W. 97
McGarritty, F. 50
McGran, H. 31
McGregor, J. 100
McKeen, W. 67
McKinstry, E.R. 72
McLaren, A. 104
McLean, J. 55
McNamara, N. 92
McNulty, M. 66
McQue, W. 80
McRae, H.N. 5
Meston, R.A. 157
Meyer, W. 6
Meyers, S.A. 164
Middleton, A.H. 52
Miller, G.H. 103
Mills, R. 136
Milman, D.E.D.H. 114
Mitchell, H. 77
Montgomerie, R.A.J. 3
Montgomery, W.H. 54
Moon, E.R. 139
Moore, W.J. 75
Moores, A. 42
Moores, J. 119
Morris, G.H. 103
Morris, J. 87
Morris, T.H. 90
Morrison, R. 89
Mountain, R. 22
Moyes, W.E. 133
Mugford, W. 8
Munro, W. 117
Murdoch, A. 128
Murphy, P.J. 141
Murray, A.P. 82
Muscat, A. 133
Nadal, L. 41
Nairn, A. 104

Narrish, E. 115
Neaber, E.W. 119
Necton, R. 35
Neilson, D. 66
Nelson, C. 65
Newby, R. 92
Newland, G. 51
Nickson, L.R. 72
Niven, J. 36
Nizam Din, 51
Noble, A.R. 111
Noble, D.J.D. 12
Nutman, W.J. 90
O'Neill, F. 9
O'Sullivan, J. 71
Oddy, A. 130
Oldershaw, G. 135
Olsen, E.M.O. 151
Orde, C.R. 52
Osborne, W. 40
Ovens, G.H. 81
Owen, W.P. 113
Palmer, D. 14
Park, A. 85
Parker, G. 70
Parker, H.L. 141
Parkes, G. 33, 50
Parks, R. 84
Parnaby, C. 101
Parr, W.H. 12
Parsons V.G.A. 150
Paterson, H.P. 147
Paterson, J. 59
Paxton, J. 15
Payne, R.L. 97
Pearce, D. 114
Pearce, T.R. 47
Pearson, F.E. 138
Pearson, R.C. 28
Pennett, W. 79
Perry, C.J. 84
Petersen, C. 104
Petersen, C. 108
Pett, G. 110
Phillips, J.A. 97
Picton, S.E. 150

Piers, H. 73
Pitmam, R.G. 107
Place, W.T. 54
Pochin, J.W. 69
Porter, W. 70
Poulden, E. 31
Power, J. 79
Price, T. 115
Pride, I. 45
Prince, A. 168
Prosser, E. 50
Pryor, W.S. 145
Purdie, A. 71
Rafter, S. 132
Ramaswami, 56
Ravani, A.E. 27
Rawson, H.H. 34
Reed, R.T. 165
Renouf, E. de F. 131
Reynolds, P.J.W. 137
Rich, F. St. G. 64
Richards, J. 153
Richardson, H.N.A. 21
Richardson, J. 124
Ritchie, H.L. 16
Robbins, J. 162
Roberts, T.M. 28
Roberts, W.C. 138
Robinson, J. 69
Robson, H. 41
Robson, W. 109
Roe, J.N. 92
Rogers, F.H. 2
Rose, I. 77
Rotch, S.F.S. 98
Rourke, J. 48
Rowe, F.I. 67
Rowley, M. 135
Russell, W. 77
Rutherford, J.A. 79
Ryan, V. 145
Ryle, I.M. 156
Samuels, C. 103
Saraj Din, 62
Saul, A.E. 47
Saunders, H.W. 169

Savill, H. 34
Sawdie, G. 54
Schembri, R. 121
Sclanders, D.G. 102
Scotcher, C.G. 139
Scotcher, G. 44
Scott, J. 58
Scrase-Dickens, S.W. 7
Sears, H. 63, 65
Seed, W. 80
Selous, R. 92
Senior, G. 132
Senior, H. 4
Senior, W. 109
Shaik Mahomed Shaik Ally 115
Shapter, J. 66
Shearme, J. 11
Sheedy, D. 57
Shooter, F. 59
Short, E. 64
Shortland, T.W. 44
Shortle, R. 78
Sibson, J.N. 165
Simpson, J.R. 80
Simpson, W. 5
Sinclair, J.M.H. 160
Sinclair, W.H.M. 82
Singleton, C.H.C. 19
Skillicorn, E. 64
Slater, J. 88
Smith, C.A. 35
Smith, G.H. 13
Smith, H. 18
Smith, J. 80
Smith, J. 120
Smith, M. 62
Smith, R. 76
Smith, S.G. 33
Smith, W.E. 42
Souter D.L. 18
Sparks, A.E. 103
Speed, G.E. 36
Spencer, B.R. 20
Startin, J. 60
Steel, M. 37
Stenning G.J.F. 119

Steytler, J.M. 167
Stockton, J. 12
Storey, G.W.B. 3
Strickland, J. 43
Stuart, S. 52
Stucley, H.N.G. 71
Summerfield, C. 84
Sutcliffe, T. 74
Sutherland, A. 75
Swaine, A. 56
Swan, W.C. 105
Swanger, A. 99
Swann, A.J. 93
Sworn, S. 130
Tallant, J. 127
Tardival, F. 50
Tate, S. 113
Taylor, E.A. 121
Taylor, J.T. 137
Teague, T. 53
Thomas, A.W. 125
Thomas, B. 141
Thomas, C.J. 125
Thomas, Daniel 45
Thomas, David 100
Thomas, E.A. 166
Thomas, J. 87
Thompson, F.G. 127
Thomson, B.H. 78
Thomson, L.R. 19
Thornton, E.C. 139
Tinney, L.H.J. 102
Todd, A. 128
Tomkinson, W. 14
Tomlinson, J.W. 148
Tonge, A.J. 125
Torrey Baz, 63
Toy, J.L. 143
Traill, W.A. 89
Treagus, T.H. 145
Trench, F.P. 55
Troubridge, E.C.T. 70
Tuckfield, H.R. 136
Tudor, F.C. 57
Tuff, J. 116
Turner, A.H. 87

Twentyman, E. 16
Tyler, A. 149
Varcoe, V. 149
Voisard, E. 49
Walker, T.B. 95
Walker, W. 113
Wallis, C.B. 106
Walmsley, R. 144
Walsh, W. 64
Warburton, J. 48
Washington, C. 128
Waters, M. 70, 80
Watkins, W. 112
Watkinson, W.J. 144
Watson, E.L. 161
Watts, J. 88
Waugh, J. 132
Webb, A.H.W. 150
Webb, M. 2
Webster, A.W. 118
Webster, C.G. 155
Webster, J.S. 87
Webster, R.V. 109
Weller, S. 104
Werner, 80
West, A.H. 134
Westaway, J.G. 39
Westley, Y.P. 51
Wheal, R. 89
White, G. 46
White, J. 64
Whitehead, F.P. 88
Whitelaw, A. 74
Whiteside, F. 68
Whiteside, J. 68

Whitlock, H.C. 34
Whyte, W. 61
Williams, A. 76
Williams, B.T. 67
Williams, J. 100
Williams, J.F. 126
Williams, R. 90
Williams, R.R. 123
Williams, Sergeant 102
Williams, W.M. 115
Wilmot, W.F. 69
Wilson, F. 82
Wilson, F. 138
Wilson, W. 117
Winborn, A.T. 127
Windham, W.G. 92
Wintle, M.C.A. 146
Wintz, L.E. 3
Withers, W.R. 153
Wodehouse, N.A. 132
Wood, R.T. 39
Woolfield, E. 116
Woolley, W.D. 127
Wootton, L.A. 92
Worman, H. 89
Wright, E. 147
Wright, R.K. 135
Wright, W.J. 142
Wylie, M. 83
Yame 104
Yeates, G.F. 137
Yonge, G.H. 34
Young, G.E. 129

* * * * *

INDEX TO BRONZE MEDALS

Addison, L.P. 141
Ahern, T. 57
Archer, G. 164
Archer, G. 25
Baldwin, D. 43
Barber, A.E. 128
Barlow, M. 88
Bateman, J. 88
Bennett, F. 101
Black, C. 101
Blake, F. 132
Blower, J.F. 129
Bolton, J. 88
Booth, G. 111
Bradley, J.D. 119
Brook, W.H. 141
Brosnahan, Sub-constable 44
Bugeja, S. 122
Bullock, H.J. 132
Bullough, E. 125
Bullough, J. 125
Burnham, P. 135
Campbell, M. 166
Carter, J. 88
Clarke, D. 151
Clarke, G.A. 111
Cooper, F.E. 102
Cooper, S. 101
Corner, W. 125
Cox, F. 97
Creeth, G.W. 120
Davies, R. 140
Davies, W. 140
Davis, J. 96
Dawson, R. 137
Delahaye, F. 34
Dhan Singh 62
Diedricks, A. 106
Dixon, G.W. 125
Dixon, H.O. 125
Dowler, R. 132
Down, R. Sgt 92
Drake, F.C. 25
Driver, P. 79

Dyer, A.R. 128
Eden, T. 135
Edmunds, E. 152
England, E.E. 150
Eustaquio, T. 106
Evans, J. 90
Fisher, F. 123
Flatwell, C. 106
Ford, J. 140
Fowler, R.W. 141
Frankland, W. 130
Gane, J. 121
Gard, C.W. 162
Gerrard, J. 125
Gibson, R. 96
Gobedi, F. 157
Godden, E. 110
Gordon, A.W. 128
Green, H. 141
Greenhalgh, R. 125
Griffiths, G. 153
Hardman, J. 125
Harmer, E. 110
Hart, Mr 84
Hartley, J. 125
Harvey, H.G.L. 156
Hazell, M. 25
Hazell, M. 164
Heath, T. 105
Hennessey, Seaman 67
Henstock, G. 111
Herring, J. 125
Hibberd, C.F.W. 141
Hilton, J. 125
Hinkley, A. 88
Holliday, C. 125
Hoole, R. 88
Howe, Mr 160
Howells, R. 90
Hubbard, R.L.F. 123
Hunns, W.J. 100
Imdilla jnr. 106
Ingham, G. 17
Irwin, J. 100

179

Isaacs, S. 46
Johansson, M. 141
John, T. 90
Johnson, J. 88
Jones, D. 100
Jones, E. 90
Jones, E.J. 140
Joughin, T. 123
Kelly, T. 135
Kemp, J. 158
Kirk, H. 17
Langmead, E. 43
Langshaw, T. 88
Lawson, R. 10
le Clercq, P. 162
Leigh, W.H. 125
Lewis, L. 90
Lichfield, W. 132
Linnell, Mr 160
Lusty, A.C. 165
MacFarlane, G. 147
Maddock, J. 88
Mandala, J. 157
Mangnall, B. 125
Mansfield, S. 96
Markland, W. 125
Marsh, W. 125
Martin, Coxn 67
Mathieson, A. 106
McDonnell, W. 79
McLeod, Mr 62
Miller, B. 17
Miller, M. 155
Mills, Pte 69
Milner, H.F. 17
Moffat, J. 155
Moran, R. 141
Morris, E. 90
Moss, J. 125
Mullany, Sub-constable 44
Munday, C. 43
Naylor, J. 119
Nel, D.A. 141
Newberry, W.F. 128
Nilsen, G.M. 141
Noseworthy, W. 43

Nunn, H. 135
O'Brien, H. 127
O'Connor, B. 127
Oldfield, A. 27
Osea 104
Parke, L. 102
Parsons, E. 170
Payne, A. 122
Peck, A.G. 128
Perrin, H. 95
Perry, M.J.F. 141
Pittaway, J. 128
Polley, J.H. 125
Poole, B. 120
Pound, L.D. 152
Powell, J. 101
Quirke, J. 57
Ratan Singh 110
Regan, P. 135
Roberts, C. 108
Roberts, R. 125
Roddy, G. 102
Rosser, R. 91
Rowley, G. 88
Russell, J.C. 125
Ryan, M. 166
Schofield, W. 125
Sclater, R. 132
Scott, W. 132
Scragg, J. 140
Shaw, E. 130
Sherevera, P. 21
Simpson, D. 132
Smith, Mr 84
Spiteri, G. 122
Sproston, J. 88
Staton, Pte 69
Stewart, C.T. 141
Stott, A. 125
Thompson, C. 79
Tiltman, Mr 68
Tong, J. 110
Tremayne, J.H. 102
Tucker, J. 121
Turton, J. 125
Twitt, E. 170

Tyler, W.G. 149
Wall, W. 101
Ward, C. 106
Watson, P. 96
Watts, A. 111
Weddle, J. 10
Whittington, L. 101
Williams, G. 132
Williams, J. 125
Williams, L. 125

Williams, M. 90
Williams, T. 90
Williams, W. 91
Wilson, L. 101
Winter, H. 166
Wise, F.H. 102
Wood, Mr 159
Wood, P.C. 160
Workman, P.C. 141

* * * * *

INDEX TO TESTIMONIALS

Ash, A.E. 150
Ballard, C.G. 120
Baxter, J. (M) 12
Bigg, R.J. (M) 109
Blackhall, G. (M) 116
Bretherton, R.W. 12
Brown, J. (M) 129
Brown, W. (M) 77
Cawsey, W. (M) 104
Chew, J. (M) 76
Christopher, T. 25
Christopher, T. 164
Clow, Mr (M) 160
Cole, W. 150
Cowie, A. 117
Crisp, R. 120
Darton, E.J. (M) 132
Davlin, F. 159
Farbrother, H. (M) 78
Gayton, A. (M) 160
Grech, G. 122
Griffith, H.D. 120
Hansen, C. (M) 104
Haseldine, A.V. 160
Hill, C. 120
Hill, H. (M) 109
Hutchinson, W. (M) 104
Hyde, R. 99
Johnson, Constable 101
Jones, E. 164
Jones, E. 25

King, W. 160
Legh, J.A.P. (M) 26
Lekobo, D. 146
Libby, R.F. (M) 128
McCarthy, J. 153
McLaren, W. (M) 128
Mifsud, S. 122
Milman, R. (R) 114
Mitchell, J. 12
Nicolle, St. 56
O'Reilly, A.R.C. 146
Peacock, J. 120
Peacock, R. 120
Penny, C. (M) 17
Reeves, W.G.E. 160
Richards, L. 25
Richards, L. 164
Roberts, S.A. 166
Smart, G. (M) 160
Smith, F. 166
Smith, W. (M) 166
Southern, J.H. 120
Stewart, W.S. (M) 163
Timm, A. (M) 17
Treadwell, R.H. 26
Turner, R.G. 120
Turton, W. (M) 125
Upton, A.W. (M) 141
Walker, G. (M) 109
Wiltshire, J. 120
Wright, J.R. 22

Note: (M) = In Memorium Testimonial
(R) = Resuscitation Certificate

* * * * *

www.ingramcontent.com/pod-product-compliance
Lightning Source LLC
Chambersburg PA
CBHW080401170426
43193CB00016B/2783